普通高等学校测控技术与仪器专业规划教材

测控专业英语

Professional English for Measurement and Control

主 编 王丽君 梁福平
参 编 刘嘉敏 韩晓娟
　　　 郭阳宽 运红丽

http://www.hustp.com

中国·武汉

内容简介

本书从测控技术与仪器专业的角度，选编了关于机械、电子、测量、控制及计算机等方面的英文资料，基本上覆盖了和测控技术与仪器相关的各个领域，旨在使学生能够通过专业英语的学习，熟悉并掌握测控技术与仪器方面的基本英语词汇及用法，培养和提高学生阅读和翻译专业英语文献资料的能力。

本书分为9个部分，每个部分均由课文及阅读材料组成，供上课讲解和课后阅读使用。第一部分为概述，介绍了测量与控制技术；第二部分为机械部分，由机构、工程材料、机械设计、工程制图和加工等5课组成；第三部分为测量，由测量、传感器、通用仪器、虚拟仪器、激光技术和标定技术等6课组成；第四部分为信号调理，由数据采样、运算放大器、滤波器、D/A和A/D转换、仪表装置和接地等5课组成；第五部分为控制，由自动控制简介、开环和闭环控制、离散时间控制、过程控制、PID控制器和可编程控制器等6课组成；第六部分为计算机，由计算机硬件和软件、微处理器、总线网络技术、计算机网络和数字信号处理等5课组成；第七部分为执行机构，由电动执行机构、液压执行机构和气动执行机构等3课组成；第八部分为新技术，由机器人技术简介、分布式控制系统中的先进控制技术、遥感技术、机器视觉简介和21世纪的航空技术等5课组成；第九部分为翻译与写作，介绍了专业英语的特点、专业英语的翻译概论和科技论文的写作方法。

本书适合于高校测控技术与仪器相关专业的学生作为专业英语教材，也可供大专、职业大学、成人大学等相关专业选用，还可供研究生及从事相关专业的工程技术人员阅读参考。

普通高等学校测控技术与仪器专业规划教材

编委会

主　任：
钟毓宁
（湖北工业大学副校长，教育部高等学校仪器科学与技术专业教学指导委员会委员）

副主任：
孔　力
（华中科技大学教授，教育部高等学校仪器科学与技术专业教学指导委员会委员）
许贤泽
（武汉大学教授，教育部高等学校仪器仪器科学与技术专业教学指导委员会委员）

委　员：（以姓氏笔划为序）
王连弟（华中科技大学出版社）　王先培（武汉大学）
史红梅（北京交通大学）　　　　李威宣（武汉理工大学）
杨　帆（武汉工程大学）　　　　张思祥（河北工业大学）
何　涛（湖北工业大学）　　　　周荣政（江汉大学）
胡春海（燕山大学）　　　　　　郭天太（中国计量学院）
康宜华（华中科技大学）　　　　梁福平（北京信息科技大学）
董浩斌（中国地质大学）　　　　曾以成（湘潭大学）

秘　书：
刘　锦　万亚军

普通高等学校测控技术与仪器专业规划教材

总 序

  测控技术与仪器专业是在合并原来的11个仪器仪表类专业的基础上新设立的专业，目前设有该专业的高校已经超过250所，是当前发展较快的本科专业之一。经过两届全国高等学校仪器科学与技术教学指导委员会的努力，形成了《测控技术与仪器专业本科教学规范》（以下简称《专业规范》）。《专业规范》颁布后，各高校开始构建面向21世纪的测控技术与仪器本科专业的课程体系，并进行教学改革，以更好地满足科学技术和国民经济发展的需要。

  华中科技大学出版社邀请多位全国高等学校仪器科学与技术教学指导委员会委员和具有丰富教学经验的专家编写了这套"普通高等学校测控技术与仪器专业规划教材"，这对于满足各高校测控专业建设需要，加强高校测控专业的建设，进一步落实《专业规范》精神，具有积极的作用。

  这套教材基本涵盖了测控技术与仪器专业的专业基础课程和部分专业课程，编写定位清晰，内容适应了加强工程教学的趋势，注重了教材的实用性和创新性教育的推进。这套教材的出版，是测控专业教学领域"百花齐放、百家争鸣"的一个体现，它为测控专业教学选用教材又提供了一个选择。

  由于时间所限，这套教材可能存在这样那样的问题。随着这套教材投入教学使用和通过教学实践的检验，它将不断得到改进、完善和提高，为测控专业人才的培养做出积极的贡献。

  谨为之序。

全国高等学校仪器科学与技术教学指导委员会主任委员

胡小唐

2009年7月

前　言

　　测控专业英语是测控技术与仪器专业及相关专业的一门专业课程,是本科英语教学中必不可少的一个教学环节。为了使学生熟悉和掌握本专业及相关专业的常用专业词汇、词组及相关的科技文献资料,培养学生顺利阅读专业文献、进行信息交流、完成专业翻译及写作的能力,了解当前国内外的一些新的测量技术及方法,特编写了《测控专业英语》一书。

　　本书的主要特点体现在:①选材力求丰富多样,内容和专业词汇的涵盖面广,选取的文章具有代表性、新颖性,既有利于培养学生学习兴趣,又有利于学生丰富专业知识并积累相关的专业词汇。②本书的大多数资料选自国外原版的教材、专著、论文或本专业相关网站提供的技术资料,保证了课文的实用性和可读性。③本书共提供课文36课,每课内容都由课文、生词和短语、重点和难点的翻译与解释及阅读材料组成,既便于各学校根据自己的特点机动地组织教学,也便于学生自学。

　　本书由华北水利水电学院王丽君副教授、北京信息科技大学梁福平教授任主编,具体编写分工为:华北电力大学的韩晓娟副教授编写第一部分和第六部分,华北水利水电学院的运红丽讲师编写第二部分,北京信息科技大学的梁福平教授编写第三部分和第九部分,北京信息科技大学的郭阳宽副教授编写第四部分,华北水利水电学院的王丽君副教授编写第五部分和第七部分,重庆大学的刘嘉敏副教授编写第八部分。全书由王丽君和梁福平统稿,由武汉大学的马志敏教授主审,郑州轻工业学院丁静老师、北京信息科技大学刁素坤老师、研究生马丽丽等为本书的编写提供了许多资料和帮助,参编的各个单位的领导也给予大力支持,在此一并表示感谢。

　　由于水平有限,书中错误和不当之处在所难免,欢迎广大读者多提宝贵意见。

编　者

2009 年 4 月

目 录

PART ONE Overview ·· (1)
Lesson 1 An Introduction to Measurement & Control Technology ··················· (1)
PART TWO Machinery ··· (7)
Lesson 1 Mechanism ··· (7)
Lesson 2 Engineering Materials ··· (12)
Lesson 3 Machine Design ·· (18)
Lesson 4 Engineering Drawing ··· (23)
Lesson 5 Machining ·· (28)
PART THREE Measurement ·· (35)
Lesson 1 Measurement ··· (35)
Lesson 2 Sensors ··· (43)
Lesson 3 Common Instruments ·· (50)
Lesson 4 Virtual Instruments ··· (59)
Lesson 5 Laser Technology ··· (68)
Lesson 6 Calibration Technology ·· (76)
PART FOUR Signal Conditioning ··· (85)
Lesson 1 An Introduction to Data Acquisition ·· (85)
Lesson 2 Operational Amplifier ·· (92)
Lesson 3 Filters ·· (98)
Lesson 4 DAC and ADC ·· (105)
Lesson 5 Instrumentation and Ground ·· (113)
PART FIVE Control ··· (120)
Lesson 1 An Introduction to Automatic Control ·· (120)
Lesson 2 Open-Loop and Closed-Loop Control ··· (125)
Lesson 3 Discrete-Time Control ··· (130)
Lesson 4 Process Control ··· (136)
Lesson 5 PID Controller ·· (142)
Lesson 6 PLC ··· (147)
PART SIX Computer ··· (153)
Lesson 1 Computer Hardware and Software ·· (153)
Lesson 2 Microprocessor ·· (160)
Lesson 3 Bus Network Technology ··· (167)
Lesson 4 Computer Network ··· (174)
Lesson 5 Digital Signal Processing ··· (181)
PART SEVEN Actuators ··· (188)

Lesson 1　Electric Actuators ……………………………………………………………(188)
Lesson 2　Hydraulic Actuators …………………………………………………………(193)
Lesson 3　Pneumatic Actuators …………………………………………………………(199)
PART EIGHT　New Technology ……………………………………………………(205)
Lesson 1　An Introduction to Robotics Technology …………………………………(205)
Lesson 2　Advanced Control Technologies in DCS …………………………………(211)
Lesson 3　Remote Sensing Technology ………………………………………………(217)
Lesson 4　Machine Vision in Brief ……………………………………………………(223)
Lesson 5　Aeronautical Technologies for the 21st Century …………………………(227)
PART NINE　Translation and Writing ……………………………………………(233)
　第一章　专业英语的特点……………………………………………………………(233)
　　第一节　引言………………………………………………………………………(233)
　　第二节　专业英语的特点…………………………………………………………(234)
　　第三节　专业英语的语法特点……………………………………………………(236)
　　第四节　专业英语的词汇特点……………………………………………………(238)
　　第五节　符号、公式及其他………………………………………………………(243)
　第二章　专业英语翻译概论…………………………………………………………(246)
　　第一节　翻译的过程、标准及对译者的要求……………………………………(246)
　　第二节　专业英语翻译的基本方法………………………………………………(250)
　第三章　科技论文的写作方法………………………………………………………(258)
　　第一节　科技论文的结构…………………………………………………………(258)
　　第二节　题目、摘要与关键词的写法……………………………………………(259)
　　第三节　正文的写法………………………………………………………………(261)
　　第四节　致谢、附录及参考文献…………………………………………………(264)
　　第五节　专业术语和专有名词的译法……………………………………………(265)
References ………………………………………………………………………………(268)

PART ONE Overview

Lesson 1 An Introduction to Measurement & Control Technology

"Measurement & Control Technology and Instruments" is the unique major of instrument science and technology in China. Instrument and meter is an essential part of IT industry. Instrument and meter technology is a comprehensive subject which is based on mechanics, computer science and information technology. And it shows greater and greater power in the development of national economy, national defense and everyday life.

Understanding is a powerful aid to prediction. Models lead to understanding, and observations ground models. Instruments and measurement techniques extend direct observation to the benefit of understanding and prediction. Develop skill in utilization of instrumentation and learn to specify or invent new instrumentation and you will aid observation. Better techniques of measurement lead to greater and more accurate understanding of the natural system. The short term benefit of such understanding is the ability to predict response. In the long term, understanding is a general guard against blunders in our own behavior as a society. And understanding can lead to opportunities for human use and individual appreciation to social benefit.

1. Trends in Measurement and Control System Equipment and Future Outlook

The wave of digitization has become widely disseminated in many fields since 1975, encompassing power systems including nuclear and thermal power systems; industrial systems including petrochemicals, steel, foods, and pharmaceuticals; and infrastructure systems including water and sewage, road, and airport control systems. Substantial progress has been made in open system technologies, information technologies, and integration technologies, and methods of configuring control systems under total system optimization including information systems are now attracting global attention.

2. Industrial Controllers—Advances in Development of High-Speed and High-Reliability Controller Technologies

Technologies have been progressing for the standardization and realization of open architectures for programmable logic controllers (PLCs) and distributed control systems (DCS), both of which are representative industrial control equipment. Moreover, taking technical trends and the social environment into consideration, we have studied hardware and software technologies to improve management and applicability to factory automation (FA) and process automation (PA) systems, and proposed the development of products to be released in the future.

3. New Developments for Industrial Computers

The application of industrial computers has expanded to encompass not only factory automation systems but various other fields, including social infrastructure systems such as broadcasting and communication systems, transportation management systems, water supply and sewerage monitoring systems, electric power generation and supply systems, and building management systems; as well as automated equipment, inspection and analysis equipment, and so on. In monitoring and control systems, and equipment with embedded computers, there is an accelerating trend toward open systems and an increasing number of systems using PCs and PC servers. As a result, the requirements for industrial computers have expanded and diversified according to such factors as the purpose of use and the scale of application.

4. Latest Field Measurement Technologies

Various types of field measurement devices such as flowmeters, pressure transmitters, thermometers, and density meters are widely applied in manufacturing process systems.

5. Instrument and Control Products Contributing to Effective Operation of Water and Sewage Plants

Water and sewage systems are an important part of the social infrastructure and indispensable in people's daily lives. A water system must provide safe water at all times, while a sewage system must purify sewage and rainwater collected by sewerage pipes and transform them into clear water before discharge into a river or ocean. At the same time, reduction of electricity consumption by water and sewage plants is important to reduce greenhouse gas emissions, which lead to global warming. It is also necessary to prevent overdosing of chemicals in treated water from the standpoint of environmental protection. In addition, the reduction of chemical consumption is important from the viewpoint of reducing the operating and maintenance costs of plants.

6. Monitoring and Control of Building Automation System

The architecture of building automation and control systems is evolving into the Building Energy Management System (BEMS), including energy-saving control and energy management. BEMS measures the status of the building facilities and space environment, performs accurate control, and stores data for reporting and analysis.

7. Solutions for Measurement and Control Systems in Industrial Processing Fields

Thirty years have passed since digital technology was introduced in the field of measurement and control systems. On the one hand, investment in plant and equipment has been rising in raw material industries such as steel and petrochemicals due to the recent growth of the Chinese economy, and this in turn has promoted the renewal of instrument systems. On the other hand, the operators who have supported the high-growth period of the Japanese economy are now aging, and it is becoming increasingly difficult to maintain safe and stable operations as well as the uniformly high quality realized by the experience and skill of these expert operators up to now. In particular, problems are expected to arise from 2007 onward with regard to the renewal of distributed control systems (DCS).

8. Current Project Areas

Below is a list of current research projects in the Systems, Measurement and Control Areas:

Modeling and System Identification
- Modeling and controling of fuel cell power systems;
- Modeling of machining chatter;
- Autonomous modeling of complex manufacturing processes;
- Real-time predictive modeling and simulation for prognosis in smart ships;
- Real-time load and damage identification in filament wound rocket motor casings;
- Modeling and identification of seat head rest rattle in passenger bucket seat;
- Modeling and identification of morphing aircraft structure.

Measurements and Diagnostics
- Nonlinear observer design and neural networks for virtual sensing, modeling, fault detection, diagnostics, and adaptive robust fault-tolerant control;
- Diesel engine diagnostics and prognostics using information-rich input signals;
- Estimating particulate load in a diesel particulate filter for regeneration control;
- Vehicle health management technologies;
- Integrated diagnostics and reliability forecasting for heterogeneous structures;
- A facility for theoretical and experimental environmental conditioning, modeling and prognostics of advanced heterogeneous structures;
- Sensing and diagnostics of electrical machines;
- Autonomous selection of sensors and sensor features for intelligent monitoring and diagnostics for manufacturing processes;
- Integrated prognostics health management technologies for commercial and defense systems;
- Integrated sensing and diagnostics for life cycle health management of gas turbine engines:application to wire harnesses and connectors;
- Modeling and diagnostics of mechanically attached structural components;
- Diagnostics & prognostics for assessing vehicle products in real time with feedback for manufacturing to reduce conservatism.

Control Theory
- Nonlinear adaptive robust control theory;
- Multi-level fuzzy control;
- Multivariable intelligent control;
- Neural network-based adaptive control;
- Observer-based adaptive control.

Control Applications
- Engine controls;

- Energy-saving nonlinear control of electro-hydraulic systems;
- Intelligent and precision control of high-speed linear motor drive systems, machine tools, and piezo-electric actuators for precision manufacturing;
- Nonlinear control of high-density hard disk drives;
- Coordinated control of robot manipulators;
- Feedforward/feedback motion control for high-speed automation;
- High-speed motion control for flexible robotic manipulators;
- Precision control of piezo-electric actuators for scanning microscopes;
- Control of medical devices;
- Control of mechatronic devices.

Words and Expressions

pharmaceuticals [ˌfɑːməˈsjuːtikəlz] n. 医药品
infrastructure [ˈinfrəˈstrʌktʃə] n. 下部构造,下部组织,基础结构,基础设施
programmable logic controllers 可编程控制器
factory automation(FA) 工厂自动化
process automation(PA) 过程自动化
flowmeter [ˈfləumiːtə] n. 流量计
transmitter [trænzˈmitə] n. 发报机;发射机;发送器;话筒;变送器
sewage [ˈsjuː(ː)idʒ] n. 脏水,污水
Building Energy Management System 建筑节能管理系统
distributed control systems(DCS) 分布式控制系统
piezo-electric 压电的
energy-saving 节能的

Notes

1. The wave of digitization has become widely disseminated in many fields since 1975, encompassing power systems including nuclear and thermal power systems; industrial systems including petrochemicals, steel, foods, and pharmaceuticals; and infrastructure systems including water and sewage, road, and airport control systems.

(1) 句中的 encompassing 是现在分词作状语,它在句子中作一个伴随状语。including 是现在分词作定语。

(2) 全句可翻译为:1975年以来,数字化浪潮已在许多领域广为传播,包含了核能和热力发电的电力系统;石化、钢铁、食品和药品的工业系统;以及供水、污水处理、道路和机场控制的基础设施系统。

2. Moreover, taking technical trends and the social environment into consideration, we have studied hardware and software technologies to improve management and applicability to factory automation (FA) and process automation (PA) systems, and proposed the development of products to be released in the future.

(1) 句中 taking... into consideration:考虑……。

（2）全句可翻译为：此外，考虑到技术发展趋势和社会环境，我们研究了硬件和软件技术来改善工厂自动化和过程自动化系统的管理和应用，提出了未来产品的开发方案。

3. It is also necessary to prevent overdosing of chemicals in treated water from the standpoint of environmental preservation.

（1）句中 from the standpoint of："从……角度"。overdosing 是动名词，这里翻译成"超（剂）量"。例如：He's been overdosing himself. 他用药一直过量。

（2）全句可翻译为：从保护环境的角度来看，也必须防止用过量的化学品处理水。

Reading Material

A Workshop on Process Measurement and Control

In recognition of the recent growth and the perceived new opportunities in process measurement and control, a workshop on this topic was held at the Sheraton New Orleans on March 6-8, 1998. Sixteen invited speakers and discussants from academia, industry and national laboratories presented their perspectives on the current state-of-the-art applications in industry and future needs in various areas of process measurement and control. Thirty additional participants, also representing academia, industry and national laboratories, attended and participated in the workshop. Many of these individuals were invited; however, some were unsolicited applicants who learned of the workshop through colleagues and responded to a web-based call for participation located at the web site http://udel.edu/~fdoyle/V2020.html.

The goals of the workshop were five-fold:

- To identify the current state-of-the-art for process measurement and control, including their current impact on academic and industrial research and development;
- Project where these methods can be in 25 years, and the expected impact of these methods over that period;
- Identify the challenges and roadblocks that delay advancements in these technology areas;
- Identify strategic research investments that might facilitate the achievement of these latter capabilities and ensure their widespread utility to both academic and industrial communities;
- Produce a report to the research community served by the NSF, NIST, and NIST ATP concerning the findings of 1-4.

A unique feature of this workshop was that chemists and chemical engineers were brought together in a common forum to address the common interests in process measurements for control. Individual breakout groups were comprised of a mixed group from academia, industry, and the government labs. Furthermore, each group was split between measurement scientists and control engineers, and the groups each addressed one control topic and one measurement topic. In this manner, a "single track" was achieved. In the remainder of this preliminary report, the summary findings of the workshop will be discussed. Several speakers were asked to provide overviews of, and assess the state-of-the-art in, process measurement and control. Others were asked to describe successes of current methods in industry and academia, and to assess needs into the future. This was done around eight topical areas, and the balance of this report is organized around those areas:

- Nonlinear model predictive control;
- Performance monitoring;
- Estimation and inferential control;
- Identification and adaptive control;
- Molecular characterizations and separations;
- Process sensors;
- Micro-fabricated instrumentation;
- Information and data handling.

PART TWO   Machinery

Lesson 1   Mechanism

A mechanism has been defined as "a combination of rigid or resistant bodies so formed and connected that they move upon each other with definite relative motion". That is the component of machinery. Activity connections between two members that have the relative motion are to be called the motion pairs. All motion pairs contacting with planes are called lower pairs and all motion pairs contacting with points or lines are called higher pairs. Lower pairs include revolute or pin connections, for example, a shaft in a bearing or the wrist pin joining a piston and connecting rod. Both elements joined by the pin may be considered to have the same motion at the pin center if clearance is neglected. Other basic lower pairs include the sphere, cylinder, prism, helix, and plane. The Hook-type universal joint is a combination of two lower pairs. Examples of higher pairs include a pair of gears or a disk cam and follower.

The motion specific property of mechanism chiefly depends on the relative size between the members, and the character of motion pairs, as well as the mutual disposition method etc. The member is used to support the member of motion in the mechanism to be called the machine frame and used as the reference coordinate to study the motion system. The member that possesses the independence motion is called motivity member. The members except machine frame and motivity member being compelled to move in the mechanism are called driven members. The independently parameter which is essential for description or definite mechanism motion is called the free degree of mechanism. For gaining the definite relative motion between the members of mechanism, it must make the number of driving parts of mechanism equal to the number of free degrees. An unconstrained rigid body has six degrees of freedom: translation in three coordinate directions and rotation about three coordinate axes. If the body is restricted to motion in a plane, there are three degrees of freedom: translation in two coordinate directions and rotation within the plane.

Mechanisms may be categorized in several different ways to emphasize their similarities and differences. One such grouping divides mechanisms into planar, spherical, and spatial categories. All three groups have many things in common; the criterion which distinguishes the groups, however, is to be found in the characteristics of the motions of the links.

A planar mechanism is one in which all particles describe plane curves in space and all these curves lie in parallel places, i. e., the loci of all points are plane curves parallel to a single common plane. This characteristic makes it possible to represent the locus of any chosen point of a planar mechanism in its true size and shape on a single drawing or figure.

The motion transformation of any such mechanism is called coplanar. The plane four-bar linkage, the plate cam and follower, and the slider-crank mechanism are familiar examples of planar mechanism. The vast majority of mechanisms in use today are planar.

1. Four-Bar Mechanisms

When one of the members of a constrained linkage is fixed, the linkage becomes a mechanism capable of performing a useful mechanical function in a machine. On pin-connected linkages the input (driver) and output (follower) links are usually pivotally connected to the fixed link; the connecting links (couplers) are usually neither inputs nor outputs. Since any of the links can be fixed, if the links are of different lengths, four mechanisms, each with a different input-output relationship, can be obtained with a four-bar linkage. These four mechanisms are said to be inversions of the basic linkage, as shown in Figure 2.1.

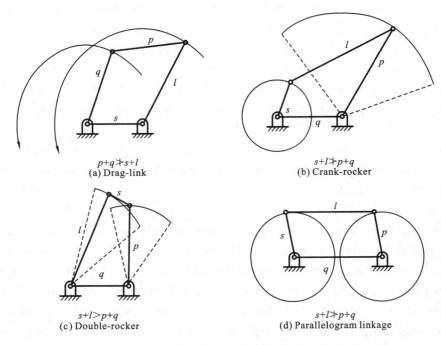

Figure 2.1 The inversions of the four-bar mechanisms

2. Slider-Crank Mechanism

When one of the pinconnections in a four-bar linkage is replaced by a sliding joint, a number of useful mechanisms can be obtained from the resulting linkage. In Figure 2.2, the connection between links 1 and 4 is a sliding joint that permits block 4 to slide in the slot in link 1. If link 1 is fixed, the resulting slider-crank mechanism is a reciprocating engine. The block 4 represents the piston; link 1 is the block that contains the crankshaft bearing at A and the cylinder; link 2 is the crankshaft and link 3 the connecting rod. The crankpin bearing is at B, the wrist pin bearing at C. The stroke of the piston is twice AB, the stroke of the crank.

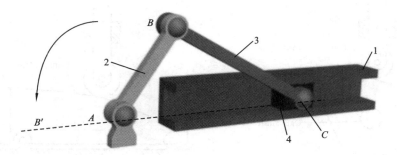

Figure 2.2 Slider-crank mechanism

The slider-crank mechanism provides means for converting the translatory motion of the piston in a reciprocating engine into rotary motion of the crankshaft, or the rotary motion of the crankshaft, or the rotary motion of the crankshaft in a pump into a translatory motion of the pistons. In Figure 2.2, when B is in position B′, the connecting rod would interfere with the crank if both were in the same plane. This problem is solved in engines and pumps by offsetting the crankpin bearing from the crankshaft bearing. By using an eccentric-and-rod mechanism in place of a crank, no offsetting is necessary and very small throws can be obtained.

3. Cam Systems

A cam is a machine member that drives a follower through a specified motion. By the proper design of a cam, any desired motion to a machine member can be obtained. As such, cams are widely used in almost all machinery. They include internal combustion engines, a variety of machine tools, compressors and computers. In general, a cam can be designed in two ways.

(1) The profile of a cam is so designed to give a desired motion to the follower.

(2) To choose a suitable profile to ensure a satisfactory performance by the follower.

A rotary cam is a part of a machine, which changes cylindrical motion to straight-line motion. The purpose of a cam is to transmit various kinds of motion to other parts of machine.

Practically every cam must be designed and manufactured to fit special requirements. Though each cam appears to be quite different from the other, all of them work in similar way. In each case, as the cam is rotated or turned, another part connected with the cam, called a follower, is moved either right or left, up and down, or in and out. The follower is usually connected to other parts on the machine to accomplish the desired action. If the follower loses contact with the cam, it will fail to work.

Cams are classified according to their basic shapes. Figure 2.3 illustrates two different types of cams.

A spherical mechanism is one in which each link has some points which remain stationary as the linkage moves and in which the stationary points of all links lie at a common location, i.e., the locus of each point is a curve contained in a spherical surface, and the

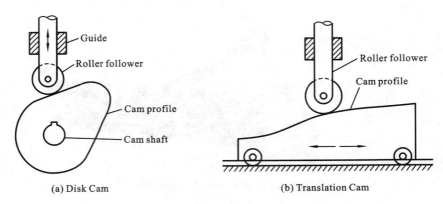

Figure 2.3　Two types of cams

spherical surfaces defined by several arbitrarily chosen points are all concentric. The motions of all particles can therefore be completely described by their radial projections, or "shadows", on the surface of a sphere with properly chosen center.

Spatial mechanisms, on the other hand, include no restrictions on the relative motions of the particles. The motion transformation is not necessary coplanar, nor must it be concentric. A spatial mechanism may have particles with loci of double curvature. Worm gear pairs, as an example, transmit motion between two shafts. The shafts are usually at right angles to each other but do not lie in the same plane.

Words and Expressions

mechanism ['mekənizəm] n. 机械装置，机构
wrist pin　活塞销
clearance ['kliərəns] n. 空隙，间隙
sphere [sfiə] n. 球，球体
cylinder ['silində] n. 圆筒；圆柱体
prism ['prizəm] n. 棱柱
helix ['hi:liks] n. 螺旋，螺旋线
universal joint　万向接头
machine frame　机座，机架
coordinate [kəu'ɔ:dinit] n. 同等者，同等物；坐标
free degree　自由度
categorize ['kætigəraiz] vt. 把……归类，分类
spherical ['sferikəl] a. 球的，球形的
spatial ['speiʃəl] a. 空间的
criterion [krai'tiəriən] n. （判断的）标准，准则，规范
slider-crank　曲柄滑块
coupler ['kʌplə] n. 连结器；配合者
inversion [in'və:ʃən] n. 反向；转换；（四杆机构的）机架变换
slot [slɔt] n. 缝；狭槽；细长的孔

reciprocating [riˈsiprəkeitiŋ] a. 往复的，来回的，交替的
crankshaft [ˈkræŋkʃɑːft] n. 曲轴，曲柄轴
stroke [strəuk] n. 冲程，行程
translatory [ˈtrænslətəri] a. 平移的，平动的
eccentric-and-rod 偏心杆（棒）
spherical [ˈsferikəl] a. 球的，球形的

Notes

1. A mechanism has been defined as "a combination of rigid or resistant bodies so formed and connected that they move upon each other with definite relative motion".
（1）resistant bodies：有承载能力的物体
（2）that 引导目的状语从句。
（3）全句可翻译为：机构被定义为"是由刚体或具有承载能力的物体联接而成的组合体，使得它们在运动时彼此之间具有确定性的相对运动"。

2. When one of the members of a constrained linkage is fixed, the linkage becomes a mechanism capable of performing a useful mechanical function in a machine.
（1）linkage：杆系，连杆机构
（2）全句可翻译为：当受约束的连杆机构中的一个杆件被固定时，连杆机构就变成了机器里能够完成某种有用的机械功能的机构。

3. This problem is solved in engines and pumps by offsetting the crankpin bearing from the crankshaft bearing.
（1）offset...from...：使……偏置于……
（2）crankpin bearing：曲柄销轴承，即文中的 B 点
（3）crankshaft bearing：曲柄轴承，即文中的 B′点
（4）全句可翻译为：在发动机和泵中，这个问题可以通过将曲柄销轴承偏置于曲柄轴承得到解决。

Reading Material

Types of Gears

Gears are used to transmit power positively from one shaft to another by means of successively engaging teeth (in two gears). They are used in place of belt drives and other forms of friction drives when exact speed rations and power transmission must be maintained. Gears may also be used to increase or decrease the speed of the driven shaft, thus decreasing or increasing the torque of the driven member.

Spur gears are generally used to transmit power between two parallel shafts. The teeth on these gears are straight and parallel to the shafts to which they are attached. When two gears of different sizes are in mesh, the larger one is called the gear while the smaller one is called the pinion. Spur gears are used where slow- to moderate-speed drives are required.

Internal gears are used where the shafts are parallel and the centers must be closer together than could be achieved with spur or helical gearing. This arrangement provides a stronger drive since there is a greater area of contact than with the conventional gear drive. It also provides speed reduction with a minimum space requirement. Internal gears are used on heavy-duty tractors where much torque is required.

Helical gears may be used to connect parallel shafts or shafts that are at an angle. Because of the progressive rather than intermittent action of the teeth, helical gears run more smoothly and quietly than spur gears. Since there is more than one tooth in engagement at any time, helical gear are stronger than spur gears of the same size and pith. However, special bearings (thrust bearings) are often required in shafts to overcome the end thrust produced by these gears as they turn.

In most installations where it is necessary to overcome end thrust, herringbone gears are used. This type of gear resembles two helical gears placed side by side, with one-half having a left-hand helix and the other half a right-hand helix. These gears have a smooth continuous action and eliminate the need for thrust bearings.

In order to achieve line contact and improve the load carrying capacity of the crossed-axis helical gears, the gear can be made to curve partially around the pinion, in somewhat the same way that a nut envelops a screw. The result would be a cylindrical worm and gear. Worm gears provide the simplest means of obtaining large ratios in a single pair. They are usually less efficient than parallel-shaft gears, however, because of an additional sliding movement along the teeth. Because of their similarity, the efficiency of a worm and gear depends on the same factors as the efficiency of a screw.

For transmitting rotary motion and torque around corners, bevel gears are commonly used. The connected shafts, whose axes would intersect of extended, are usually but not necessarily at right angles to one another. The profiles of the teeth on bevel gears are not involutes; they are of such a shape that the tools for cutting the teeth are easier to make and maintain than involute cutting tools. Since bevel gears come in pairs, as long as they are conjugate to one another they need not be conjugate to other gears with different tooth numbers.

Lesson 2 Engineering Materials

Materials are substance of the universe. These substances have properties that make them useful in structure, machines, devices, products, and systems. The term property describes behavior of materials when subjected to some external force or condition. Materials may be grouped in several ways. For industrial purpose, materials are divided into engineering materials and nonengineering materials. Engineering materials are those used in manufacture and become parts of products. Nonengineering materials are the chemicals, fuels, lubricants, and other materials used in the manufacturing process which do not become parts of the products.

Engineering materials may be further subdivided into five groups: metals, polymers, ceramics, composites, and materials that do not fit well into the forecited four groups.

All materials have their own properties or characteristics that help modify and distinguish one material from another. All properties are observable and most can be measured quantitatively. Properties are classified into three main groups: physical, chemical and mechanical properties.

1. Physical Properties

Physical properties are restricted to those describe the basic features of the material. These features are measured or observed without the use of extensive scientific experiments. The common physical properties are size, shape, density and porosity.

Size is the overall dimensions of an object. These dimensions, for most materials, are given as thickness, width, and length or as diameter and length.

Shape is the contour or outline of an object. Contour is given to an object by curved, notched, sloped, or other irregular surfaces.

Density or specific gravity measures the mass of an object. The measurement is by weight for a unit or a certain volume. Typically, density is measured by pounds per cubic foot or kilograms per cubic meter of material. Density allows the mass of one material to be compared with other materials.

Porosity is a measure of voids (open pores) in the material. It is generally described as a ratio of open pore volume to total volume of a material. This ratio is expressed as a percentage. Porosity will provide a measure of liquid-holding power, or the ability of air or gas to move through the material.

2. Chemical Properties

Chemical properties cannot be determined just by viewing or touching the substance. This is contrasted with physical properties, which can be discerned without changing the substance's structure. The chemical properties of material must be affected by its structure, which becomes evident during a chemical reaction.

All materials are used in some type of environment. All environments, except a pure vacuum, contain chemicals. These chemicals may be gases (oxygen, hydrogen, chlorine, and nitrogen), liquids (water, acids, and oils) or solids (other engineering materials). The reaction between the chemicals and a material in an environment is called corrosion. In general, there are several types of chemical reactions, as follows:

(1) Oxidation—corrosion caused by a reaction between the material and oxygen in the air. Iron oxidizes to form iron oxide. Some polymers are weakened and destroyed by a combination of sunlight and oxygen. Rubber is particularly prone to oxidation which is called aging. As rubber ages it loses its flexibility and strength.

(2) Electrochemical corrosion—caused by electrical currents set up in a material in a liquid or moist environment. Electrical current flows from one point on the material to another part. The current removes materials from the anodic area and deposits it at the cathodic area. This action is similar to the operation of the storage battery.

(3) Water absorption—the tendency of polymers and ceramic materials to absorb water.

This action increases the material's weight and volume. Water absorption will cause many materials to warp and swell, and lose desirable mechanical and electrical properties.

3. Mechanical Properties

Mechanical properties are defined as a measure of a material's ability to carry or resist mechanical forces or stresses. Mechanical properties are structure-sensitive in the sense that they depend upon the type of crystal structure and its bonding forces, and especially upon the nature and behavior of the imperfections that exist within the crystal itself or at the grain boundaries. The bonding forces in this structure resist any attempt to disrupt this equilibrium. One such attempt may be an external force or load. Stress results from forces such as tension, compression, or shear that pull, push, twist, cut, or in some way deform or change the shape of a piece of material.

Stress and Strain Stress is defined as the resistance offered by a material to external forces or loads. It is measured in terms of the force exerted per area. Normal stress is that applied perpendicular to the surface to which it is applied, i.e., tension or compression. Another way of defining it is to say that stress is the amount of force divided by the area over which it acts. An assumption is made that the stress is the same on each particle of area making up the total area. If this is so, the stress is uniformly distributed. The force and the area over which the force acts can be used to calculate the stress produced in the material.

Strain is the unit change in the size or shape of a material which under stress. Many times, we assume that a solid body is rigid; that is, when the body is loaded with some force, the body keeps its size and shape. This is far from correct. Regardless of how small the force, a body will alter its shape when subjected to a force. The change in a physical dimension is called deformation.

The stress-strain relationship is often used to study many mechanical properties. Figure 2.4 is a stress-strain diagram for low-carbon steel.

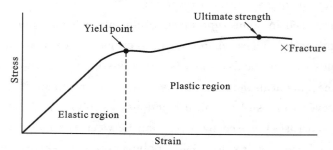

Figure 2.4 Stress-strain curve for mild steel

The straight-line portion of the diagram up to almost the yield point is known as the elastic region of the material. Within this range of stresses, the material will return to its original dimensions once the load has been removed.

Beyond the yield point, the material will continue to deform. In this region, known as the plastic region, plastic deformation takes place and when the load is removed, the material will not return to its original dimensions.

The yield point represents the dividing line or transition from the elastic to the plastic region of the curve. When the stress reaches the yield point, a large increase in strain occurs with no increase in stress.

Ultimate strength or tensile strength is the maximum stress developed in a material during a tensile test. It is a good indicator of the presence of defects in the crystal structure of a metal material, but it is not used too much in design because considerable plastic deformation has occurred in reaching this stress. In many applications the amount of plastic deformation must be limited to much smaller values than that accompanying the maximum stress.

Shear Stress   A second family of stresses is known as shear stress or shearing stress. A shearing force produces a shear stress in a material, which, in turn, results in a shearing deformation.

Ductility   A material that can undergo large plastic deformation without fracture is called a ductile material. A brittle material, on the other hand, shows an absence of ductility, and shows little evidence of forthcoming fracture by yielding.

Toughness   The ability or capacity of a material to absorb energy during plastic deformation is known as toughness. Most metals have good toughness and thus have good impact resistance. Compounds of metals and nonmetals, due to their inherent nature, ceramics do not possess the ability to redistribute stresses and plastically deform. So they have poor toughness, poor impact resistance, and poor fracture toughness.

Words and Expressions

chemical ['kemikəl] *n.* 化学制品；化学药品
fuel [fjuəl] *n.* 燃料
lubricant ['luːbrikənt] *n.* 润滑剂
polymer ['pɔlimə] *n.* 聚合物
ceramic [si'ræmik] *n.* 陶瓷制品，陶瓷 *a.* 陶器的
composite ['kɔmpəzit] *n.* 合成物
forecited ['fɔːˌsaitid] *a.* 前面会引用的，前述的
mechanical property   机械性能，力学性质
porosity [pɔː'rɔsiti] *n.* 多孔性，孔隙率[度]，(疏)松度
diameter [dai'æmitə] *n.* 直径
contour ['kɔntuə] *n.* 轮廓；周线，等高线
notch [nɔtʃ] *n.* 槽口，凹口
slope [sləup] *n.* 斜坡，斜面，倾斜 *v.* 倾斜
specific gravity   比重
cubic foot   立方尺
kilogram ['kiləgræm] *n.* 千克，公斤
chemical reaction   化学反应
vacuum ['vækjuəm] *n.* 真空

hydrogen ['haidrəudʒən] n. 氢
chlorine ['klɔ:ri:n] n. 氯
nitrogen ['naitrədʒən] n. 氮
corrosion [kə'rəuʒən] n. 侵蚀，腐蚀状态
oxidation [ɔksi'deiʃən] n. 氧化
oxide ['ɔksaid] n. 氧化物
electrochemical corrosion 电化学腐蚀
anodic [ə'nɔdik] a. 阳极的
cathodic [kə'θɔdik] a. 阴极的，负极的
water absorption 吸水性[率]
warp [wɔ:p] n. 弯曲；歪曲
swell [swel] n. 增大；膨胀
equilibrium [ˌi:kwi'libriəm] n. 平衡，均衡
stress [stres] n. 应力
strain [strein] n. 应变
perpendicular [ˌpə:pən'dikjulə] a. 垂直的，正交的
elastic [i'læstik] a. 弹性的
plastic ['plæstik] a. 塑性的，成型的
ductility [dʌk'tiliti] n. 展延性，柔软性
toughness ['tʌfnis] n. 韧性，刚性

Notes

1. Rubber is particularly prone to oxidation which is called aging.
（1）prone to：倾向于……，易于……
（2）aging：老化
（3）全句可翻译为：橡胶特别容易氧化，也就是老化。

2. Mechanical properties are structure-sensitive in the sense that they depend upon the type of crystal structure and its bonding forces, and especially upon the nature and behavior of the imperfections that exist within the crystal itself or at the grain boundaries.
（1）in the sense that：从某种意义上来说
（2）bonding force：键力，结合力
　　grain boundary：晶界
（3）全句可翻译为：机械性能是结构敏感的，从某种意义上来说机械性能取决于晶体结构的类型和晶体的键力，特别是取决于晶体本身或者晶界上的不完整性产生的特性和习性。

3. It is measured in terms of the force exerted per area.
（1）in terms of：根据，按照
（2）全句可翻译为：应力可以根据单位面积上施加的力来测量。

4. A brittle material, on the other hand, shows an absence of ductility, and shows little evidence of forthcoming fracture by yielding.
（1）on the other hand：另一方面，相反

（2）全句可翻译为：相反，脆性材料缺乏延展性，并且在屈服点几乎不表现出即将断裂的迹象。

Reading Material

Metals

In a strict definition, metal refers only to an element such as iron, gold, aluminum, and lead. The definition used for a metal will differ depending on the field of study. Chemists might use a different definition for metals than that used by physicists.

While metals comprise about three-fourths of the elements that we use, few find service in their pure form. There are several reasons for not using pure metals. Pure metals may be too hard or too soft, or they may be too costly because of their scarcity, but the key factor normally is that the desired property sought in engineering requires a blending of metals and elements. Thus, the combination forms (alloys) find the greatest use. For example, steel is an iron alloy made by combining iron, carbon, and some other elements. Aluminum-lithium alloys provide a 10% saving in weight over conventional aluminum alloy.

Metals are divides into two general types—ferrous and nonferrous. Ferrous metals are those which contain at least 50% iron, such as cast iron, wrought iron, steel, and stainless steel. Nonferrous metals are those which do not contain iron. However, some nonferrous metals may contain a small amount of iron as an impurity.

Steel is an alloy containing chiefly iron, carbon, and certain other elements in varying amounts. A wide range of physical properties may be obtained in steel by controlling the amount of carbon and other alloying elements and by subjecting the steel to various heat treatments. Plain carbon steels usually contain, besides iron and carbon, small amounts of silicon, sulphur, phosphorus, and manganese.

Carbon is by far the most important alloying element in steel. It is the amount of carbon present which largely determines the maximum hardness obtainable. The higher the carbon content, the higher the tensile strength and the greater the hardness to which the steel may be heat-treated. Table 2.1 is a classification of ferrous materials according to their carbon content.

Table 2.1 The carbon content of ferrous materials

Ferrous Material	Carbon Content
Wrought iron	Trace to 0.08%
Low-carbon steel	0.04% to 0.30%
Medium-carbon steel	0.30% to 0.60%
High-carbon steel	0.60% to 1.70%
Cast iron	1.70% to 4.50%

Low-carbon steels are usually used for low-strength parts requiring a great deal of forming. Medium-carbon steels are used for forgings and other applications where increased strength and a certain amount of ductility are necessary. High-carbon steels are used for high-strength parts such as spring, tools, and dies.

The nonferrous materials include common lightweight metals such as titanium and beryllium and common heavier metals such as copper, lead, tin and zinc. Among the heavier metals is a group of white metals, including tin, lead, and cadmium; they have lower melting points, about 230 ℃ to 330 ℃.

Lesson 3 Machine Design

Machine design is the application of technical science through designing the new product or improving the old product to meet the human need. The complete design of a machine is a complex process. It involves the project technology of much domain which not only studies the product in terms of its size, shape and construction details, but also concerns the various factors involved in the manufacture, marketing and use of the product.

People who perform the various functions of machine design are usually called designers or machine design engineers. Machine design is a creative work. The designer must have a good background in such fields as statics, kinematics, dynamics, and strength of materials, and in addition, be familiar with the fabrication materials and processes.

The design process for a machine first requires a clear understanding of the functions and the performance expected of that machine. The machine may be new, or it may be a revised version of an existing product. The design process, as shown in Figure 2.5, begins with the development of an original product concept. An innovation approach to design is

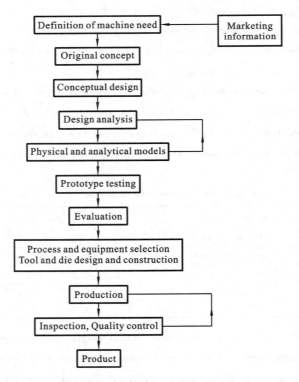

Figure 2.5 Steps in machine design

highly desirable, and even essential, at this stage for the product to be successful in the marketplace. A good designer should dare to propose the new idea, moreover is willing to undertake a certain amount of risk, when the new method is not suitable the existing method can be reinstated. Therefore, a designer must have patience, since there is no assurance of success for the time and effort expended.

Conceptual design is the generation of solution to meet the specified requirements. It can represent the sum of all subsystems and component parts which go on to make up the whole system. It is important to generate as many concepts and ideas as possible or economically expedient. There is a temptation to accept the first promising concept and proceed towards detailed design and the final product. This should be resisted as such results can invariably be better. It is worth noting that sooner or later your design will have to compete against those from other manufacturers, so the generation of developed concepts is prudent. Concepts are often most effectively generated by working individually and then coming together with other members of the design team at a later stage to evaluate the collective concepts.

Having generated the conceptual solution, the next step is the detailed design phase for machine. It often involves preparing analytical and physical models of the machine, as an aid to analyzing factors such as forces, stresses, deflections, and optimal part shape. The analysis will include as its objective satisfactory or superior performance, plus safety and durability with minimum weight, and a competitive cost. Optimum proportions and dimensions will be sought for each critically loaded section, together with a balance between the strengths of the several components.

The necessity for physical and analytical models depends on machine complexity. Today, constructing and studying analytical models is made easy by the use of computer-aided design and manufacturing techniques. Based on these models, the designer selects and specifies the final shape and dimensions of the product, its surface finish and dimensional accuracy, and the materials to be used.

Careful calculations are necessary to ensure the validity of a design. Calculations never appear on drawings, but are filed away for several reasons. In case of any part failures, it is desirable to know what was done in originally designing the defective components. Also, an experience file can result from having calculations from past projects. When a similar design is needed, past records are of great help. The checking of calculations is of utmost importance. The misplacement of one decimal point can ruin an originally acceptable project. All aspects of design work should be checked and rechecked.

An important design consideration is how a particular component is to be assembled into the final machine. Lift the hood of your car and observe how hundreds of components are put together in a limited space. Note also how difficult it is on some cars to remove a spark plug or an oil filer, much less to make repairs or perform maintenance on the engine.

The components of a product may be assembled by a variety of means, such as with bolts, screws, and rivets or by welding, soldering, or adhesive, bonding. The method of assembly should be reliable and economical and require as little time as possible to perform, particularly for mass-produced items.

Materials and their treatment will be chosen. Numerous materials are available to today's designers. The function of the product, its appearance, the cost of the material, and the cost of fabrication are important in making a selection. In this stage, a practical, workable design is developed, and materials are selected and specified for the various components. Although it is expected that the testing of prototype shows that some changes may have to be made in materials before the product is advanced to the production-design stage, this should not be taken as an excuse for not doing a thorough job of material selection.

The next step in the design process is to make and test a prototype, that is, an original working model of the machine. Testing is now done statistically, and the proper interpretation of test results is crucial to maintaining the quality of a product. Total quality control of a machine is one of the most important considerations in engineering design.

Tests must be designed to simulate as closely as possible the conditions under which the machine is to be used. These include environmental conditions such as temperature and humidity, as well as the effects of vibration and repeated use and misuse of the machine. Computer-aided design techniques are now capable of comprehensively and rapidly performing such simulations. During this stage, modifications in the original design, materials selected, or production methods may be necessary. Difficulties are often encountered in making the machine function properly while fulfilling design, quality, and service requirements, especially producing it economically.

Evaluation is a significant phase of the total design process. Evaluation is the final proof of a successful design, which usually involves the testing of a prototype in the laboratory. Here we wish to discover if the design really satisfies the need. Is it reliable? Will it compete successfully with similar products? Is it economical to manufacture and to use? Is it easily maintained and adjusted? Can a profit be made from its sale or use?

As a result of the tests and evaluations performed on the prototype, the engineer should have a quantitative measure of the success or failure of the design. The engineer will likely know whether the design should be abandoned or whether it should be retained for further improvement. This step leads back to the conceptual design step. Since a number of different design ideas may be tried, modified, and improved before a final design choice is made, the design process is quite iterative.

After this phase has been completed, appropriate manufacturing methods, equipment, and tooling should be selected with the cooperation of manufacturing engineers, process planners, and all others that are to be directly involved in production.

"Quality control" may be defined in its broadest sense as all those activities within an organization that positively affect the quality of the products produced. Thus, quality control includes those processes or operations of testing, measuring, and comparing the manufactured parts or apparatus with a standard, and then determining whether it should be accepted, rejected, adjusted, or reworked. Other quality control activities include the initial specifications applying to allowable tolerances and the extent of inspections considered essential of feasible. Every successful product is a reflection of the effectiveness of quality control. Consequently, the production-design engineer is vitally interested in this activity. The high reliability of ball and roller bearings is taken for granted today because of many years of careful control of materials, processes, and workmanship.

Words and Expressions

statics ['stætiks] *n.* 静力学
kinematics [,kaini'mætiks] *n.* 运动学
dynamics [dai'næmiks] *n.* 动力学
fabrication [,fæbri'keiʃən] *n.* 制造;构成
original [ə'ridʒənəl] *a.* 最初的,原始的;独创的,新颖的
reinstate ['ri:in'steit] *v.* 使恢复原状
conceptual design 概念(方案)设计
expedient [ik'spi:diənt] *n.* 权宜之计;对策
It is worth noting that... 值得注意的是……
prudent ['pru:dənt] *a.* 谨慎的
analytical [,ænə'litikəl] *a.* 分析的;解析的
deflection [di'flekʃən] *n.* 转向;偏斜;变形
optimum proportion 最优掺合量比,最佳比例
surface finish 表面加工
decimal ['desiməl] *a.* 十进制的,小数的
hood [hud] *n.* 车篷,引擎罩
bolt [bəult] *n.* 螺钉
screw [skru:] *n.* 螺杆,螺孔
rivet ['rivit] *n.* 铆钉
soldering ['sɔldəriŋ] *n.* 软焊,锡焊,低温焊接,钎焊
adhesive [əd'hi:siv] *n.* 粘合剂
bonding ['bɔndiŋ] *n.* 连(搭,焊,胶,粘)接
statistically [stə'tistikli] *ad.* 统计上地,统计地
vibration [vai'breiʃən] *n.* 振动
iterative ['itərətiv] *a.* 重复的,反复的
apparatus [,æpə'reitəs] *n.* 器械,设备,仪器
allowable tolerance 允许公差

Notes

1. An innovation approach to design is highly desirable, and even essential, at this stage for the product to be successful in the marketplace.

(1) and even essential:插入语,更为必要

（2）全句可翻译为：在设计中采用创新的方法对于成功地开创市场是极为理想的，甚至是很有必要的。

2. Note also how difficult it is on some cars to remove a spark plug or an oil filer, much less to make repairs or perform maintenance on the engine.

（1）how difficult...an oil filter 是 note 的宾语从句。

（2）全句可翻译为：也应该注意到要在某些汽车上卸下火花塞或滤油器是多么困难，更不用说要对发动机进行修理和维护了。

3. Testing is now done statistically, and the proper interpretation of test results is crucial to maintaining the quality of a product.

全句可翻译为：目前，测试是按统计方法进行的，且对检测结果进行恰当的整理分析是保证产品质量的关键。

4. Difficulties are often encountered in making the machine function properly while fulfilling design, quality, and service requirements, especially producing it economically.

全句可翻译为：要使产品获得满意的功能，在进行正确的设计、质量控制及管理服务等方面，尤其是在经济地制作产品方面常会遇到一些困难。

Reading Material

Safety Factors in Engineering Designs

Engineering design is a systematic process by which solutions to the needs of humankind are obtained. The process is applied to problems of varying complexity. For example, mechanical engineers will use the design process to find an effective method to convert reciprocating motion to circular motion for the drive train in an internal combustion engine; electrical engineers will use the process to design electrical generating systems using falling water as the power source; and materials engineers use the process to design ablative materials which enable astronauts to safely reenter the earth's atmosphere.

Engineering design is the process of devising a system, component, or process to meet desired needs. It is a decision making process, in which the basic sciences, mathematics, and engineering sciences are applied to convert resources optimally to meet a stated objective.

Any consideration of engineering design of systems utilizing materials must initially deal with Murphy's Law for materials systems and the law of materials applications:

Murphy's Law: If any material can fail, it will.

Laws of materials applications:

(1) All materials are unstable.

(2) The materials system is only as strong or as stable as its weakest or most unstable component.

All materials are indeed unstable. Even such materials as platinum can be degraded in particular environments. Under stress, all materials respond to that stress. Given enough time, failure can be calculated to occur in all materials under creep stress. Stress and environment can act in concert to cause failure, for example, stress corrosion cracking. Creep temperature effects and stress-temperature effects can contribute to the degradation of properties and components and system failure.

The concept of safety factors is normally applied to the evaluation and consideration of strength of materials used in a design. Safety factors are normally applied to the yield strength of a material but can be applied to the ultimate tensile strength. The yield stress is the stress above which the material will deform permanently. Having exceeded the yield stress or yield strength, materials begin to creep. That is, dislocation will be created, and application of a load to continue the stress above yield will allow the material to slip. So if a material is used in a service environment in which the yield stress is never exceeded, it is unlikely it will fail by being over stressed.

Quality cannot be inspected into a product after it is made. The practice of inspecting products after they are made is now being replaced rapidly by the broader view that quality must be built into a product—from the design stage through all subsequent stages of manufacture and assembly. Producing defective products can be very costly to the manufacturer, creating difficulties in assembly operations, necessitating repairs in the field, and resulting in customer dissatisfaction. Contrary to general public opinion, high-quality products do not necessarily cost more than poor-quality products.

Total quality control and quality assurance have become the responsibility of everyone involved in designing and manufacturing a product. Our awareness of the technological and economic importance of built-in product quality has been heightened further by recent pioneers in quality control. They pointed out the importance of the management's commitment to product quality, pride of workmanship at all levels of production, and the use of modern statistical techniques to identify the causes of quality control problems.

Lesson 4 Engineering Drawing

Engineering drawing is a cornerstone of engineering. It is a graphical language used by engineers and other technical personnel associated with the engineering profession. The purpose of engineering drawing is to convey graphically the ideas and information necessary for the construction or analysis of machines, structures, or systems.

Study of the fundamentals of engineering drawing is one key to your success as an engineer. Being able to describe an idea with a sketch is a prerequisite of the engineering profession. The ability to put forth a three-dimensional geometry in a form that can be communicated to other engineers, scientists, technicians, and nontechnical personnel is a valuable asset. Of equal importance is to know how to read and understand the graphics prepared by others. The ability to communicate is the key to success for a practicing engineer. Graphic communication, along with written and oral communication, constitutes an important part of a program of study in engineering. The fundamentals of the drawing language are universal in the industrialized world, an advantage not afforded by the written and spoken language. Thus engineering drawing may be said to be "a language for engineers".

The basis for much engineering drawing is orthographic representation (projection). Objects are depicted by front, top, side, auxiliary, or oblique views, or combination of these. The complexity of an object determines the number of views shown. At times, pictorial views are also shown.

Engineering drawings often include such features as various types of lines, dimensions, lettered notes, sectional views, and symbols. They may be in the form of carefully planned and checked mechanical drawing, or they may be freehand sketches. Usually a sketch precedes the mechanical drawing. Final drawings are usually made on tracing paper, cloth or Mylar film, so that many copies can be made quickly and cheaply by such processes as, blueprinting, ammonia-developed printing, or lithography.

1. Section Drawings

Many objects have complicated interior detail which cannot be clearly shown by means of front, top, side, or pictorial views. Section views enable engineer or detailer to show the interior detail in such cases. Features of section drawing are cutting-plane symbols, which show where imaginary cutting planes are passed to produce the sections, and section-lining, which appears in the section view on all portions that have been in contact with the cutting plane. When only a part of the object is to be shown in section, conventional representation such as a revolved, rotated, or broken-out section is used. Details such as flat surfaces, knurls, and threads are treated conventionally, which facilitates the making and reading of engineering drawings by experienced personnel. Figure 2.6 shows a section view, and how a cutting plane works.

When a cutting plane cuts an object lengthwise, the section obtained is commonly called a longitudinal section; when crosswise, it is called a cross section. It is designated as being either a full section, a half section, or a broken section. If the plane cuts entirely across the object, the section represented is known as a full section. If it cuts only halfway across a symmetrical object, the section is a half section. A broken section is a partial one, which is used when less than a half section is needed.

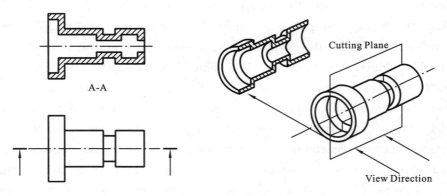

Figure 2.6　A section drawing

2. Hatching

On sections and sectional views solid area should be hatched to indicate this fact. Hatching is drawn with a thin continuous line, equally spaced (preferably about 4 mm apart, though never less than 1 mm) and preferably at an angle of 45 degrees.

When you are hatching an object, but the object has areas that are separated, all areas of the object should be hatched in the same direction and with the same spacing. When hatching assembled parts, the direction of the hatching should be reversed on adjacent parts. If more than two parts are adjacent, then the hatching should be staggered to emphasize the fact that these parts are separate. Sometimes, it is difficult to hatch very thin sections. To emphasize solid wall the wall can be filled in. This should only be used when the wall thickness size is less than 1 mm. When hatching large areas, the hatching can be limited to the area near the edges of the part.

3. Dimensioning

In addition to describing the shape of objects, many drawings must show dimensions. A dimensioned drawing should provide all the information necessary for a finished product or part to be manufactured. Dimensions are always drawn using continuous thin lines. Two projection lines indicate where the dimension starts and finishes. Projection lines do not touch the object and are drawn perpendicular to the element you are dimensioning. This is accomplished by placing the required values along dimension lines and by giving additional information in the form of notes which are referenced to the parts in question by angled lines called leaders. In general units can be omitted from dimensions if a statement of the units is included on your drawing. The general convention is to dimension in mm. All dimensions less than 1 should have a leading zero, i.e., .35 should be written as 0.35.

In general all notes should be written in capital letters to aid legibility. All lettering should be of the same size and preferably no smaller than 3 mm. Working types of drawing may differ in styles of dimensioning, lettering, positioning of the numbers, and in the type of fraction used. If special precision is required, an upper and a lower allowable limit are shown. Such tolerance, or limit, dimensioning is necessary for the manufacture of interchangeable mating parts.

4. Layout drawings

It is important that you follow some simple rules when producing an engineering drawing which although may not be useful now, will be useful when working in industry. All engineering drawings should feature an information box. An example is shown below in Figure 2.7.

Title The title of the drawing.

Name The name of the person who produced the drawing. This is important for quality control so that problems with the drawing can be traced back to their origin.

Checked In many engineering firms, drawings are checked by a second person before they are sent to manufacture, so that any potential problems can be identified early.

Version Many drawings will get amended over the period of the parts life. Giving each

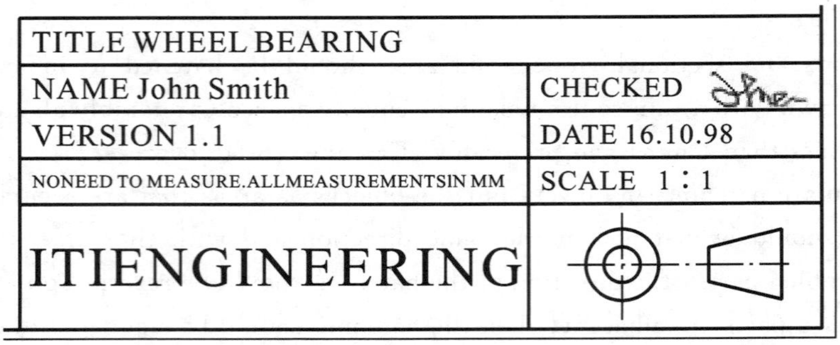

TITLE WHEEL BEARING	
NAME John Smith	CHECKED
VERSION 1.1	DATE 16.10.98
NO NEED TO MEASURE. ALL MEASUREMENTS IN MM	SCALE 1∶1
ITIENGINEERING	

Figure 2.7 Common information recorded on an engineering drawing

drawing a version number helps people identify if they are using the most recent version of the drawing.

Date   The date the drawing was created or amended on.

Scale   The scale of the drawing. Large parts won't fit on paper so the scale provides a quick guide to the final size of the product.

Projection System   The projection system used to create the drawing should be identified to help people read the drawing. (Projection systems will be covered later).

Company Name   Many CAD drawings may be distributed outside the company so the company name is usually added to identify the source.

5. Assembly Drawings

A drawing that shows the parts of a machine or machine unit assembled in their relative working positions is an assembly drawing. Detailed dimensions required for manufacture are excluded from assembly drawings. But overall dimensions of the assembled object are usually indicated. If the spatial relationship between parts is important for the product to function correctly then these should also be indicated on the drawing. For example, indicating the maximum and minimum clearance between two parts. If there are internal assemblies, sectional views should be used.

Each part is given a unique number, indicated on the drawing by a circle with the number in it and a leader line pointing to the part. The leader line terminates in an arrow if the line touches the edge of the component or a dot if the line terminates inside the part. A table of parts should be added to the drawing to identify each part.

Words and Expressions

fundamental [ˌfʌndəˈmentl] n. 基本原理 a. 基础的,基本的
sketch [sketʃ] n. 略图,草图
prerequisite [ˈpriːˈrekwizit] n. 先决条件 a. 必备的
put forth   提出;发表;拿出
practicing [ˈpræktisiŋ] a. 开业的,从业的,在工作的
orthographic [ˌɔːθəˈɡræfik] a. 垂直线的
orthographic representation   正视表示法

depict [di'pikt] *vt.* 描述,描写
auxiliary [ɔːg'ziljəri] *a.* 辅助的;补助的
oblique [ə'bliːk] *a.* 倾斜的
pictorial [pik'tɔːriəl] *a.* 图示的
sectional view   剖视图
tracing paper   描图纸
Mylar ['mailɑː] *n.* 迈拉(一种聚酯类高分子物的商品名)
lithography [li'θɔgrəfi] *n.* 平版印刷术
knurl [nəːl] *n.* 硬节,压花
thread [θred] *n.* 螺纹
symmetrical [si'metrikəl] *a.* 对称的,均匀的
hatching ['hætʃiŋ] *n.* 阴影,剖面线
staggered ['stægəd] *a.* 错列的,交叉排的
perpendicular to   垂直于
allowable limit   允许极限
tolerance ['tɔlərəns] *n.* 公差

Notes

1. When a cutting plane cuts an object lengthwise, the section obtained is commonly called a longitudinal section; when crosswise, it is called a cross section.

（1）longitudinal section:纵剖面
    cross section:横剖面

（2）全句可翻译为:当切平面纵向切开一个物体时,所获得的剖面一般叫做纵剖面;当横向切开一个物体时,就称为横剖面。

2. This is accomplished by placing the required values along dimension lines and by giving additional information in the form of notes which are referenced to the parts in question by angled lines called leaders.

（1）which 指代 notes。

（2）全句可翻译为:这一工作可以通过沿尺寸线放置所需要的值及以标注的形式给出附加信息来完成。标注就是用称为引出线的折线给有疑问的零件加附注。

3. If the spatial relationship between parts is important for the product to function correctly then these should also be indicated on the drawing.

全句可翻译为:如果零件间的空间关系对于产品的正常运行非常重要,那么也要在图中标明。

Reading Material

CAD

CAD is a term which means computer-aided design. It is the technology concerned with the use of digital computer to perform certain function in design. The computer system consist of the hardware and software to perform the specialized design functions required by particular user firm. The CAD hardware typically includes the computer, one or more graphics display terminals, keyboards, and other peripheral equipments. The CAD software consists of the computer programs to implement computer graphics on the system plus application programs to facilitate the engineering functions of the user company. Examples of these application programs include stress-strain analysis of components, dynamic response of mechanisms, heat-transfer calculations, and numerical control part programming. The collection of application programs will vary from one user firm to the next because their product lines, manufacturing processes, and customer markets are different. These factors give rise to differences in CAD system requirements.

CAD systems can entail a whole new set of drafting philosophies, all of which enhance productivity. For instance, most systems now on the market have a number of built-in functions that make new and useful drafting techniques automatic. Layering, for example, enable drafters to create drawings in logical segments that can be stored separately for easy identification; but the segment can still be output together, in one single piece, which illustrates the entire drawing at once. Layering with a graphics system uses the same principle except the overlays are logical rather than physical.

Working in three dimensions with the computer, graphics will be produced easily in two-dimensional or three-dimensional modes depending upon the application. Three-dimensional geometric modeling involves wireframe, surface, and solid models. From a solid model, a complete analysis of performance of the object can be performed on the computer with appropriate software, for example CAD.

Another example of a productivity enhancement for drafting might involve automating auxiliary views of a design. By pressing the right button or by entering the right command, a drawing could be turned 90 degrees in one direction or another. Three-dimensional designs could be rotated on any axis or displayed in any of several projections.

The potential is really endless. Productivity increases are limited only when system management philosophies are limited. As an additional example, consider a drafting center for an architectural firm that specializes in designing warehouses. Much of the design work is repetitive and can be carried over from one job to the next. In such a situation, standard components of each drawing can be automated by creating macros. These macros are nothing more than a series of graphics system commands strung together and executed as a single unit to build.

Other macro programs could be useful. A set of commands might be put together that change the dimensioning of a drawing automatically from English to metric unit, or that automatically scale an entire drawing and rotate it to a desired orientation, or that generate a bill of materials list for complicated engineering drawings.

Lesson 5 Machining

1. Introduction

All machining processes remove material to form shapes. As metals are still the most widely used materials in manufacturing, machining processes are usually used for metals. However, machining can also be used to shape plastics and other materials which are becoming more widespread. Basically all the different forms of machining involve removing material from a component by using a rotating cutter. The differences between the various types arise from the relative motion between cutting tool and workpiece and the type of cutting tool used.

Typically machining will be done by using a machine tool. This tool holds the workpiece and the rotating cutting tool and allows relative movement between the two. Usually machine tools are dedicated to one type of machining operation, although some more flexible tools allow more than one type of machining to be performed. The machine tools can either be under manual or automatic (Computer Numeric Control—CNC) control. Automatic control is more expensive because of the investment in the necessary control mechanisms, however it becomes more desirable as the number of components produced increases and labour costs can be reduced.

The speed at which a machine tool can process individual components is a function of the cutting speed of the tool and the downtime involved in changing the workpiece and maintaining the tool (this will usually involve changing the cutting edges of the tool). Some very flexible tools allow automatic changing of components and cutting tools, however they greatly add to initial purchase price of the machine tool.

The cutting speed of the tool is usually dictated by the type of material being machined. In general, the harder the material is, the longer the machining time is. Machining speed can be increased by increasing the rotational speed of the cutter, however this will be at the expense of the tool life. Hence for machining processes there is an optimum cutting speed that balances tooling costs with cutting speed.

In order to dissipate the heat generated between the workpiece and the cutting tool, cutting fluids are sprayed onto the tool. The cutting fluid also acts to remove cut material away from the cutting region and lubricates the tool-workpiece interface but may require that the component is cleaned afterwards.

The advantage of machining processes is high precision components to be rapidly produced. However, machining processes are not suitable for removing large amounts of material. Because there can be a large amount of wastage.

2. Turning

Turning is widely used in industry to produce all kinds of machine parts. In this process, the workpiece is held in two rotating spindles and made contact with a cutting edge removing material from the surface of the workpiece. By moving the cutting tool along the length of the workpiece, circular section components are rapidly produced, as shown in Figure 2.8. The

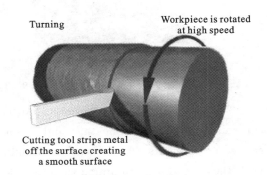

Figure 2.8　The abridged general view of turning

tool can be held at varying distance from the workpiece to create components of varying diameter. By changing the position of the cutting tool as the tool moves along the workpiece, conical components can be produced. The machine tool used for this process is called a lathe.

Turning can be used to produce components such as shafts and rods. It can also be used to create internal cuts. This process is called boring. Boring can not actually produce the initial "hole" in the component, this has to be done with some other process such as drilling. However, boring can be used to increase the dimensions of an internal circular cut. Another turning process is thread cutting, which can be done on most lathes.

Lathe control can either be manual or automatic. Modern multi-spindle machines allow rapid processing of a number of components.

3. Milling

Milling is carried out by means of a multiedge rotating tool known as a milling cutter. In this process, metal removal is achieved through combining the rotary motion of the milling cutter and linear motions of the workpiece simultaneously. Milling operations are employed in producing flat, contoured and helical surfaces as well as for thread-and gear-cutting operations.

Each of the cutting edges of a milling cutter acts as an individual single-point cutter when it engages with the workpiece metal. Therefore, each of those cutting edges has appropriate rake and relief angles, as shown in Figure 2.9. Since only a few of the cutting edges are engaged with the workpiece at a time, heavy cuts can be taken without adversely affecting the tool life. In fact, the permissible cutting speeds and feeds for milling are three to four times higher than those for turning or drilling. Moreover, the quality of the surface machined by milling is generally superior to the quality of surfaces machined by turning, shaping, or drilling.

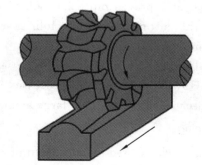

(a) cylindrical mill   (b) form milling cutter

Figure 2.9 Types of milling cutters

Control of the milling machine tool can be either manual or automatic. Modern CNC controlled milling machines are highly sophisticated, capable of producing highly complex shaped components. A wide variety of milling cutters is available in industry. This, together with the fact that a milling machine is a very versatile machine tool, makes the milling machine the backbone of a machining workshop.

4. Grinding

This process uses a rotating grinding wheel which has abrasive grit particles on its surface to remove material from a component. It is a specialized form of machining in that instead of a single or several cutting tools being used, the cutting surface is provided by the grit particles.

In metal cutting terms, grinding is a hybrid between turning and milling. Like milling, the grinding tool is in motion, and like turning, the workpiece is also nearly always moving, although not necessarily rotating. That distinction between rotating workpieces, and those moving in a linear or oscillating fashion under the grinding tool, but otherwise fixed, defines the most basic division in grinding application. The former is generically described as "cylindrical" grinding, while the latter is "surface" grinding, even though both types can produce precision surfaces on the workpiece.

Because only small amounts of material can economically be removed, grinding is usually used as a finishing process. In addition, the dimensional accuracy of the workpiece is improved since tolerances of 0.000 25 mm are possible in grinding operations. Grinding can be performed on flat, cylindrical, or even internal surfaces by employing specialized machine tools, which are referred to as grinding machines. Obviously, grinding machines differ in construction as well as capabilities, and the type to be employed is determined mainly by the geometrical shape and nature of the surface to be ground. The process can either be automated or under manual control.

5. Drilling

This is a very common machining process used to produce holes in components. A drill bit is rotated at high speeds to create a hole. The screw thread shape of the drill bit causes materials to be cut away as the drill bit is pushed into the workpiece and also to allow lubricants and coolants to reach the cutting edges and the surface being machined.

There are several types of drill available. Hand held drills are useful for drilling holes in any location, but require accurate use. Pillar drills used in workshops are fixed orientation drills. The workpiece is clamped so that it can't move which makes it easier to drill more accurate holes. The problem with pillar drills is that the workpiece has to be small enough to fit on to the table. Note that different materials have their own drill bits.

Words and Expressions

cutter ['kʌtə] n. 刀具
arise from 由……引起，源于
workpiece ['wəːkpiːs] n. 工件，加工件
machine tool 机床
flexible tool 柔性机床，灵活机床
dissipate ['disipeit] v. 驱散，耗散
spray [sprei] vt. 喷射，喷溅

turning ['tə:niŋ] n. 车削
spindle ['spindl] n. (主)轴,杆,心轴
cutting edge 切削刃
circular ['sə:kjulə] a. 圆形的
conical ['kɔnikəl] a. 圆锥的,圆锥形的
lathe [leið] n. 车床
milling ['miliŋ] n. 铣(削),铣削法
helical ['helikəl] a. 螺旋状的
engage [in'geidʒ] v. 啮合,衔接
rake [reik] n. 斜度
rake angle 刀面角,前角
relief angle 后角
grinding ['graindiŋ] n. 研磨,磨削
grinding wheel 砂轮
abrasive grit 铁粒,研磨用砂粒
hybrid ['haibrid] n. 混合物 a. 混合的
oscillate ['ɔsileit] v. (来回)摆动,振荡
cylindrical grinding 圆柱面磨削,外圆磨削
surface grinding 平面磨削
drilling ['driliŋ] n. 钻孔
drill bit 钻头
pillar drill 柱式钻床

Notes

1. The speed at which a machine tool can process individual components is a function of the cutting speed of the tool and the downtime involved in changing the workpiece and maintaining the tool (this will usually involve changing the cutting edges of the tool).

(1) the speed at:在某方面的速度

(2) 全句可翻译为:机床加工单独一个零件的速度是刀具的切削速度和包括更换工件、调整刀具(通常包括改变刀具的切削刃)在内的停工时间的函数。

2. Machining speed can be increased by increasing the rotational speed of the cutter, however this will be at the expense of the tool life.

(1) at the expense of:以(损害)……为代价

(2) 全句可翻译为:加工速度可以通过增大刀具的转速得到提高,然而这是以损害刀具的寿命为代价。

3. That distinction between rotating workpieces, and those moving in a linear or oscillating fashion under the grinding tool, but otherwise fixed, defines the most basic division in grinding application.

(1) but otherwise fixed 为插入语,作补充说明。

(2) 全句可翻译为:旋转工件与相对磨削工具作直线或往复运动(否则固定安装)的工件

相比,它们之间的区别正是磨削在应用方面的基本分类依据。

Reading Material

Numerical Control

Numerical control (NC) is a method of controlling the movements of machine components by directly inserting coded instructions in the form of numerical data into the system. The system automatically interprets these data and converts it to output signals. These signals, in turn, control various machine components, such as turning spindles on and off, changing tools, moving the workpiece or the tools along specific paths, and turning cutting fluids on and off.

In numerical control, data concerning all aspects of the machining operation, such as locations, speeds, feeds, and cutting fluid, are stored on magnetic tape, cassettes, floppy or hard disks, or paper or plastic tape. Data are stored on punched 25 mm wide paper or plastic tape, as originally developed and still used. An organized list of commands constitutes an NC program. The program may be used repeatedly to obtain identical results. Manual operation of machine tools may be unsurpassable in producing fine-quality work, but such qualities are not consistent. NC is not a machine method; it is a means for machine control. NC is considered as one of the most dramatic and productive developments in manufacturing in this century.

NC starts with the parts programmer who, after studying the engineering drawing, visualizes the operations needed to machine the workpiece. The program is prepared before the part is manufactured and consists of a sequence of symbolic codes that specify the desired action of the tool, workpiece and machine. The engineering drawing of the workpiece is examined, and processes are selected to transform the raw material into a finished part that meets the dimensions, tolerances, and specifications. This process planning is concerned with the preparation of an operations sheet or a route sheet or traveler. Once the operations are known, those that pertain to NC are further engineered in that detail sequences are selected.

A program is prepared by listing codes that define the sequence. A part programmer is trained about manufacturing processes and is knowledgeable of the steps required to machine a part, and documents these steps in a special format. These are two ways to program for NC, by manual or computer assisted part programming. The part programmer must understand the processor language used by the computer and the NC machine.

If manual programming is required, the machining instructions are listed on a form called a part program manuscript. This manuscript gives instructions for the cutter and workpiece, which must be positioned relative to each other for the path instructions to machine the design. Computer assisted part programming, on the other hand, does much of the calculation and translates brief instruction into a detailed instruction and coded language for the control tape.

There are two basic types of numerical control systems: point to point and contouring.

Point to point control system, also called positioning, are simpler than contouring control system. Its primary purpose is to move a tool or workpiece from one programmed point to another. Point to point systems are suitable for hole machining operations such as drilling, countersinking, couterboring, reaming, boring and tapping, hole punching machines, spotwelding machines, and assembly machines also use point to point NC systems.

Contouring system, also known as the continuous path system, positioning and cutting operations are both along controlled paths but at different velocities. Because the tool cuts as it travels along a prescribed path, accurate control and synchronization of velocities and movements are important. The contouring system is used on lathes, milling machines, grinders, welding machinery, and machining centers. Movement along the path, or interpolation, occurs incrementally, by one of several basic methods. There are a number of interpolation schemes that have been developed to deal with the various problems that are encountered in generating a smooth continuous path with a contouring type NC system. They include linear interpolation, circular interpolation, helical interpolation, parabolic interpolation and cubic interpolation. In all interpolations, the path controlled is that of the center of rotation of the tool. Compensation for different tools, different diameter tools, or tool wear during machining, can be made in the NC program.

PART THREE Measurement

Lesson 1 Measurement

1. Measurement

Measurement is the process of associating numbers with physical quantities and phenomena.

Measurement is fundamental to the sciences; to engineering, building, and other technical matters; and to much everyday activity. For that reason the elements, conditions, limitations, and theoretical foundations of measurement have been much studied.

Measurements may be made by unaided human senses—in which case they are often called estimates—or, more usually, by the use of instruments, which may range in complexity from simple rules for measuring lengths to highly sophisticated systems designed to detect and measure quantities entirely beyond the capabilities of the senses, such as radio waves from a distant star or the magnetic moment of a subatomic particle.

Measurement begins with a definition of the measurand, the quantity that is to be measured, and it always involves a comparison of the measurand with some known quantity of the same kind. If the measurand is not accessible for direct comparison, it is converted or "transduced" into an analogous measurement signal. Since measurement always involves some interaction between the measurand and the observer or observing instrument, there is always an exchange of energy, which, although in everyday applications is negligible, can become considerable in some types of measurement and thereby limit accuracy.

In general, measuring systems comprise a number of functional elements. One element is required to discriminate the measurand and sense its dimensions or frequency. This information is then transmitted throughout the system by physical signals. If the measurand is itself active, such as water flow, it may power the signal; if passive, it must trigger the signal by interaction either with an energetic probe, such as a light source or X-ray tube, or with a carrier signal. Eventually the physical signal is compared with a reference signal of known quantity that has been subdivided or multiplied to suit the range of measurement required. The reference signal is derived from measurands of known quantity by a process called calibration. The comparison may be an analogue process in which signals in a continuous dimension are brought to equality. An alternative comparison process is quantization by counting, i. e., dividing the signal into parts of equal and known size and adding up the number of parts.

Other functions of measurement systems facilitate the basic process described above. Amplification ensures that the physical signal is strong enough to complete the measurement. In order to reduce degradation of the measurement as it progresses through the system, the signal maybe converted to coded or digital form. Magnification, enlarging the measurement signal without increasing its power, is often necessary to match the output of one element of the system with the input of another, such as matching the size of the readout meter with the discerning power of the eye.

One important type of measurement is the analysis of resonance, or the frequency of variation within a physical system. This is determined by harmonic analysis, commonly exhibited in the sorting of signal by a radio receiver. Computation is another important measurement process, in which measurement signals are manipulated mathematically, typically by some form of analogue or digital computer. Computers may also provide a control function in monitoring system performance.

Measuring systems may also include devices for transmitting signals over great distances. All measuring systems, even highly automated ones, include some method of displaying the signal to an observer. Visual display systems may comprise a calibrated chart and a pointer, all integrated display on a CRT (cathode-ray tube), or a digital readout. Measurement systems often include elements for recording. A common type utilizes a writing stylus that records measurements on a moving chart. Electrical recorders may include feedback reading devices for greater accuracy.

The actual performance of measuring instruments is affected by numerous external and internal factors. Among external factors are noise and interference, both of which tend to mask or distort the measurement signal. Internal factors include linearity, resolution, precision, and accuracy, all of which are characteristic of a given instrument or system, and dynamic response, drift, and hysteresis, which are effects produced in the process of measurement itself. The general question of error in measurement raises the topic of measurement theory.

2. Theory of measurement

Measurement theory is the study of how numbers are assigned to objects and phenomena, and its concerns include the kinds of things that can be measured, how different measures relate to each other, and the problem of error in the measurement process. Any general theory of measurement must come to grips with three basic problems: error; representation, which is the justification of number assignment; uniqueness, which is the degree to which the kind of representation chosen approaches being the only one possible for the object or phenomenon in question.

Various systems of axioms, or basic rules and assumptions have been formulated as a basis for measurement theory. Some of the most important types of axioms include axioms of order, axioms of extension, axioms of difference, axioms of conjointness, and axioms of geometry. Axioms of order ensure that the order imposed on objects by the assignment of numbers is the same order attained in actual observation or measuremEmt. Axioms of extension deal with the representation of such attributes as time duration, length, and mass, which can be combined, or concatenated, for multiple objects exhibiting the attribute in question. Axioms of difference govern the measuring of intervals. Axioms of conjointness postulate that attributes that cannot be measured empirically (for example, loudness, or intelligence, or hunger) can be measured by observing the way their component dimensions change in relation to each other. Axioms of geometry govern the representation of dimensionally complex attributes by pairs of numbers, triples of numbers, or even n-tuples of numbers.

The problem of error is one of the central concerns of measurement theory. At one time it was believed that errors of measurement could eventually be eliminated through the refinement of scientific principles and equipment. This belief is no longer held by most scientists, and almost all physical measurements reported today are accompanied by some indication of the limitation of accuracy or the probable degree of error. Among the various types of error that must be taken into account are errors of observation (which include instrumental errors, personal errors, systematic errors, and random errors), errors of sampling, and direct and indirect errors (in which one erroneous measurement is used in computing other measurements).

Measurement theory dates back to the 4th century BC, when a theory of magnitudes developed by the Greek mathematicians Eudoxus of Cnidus and Thaeatetus was included in Euclid's *Elements*. The first systematic work on observational error was produced by the English mathematician Thomas Simpson in 1757, but the fundamental work on error theory was done by two 18th-century French astronomers, Joseph-Louis, Count de Lagrange, and Pierre-Simon, Marquess de Laplace. The first attempt to incorporate measurement theory into the social sciences also occurred in the 18th century. When Jeremy Bentham, a British utilitarian moralist, attempted to create a theory for the measurement of value. Modem axiomatic theories of measurement derive from the work of two German scientists, H. L. F. von Helmholtz and L. O. Hölder and contemporary work on the application of measurement theory to psychology and economics derives in large part from the work of Oskar Morgenstern and John von Neumanm.

Since most social theories are speculative in nature, attempts to establish standard measuring sequences or techniques for them have met with limited success. Some of the problems involved in social measurement include the lack of universally accepted theoretical frameworks and thus of quantifiable measurands, sampling errors, problems associated with the intrusion of the measurer on the object being measured, and the subjective nature of the information received from human subjects. Economics is probably the social science that has had the most success in adopting measurement theories, primarily because many economic variables (like price and quantity) can be measured easily and objectively. Demography has successfully employed measurement techniques as well, particularly in the area of mortality tables.

3. Weights and measures

Measurement is accomplished through the comparison of a measurand with some known quantity of the same kind. The term weights and measures signifies those standard quantities by which such comparisons are achieved. Standard quantities may be established arbitrarily or by reference to some universal constant. Standards for different kinds of quantities may develop separately or may be integrated into logical systems of units. Originally standard measures were four in number: those for mass(weight), volume(liquid or dry measure), length, and area. To these have been added standard measurements of temperature, luminosity, pressure, electric current, and others.

The earliest standard measurements appeared in the ancient Mediterranean cultures and were based on parts of the body, or on calculations of what man or beast could haul, or on the volume of containers or the area of fields in common use. The Egyptian cubit is generally recognized to have been the most widespread unit of linear measurement in the ancient world. It came into use around 3000 BC and was based on the length of the arm from the elbow to the extended finger tips. It was standardized by a royal master cubit of black granite, against which all cubit sticks in Egypt were regularly checked. One of the earliest known weight measures was the Babylonian mina. Two surviving examples vary widely—one weighs 640 g(about 1.4 pounds), and the other 978 g(about 2.15 pounds).

The terms ounce, inch, pound and mile come from the Roman adoption of earlier Greek measuring units. The Roman system of measurement persisted into the Middle Ages in Europe, but there was great diversity of standards. Thereafter various national governments made efforts to standardize their systems, producing a welter of often confusing units and standards. The British Imperial and U.S. Customary are two of the most elaborate such systems.

The first proposal for what would later become the metric system was made by a French clergyman, Gabriel Mouton, around 1670. He suggested a standard linear measurement based on the length of the arc of one minute of longitude on the Earth's surface and divided decimally. Mouton's proposal was much discussed and refined, but it was not until 1795 that France officially adopted the metric system. Its spread throughout the rest of Europe was accelerated by the military successes of the French Revolution and Napoleon, but in many places it took a long time to overcome the nonrational customary systems of weights and measures that had been used for centuries.

Now the standard system in most nations, the metric system has been modernized to take into account 20th-century technological advances. In Paris in 1960 an international convention agreed on a new metric-based system of units. This was the Système Internationale (SI). Six base units were adopted: the metre(length), the kilogram(mass), the second(time), the ampere(electric current), the degree Kelvin(temperature), and the candela (luminosity). Each was keyed to a standard value. The kilogram was represented by a cylinder of platinum-iridium alloy kept at the International Bureau of Weights and Measures in Sèvres, France, with a duplicate at the U.S. National Bureau of Standards. The kilogram is the only one of the six units represented by a physical object as a standard. In contrast, the metre was set to be 1 650 763.73 wavelengths in vacuum of the orange-red line of the spectrum of krypton-86, and the other units were related to similarly derived natural standards.

Other units derived from basic SI units include the coulomb(charge), joule(energy), newton(force), hertz(frequency), watt(power), ohm(resistance), and cubic metre(volume).

Words and Expressions

measurand ['meʒərənd] n. 被测的物理量；被测对象
active ['æktiv] a. 积极的，主动的；有源的
passive ['pæsiv] a. 被动的，消极的；无源的
discriminate [dis'krimineit] v. 区别，识别；求解；区别对待
amplification [ˌæmplifi'keiʃən] n. 放大；扩大；加强，增强
resonance ['rezənəns] n. 共鸣，共振，谐振
harmonic [hɑː'mɔnik] a. 调和的，谐波的，音乐般的，和声的，悦耳的 n. 调和函数；谐波
harmonic analysis   谐波分析
chart [tʃɑːt] n. 图表，有刻度的记录纸 v. 制成图表
CRT(cathode-ray tube)   阴极射线管，示波管
feedback ['fiːdbæk] n. 反馈
mask [mɑːsk] n. 口罩；假面具；掩饰 v. 戴面具，掩饰，掩盖，屏蔽；[计算机]掩码
distort [dis'tɔːt] v. 扭曲，失真，畸变
hysteresis [ˌhistə'riːsis] n. 磁滞现象
come to grips with   努力钻研，认真对待
axiom ['æksiəm] n. 定理，原理，公理，格言
be taken into account   考虑(到)，注意(到)，计及
Euclid ['juːklid] n. 欧几里得
demography [di'mɔgrəfi] n. 人口统计学
weights and measures   度量衡，权度
luminosity [ˌljuːmi'nɔsiti] n. 光明，光辉；[计算机] 光度
mediterranean [ˌmeditə'reinjən] a. 地中海的 n. 地中海
haul [hɔːl] n. 用力拖拉；努力的结果 v. 拖，改变方向
granite ['grænit] a. 花岗岩的 n. 花岗石
clergyman ['kləːdʒimən] n. 牧师
nonrational [nɔn'ræʃənl] a. 不合理的，非理性的
duplicate ['djuːplikeit] n. 副本；复制品 a. 复制的；二重的 v. [计算机] 复制

Notes

1. Measurement begins with a definition of the measurand, the quantity that is to be measured, and it always involves a comparison of the measurand with some known quantity of the same kind.

(1) comparison...with...：与……相比较
(2) 全句可翻译为：测量从对被测的物理量也即待测量的定义开始，它始终涉及到需将被

测对象与一些已知量的同类物理量进行比较的过程。

2\. The reference signal is derived from measurands of known quantity by a process called calibration.

(1) be derived from…：由……（派生）而来，从……产生，来源于

(2) 全句可翻译为：参考信号由称作定标过程得到的已知物理量派生而来。

3\. Magnification, enlarging the measurement signal without increasing its power, is often necessary to match the output of one element of the system with the input of another, such as matching the size of the readout meter with the discerning power of the eye.

全句可翻译为：放大，是在不增加能量的情况下放大测量信号，为使系统的输出与另一个输入相匹配常常必需进行放大，例如，将仪表的示值读数的大小与眼睛的分辨力相匹配。

4\. Measurement systems often include elements for recording. A common type utilizes a writing stylus that records measurements on a moving chart. Electrical recorders may include feedback reading devices for greater accuracy.

全句可翻译为：测量系统通常还包括记录单元。普通型是用记录笔,将测量结果记录在运动的记录纸上。电记录仪还包括以获得更高的精度的反馈读数装置。

5\. Among external factors are noise and interference, both of which tend to mask or distort the measurement signal.

全句可翻译为：在外部因素中有噪音和干扰，两者均可使测量信号湮没或产生畸形(失真)。

6\. Some of the most important types of axioms include axioms of order, axioms of extension, axioms of difference, axioms of conjointness, and axioms of geometry.

全句可翻译为：公理中一些最重要的类型包括次序公理、外延公理、差分公理、结合公理和几何公理。

7\. Measurement theory dates back to the 4th century BC, when a theory of magnitudes developed by the Greek mathematicians Eudoxus of Cnidus and Thaeatetus was included in Euclid's *Elements*.

(1) date back to：追溯到

(2) BC（或 B.C.）:(Before Christ)公元前

(3) 全句可翻译为：测量理论可以追溯到公元前 4 世纪,那时,由希腊数学家优多休斯(Eudoxus)和西特塔斯(Thaeatetus)研究的量值理论已由欧几里得的《元素》(Elements)所收录。

8\. The Egyptian cubit is generally recognized to have been the most widespread unit of linear measurement in the ancient world.

全句可翻译为：普遍认为埃及库比特(cubit)是古代世界最广泛采用的长度测量单位。

9\. The kilogram was represented by a cylinder of platinum-iridium alloy kept at the International Bureau of Weights and Measures in Sèvres, France, with a duplicate at the U.S. National Bureau of Standards.

全句可翻译为：千克由铂铱合金圆柱体作为代表，该铂铱合金圆柱体存放于法国瑟弗利斯(Sèvres)的国际标准计量局里，而它的复制品存放在美国国家计量局里。

[注]存放于法国的标志着 1 千克质量的铂铱合金圆柱形砝码，由铂铱合金制成，直径和高

度均为 3.9 厘米。在 1889 年第一届国际计量大会上被定为 1 千克的标准，并沿用至今。它现在被安放在法国巴黎塞夫尔一个城堡中的三层锁保险箱中，极少见光。世界上所有使用公制计量单位的国家全都要依照它来制定 1 千克的质量。但据报导，2007 年 9 月发现它神秘"变轻"，其质量比原来少了 50 微克。

对于 1 千克标准确定方法的未来，有人建议说，可以制造一种硅-28 的球状晶体的新型国际标准砝码，取代原有的铂铱合金圆柱形砝码。新砝码的质地单一，可以避免在两种元素配比过程中由于比率差错而产生的问题，使科学家能够精确确定其中的原子类型和数量。

Reading Material

Instrumentation

Instrumentation, in technology, is the development and use of precise measuring equipment. Although the sensory organs of the human body can be extremely sensitive and responsive, modern science and technology rely on the development of much more precise measuring and analytical tools for studying, monitoring or controlling all kinds of phenomena.

Some of the earliest instruments of measurement were used in astronomy and navigation. The armillary sphere, the oldest known astronomical instrument, consists essentially of a skeletal celestial globe whose rings represent the great circles of the heavens. The armillary sphere was known in ancient China; the ancient Greeks were also familiar with it and modified it to produce the astrolabe, which could tell the time or length of day or night as well as measure solar and lunar altitudes. The compass, the earliest instrument for direction finding that did not make reference to the stars, was a striking advance in instrumentation made about the 11th century. The telescope, the primary astronomical instrument was invented about 1608 by the Dutch optician Hans Lippershey and first used extensively by Galileo.

Instrumentation involves both measurement and control functions. An early instrumental control system was the thermostatic furnace developed by the Dutch inventor Cornelius Drebbel (1572—1634), in which a thermometer controlled the temperature of a furnace by a system of rods and levers. Devices to measure and regulate steam pressure inside a boiler appeared at about the same time. In 1788 the Scotsman James Watt invented a centrifugal governor to maintain the speed of a steam engine at a predetermined rate.

Instrumentation developed at a rapid pace in the Industrial Revolution of the 18th and 19th centuries, particularly in the areas of dimensional measurement, electrical measurement, and physical analysis. Manufacturing processes of the time required instruments capable of achieving new standards of linear precision, met in part by the screw micrometer, special models of which could attain a precision of 0.000 025 mm (0.000 001 inch). The industrial application of electricity required instruments to measure current, voltage, and resistance. Analytical methods, using such instruments as the microscope and the spectroscope, became increasingly important; the latter instrument, which analyzes by wave length the light radiation given off by incandescent substances, began to be used to identify the composition of chemical substances and stars.

In the 20th century the growth of modern industry, the introduction of computerization, and the advent of space exploration have spurred still greater development of instrumentation, particularly of electronic devices. Often a transducer, all instrument that changes energy from one form into another (such as the photocell, thermocouple, or microphone) is used to transform a sample of the energy to be measured into electrical impulses that are more easily processed and stored. The introduction of the electronic computer in the 1950s, with its great capacity for information processing and storage, virtually revolutionized methods of instrumentation, for it allowed the simultaneous comparison and analysis of large amounts of information. At much the same time, feedback systems were perfected in which data from instruments monitoring stages of a process are instantaneously evaluated and used to adjust parameters affecting the process. Feedback systems are crucial to the operation of automated processes.

Most manufacturing processes rely on instrumentation for monitoring chemical, physical, and environmental properties, as well as the performance of production lines. Instruments to monitor chemical properties include the refractometer, infrared analyzers, chromatographs, and pH sensors. A refractometer measures the bending of a beam of light as it passes from one material to another; such instruments are used, for instance, to determine the composition of sugar solutions or the concentration of tomato paste in catsup. Infrared analyzers can identify substances by the wavelength and amount of infrared radiation that they emit or reflect. Chromatography, a sensitive and swift method of chemical analysis used on extremely tiny samples of a substance, relies on the different rates at which a material will absorb different types of molecules. The acidity or alkalinity of a solution can be measured by pH sensors.

Instruments are also used to measure physical properties of a substance, such as its turbidity, or amount of particulate matter in a solution. Water purification and petroleum-refining processes are monitored by a turbidimeter, which measures how much light of one particular wavelength is absorbed by a solution. The density of a liquid substance is determined by a hydrometer, which measures the buoyancy of an object of known volume immersed in the fluid to be measured. The flow rate of a substance is measured by a turbine flowmeter, in which the revolutions of a freely spinning turbine immersed in a fluid are measured, while the viscosity of a fluid is measured by a number of techniques including how much it dampens the oscillations of a steel blade.

Instruments used in medicine and biomedical research are just as varied as those in industry. Relatively simple medical instruments measure temperature, blood pressure (sphygmomanometer), or lung capacity (spirometer). More complex instruments include the familiar X-ray machines and electroencephalographs and electrocardiographs, which detect electrical signals generated by the brain and heart, respectively. Two of the most complex medical instruments now in use are the CAT (computerized axial tomography) and NMR (nuclear magnetic resonance) scanners, which can visualize body parts in three dimensions.

The analysis of tissue samples using highly sophisticated methods of chemical analysis is also important in biomedical research.

Lesson 2 Sensors

Transducers change physical qualities such as motion or heat into electrical signals that can be measured to gage the corresponding physical characteristic. Common transducers measure pressure, temperature, light or magnetic fields.

1. Pressure sensors

Solid-state pressure transducers consist of a thin pressure-sensing diaphragm etched in a chip substrate. Strain-gage resistor bridges are then either deposited on the diaphragm surface or diffused into the diaphragm material. Amplifiers and power-circuit ICs are then attached to the chip to form a hybrid-circuit transducer. However, including high-precision A/D converters on the transducer diaphragm chip would entail high-temperature semiconductor diffusions which would degrade the diaphragm temperature characteristics and pressure sensitivity.

In general, strain-gage pressure transducers are more accurate than other types. But their performance depends on the complete "system", which includes the pressure-force summing element, such as a diaphragm and cantilever beam assembly; the strain-sensitive element, which is also the electrical transduction element (a thin metal wire, metal foil, semiconductor, or thin film); and the case.

In operation, pressure exerted by gas or liquid upon a force-summing element is transmitted to the strain-sensitive element attached to it. The change in the electrical resistance of the sensing element brought about by the resulting increase (or decrease) in the length of the sensor element is directly proportional to applied pressure. If a voltage is applied to the strain-sensitive element, mechanical strain is converted into an easily measurable electrical output. Normally, strain-sensitive elements are connected in a Wheatstone bridge circuit. Either one, two, or four of the arms of the bridge may be active elements.

Strain-gage pressure transducers are classified according to their sensing elements and how these elements are attached to the force-summing devices. Figure 3.1 shows two different type of pressure sensors.

2. Temperature sensors

Temperature sensors used in industry today are likely to be one of three types: thermocouples, resistive temperature detectors (RTDs), or thermistors. Each of these devices has limits associated with measurement accuracy. The character and amount of error associated with a given measurement approach is an important factor that must be considered when choosing a sensor for a given application.

Thermocouples are the most widely used devices for temperature measurement despite of

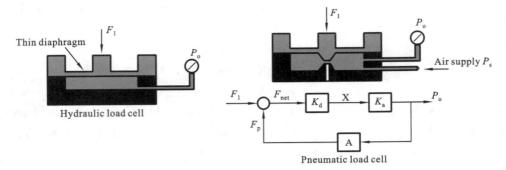

Figure 3.1 Different type of pressure sensors

low sensitivity and moderate accuracy. They feature a wide temperature span, up to 1 800 ℃ (3 270 ℉) for noble (precious) metal types and low cost for basemetal types J, K, T, and E. They are available in sizes ranging from fine wire for millisecond, response times, up to heavy gages for durability and high temperatures. They are particularly useful for point-sensing temperature measurements.

Thermocouples generate a voltage proportional to temperature differences rather than to absolute temperature. They consist of two wires, each made from dissimilar metals of known composition, electrically connected at one end to form the measurement, or hot, junction. The other ends, though not electrically connected, must be kept at the same temperature. This isothermal connection is called reference or "cold" junction. The National Bureau of Standards tables fix the reference junction at the ice-point of water (0 ℃).

The thermocouple, with its junctions at the measurement temperature and ambient, is compensated by a voltage equal to that generated by the same thermocouple with its measurement junction at ambient and its reference junction at the ice point. This is called ice-point or cold-junction compensation.

Thermocouples produce nonlinear voltage output over their temperature span. Special circuits must compensate for this nonlinearity and provide a digital output conforming closely to the NBS tables.

The upper temperature limit of base-metal thermocouples in air is generally determined by their oxidation resistance. This limit varies with wire size. The type K thermocouple has become the most widely used due to its oxidation resistance and high melting point. Even so, decalibration drifts of 10 ℃ have been recorded with as little as 50 hours of exposure at 1 250 ℃.

3. Light sensors

Optoelectronic light sources and detectors are one of the most widely used sensors for detecting motion. For these applications, light emitters and detectors are often combined in a single U-shaped "interrupter" module. A plate containing optical slits moves through the light beam to register motion. The light-intensity change induces detector output voltage pulses as transparent slits transmit light.

Most optoelectronic sensors use a light-emitting diode (LED) that transmits infrared as opposed to visible light, since silicon light detectors are most sensitive to infrared light more efficiently than visible light. Light-detector elements can be either photo-transistors, photodarlingtons, photo-diodes, or selenium cells. Selenium cells respond to light slowly and generally are not used to sense motion.

Maximum sensing speed is one of the most important transducer characteristics when sensing motion or velocity. In optoelectronics, the light detector and its biasing limits switching speed. Depending on the detector current, detector output rise and fall times can range from 5 μs for low-power(about 50 mW)devices to 125 μs for high-power(100~150 mW)detectors. These rise and fall times correspond to maximum switching speeds of 8 kHz and 100 kHz, respectively. Many interrupter modules are biased to produce signal levels compatible with TTL or CMOS logic levels, and the biasing required to produce these levels often determines switching speed. Some manufacturers also produce interrupters containing Schmitt trigger outputs, which "snap" the output voltages between high and low levels when triggered by input signals.

Resolution and accuracy attained in optoelectronic velocity and position sensing applications is often determined by the optics between the detector and light source. High-precision systems generally use a light shutter composed of two grating patterns, one moving in front of the other, between the light source and detector. The opaque and clear segments on these gratings can be on the order of 0.05mil, so that a 0.05-mil change in position registers a light pulse on the detector. Some light detectors also contain integral lenses to reduce the field of detected light, thereby increasing light-pulse resolution.

When high ambient light levels are present, pulsing the LED at a particular frequency enables the light detector to distinguish between the LED signal and ambient light. Here, the light detector output voltage goes through a circuit filter that passes only signal frequencies corresponding to the LED output. Many light detectors incorporate built-in lenses that restrict the detector's field of view, thereby reducing ambient-light effects. Some applications, such as smoke detectors, use high-amplitude, short-duration current spikes (typically 1A for 100 μs on a 1% duty cycle) to energize the light source. The spikes produce high-intensity light pulses, but average LED current for this application is low (about 10mA), an advantage for battery-powered devices. If LED current was not pulsed, light intensity would be too low to illuminate smoke particles.

Optoelectronic transducers also find application as proximity sensors. One manufacturer, for example, offers a liquid-level sensor comprised of an LED positioned at one end of a transparent plastic rod. LED light shines through the rod to the conical rod end, and passes through the cone when the tip contacts a liquid or reflects back through the rod to actuate a light detector when the tip contacts air. Originally developed to sense low oil levels in crankshaft cases of off-road diesels, the transducer also sense such liquids as water and fuel.

Like many other silicon based devices, optoelectronic sensors must operate in temperatures below about 100 ℃. Some light-source outputs also diminish with time, necessitating compensation for worst-case output. Light-detector output can also change with time, but can generally be corrected with additional circuitry. Optoelectronic interrupters may also be ineffective in dirty environments where debris such as cutting chips or heavy particles can interfere with the light beam.

4. Magnetic sensing

Metal sensors that detect moving ferrous metal are often used in environments where optoelectronic devices are impractical. The simplest metal sensor consists of a wire coiled around a permanent magnet, although many variations of this approach are available. A ferrous object approaching the sensor changes magnetic flux through the coil, generating a voltage at the coil terminals.

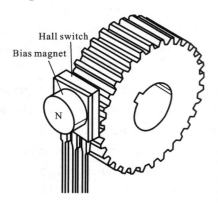

Figure 3.2   Hall sensor

Magnetic pick-ups require no external power source and can sense linear or rotary motion. They also have high resolution, generating many pulses per inch of target travel, and can sense very small ferrous objects. One manufacturer, for example, makes sensors responding to 96-pitch gears, whereas Hall-effect sensors can only register 16-pitch gear teeth as shown in Figure 3.2. In this application, magnetic transduction can be accurate to hundredths of a mechanical degree. For sensing rotating shaft speed, output-pulse frequency is proportional to shaft speed and can be converted to rpm by digital-conversion electronics at an accuracy of less than 0.1%.

Magnetic sensors have successfully measured speeds up to 600 000 rpm. Maximum sensor frequency is in the megahertz region, with usable frequencies limited by the internal sensor impedance and external load.

Magnetic sensors do not sense speeds near zero because output voltage depends on the rate-of-change of flux through the coil. As frequency approaches zero, sensor outputs typically drop to the millivolt range.

Words and Expressions

transducer [trænz'dju:sə] n. 传感器,变送器,换能器,转换器
diaphragm ['daiəfræm] n. 膜片,隔膜,薄膜
cantilever ['kæntili:və] n. 悬臂,伸臂,突梁
hybrid ['haibrid] n. 混血儿,杂种,混合物 a. 混合的,杂种的,混合语的
hybrid-circuit   混合电路
Wheatstone bridge   惠斯通电桥
thermistor ['θə:mistə] n. 热敏电阻,热变电阻器
isothermal [ˌaisəu'θə:məl] a. 等温的,等温线的 n. 等温线
cold-junction compensation   冷端补偿
photodarlington n. 光电达林顿管,光电复合晶体管

selenium[si'li:niəm, -njəm] n. [化]硒（非金属元素，符号 Se，原子序 34）selenium cell 硒光电管

Schmitt trigger 施密特触发器

duty cycle 脉冲保持时间与间歇时间之比，脉冲占空比

off-road ['ɔ:f,rəud] a. 越野的

Notes

1. Transducers change physical qualities such as motion or heat into electrical signals that can be measured to gage the corresponding physical characteristic.

（1）change...into...：将……转换（变）成……

（2）such as motion or heat 修饰 physical qualities

（3）全句可翻译为：传感器将如运动或热这样的物理量转换成可测量的电信号，并由这些电信号计量相对应的物理特性。

2. The character and amount of error associated with a given measurement approach is an important factor that must be considered when choosing a sensor for a given application.

（1）be associated with：与……有关系；涉及；伴随……产生，在……的同时

（2）全句可翻译为：在为给定的应用选择传感器时，与给定的测量方法有关的误差特性和总误差是必须考虑的重要因素。

Reading Material

Incremental encoders

Figure 3.3 shows incremental encoders how to work. Optical sensors generally operate by light interruption or reflection. Interruption schemes depend on a separate vane or grid to interrupt a light beam passing between an LED and light detector, and reflection schemes use the sensed surface to reflect LED light to the detector.

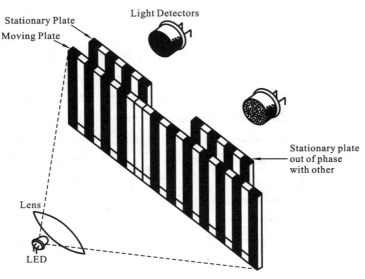

Figure 3.3 Incremental encoders

Rotary and linear optical encoders are most widely used position and motion sensors. Here, a disc plate containing opaque and transparent segments spins between an LED and detector to pulse light.

Encoders can be classified as either incremental or absolute. Absolute encoders use discs that simultaneously actuate several detectors whose outputs form a digital word representing the absolute position of the encoder shaft. Incremental encoder discs contain uniform patterns of equally spaced radial lines to produce detector pulses that are counted to determine shaft position relative to a reference.

Of the two, incremental encoders are more widely used because they cost less. Incremental encoder outputs can be sine waves, square waves, or a series of equally spaced pulses. Light detectors in practical devices intercept light passed by 20 or more slits, instead of through one slit, to provide easy alignment and to nullify the effects of disc imperfections such as scratches or dust.

Incremental-encoder light interrupters generally consist of a stationary mask and moving disc, both containing a grid of opaque and transparent areas. As the disc moves past the mask, it induces triangular-shaped output waveforms.

Encoder outputs are often digitized by producing a pulse each time the triangular detector output wave passes through a predetermined value. Additional circuitry counts the resulting series of pulses to measure mechanical movement.

Hall-effect sensors

Analog Hall-effect sensors provide a dc output proportional to magnetic field strength. Digital types provide digital voltages triggered by a specific magnetic field strength. Some Hall-effect sensors combine digital signal-conditioning circuits on the Hall-sensor chip. Typical circuits consist of an amplifier, flip-flop offset voltage adjustment, and comparator. Since Hall-element voltages are small (about 1mV for a 50-Gs field), an amplifier whose temperature coefficient cancels that of the Hall element amplifiers the Hall voltage to produce a linear temperature-compensated dc signal.

The amplifier output feeds a hysteresis flip-flop and comparator that provide a precise switching action between on and off states, thereby preventing oscillation as the magnetic field approaches threshold. The comparator output switches from low to high as the amplified Hall voltage exceeds the offset voltage, which is adjusted during manufacture to allow output switching at required magnetic-field levels. The comparator output is fed back to the hysteresis flip-flop, which in turn changes state. The sum of the amplifier, flip-flop, and offset voltages fix the comparator in a high state. When a reduced magnetic field decrease the amplifier output comparator output drops and the hysteresis circuit switches to stabilize the output at low level.

New developments in Hall-effect sensors aim mainly at increasing sensitivity, reducing sensor weight and more sophisticated switching functions through the use of ICs.

Low-cost (on the order of a dollar) Hall-effect sensors are now available in plastic packages that include 3-pin transistors and 4-pin dual in-line packages. Other more expensive sensors are packaged in metallic enclosures to withstand hostile environments.

Piezoelectric Sensors

The Piezoelectric effect is an effect in which energy is converted between mechanical and electrical forms. It was discovered in the 1880's by the Curie brothers. Specifically, when a pressure (piezo means pressure in Greek) is applied to a polarized crystal, the resulting mechanical deformation results in an electrical charge. Piezoelectric microphones serve as a good example of this phenomenon. Microphones turn an acoustical pressure into a voltage. Alternatively, when an electrical charge is applied to a polarized crystal, the crystal undergoes a mechanical deformation which can in turn create an acoustical pressure. An example of this can be seen in piezoelectric speakers. (These are the cause of those annoying system beeps that are all too common in today's computers).

Electrets are solids which have a permanent electrical polarization. (These are basically the electrical analogs of magnets, which exhibit a permanent magnetic polarization). Figure 3.4 shows a diagram of the internal structure of an electret. In general, the alignment of the internal electric dipoles would result in a charge which would be observable on the surface of the solid. In practice, this small charge is quickly dissipated by free charges from the surrounding atmosphere which are attracted by the surface charges. Electrets are commonly used in microphones.

Permanent polarization as in the case of the electrets is also observed in crystals. In these structures, each cell of the crystal has an electric dipole, and the cells are oriented such that the electric dipoles are aligned. Again, this results in excess surface charge which attracts free charges from the surrounding atmosphere making the crystal electrically neutral. If a sufficient force is applied to the piezoelectric crystal, a deformation will take place. This deformation disrupts the orientation of the electrical dipoles and creates a situation in which the charge is not completely canceled. This results in a temporary excess of surface charge, which subsequently is manifested as a voltage which is developed across the crystal.

In order to utilize this physical principle to make a sensor to measure force, we must be able to measure the surface charge on the crystal. Figure 3.5 shows a common method of using a piezoelectric crystal to make a force sensor. Two metal plates are used to sandwich the crystal making a capacitor. As mentioned previously, an external force causing a deformation of the crystal results in a charge which is a function of the applied force. In its operating region, a greater force will result in more surface charge. This charge results in a voltage $V = \frac{Q_f}{C}$, where Q_f is the charge resulting from a force f, and C is the capacitance of the device.

In the manner described above, piezoelectric crystals act as transducers which turn force, or mechanical stress into electrical charge which in turn can be converted into a voltage. Alternatively, if one was to apply a voltage to the plates of the system described above, the resultant electric field would cause the internal electric dipoles to re-align which

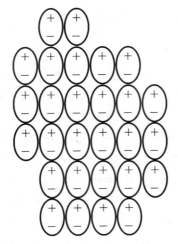
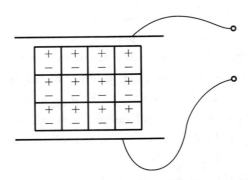

Figure 3.4　Internal structure of an electret　　Figure 3.5　A sensor based on the piezoelectric effect

would cause a deformation of the material. An example of this is the fact that piezoelectric transducers find use both as speakers (voltage to mechanical) and microphones (mechanical to electrical).

Lesson 3　Common Instruments

1. Introduction

The oscilloscope is basically a graph-displaying device—it draws a graph of an electrical signal. In most applications the graph shows how signals change over time. From the graph it is possible to:
- determine the time and voltage values of a signal;
- calculate the frequency of an oscillating signal;
- see the "moving parts" of a circuit represented by the signal;
- tell if a malfunctioning component is distorting the signal;
- find out how much of a signal is d.c. or a.c.;
- tell how much of the signal is noise and whether the noise is changing with time.

Oscilloscopes are used by everyone from television repair technicians to physicists. They are indispensable for anyone designing or repairing electronic equipment. The usefulness of an oscilloscope is not limited to the world of electronics. With the proper transducer (i.e. a device that creates an electrical signal in response to physical stimuli, such as sound, mechanical stress, pressure, light or heat), an oscilloscope can measure any kind of phenomena. An automobile engineer uses an oscilloscope to measure engine vibrations; a medical researcher uses an oscilloscope to measure brain waves, and so on.

2. The Types of Oscilloscopes

Electronic equipment can be classified into two categories: analog and digital. Analog equipment works with continuously variable voltages, while digital equipment works with discrete binary numbers that represent voltage samples.

Oscilloscopes are available in both analogue and digital types. An analogue oscilloscope works by directly applying a voltage being measured to an electron beam moving across the oscilloscope screen. The voltage deflects the beam up or down proportionally, tracing the waveform on the screen. This gives an immediate picture of the waveform.

In contrast, a digital oscilloscope samples the waveform and uses an analogue to digital converter to convert the voltage being measured into digital information. It then uses this digital information to reconstruct the waveform on the screen. Digital oscilloscopes can be further classified into digital storage oscilloscopes (DSOs), digital phosphor oscilloscopes (DPOs) and digital sampling oscilloscopes.

For many applications either an analogue or digital oscilloscope is appropriate. However, each type does possess some unique characteristics making it more or less suitable for specific tasks.

Analogue oscilloscopes are often preferred when it is important to display rapidly varying signals in "real time" (i.e. as they occur).

Digital oscilloscopes allow the capture and viewing of events that happen only once. They can process the digital waveform data or send the data to a computer for processing. Also, they can store the digital waveform data for later viewing and printing. Digital storage oscilloscopes are explained in Section 5.

3. Analogue oscilloscopes

When an oscilloscope probe is connected to a circuit, the voltage signal travels through the probe to the vertical system of the oscilloscope. Figure 3.6 shows a simple block diagram that shows how an analogue oscilloscope displays a measured signal.

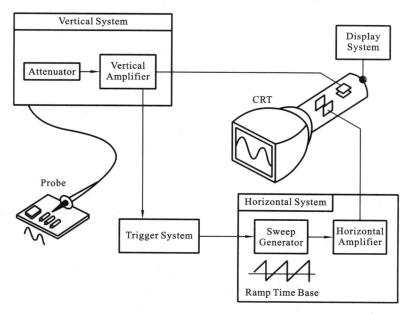

Figure 3.6 Diagram of an analogue oscilloscope

Depending on how the vertical scale(volts/division control) is set, an attenuator reduces the signal voltage or an amplifier increases the signal voltage. Next, the signal travels directly to the vertical deflection plates of the cathode ray tube(CRT). Voltage applied to these deflection plates causes a glowing dot to move. (An electron beam hitting phosphor inside the CRT creates the glowing dot.) A positive voltage causes the dot to move up while a negative voltage causes the dot to move down.

The signal also travels to the trigger system to start or trigger a "horizontal sweep". Horizontal sweep is a term referring to the action of the horizontal system causing the glowing dot to move across the screen. Triggering the horizontal system causes the horizontal time base to move the glowing dot across the screen from left to right within a specific time interval. Many sweeps in rapid sequence cause the movement of the glowing dot to blend into a solid line. At higher speeds, the dot may sweep across the screen up to 500 000 times each second.

Together, the horizontal sweeping action (i.e. the X direction) and the vertical deflection action (i.e. the Y direction), traces a graph of the signal on the screen. The trigger is necessary to stabilise a repeating signal. It ensures that the sweep begins at the same point of a repeating signal, resulting in a clear picture.

In conclusion, to use an analogue oscilloscope, three basic settings to accommodate an incoming signal need to be adjusted:

- the attenuation or amplification of the signal—use the volts/division control to adjust the amplitude of the signal before it is applied to the vertical deflection plates;
- the time base—use the time/division control to set the amount of time per division represented horizontally across the screen;
- the triggering of the oscilloscope—use the trigger level to stabilise a repeating signal, as well as triggering on a single event.

Also, adjusting the focus and intensity controls enable a sharp, visible display to be created.

(1) With direct voltage measurements, only the Y amplifier "volts/cm" switch on the oscilloscope is used. With no voltage applied to the Y plates the position of the spot trace on the screen is noted. When a direct voltage is applied to the Y plates the new position of the spot trace is an indication of the magnitude of the voltage. For example, in Figure 3.7(a), with no voltage applied to the Y plates, the spot trace is in the centre of the screen(initial position) and then the spot trace moves 2.5 cm to the final position shown, on application of a d.c. voltage. With the "volts/cm" switch on 10 volts/cm the magnitude of the direct voltage is 2.5 cm × 10 volts/cm, i.e. 25 volts.

(2) With alternating voltage measurements, let a sinusoidal waveform be displayed on an oscilloscope screen as shown in Figure 3.7(b). If the "time/cm" switch is on, say, 5 ms/cm then the periodic time T of the sinewave is 5 ms/cm × 4 cm, i.e. 20 ms or 0.02 s. Since frequency

$$f = \frac{1}{T}, \quad frequency = \frac{1}{0.02} = 50 \text{ Hz}.$$

If the "volts/cm" switch is on, say, 20 volts/cm then the amplitude or peak value of the sinewave shown is 20 volts/cm × 2 cm, i.e. 40 V. Since

$$r.m.s.\ voltage = \frac{peak\ voltage}{\sqrt{2}}$$

$$r.m.s.\ voltage = \frac{40}{\sqrt{2}} = 28.28 \text{ volts}.$$

Double beam oscilloscopes are useful whenever two signals are to be compared simultaneously. The c. r. o. demands reasonable skill in adjustment and use. However its greatest advantage is in observing the shape of a waveform—a feature not possessed by other measuring instruments.

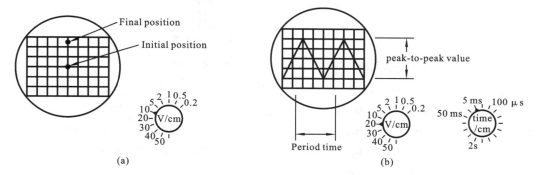

Figure 3.7 An oscilloscope screen

4. Digital oscilloscopes

Some of the systems that make up digital oscilloscopes are the same as those in analogue oscilloscopes; however, digital oscilloscopes contain additional data processing systems—as shown in the block diagram of Figure 3.8. With the added systems, the digital oscilloscope collects data for the entire waveform and then displays it.

When a digital oscilloscope probe is attached to a circuit, the vertical system adjusts the amplitude of the signal, just as in the analogue oscilloscope. Next, the analogue to digital converter (ADC) in the acquisition system samples the signal at discrete points in time and converts the signals' voltage at these points to digital values called sample points. The horizontal systems' sample clock determines how often the ADC takes a sample. The rate at which the clock "ticks" is called the sample rate and is measured in samples per second.

The sample points from the ADC are stored in memory as waveform points. More than one sample point may make up one waveform point.

Together, the waveform points make up one waveform record. The number of waveform points used to make a waveform records called a record length. The trigger system determines the start and stop points of the record. The display receives these record points after being stored in memory.

Depending on the capabilities of an oscilloscope, additional processing of the sample

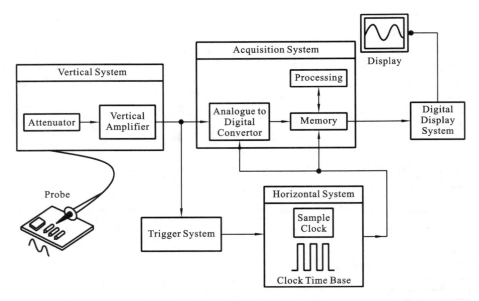

Figure 3.8 Diagram of a digital oscilloscope

points may take place, enhancing the display. Pre-trigger may be available, allowing events to be seen before the trigger point.

Fundamentally, with a digital oscilloscope as with an analogue oscilloscope, there is a need to adjust vertical, horizontal, and trigger settings to take a measurement.

5. Virtual test and measuring instruments

Computer-based instruments are rapidly replacing items of conventional test equipment in many of today's test and measurement applications. Probably the most commonly available virtual test instrument is the digital storage oscilloscope (DSO). Because of the processing power available from the PC coupled with the mass storage capability, a computer-based virtual DSO is able to provide a variety of additional functions, such as spectrum analysis and digital display of both frequency and voltage. In addition, the ability to save waveforms and captured measurement data for future analysis or for comparison purposes can be extremely valuable, particularly where evidence of conformance with standards or specifications is required.

Unlike a conventional oscilloscope (which is primarily intended for waveform display) a computer-based virtual oscilloscope effectively combines several test instruments in one single package. The functions and available measurements from such an instrument usually includes:

- real time or stored waveform display;
- precise time and voltage measurement (using adjustable cursors);
- digital display of voltage;
- digital display of frequency and/or periodic time;
- accurate measurement of phase angle;
- frequency spectrum display and analysis;

- data logging (stored waveform data can be exported in formats that are compatible with conventional spreadsheet packages, e. g. as . xls files);
- ability to save/print waveforms and other information in graphical format (e. g. as . jpg or. bmp files).

Virtual instruments can take various forms including:
- internal hardware in the form of a conventional PCI expansion card;
- external hardware unit which is connected to the PC by means of either a conventional 25-pin parallel port connector or by means of a serial USB connector.

The software (and any necessary drivers) is invariably supplied on CD-ROM or can be downloaded from the manufacturer's web site. Some manufacturers also supply software drivers together with sufficient accompanying documentation in order to allow users to control virtual test instruments from their own software developed using popular programming languages such as Visual BASIC or C++.

Words and Expressions

oscilloscope [ɔ'silɔskəup] n. 示波器
malfunction [mæl'fʌŋkʃən] n. 故障 v. 发生故障,不起作用
stimuli ['stimjulai](stimulus 的复数) n. 刺激,激励,刺激品(刺激物,刺激源,促进因素,色质)
deflect [di'flekt] v. (使)偏斜,(使)转向,(使)弯曲,打歪
phosphor ['fɔsfə] n. 磷(荧)光体,磷
digital phosphor oscilloscope 数字荧光示波器
attenuator [ə'tenjueitə] n. 衰减器,阻尼器
cathode ray tube(CRT) 阴极射线管
stabilise=stabilize ['steibilaiz] v. 使稳定;使坚固
electron beam 电子束
phosphorescent screen 荧光屏
deflection plate 偏转板
trigger ['trigə] n. 触发器
discrete [di'skri:t] a. 不连续的;[数]离散的,单个的;[计算机] 分离
digital phosphor oscilloscope(DPO) 数字荧光示波器
sweep [swi:p] v. n. 扫描;扫,扫频
cursor ['kə:sə] n. 光标

Notes

1. ... tell if a malfunctioning component is distorting the signal...
(1) if 相当于 weather,所引导的从句为 tell 的宾语从句。
(2) 全句可翻译为:……断定是否有有故障的元件使信号失真

2. An analogue oscilloscope works by directly applying a voltage being measured to an electron beam moving across the oscilloscope screen.

(1) apply...to,把……施加(应用)于;being measured 是修饰 voltage 的分词短语。

(2) 全句可翻译为:模拟示波器是通过直接将被测电压施加在电子束上使之撞击示波器的荧屏来运行的。

3. In contrast, a digital oscilloscope samples the waveform and uses an analogue to digital converter to convert the voltage being measured into digital information.

(1) in contrast,可是,比较起来,相反;to convert...into...,将……转换为……

(2) 全句可翻译为:可是,数字示波器对波形采样,并且使用模数转换器将待测量的电压转换为数字信息。

4. Voltage applied to these deflection plates causes a glowing dot to move. (An electron beam hitting phosphor inside the CRT creates the glowing dot.)

全句可翻译为:施加在这些偏转板上的电压使得发光点移动(电子束撞击阴极射线管内壁的荧光体就产生发光点)。

5. The c.r.o. demands reasonable skill in adjustment and use.

(1) c.r.o.＝cathode-ray oscilloscope:阴极射线示波器

(2) 全句可翻译为:在调整和使用阴极射线示波器时,需要有比较好的技能。

6. Because of the processing power available from the PC coupled with the mass storage capability, a computer-based virtual DSO is able to provide a variety of additional functions, such as spectrum analysis and digital display of both frequency and voltage.

全句可翻译为:由于个人计算机与大容量的贮存相结合具有有效的处理能力,因此,基于计算机的数字存储示波器能提供各种各样的附加功能,例如频谱分析,频率和电压的数字显示。

Reading Material

What Is Instrumentation, and Why Is It Important?

Instruments are the key to the advancement of scientific, engineering, and medical research and the development of new and improved technologies. Progress in research impacts every aspect of our modern lives—from agriculture and health to national and homeland security. Instrumentation is a critical component of the research enterprise and thus is in part responsible for the benefits that research brings to society.

Instruments have revolutionized how we look at the world and refined and extended the range of our senses. From the beginnings of the development of the modern scientific method, its emphasis on testable hypotheses requiring the ability to make quantitative and ever more accurate measurements—for example, of temperature with the thermometer (1593), of cellular structure with the microscope (1595), of the universe with the telescope (1609), and of time itself (to discern longitude at sea) with the marine chronometer (1759). Instruments have been an integral part of our nation's growth since explorers first set out to map the continent. The establishment of the U.S. Geological Survey had its roots in the exploration of the western United States, and its activities depended critically on advanced surveying instruments.

A large fraction of the differences between 19th century, 20th century, and 21st century science stems directly from the instruments available to explore the world. The scope of research that instrumentation enables has expanded considerably, now encompassing not only the natural (physical and biologic) world but also many facets of human society and behavior. Instrumentation has often been cited as the pacing factor of research; the productivity of researchers is only as great as the tools they have available to observe, measure, and make sense of nature. Cutting-edge instruments not only enable new discoveries but help to make the production of knowledge more efficient. Many newly developed instruments are important because they enable us to explore phenomena with more precision and speed. The development of instruments maintains a symbiotic relationship with science as a whole; advanced tools enable scientists to answer increasingly complex questions, and new findings in turn enable the development of more powerful, and sometimes novel, instruments.

Electronic Gauges/Tooling

1) It's generation of the most popular gage readout in manufacturing

One of the workhorses in manufacturing since the 1970s is our legendary Trendsetter™ analog column amplifier. Trendsetter II streamlines the best features of the earlier generation model and provides new benefits to the user. It is now a digital unit that is selectable for any one of eight scale ranges. With a quick module change, the column can be used with electronic or air gaging tools. Inch or metric results are displayed on the tri-color LED bar graph as a deviation from a nominal size. "Good", "oversize", and "undersize" conditions are recognized instantly by either green, red, or yellow bar colors. With its RS-232 output, the information can be downloaded to a variety of media for storage or further analysis.

2) One unit displays a host of dimensional measurement

Trendsetter II is a programmable single feature gaging amplifier featuring two quick-change modules. One is an electronic module that accepts up to two Edmunds LVDT inputs for measuring simple single element dimensions or a combination of the two inputs, such as when checking diameters. The other module is designed for single input air gaging and contains an air-to-electronic transducer, capable of accepting almost any brand tooling. It changes the air pressure signal to voltage for the column display. Typical dimensions that can be measured using the Trendsetter II include diameters, width, length, height, and thickness. Also, because of the Trendsetter II's ability to lock and display dynamic values, users can also measure geometric forms such as a T.I.R., parallelism, roundness and tapers or max or min peaks.

3) Multiple units for multiple measurements

The Trendsetter II comes equipped with an analog port to bus signals over I/O matrix lines, providing the ability to communicate column to column. In practice, several Trendsetter II units can be connected together for measuring multiple dimensional features. A typical example of this set up is if you wish to measure clearance between two mating parts. The electronic module also doubles for summing or calculating differences from other

Figure 3.9 Measurement column

column outputs. Figure 3.9 shows a measurement column device.

4) Automatic gaging? No problem!

While most of our Trendsetter Ⅱ readouts are used in single element manual gaging applications, we can configure them for use in multi-dimensional automatic measuring applications. Part status may be communicated with the use of an optional internal plug-in board. Such conditions can be informed by communicating with a light or audibly by ringing a bell or even open a sorting gate to separate good and reject parts. Obviously, automatic gaging is a much more comprehensive and complex solution and requires expertise in which Edmunds Gages is world-renowned.

5) More selectable scales

We are pleased to offer eight easily selectable full scale values with the Trendsetter Ⅱ, and give you the flexibility to measure a host of jobs with varying tolerance ranges, now and in the future. These scales, in both inch and metric, span most every tolerance range by today's manufacturing standards:

Inch	Metric
0.0002″	0.005 mm
0.0005″	0.01 mm
0.001″	0.02 mm
0.002″	0.05 mm
0.005″	0.10 mm
0.01″	0.20 mm
0.02″	0.50 mm
0.05″	1.0 mm

6) Integration with peripheral devices for ultimate data control and manipulation

The Trendsetter Ⅱ can be easily setup right at the unit with the use of six keys on the front panel. And, for your convenience, data can be offloaded to a PC or hand held PDA for transferring to a remote storage device. You can also download data to a printer or other synchronizing devices. Some customers crunch results through sophisticated SPC programs on their desktop computers to analyze the data even further. Whatever your measurement goals with Trendsetter Ⅱ, we can help you achieve them.

7) Accessories: Electronic Bore Plug Gages

Edmunds Electronic Bore Plug Gages are manufactured with hardened steel, chrome-plated body and tungsten carbide contacts, and designed for rigorous production use. An insulated handle contains and protects an Edmunds cartridge type electronic probe. Changing between sizes requires change of the plug only. Our electronic plugs are available in two styles and several sizes. Figure 3.10 shows the electronic bore plug gages.

Figure 3.10 Electronic Bore Plug Gages

Lesson 4 Virtual Instruments

1. Virtual Instruments

Combined with a PC and software, a DAQ board makes up a virtual instrument, as shown in Figure 3.11. Unlike "virtual reality", or imitation world that can be experienced through computer peripherals (e. g. screen, speakers), a virtual instrument is an actual appliance. It is "virtual" because you need to use a computer interface (e. g. screen, keyboard, and mouse) to communicate with this appliance, and because the board is hidden inside the PC (except external boards with the USB or IEEE-1394 interface). A virtual instrument has input terminals to connect input signals. Virtual instruments usually provide better measurement performance or utility characteristics than their conventional digital counterparts. In a virtual instrument, readings are displayed on the computer screen, and manual adjustment of settings, such as input range or trigger level, is performed using the mouse.

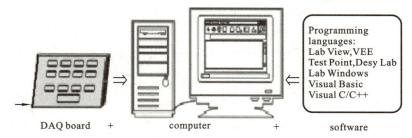

Figure 3.11 The structure of a virtual instrument

While the computer DAQ board concept raises no controversy, there are various definitions of the virtual instrument category. In addition to the "virtual instrument = DAQ board + computer + software" concept described above, the following are sometimes classified as virtual instruments:

- A computer-based measurement system incorporating one or more instruments (such as a digital voltmeter), interfaced to a computer and operated remotely from a GUI control panel, by means of computer peripherals;
- Measurement simulation software whose graphical form (control panel) may be identical to actual measurement systems.

We opt for the narrower meaning of the virtual instrument concept. Although we do not question the usefulness of simulation software for teaching purposes, we do not classify it in the instrument category. Furthermore, we believe that remote operation of an instrument (e. g., a digital voltmeter), interfaced to a computer does not necessarily make it a virtual instrument. There are usually two operating modes available: remote or local, as in the IEEE-488 system.

Instead of a DAQ board, a virtual instrument can incorporate stand-alone devices, interfaced to the chosen PC bus, via cable and providing the same functionality as a DAQ board. Such data acquisition devices are often delivered under brand names, such as WaveBook (designed for PC operation only), or LogBook (operating as a PC peripheral or stand-alone) from IOtech.

In addition to a computer, a DAQ board and a connector, as shown in Figure 3.12, virtual instrument-based measurement system hardware may and usually does include additional components:

Figure 3.12 Two types of DAQ board connectors: (left) with terminals and BNC coax connectors, and (right) with screw terminals for unshielded cables

- A conditioner card to match the input levels to the DAQ board's input range;
- A conditioner card for temperature, pressure, or displacement sensors;
- Expansion cards to provide additional analog inputs, high-voltage inputs, or low-voltage inputs;
- An optically isolated analog/digital input card;
- A BNC coax input card;
- A low pass filter card or other cards.

Figure 3.13 shows a measurement system with a virtual instrument and additional cards. An adapter board is used to connect more than one conditioner card or expansion card to the DAQ board input. A virtual instrument-based measurement system, as shown in Figure 3.13, can be used to measure and process various physical qualities (e. g.,

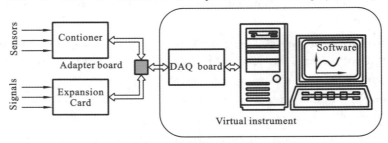

Figure 3.13 A virtual instrument-based measurement system

temperature, pressure, or displacement) and electrical signals spanning a wide range, by means of limited technical resources. The measurement performance of such a system depends not only on the specifications of the boards used, but also on the characteristics of the system's application software. By using signal filtration and averaging, statistical calculations, and other procedures, the quality of final measurement results may be significantly improved.

2. Programming of Measurement Systems and Virtual Instruments

Software is an indispensable part of a computer-based measurement system and of a virtual instrument. High-level graphical programming languages, known as measurement system development environments, provide extensive software development capabilities and make it easy to program a measurement system or a virtual instrument. Furthermore, the major instrumentation manufacturers offer proprietary programming languages (environments), such as LabVIEW or LabWindows from National Instruments, VEE (formerly HP VEE) from Agilent Technologies, and TestPoint from Keithley. All these languages have a number of advantages but they are rather expensive. The price is several thousand dollars for a basic version. Graphically rich general-purpose programming languages, such as Visual C++ or Visual Basic, and commands from the list of Standard Commands for Programmable Instruments (SCPI), can also be used to develop virtual instrument software. LabVIEW, LabWindows, VEE, and TestPoint all come with libraries of drivers for specific instruments, such as multimeters, digital oscilloscopes, analyzers, DAQ boards, and generators. Instrumentation manufacturers ensure that the drivers for their instruments are available in the libraries of most popular development environments. The development issues are so elaborate that each package comes with a two-volume documentation and requires a comprehensive manual.

3. Software Development in the LabVIEW Environment

The principles of developing measurement system (or virtual instrument) software in a development environment are described briefly in the example of using LabVIEW to build a virtual instrument (a spectrum analyzer) with a DAQ board. Each software developed in LabVIEW consists of two main parts:

- The Graphical User Interface (GUI), which provides an integrated front panel of the instruments making up the measurement system or virtual instrument. Figure 3.14 shows a sample front panel of a virtual spectrum analyzer in LabVIEW 7;
- The functional diagram (block diagram), which maps the function block icons and relations between these function blocks of the virtual instrument. See Figure 3.15 for a block diagram of a spectrum analyzer. This block diagram is the source code of the virtual instrument control program.

To write a program in LabVIEW, a block diagram is created by dragging and dropping object icons or function icons from the *All Functions* palette, as shown in Figure 3.16, and the *All Controls* palette, as shown in Figure 3.17, onto the panel.

Many of these functions in the diagram can be expanded on multiple levels to set their

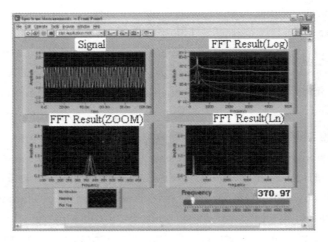

Figure 3.14 Graphical User Interface of the Virtual Instrument spectrum analyzer in LabVIEW 7(Courtesy of National Instruments)

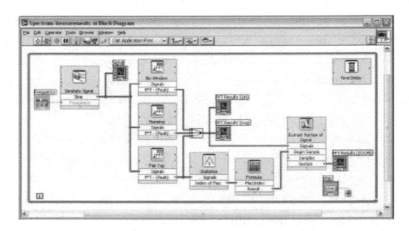

Figure 3.15 Block diagram of a virtual spectrum analyzer in LabVIEW 7 (Courtesy of National Instruments)

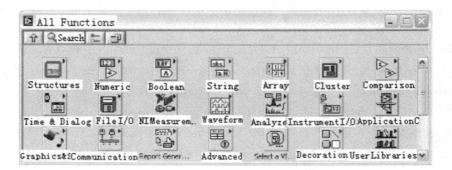

Figure 3.16 *All Functions* palette in LabVIEW 7 (Courtesy of National Instruments)

required properties. Surrounding the selected objects with a loop forces a conditional execution or repetition of the selected operations, corresponding to the effect of *if* or *while* instructions known from other programming languages. Instrument drivers which are

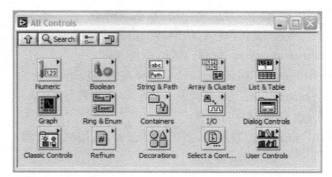

Figure 3.17 *All Controls* palette in LabVIEW 7 (Courtesy of National Instruments)

necessary for the program to run should be stored in the LabVIEW driver library. Once the icon of a specific instrument is placed on the system diagram, as shown in Figure 3.15, the program will use that instrument's driver at runtime. Figure 3.18 shows the expanded view of program menus that must be invoked to insert the HP34401A digital multimeter driver from Hewlett-Packard into the system.

Creating control programs in *VEE* or *TestPoint* is similar to the technique described earlier.

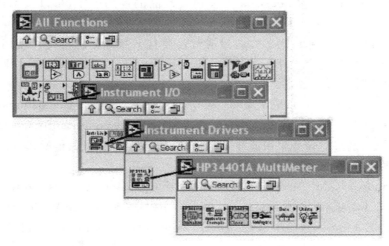

Figure 3.18 Inserting instrument drivers in LabVIEW 7 (Courtesy of National Instruments)

Words and Expressions

DAQ *abbr.* (data acquisition) 数据采集
virtual [ˈvəːtjuəl, ˈvəːtʃuəl] *a.* 虚拟的；实质的
peripherals [pəˈrifərəls] *n.* 外围设备，外部设备
USB *abbr.* (Universal Serial Bus) Intel 公司开发的通用串行总线
counterpart [ˈkauntəpɑːt] *n.* 相似之物，相关者，对应物
category [ˈkætigəri] *n.* 种类，类别
GUI *abbr.* (Graphical User Interface) 图形用户界面
trigger level 触发器电平
opt [ɔpt] *v.* 选择

stand-alone ['stændəˌləun] a. 可独立应用的,独立的
deliver [di'livə] vt. 递送,交付;提供,供给;释放;发表
displacement [dis'pleismənt] n. 位移,移动;换置,转位
VEE (Visual Environment Engineering) 一种高级编程语言
proprietary [prə'praiətəri] a. 专利的(所有的) n. 所有权(所有人)
invoke [in'vəuk] vt. 调用,引用;行使
multimeter [ˌmʌlti'mi:tə] n. 万用表,多用途计量器,通用测量仪器

Notes

1. Virtual instruments usually provide better measurement performance or utility characteristics than their conventional digital counterparts.

全句可翻译为:通常虚拟仪器所提供的测量性能或有用的特性要比相对应的数字仪器好得多。

2. Such data acquisition devices are often delivered under brand names, such as WaveBook (designed for PC operation only), or LogBook (operating as a PC peripheral or stand-alone) from IOtech.

（1）IOtech,WaveBook 和 LogBook 为公司或产品的专用名字,可以按音译或直接标出原文。

（2）全句可翻译为:这种数据采集装置通常需要打上商标铭牌再交付使用,例如 IOtech 公司的 WaveBook 牌(仅为个人计算机的操作而设计的装置)或 LogBook 牌(用作个人计算机的外围设备或独立设备)。

3. By using signal filtration and averaging, statistical calculations, and other procedures, the quality of final measurement results may be significantly improved.

全句可翻译为:通过对信号采用滤波、取平均值、统计计算以及其他操作,可使最终测量结果的品质得到明显的改善。

4. Furthermore, the major instrumentation manufacturers offer proprietary programming languages (environments), such as LabVIEW or LabWindows from National Instruments, VEE (formerly HP VEE) from Agilent Technologies, and TestPoint from Keithley.

全句可翻译为:此外,大部分仪器制造商会提供所有的程序语言(环境),例如国家仪器公司(National Instruments)的 LabVIEW 或 LabWindows,安捷伦(Agilent)公司的 VEE(早先为 HP VEE),以及吉时利(Keithley)公司的 TestPoint。

5. BNC,同轴电缆接插件,全称 Bayonet Nut Connector,刺刀螺母连接器,又称为 British Naval Connector 英国海军连接器或 Bayonet Neil Consulman,一种用于同轴电缆的连接器,比如 10Base-2 以太网系统采用的 RG-58A/U 电缆。

Reading Material

Computer DAQ Boards

1) Structure and Functions of a DAQ Board

Certain measurement tasks cannot be performed better than by means of a computer measurement board. Combined with a computer and software, such measurement boards makes up a virtual instrument. Due to its extensive data acquisition functionality, a computer measurement board is referred to as Data Acquisition (DAQ) card. Card designations often include additional symbols—DAQ.

Board designates a board that is designed for installation inside a computer (pluggable onto the PCI or ISA bus); and DAQ PC card designates a PCMCIA card. The functions of a measurement card involve much more than just A/D conversion. Modern computer DAQ boards provide the following functions:

- Digitize a single signal (voltage or sometimes current) from one of the multiple analog inputs;
- Digitize multiple signals received on multiple analog inputs;
- Perform antialiasing analog filtration of the input signal;
- Set the analog input signal trigger levels and time-outs;
- Present the required signals (voltage or current) onto analog outputs through D/A conversion;
- Read and send digital signals from/to data inputs/outputs (DIO);
- Produce signals of a preset frequency or pulses of a preset duration;
- Measure the input signal frequency or pulse duration;
- Synchronize with the triggering lines of computer-based RTSI real-time systems (optional);
- Store measurement data and configuration settings in the card's memory.

Figure 3.19 shows a functional diagram of a DAQ board. A typical DAQ board consists of an analog multiplexer, a programmable amplifier, a sample and hold (S&H) or sample-and-trace (S&T) circuit, an ADC, a DAC, a high quality reference voltage source, a

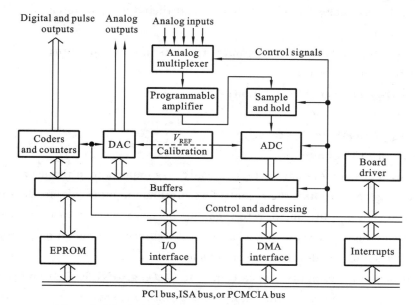

Figure 3.19 A functional diagram of a computer DAQ board

calibration circuit, a triggering block, registers, memory circuits, and a control block. Some boards provide a DMA interface for a direct access to the PC memory, without involving the CPU.

Compared to conventional digital instruments with an interface circuit, DAQ boards provide the following benefits:
- Support multichannel measurements;
- The same card can be set to function as a digital multimeter, a function generator or an oscilloscope;
- Send analog and digital activation or test signals to the measurement system;
- Require no additional space if plugged into the PCI, ISA, or PCMCIA bus inside a computer.

High-performance HiTech DAQ boards are manufactured by a number of companies, such as National Instruments, Keithley, IOtech, Advantech, and Computer Board. The prices range from \$1 000 to \$5 000. A number of small companies make dedicated DAQ boards or boards providing limited capabilities.

2) DAQ Board Specifications

The quality of A/D conversion or digital measurement can be quantified as the product of sampling rate and measurement resolution, expressed as the number of bits in a digital word after digitization. DAQ boards provide the highest value of this index. A digital oscilloscope with an ADC providing a resolution higher than 8 bits can be built as a virtual instrument only, using a DAQ board and suitable software (at least the author could not find any corresponding hardware unit in products from Tektronix, LeCroy, Agilent, and Stanford Research System). These two indices can be used to evaluate the performance of DAQ boards. The board specifications include:
- The number of analog inputs (channels) and their types: differential (DI) or single-ended (SE);
- ADC resolution expressed as the number of bits in a digital word;
- Maximum sampling rate;
- Input range and absolute resolution;
- Measurement accuracy;
- On-board EPROM storage capacity;
- The type of PC bus interface.

In addition, a dozen more parameters, usually less important to the user, are specified: the number of analog outputs, their control resolution (number of bits), analog output voltage range, analog output control rate (samples per second) and measurement triggering method (analog or digital), input impedance, input current, common-mode rejection ratio (CMRR), power supply mode, and power consumption.

The number of analog inputs ranges from 1 to 64 (e. g., NI-6031E) and can usually be increased (even up to 256) by adding more analog multiplexers on an additional expansion card. Therefore, a single DAQ board and a PC can be used to build a multipoint measurement system.

The number of bits in a digital word after digitization (bit resolution) ranges from 8 to 24 (e. g. , the NI-4350 card for temperature sensors), with the upper range significantly exceeding the resolution of digital instruments within the same price group. Usually, the number of effective bits in a digital word is quoted for the specific board model as the range of values (e. g. , from 8 to 16 bits), where the extreme word lengths apply respectively to the lowest sampling rate (the longest word, e. g. , 16 bits) and the highest sampling rate (the shortest word, e. g. , 8 bits).

Sampling rate, expressed as the number of samples per second (Sps), is what best proves the advantage of a DAQ board, based measurement system against a stand-alone voltmeter-based system. The sampling rate ranges from several thousand Sps to 100 MSps (e. g. NI-5911). The figures quoted in catalogs refer to the conversion capacity of the on-board ADC converter and DSP circuitry (unless specified otherwise). The sampling rate is specified synthetically for the whole multi-input board. When measuring voltage on multiple inputs (channels) of a multichannel board, the maximum sampling rate per input is obtained by dividing the overall sampling rate by the number of active channels. For example, if a board features the maximum overall sampling rate of 1 MSps and has eight active channels, then the maximum sampling rate per channel is 125 KSps. However, if only one channel is active on the same board, then the maximum sampling rate in this channel is 1 MSps.

The input range of a DAQ board is specified as a range of voltage values symmetrical in relation to zero, or as a positive voltage range. On various boards, the input range spans from millivolts to several hundred volts (300V on some DAQ boards from IOtech). The selected input range and bit resolution define the board's absolute resolution. Take, for example, the NI-6111E 12-bit board which supports input ranges from ± 0.2 V to ± 42 V. In the ± 1V range, the absolute resolution of ΔV voltage measurement by means of this board is:

$$\Delta V = \frac{V_{max} - V_{min}}{2^{12}} = \frac{1V - (-1V)}{4\ 096} = 0.488\ 3\ \text{mV}$$

Once the input voltage has been amplified by the programmable amplifier with the k_u factor, the absolute resolution improves from ΔV to $\Delta V k_u$.

The board's measurement accuracy is usually specified in a tabular format, since it depends on a number of factors: the selected input range, temperature, and test period (24 hours, 90 days, or 1 year). According to the theory of measurement, the board's accuracy can be roughly estimated to be between 2 and 10 times worse than its resolution.

On-board memory buffer can be used to store several hundred thousand or even many million samples before uploading the data via the bus to the PC. High sampling rate DAQ boards are provided with EPROM memory to store measurement data samples. In addition to the EPROM for the samples, boards have much smaller memory chips to store the selected configuration and settings.

The bus interface of the board is another parameter. Boards are available for the following buses: PCI, ISA, PCMCIA (PC Card), USB, or IEEE-1394. PCI, ISA, and PCMCIA boards are designed as plug-in boards for installation inside a PC, USB and IEEE-1394 boards are designed as stand alone units, to be installed outside a PC and connected via a multiwire cable.

Lesson 5 Laser Technology

Laser can be used to measure distances with hitherto unimaginable convenience and accuracy.

There are three quite different methods of distance measurement by laser: (a) interferometric methods; (b) beam modulation; (c) pulse echo.

Interferometric methods are really only applicable at present for distances up to 10m. Methods (b) and (c) are suitable for measuring distances from 10 m up to millions of kilometres.

1. Interferometric Methods

The use of the Michelson interferometer to form interference fringes has been discussed in. It is readily apparent that this instrument can be used to measure distance, or more precisely changes in distance. If either mirror of a Michelson interferometer is moved in a direction parallel to the incident beam, while still remaining normal to it, then the interference pattern will change. A movement of one fringe is caused by the mirror moving through a distance equal to half a wavelength of the light source. By a movement of one fringe, it is meant that the illumination of some point in the interference goes through one cycle, i.e. black through bright to black again.

By counting the number of fringes passing a detector when the mirror moves, and knowing the wavelength of the light in air, it is possible to calculate the distance through which the mirror has moved normal to the incident beam with great accuracy over a considerable distance. This method of measurement is not new but was severely limited by the quality of the light sources available until lasers became available. With non-laser sources, coherent lengths are restricted to a few tens of centimetres with a consequent limit on the range of distances measurable.

In practice the conventional Michelson set-up using plane mirrors is not used for two reasons. Firstly light from the laser would be reflected back into the cavity, and this would result in an undesirable modulation of the laser output. Secondly plane mirrors are extremely difficult to align.

The commercial systems available use two different arrangements of the optical components as illustrated in Figure 3.20(a) and Figure 3.20(b).

In each case the fixed part of the instrument is indicated by the components inside the dotted line while the corner-cube prism is fixed to the component whose movement is required. The arrangement shown in Figure 3.20(a) has the advantage of being easily aligned as two corner-cube retro-reflectors are used. These have the property of reflecting

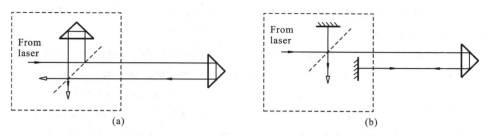

Figure 3.20 Two practical optical systems for measuring distance by fringe counting

the beam back along a direction parallel to its incident path. The lateral displacement involved is utilized to avoid returned light entering the laser. Figure 3.20(b) shows a similar arrangement which has the advantage of being less sensitive to the effects of lateral shear caused by the corner-cube having any sideways motion. It also has the further advantage of being twice as sensitive because the third mirror produces twice the fringe shift for the same movement. As a plane mirror has to be used in order that the returned beams superimpose, the alignment is more difficult and returned light entering the laser must be avoided by the use of a polarizing system incorporating a quarter wave plate.

In a conventional Michelson interferometer a change in mirror position of 1 cm causes a movement of nearly ten million fringes. These must obviously be counted electronically by means of a photo-cell detector.

It will be observed that two fringe patterns are formed in the arrangement shown in Figure 3.20(a); these are used to avoid ambiguities caused by vibration. If only one fringe pattern were detected it would not be possible to determine whether the mirror was moving towards or away from the instrument. By detecting both patterns in conjunction with a phase sensitive detector the final distance, usually indicated on a digital display, includes the effects of direction reversals caused by vibration or shock.

The speed in which a measurement can be taken depends on the velocity of the mirror. This is limited by the maximum frequency response of the detector. In practice movements of 10 cm s^{-1} are possible on commercial instruments. 3 ms^{-1} is available in the laboratory, the latter corresponding to a maximum frequency of 600 MHz. The amount of shock and vibration which can be tolerated before measurements are disrupted is clearly also dependent on detector frequency response.

In theory the maximum distances measurable with these techniques depend on the coherence length of the laser used. Providing the laser is stabilized the coherence length considerably increases on changing from multiple axial mode to single axial mode operation and distances of hundreds of kilometres could be measured if it were not for air turbulence which can make the path lengths in each arm of the interferometer vary to such an extent that no spatial coherence exists between the interfering beams and so no fringes are formed. Air turbulence results in great difficulty in measuring distances greater than 10 m.

With electronic methods of counting fringes it is possible to measure changes of 1/10 of a fringe. Thus a 10 m path length using visible laser light an accuracy of a few parts in 10^8 is possible. The realization of this accuracy will depend on knowing the wavelength of the laser to the same accuracy.

Under normal conditions a single axial mode output is easily obtained by decreasing the length of the cavity until the axial mode separation is greater than the Doppler width of the gain curve. In this situation only one axial mode can exist under the gain curve at any one instant. The presence of temperature fluctuations and microphonic disturbances will cause the laser mirrors to vary in separation thus in turn vary the wavelength and intensity of the output. So, although single axial mode operation is obtained providing great coherence length it is only possible to state that the wavelength of the output is at some value inside the Doppler linewidth. If for a helium-neon laser the Doppler width is 2 000 MHz then for a short unstabilized laser the wavelength is known only to an accuracy of 2×10^9 Hz in 5×10^{14} Hz. i. e. a few parts in 10^5.

In order to realize the full potential of interferometric measuring systems it is clearly necessary to stabilize the laser output. This can be achieved to better than 1 part in 10^7 by piezo-electric vibration of one of the following laser mirrors.

There is another form of interferometer suitable for measuring distances which is depicted in Figure 3.21.

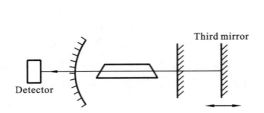

Figure 3.21 The third-mirror interferometer

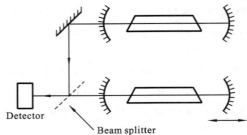

Figure 3.22 The beating of two laser outputs to measure mirror movement

In this system referred to as the third mirror system and discovered at the Services Electronics Research Laboratory, an additional mirror is placed outside the laser cavity. This third mirror reflects light back into the cavity. For certain positions the mirror reflects light back into the cavity so as to be in antiphase with the light inside. The output of the system is consequently of minimum intensity in this situation. By moving the third mirror, $\lambda/2$ along the optical axis, the returned light is now in phase and the output is a maximum. By counting the fringes the distance moved by the third mirror can be determined. Measurement of very small movements can be made by interfering two laser beams. Figure 3.22 shows how the output from two laser is combined at a photomultiplier detector. If one laser is stabilized and mirror of the other is caused to move, then a change in the beat frequency obtained at the detector will be observed.

We have

$$\frac{n\lambda}{2} = L \qquad (3.5.1)$$

where, n is the number of wavelengths in the laser cavity. This number defines the axial mode under consideration. λ is the wavelength and L is the length of the cavity.

$$\frac{nc}{2\nu} = L \tag{3.5.2}$$

differentiating Equation (3.5.2) and ignoring the negative sign:

$$\frac{dL}{d\nu} = \frac{nc}{2\nu^2} \tag{3.5.3}$$

and hence using Equation (3.5.2)

$$d\nu = \frac{\nu}{L} dL \tag{3.5.4}$$

Thus assuming that frequencies of a few tens of cycles are detectable (an audio frequency) it should be possible, in principle, to detect a mirror movement of 10^{-13} cm. In practice, thermal and microphonic effects as well as changes in the reference laser would make such measurements very difficult. The reference laser can be stabilized to hold the drift to ± 5 MHz per day and thus a 100 MHz beat could be detected with 5% accuracy. For a 10 cm laser tube this would correspond to a mirror movement of 2×10^{-6} cm.

2. Beam Modulation

A well-established method of distance measurement is to modulate a signal which, after transmission and reflection of a target, is detected. The change in phase of the impressed frequency is a dependent of the distance the wave has travelled. By modulating at a number of different frequencies an unambiguous determination of distance is obtained.

Early devices based on this principle use r.f. modulation of micro-waves or microwave modulation of incoherent sources. The use of a modulated laser beam enhances the performance of such a system for the following reasons:

(1) The high frequency of the visible light enables a modulated signal of higher frequency to be used hence to increase resolution.

(2) The narrow bandwidth of the laser output enables high discrimination against stray light, thus enabling use in daylight with increased signal to noise ratio.

(3) A high degree of selectivity is possible owing to the small divergence of the laser beam and so different parts of the target can be examined.

3. Pulse Echo

Up to this point all the distance measurement devices described have employed continuously operating gas lasers in which use has been made of high coherence or small beam divergence. The use of high power pulsed lasers is also possible in radar type systems where the time interval between transmission and detection is obtained. By multiplying half this time by the velocity of light, whose variations with refractive index, pressure, temperature and humidity are well known, the distance of the target may be ascertained.

Such systems are not novel but have been improved considerably with lasers. Q-switched ruby lasers enable hitherto unimaginable powers to be obtained in very short pulses. The shorter the pulse the more accurately can the distance be determined. The narrow linewidth enables high discrimination against unwanted light to be obtained hence increasing signal-to-noise ratio and range.

A particularly interesting application of pulse echo techniques is the determination of the distance between the earth and the moon. Until about 1957 conventional astronomical techniques such as optical parallax measurements enabled the moon's distance to be established to an accuracy of ± 3.2 km. More recently by measuring the transit time of a radar pulse a higher accuracy of ± 1.1 km has been obtained.

The advent of the laser opened up the possibility of an even more accurate determination which would provide information not only on the absolute distance but also on variations in distance. These variations enable information about the distribution of mass inside the moon, continental drift on earth and changes in the location of the earth's north pole to be ascertained.

The first attempt at laser measurement was made in 1962 at the Massachusetts Institute of Technology by using a one millisecond laser pulse. Results were disappointing due to the relatively long pulse duration. Better results were obtained in 1965 by Russian workers who used a 50 ns pulse from a Q-switched ruby laser. However the curvature and irregularity of the moon's surface limited accuracy to about 200 m.

The most accurate way of carrying out pulse echo ranging is to use a cooperative target. The amount of light returned can be greater by two orders of magnitude and higher accuracy is obtained by observing the returned beam from a selected point on the target. Cooperative ranging of the moon was possible after the astronauts in the Apollo 11 mission of 1969 placed an array of corner cube reflectors on the lunar surface.

The array actually consists of 100 individual corner cubes each 4 cm in diameter, the latter dimension being determined by considerations of thermal stability and diffraction. If the corner cube is too small, the returned beam will be very wide by the time it returns to earth and insufficient illumination of the detector might occur. On the other hand, if the corner cube reflector is too large the rotation of the earth may cause the returned beam to miss the detector altogether particularly if the laser and detector are located coincidentally. This can happen because the light takes as long as 2.5 seconds to travel from the earth to the moon and back to the earth again.

The 4 cm diameter corner cube reflector causes the reflected beam to be 16 km in diameter by the time it returns to earth.

The transmitting and receiving unit was located at the Lick Observatory at Mount Hamilton in California where the 120 inch telescope was used in reverse to expand the pulse from a ruby laser. The pulses had an energy of 8 J and lasted 10 ns.

Using this technique the earth-moon distance has been determined to an accuracy of ± 15 cm.

Words and Expressions

hitherto [ˌhiðəˈtuː] *ad.* 到目前为止，迄今

unimaginable [ˌʌniˈmædʒinəbl] a. 不能想象的,想象不到的;难以理解的
interferometric [ˈintəˌferəuˈmetrik] a. 干涉测量的;干涉仪的
incident [ˈinsidənt] n. 事件 a. 入射的;关联的
coherent [kəuˈhiərənt] a. 互相密合着的,凝聚性的,连贯的;相干的,可干涉的
corner-cube prism 角隅棱镜,三面直角棱镜
retro-reflector 反光镜,后向反射器
shift [ʃift] n. 变化;移动,移位;漂移 v. 改变;位移;转移
quarter wave plate=quarter wavelength plate 四分之一波片
ambiguity [ˌæmbiˈgjuːiti] n. 不明确,含糊,暧昧,模棱两可,模糊,不定性
disrupt [disˈrʌpt] v. 使……分裂,使……瓦解,使中断,使陷于混乱
fluctuation [ˌflʌktjuˈeiʃən] n. 波动;起伏
microphonic [ˈmaikrəˈfɔnik] a. 麦克风的,扩音器的,颤噪的
piezo-electric= piezoelectric [paiˌiːzəuiˈlektrik] a. 压电的
depict [diˈpikt] v. 描述
photomultiplier [ˈfəutəuˈmʌtiplaiə] n. 光电倍增器,光电倍增管,亦作 photomultiplier tube
beat frequency 拍频
unambiguous [ˌʌnæmˈbigjuəs] a. 不含糊的,明白的
discrimination [disˌkrimiˈneiʃən] n. 歧视;辨别,区别
echo [ˈekəu] n. 回声,回音,回波 v. 发出回声;随声附和;摹仿
parallax [ˈpærəlæks] n. 视差

Notes

1. If either mirror of a Michelson interferometer is moved in a direction parallel to the incident beam, while still remaining normal to it, then the interference pattern will change.

(1) Michelson interferometer：迈克尔逊干涉仪

(2) (be) normal to：垂直于,对……成直角

(3) 全句可翻译为：如果迈克尔逊干涉仪的两个镜子中的任一个镜子沿着平行于入射光的方向移动,而另一个静止不动的镜子保持垂直于入射光,那么,干涉条纹将会改变。

2. A movement of one fringe is caused by the mirror moving through a distance equal to half a wavelength of the light source. By a movement of one fringe it is meant that the illumination of some point in the interference goes through one cycle, i.e. black through bright to black again.

全句可翻译为：一个条纹的移动,是由于镜子移动的距离等于半个光源波长引起的。移动一个条纹,就意味着在干涉中的某些点的照度变化一个周期,即由暗到亮,再回到暗。

3. The amount of shock and vibration which can be tolerated before measurements are disrupted is clearly also dependent on detector frequency response.

这是个复合句。全句可翻译为：在测量被瓦解前能容许的冲击和振荡的量,显然也取决于探测器的频率响应。

4. If for a helium-neon laser the Doppler width is 2 000 MHz then for a short

unstabilized laser the wavelength is known only to an accuracy of 2×10^9 Hz in 5×10^{14} Hz. i. e. a few parts in 10^5.

全句可翻译为:假如氦氖激光器的多普勒线宽为 2 000 MHz,那么一台短时未加稳定措施的激光器的波长的精度只有 5×10^{14} Hz 的 2×10^9 Hz ,即 10^5 的几分之几。

5. Early devices based on this principle used r. f. modulation of micro-waves or microwave modulation of incoherent sources.

(1) r. f. = radio frequency 射频

(2) 全句可翻译为:基于这个原理的早先的设备采用微波射频调制或非相干源的微波调制。

Reading Material

Measurement with Laser

When laser is operating in the uniphase transverse mode the output beam can be regarded as a straight line of almost constant thickness. This property can be utilized for the purposes of alignment. An accurate and easily repeatable method of alignment is necessary in construction work and engineering. Examples in which a laser has been used successfully include tunnel boring, pipe laying and bridge construction. Not only can a straight line be defined but qualities such as aquareness and parallelism can also be ascertained.

Figure 3.23 Laser transit telescope (Photograph by courtesy of Spcctra-Physics, Ltd.)

For straight-edge applications laser can be used in its own right or as a light source in conjunction with optical elements. Figure 3.23 is a photograph of a commercial helium-neon laser transit telescope which can provide a 10 cm diameter beam at a distance of 1.6 km or, in conjunction with a cylindrical lens, a line 10 cm wide by 250 m high at the same distance.

It is obvious that the accuracy obtainable must depend on the ability to define the centre of the laser beam and for a readily definable centre, the symmetrical uniphase mode is obviously the most suitable as well as having minimum divergence. Thus the laser used must not only be sufficiently rugged to withstand the rigours of the environment in which it is to be used, but it must also provide a stable uniphase output. Stability is an important factor; once the instrument is set up it must be capable of providing a beam which continues to point in the initially determined direction. The successful application of the laser in construction work may well depend on this feature as conventional the odolites are capable of high accuracy. Continuous checking of the work as it proceeds is easily undertaken with a permanently set up laser and relatively unskilled personnel, whereas the constant use of a theodolite is prohibitively expensive.

For applications where extremely high accuracy is unnecessary, such as, tunnel boring, a rude method of estimating the beam centre can be used. This can take the form of a graticule of concentric rings placed in the path of the beam. The machine operator merely has to guide the machine so as to keep the beam as near as possible on the centre of the graticule.

For more precise work an electronic detecting system must be used which can take the form of four symmetrically placed silicon photocells. Diametrically opposed cells are linked so as to produce a null reading when each is illuminated by equal intensities. The beam is centred when two null readings from each diametrically opposed pair are obtained simultaneously. The device must be balanced initially by means of ballast resistors incorporated in each circuit (See Figure 3.24) to compensate temperature differences and the differing characteristics of each detector. Each cell must be accurately positioned with respect to the others. This can be achieved by allowing the beam to fall on a reflecting pyramid which can be made of glass to a high standard. The cells are then placed around the pyramid as indicated in Figure 3.24. It is important that the base of the pyramid is kept normal to the incident beam direction.

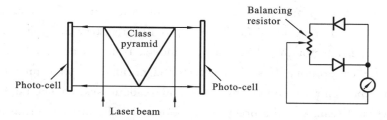

Figure 3.24 Laser beam alignment head and electronic circuit

The use of optical components in conjunction with a laser has provided an enhanced method of alignment. The optical components used have consisted either of a coarse circular diffraction grating (See Figure 3.25) or coarse Fresnel zone plates (See Figure 3.26). These are fabricated on plane surfaces and the surface positioned so as to be normal to the laser beam.

 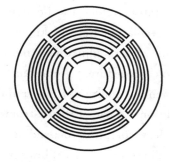

Figure 3.25 Circular diffraction grating   Figure 3.26 Fresnel zone plate

When a beam of light is incident normally on a circular diffraction grating the effect is to produce, on the far side of the grating, a circular fringe pattern in any plane parallel to the grating. The centre of this fringe pattern defines a straight line which can be used for continuous alignment in conjunction with a graticule consisting of concentric circles.

There may be situations where a number of points need to be aligned. A circular Fresnel plate can be used which consists of concentric annuli of varying width as shown in Figure 3.26.

Lesson 6　Calibration Technology

1. General

The technical issues related to calibration and evaluation of instruments used for radiation protection purposes are dealt with in this report. Certain factors such as the type of display (e. g. , analog vs. digital) and human factor design features (e. g. , weight, balance, size) which affect the selection or desirability of particular instruments, while important, are not covered here.

Most of the considerations in the report apply to fixed radiation monitors as well as to portable instruments. Fixed area detectors are frequently located on walls or other surfaces and may be mounted in proximity to sources of radiation or in areas of generally high background radiation. It may be difficult or impossible to carry out calibration of a fixed monitor *in situ*; the detector may have to be removed from its normal location to a more convenient one for calibration. If such a detector is normally cable-connected to a remote readout station, the same or equivalent cable and readout system should be used in the calibration process. Because of the presence of potential radiation scattering materials close to a fixed monitor in the field, such a monitor may be exposed to both primary and scatter-degraded radiations during actual use. If the detector in question exhibits an energy-dependent response, calibration in a laboratory setting may not assure accurate performance in the field if the energy or angular distribution in the two situations are different. Other features specific to the calibration of these monitors are not elaborated in this report.

2. Level of Calibration

Calibration refers to the determination and adjustment of instrument response in a particular radiation field of known intensity. Some obvious factors which affect response, such as meter zero adjustment and battery condition, are necessarily considered in the overall calibration procedure. Additional influencing factors, such as energy dependence and environmental conditions, may require consideration in the calibration process, depending on the conditions of use of the instrument. Thus, the procedures required for calibration may be more or less complex, depending on the need to assess the impacts of these influencing factors. Three levels of calibration are defined; these are discussed below and identified as full characterization, characterization for specific acceptance, and routine calibration.

3. Full Characterization

Full characterization of an instrument involves more than what is normally required by users of instruments. Routine calibration (See Section 2.3) often requires simply the determination of reading linearity when an instrument is exposed to a single radiation type of specified energy. Manufacturers of instruments and others may, however, have the need to characterize fully an instrument being supplied to users in the field. Such characterization should include the following:

(1) Evaluation of the energy-dependence of the response of the instrument to the radiation types to which the instrument is intended to respond; note that response, as it applies to instrument calibration, is the quotient of the instrument reading by the true value of the quantity being measured;

(2) Evaluation of linearity of instrument readings;

(3) Evaluation of the effects of other ionizing radiation types which may be encountered in field use on the instrument reading;

(4) Evaluation of the effects of environmental influences, such as temperature, pressure, and humidity, on the instrument reading;

(5) Evaluation of the effects of nonionizing radiations, particularly RF radiations, on the instrument reading;

(6) Evaluation of geotropic effects;

(7) Evaluation of the ability of the instrument to survive mechanical shock as might be encountered in field use;

(8) Evaluation of the dose rate-dependence of the response and/or dead-time characteristics; this is particularly important to avoid significant exposure when an instrument's response is depressed at high dose rates;

(9) Evaluation of the effects of other influencing factors, such as magnetic and electrostatic fields;

(10) Evaluation of the angular response of the instrument, preferably at an energy close to the minimum useful energy for the instrument.

Presently, most manufacturers provide information relating to item (1) above for portable instruments used in air kerma/dose measurements and for some instruments used in assessing alpha-and beta-emitting surface contamination. A user may have to arrange for characterization with respect to additional items from the list given above.

4. Calibration for Specific Acceptance

It may be necessary to use an instrument under specific conditions of a non-routine nature, and calibration specific to that objective may be required. An example would be the intended use of an instrument at temperatures higher than those encountered in general use. Such an application would require evaluation of the instrument response at the anticipated temperatures. Calibration might be carried out at the elevated temperature and, if the adjusted response is acceptable, the instrument approved for such use. As an alternative to calibrating the instrument at the elevated temperature, if the temperature dependence of response is known, the calibration reading at a lower temperature may be used to adjust to what would be expected at the higher temperature. In these cases, a label should be applied to the instrument noting that it may not be suitable for other uses if this is the case. Alternatively, the instrument may be calibrated for routine use and its response then evaluated under the proposed use conditions. If responses under routine and proposed use conditions are significantly different, a correction factor or chart should be supplied with the instrument for use under the proposed conditions. ANSI, in report number N42. 17C (ANSI, 1989a), discusses performance specifications for portable instruments that are to be used under extreme environmental conditions.

5. Routine Calibration

Routine calibration refers to calibration of an instrument for normal use. Normal use is characterized by the following:

(1) use of the instrument for radiation of the type for which the instrument is designed;

(2) use of the instrument for radiation energies within the range of energies for which the instrument is designed;

(3) use under environmental conditions for which the instrument is designed;

(4) use under influencing factors, such as magnetic and electrostatic fields, for which the instrument is designed;

(5) use of the instrument in an orientation such that geotropic effects are not a concern;

(6) use of the instrument in a manner that will not subject the instrument to mechanical stress beyond that for which designed.

Routine calibration commonly involves the use of one or more sources of a specific radiation type and energy (e. g., ^{137}Cs or ^{60}Co photon-emitting sources for many photon air kerma-or exposure-or dose-measuring instruments) and of sufficient activity to provide adequate field intensities for calibration on all ranges of concern.

6. Performance Check

In the interval between calibrations, however, the instrument user should validate acceptable operation by carrying out a performance check. This is merely intended to establish whether or not the instrument is operating/functioning within certain specified, rather large, uncertainty limits. Although the performance check may range from a crude determination that the instrument is responding to a source, to a more detailed determination, deviations of ± 20 percent from the expected reading are generally considered acceptable for a performance check. The initial performance check should be carried out in the calibration laboratory following calibration; the source should be held at a fixed and reproducible location and the instrument reading recorded. The source should be identified along with the instrument, and the same check source should be employed in the same fashion to demonstrate the instrument's operability on a daily basis when the instrument is in use. Beta or gamma-radiation-emitting radionuclide are commonly used in sources for performance checking of beta-and/or gamma-radiation-measuring instruments. The sources are often no more than a few hundred kBq in activity and produce a reasonable reading on the instrument when held very close to the detector. Some instruments use internally mounted sources that can be moved close to the detector by means of an external control. Alpha-emitting radionuclides are used as check sources for alpha radiation detectors. Portable neutron sources in fixed geometries or, at times, well-characterized beams at reactor facilities, are useful as check sources for neutron-measuring instruments. Tissue-equivalent proportional counters (TEPC) often use an internally mounted alpha-emitting source which serves as both a check source and a calibration source.

It is sometimes convenient to have available more than one check source for use with a given instrument or with several instruments of the same type. In such situations, the reading of the instrument, when exposed to each such check source, should be evaluated in the calibration laboratory. As above, the specific source must be identified along with the appropriate reading of a given instrument.

7. Precalibration Check

Before an attempt is made to calibrate an instrument, a series of simple operations should be completed to ensure proper condition of the instrument for calibration. Although the exact checks to be made will vary with the design of the particular instrument, a number of these are common to most instruments. These include checking for radioactive contamination, condition of the batteries, loose or broken parts, proper operation of the switches, and that the instrument zero can be adjusted in accordance with the manufacturer's instructions.

Words and Expressions

desirability [di‚zaiərə'biləti] n. 称心如意的人(事物)
in situ [拉丁语]在原地,在原来位置
elaborate [i'læbərət] a. 精细的,详尽的,精心的 v. 详尽阐述,用心地做,推敲
quotient ['kwəuʃənt] n. 商,系数
ionize ['aiənaiz] v. 离子化,(使)电离,游离(化)
RF(radio frequency) 射频
geotropic [‚dʒi(:)əu'trɔpik] a. 向地性的
dose [dəus] n. 剂量,服用量 v. 给某人一定剂量的药
dead-time n. 空载[寂静]时间
kerma ['kə:mə] n. 科玛(放射学中的一种动能,单位:焦耳/千克,尔格/克)
ANSI (American National Standards Institute) 美国国家标准协会
operability [‚ɔpərə'biliti] n. 运转或操作性能;可操作性
radionuclide [‚reidiəu'nju:klaid] – 'nu:– n. 放射性核
Bq *abbr.* 贝克,贝克勒尔(放射性活度单位)(becquerel)
radioactive contamination 放射性污染

Notes

1. Most of the considerations in the report apply to fixed radiation monitors as well as to portable instruments.

(1) apply to:适用于,适合,应用到

(2) 全句可翻译为:在本报告中所考虑的大多数事项适用于固定的辐射监测器,也适用于

便携式仪器。

2. Because of the presence of potential radiation scattering materials close to a fixed monitor in the field, such a monitor may be exposed to both primary and scatter-degraded radiations during actual use.

(1) be exposed to：容易(可能)受到……(的影响)

(2) 全句可翻译为：由于在现场存在辐射散射的材料靠近固定的监测器的可能,因此,这种监测器在实际使用时,可能同时受到原始的辐射和经散射衰减后的辐射的影响。

3. Calibration refers to the determination and adjustment of instrument response in a particular radiation field of known intensity.

(1) refer to：涉及,指的(就)是,(是,系)指,表示

(2) 全句可翻译为:定标指的就是在某一特定的已知强度的辐射场中,确定和调整仪器的响应。

Reading Material

Instrument Response Considerations

1) Linearity Measurements in Calibration

A knowledge of the response of each instrument for a wide range of dose rates is important. The ideal relationship between instrument reading and dose rate is linear, and deviations from linearity should be known. Evaluation of linearity should be carried out for all scales on which a particular instrument will be used. Characteristics of the detector and of the associated electronics can affect linearity. Nonlinear readings may be outside the acceptable accuracy limits and make an instrument unsuitable for general use.

For instruments with linear readout scales, calibration should include response evaluations and adjustment for at least two points of each scale to be calibrated. The response points should be separated by at least 40 percent of the full scale range and should be represented by points approximately equidistant from the mid-point of the scale. Acceptable results at the two points provide reasonable assurance of a linear response over the range of values covered by the selected scale. This procedure is reasonable for both analog display instruments and digital display instruments which have selectable or automatic scale-switching.

For analog instruments with multiple-decade-log-scale displays and for digital instruments with no scale selection, at least one point on each response decade should be used in calibration. The end point of a decade may be easier to read than a mid-point and such would be acceptable for calibration purposes.

2) Calibration on Selected Scales and Limited Ranges

Some instruments have selectable scales or single ranges which represent intensities known to be greater than those which will be encountered in field use. In such cases, it is considered acceptable to perform calibrations at intensities which include the highest intensities that could be encountered in field use and to exclude calibration at higher levels. The instrument should have a label affixed to it to inform the user that the instrument is not calibrated on specific ranges or above a particular intensity.

Uncertainty in the Calibration Process

The accuracy of an instrument undergoing calibration is a measure of how close the reading is to the expected (true) value of the quantity being measured. The accuracy attainable in a given calibration procedure depends on the characteristics of the radiation source(s)/field(s) used and the response characteristics of the instrument being evaluated.

The ultimate aim is to provide a calibration with sufficient accuracy that when the instrument is put into field use, its reading will yield an acceptably accurate estimate of the desired quantity(e. g. , air kerma(rate), contamination level). For an instrument whose response is independent of energy and field/detector geometry, routine use may yield measurements with accuracies close to those demonstrated in calibration. In other instances, an accurate calibration may not guarantee an acceptably accurate measurement in field use.

In Report No. 57, the NCRP recommends that instruments used for radiation protection purposes be calibrated to an accuracy of ± 5 percent (NCRP, 1978). Because of uncertainties in calibration standards and because of possible adverse effects of certain influencing factors attendant to the use of these standards, such accuracies may not be achievable. This is particularly true of beta-and neutron-dose-responding instruments. Recommendations of accuracy to be achieved in particular calibrations are presented in subsequent specific sections of this report.

NCRP Report No. 57 also recommends that when projected doses are near the level of the maximum permissible dose, a field measurement accuracy of ± 30 percent should be achieved; for projected doses less than ± 25 percent of the dose limit, inaccuracies on the order of 100 percent are acceptable; for projected doses significantly above the dose limits, accuracies of 20 percent are recommended (NCRP, 1978). Again, these accuracies may not be easily achievable, depending on the calibration accuracy achieved and the influences of the radiation field and other physical factors on the instrument response. The dose limits which apply to non-occupational exposures are considerably more restrictive than occupational limits [e. g. , NCRP (1987) recommends an annual dose limit of 1 mSv for members of the public and a monthly limit of 0. 5 mSv to a fetus]. Measurements using portable instruments for dose projections with those limits will have large uncertainties; inaccuracies exceeding 100 percent would not be unusual but may be acceptable for radiation control purposes.

It may be possible to improve field measurement accuracies by altering or extending the calibration procedure. For example, calibration with larger area sources may be a technique for reducing the error in the interpreted dose rate from distributed beta radiation sources.

The user must be aware of the response characteristics of an instrument in order to make reasonable estimates of the expected measurement accuracy based on the calibration accuracy and the differences between calibration and actual field conditions. Such estimates in the workplace can be difficult, especially if the radiation field conditions are not well known or are variable. If such factors as instrument energy dependence and field/detector geometry dependence are known, it may be possible to make estimates of the maximum errors likely in field measurements when the calibration accuracy is specified under known conditions. For example, if an air kerma rate-measuring instrument is calibrated with ^{137}Cs 662 keV photons to an accuracy of ± 10 percent on all ranges, and it is known that the instrument photon response does not vary by more than ± 20 percent (relative to the response at 662 keV) for the range of energies to be encountered in the field, and if it is known that no significant field/detector geometry dependence exists, field measurements are likely to be accurate to within ± 30 percent.

The entire subject of accuracy in field measurements is very important and could be the subject of a separate report. The present report provides limited discussion of this topic in relation to the calibration process, but no attempt is made to treat the topic in detail.

While the accuracy of any instrument measurement is judged by the extent to which the mean reading deviates from the true value of the quantity being measured, the precision associated with the measurement provides an indication of the reproducibility of the measurement. The precision associated with a group of repetitive measurements made under the same conditions refers to the closeness of agreement among the measurements. High precision is associated with tightly grouped measurement values while low (poor) precision implies a wide spread of measurement values. Random variations embodied in the measurement process are considered in quantifying precision. Such random variations may be treated by standard statistical techniques as discussed below.

Other uncertainties that are not estimable by usual statistical methods can affect the overall uncertainty in a calibration result. Such uncertainties, frequently referred to as systematic, may result from a number of causes, such as a miscalculation or an erroneous measurement of field strength, certain errors in reading an instrument scale (e. g., parallax reading error), and errors in measuring a source-to-detector distance because of a misjudgment as to the position of the source or the center of the detector. Systematic errors of this type individually result in measurements that are either consistently high or low. To the extent possible, such errors should be eliminated by thorough investigation and correction of the errors. Even when these biases are eliminated, if they can be, other uncertainties of a systematic nature may persist. Uncertainty in the half-life of a source radionuclide, inability to read a distance scale or instrument scale exactly or to measure time without error, in the case of an integral measurement, will introduce uncertainties in the calibration. Uncertainties of this type may just as likely be positive as negative. In general, it may be impossible or unrealistically difficult to evaluate exactly all systematic errors that might affect a measurement; in such cases, the maximum values of such errors should be estimated.

The overall uncertainty "... of a reported value refers to its likely inaccuracy in terms of credible limits, and combines both ① components based on data that are amenable to statistical treatments and ② components due to systematic errors that cannot be treated statistically" (NCRP Report No. 58, 1985). The appropriate method to be used for combining random and systematic errors is not always clear and is a subject of some debate.

The ICRU suggested that the overall uncertainty be expressed as "the arithmetic sum of the uncertainties due to random and assessable systematic errors". (ICRU, 1968). In 1980, representatives from eleven national standardizing laboratories met at the International Bureau of Weights and Measures (BIPM) as a Working Group on the Statement of Uncertainties. This group concluded that persistent systematic uncertainties behave as do random uncertainties and, with sufficient methods, their stochastic nature would be evident. It was recommended that systematic uncertainties be measured by quantities u, which are interpreted as estimates of the respective variances; the quantities u_j^2 are treated as if they are standard deviations. The general laws governing propagation of errors are assumed to apply to both random and systematic uncertainties in the same fashion. There is an ongoing effort by a working group of the International Standards Organization to promote international adoption of this approach. In this report the NCRP has adopted some of the recommendations of the BIPM working Group with respect to the treatment of systematic uncertainties in calibration. The assumption is made that all identifiable biases in the calibration process have been corrected. The use of confidence levels and, by inference therefore, the quantities of concern, associated with calculated uncertainties, are assumed to have values that are normally distributed. (The BIPM Working Group on the statement of uncertainties has recommended against the use of confidence levels when quantities are not normally distributed.) With respect to systematic uncertainties, as they are discussed below, the value of u (the apparent "standard deviation" representative of the systematic uncertainty) has been estimated as 1/3 the value of the estimated maximum systematic uncertainty. For purposes of defining the "95 percent confidence level", $\pm 2u$ has been selected as the range of uncertainty about the mean. This selection is somewhat arbitrary but, given the frequently indefinite magnitudes of systematic uncertainties, more precise specification is not necessary. The use of quotation marks around the phrases "standard deviation" and "confidence interval" will be used in this report to indicate that the quantity referred to includes systematic uncertainties as described above.

The random error is assumed to be the value $t\sigma_{\bar{I}}$ where $\sigma_{\bar{I}}$ is the standard deviation in the mean value (also known as the standard error), and t is the student's t-factor. The table value of t for a given number of measurements is associated with a particular confidence level. For example, for a set of 10 measurements ($n=10$) there is a 95 percent confidence that the true mean value falls in the interval $\bar{I} \pm 2.26_7$. (Note that here and in the discussion below, the symbol σ is used in relationship to errors associated with a finite number of measurements; it represents an estimate of the standard deviation and is sometimes denoted by $\overset{\circ}{\sigma}$ or s). If δ is the estimated maximum magnitude of the systematic error, the value of u is estimated by

$$u = \delta/3$$

and the overall uncertainty is given by

$$\pm [(t\sigma_{\bar{I}})^2 + (ku)^2]^{1/2}$$

The value of k, at the "95 percent confidence level", has been taken as 2.

Notes

1. NCRP: National Council on Radiation Protection and Measurements
2. ANSI: American National Standards Institute
3. ICRU: The International Commission on Radiation Units and Measurements

PART FOUR Signal Conditioning

Lesson 1 An Introduction to Data Acquisition

In many situations, it becomes necessary to alter the frequency at which particular channels are sampled depending upon the values of data signals received from a particular input sensor. Thus a channel might normally be sampled once every 10 minutes. If, however, the sensor signals approach the alarm limit, then it is obviously desirable to sample that channel once every minute or even faster so that the operator can be informed, thereby avoiding any catastrophes. Microcomputer controlled intelligent data loggers may be programmed to alter the sampling frequencies depending upon the values of process signals. Other data loggers include self-scanning modules which can initiate sampling.

The conventional hardwired data loggers, without any programming facilities, simply record the instantaneous values of transducer outputs at a regular sampling interval. This raw data often means very little to the typical user. To be meaningful, this data must be linearised and scaled, using a calibration curve, in order to determine the real value of the variable in appropriate engineering units. Prior to the availability of programmable data loggers, this function was usually carried out in the off-line mode on a mini-or mainframe computer. The raw data values had to be punched out on paper tape, in binary or octal code, to be input subsequently to the computer used for analysis purposes and converted to the engineering units. Paper tape punches are slow speed mechanical devices reducing the speed at which channels can be scanned. An alternative was to print out the raw data values further reducing the data scanning rate. It was not possible to carry out any limit comparisons or provide any alarm information. Every single value acquired by the data logger had to be recorded even though it might not serve any useful purpose during subsequent analysis; many data values only need recording when they lie outside the pre-set low and high limits.

If the analog data must be transmitted over any distance, differences in ground potential between the signal source and final location can add noise to the interface design. In order to separate common-mode interference from the signal to be recorded or processed, devices designed for this purpose, such as instrumentation amplifiers, may be used. An instrumentation amplifier is characterized by good common-mode-rejection capability, a high input impedance, low drift, adjustable gain, and greater cost than operational amplifiers. They range from monolithic ICs to potted modules, and larger rack-mounted modules with manual scaling and null adjustments. When a very high common-mode voltage is present or the need for extremely-lowcommon-mode leakage current exists (as in many medical-electronics applications), an isolation amplifier is required. Isolation amplifiers may use optical or transformer isolation.

Analog function circuits are special-purpose circuits that are used for a variety of signal conditioning operations on signals which are in analog form. When their accuracy is adequate, they can relieve the microprocessor of time-consuming software and computations. Among the typical operations performed are multiplications, division, powers, roots, nonlinear functions such as for linearizing transducers, rims measurements, computing vector sums, integration and differentiation, and current-to-voltage or voltage-to-current conversion. Many of these operations can be purchased in available devices as multiplier/dividers, log/antilog amplifiers, and others.

When data from a number of independent signal sources must be processed by the same microcomputer or communications channel, a multiplexer is used to channel the input signals into the A/D converter.

Multiplexers are also used in reverse, as when a converter must distribute analog information to many different channels. The multiplexer is fed by a D/A converter which continually refreshes the output channels with new information.

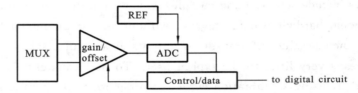

Figure 4.1 The basic components in a data-acquisition system

In many systems, the analog signal varies during the time that the converter takes to digitize an input signal. The changes in this signal level during the conversion process can result in errors since the conversion period can be completed some time after the conversion command. The final value never represents the data at the instant when the conversion command is transmitted. Sample-hold circuits are used to make an acquisition of the varying analog signal and to hold this signal for the duration of the conversion process. Sample-hold circuits are common in multichannel distribution systems where they allow each channel to receive and hold the signal level.

In order to get the data in digital form as rapidly and as accurately as possible, we must use an analog/digital (A/D) converter, which might be a shaft encoder, a small module with digital outputs, or a high-resolution, high-speed panel instrument (See Figure 4.1). These devices, which range from IC chips to rack-mounted instruments, convert analog input data, usually voltage, into an equivalent digital form. The characteristics of A/D converters include absolute and relative accuracy, linearity, monotonic, resolution, conversion speed, and stability. A choice of input ranges, output codes, and other features are available. The successive-approximation technique is popular for a large number of applications, with the most popular alternatives being the counter-comparator types, and dual-ramp approaches. The dual-ramp has been widely-used in digital voltmeters.

D/A converters convert a digital format into an equivalent analog representation. The basic converter consists of a circuit of weighted resistance values or ratios, each controlled by a particular level or weight of digital input data, which develops the output voltage or current in accordance with the digital input code. A special class of D/A converter exists which have the capability of handling variable reference sources. These devices are the multiplying DACs. Their output value is the product of the number represented by the digital input code and the analog reference voltage, which may vary from full scale to zero, and in some cases, to negative values.

In the past decade, data-acquisition hardware has changed radically due to advances in semiconductors, and prices have come down too; what have not changed, however, are the fundamental system problems confronting the designer. Signals may be obscured by noise, RFI, ground loops, power-line pickup, and transients coupled into signal lines from machinery. Separating the signals from these effects becomes a matter for concern.

Data-acquisition systems may be separated into two basic categories: ①those suited to favorable environments like laboratories; ②those required for hostile environments such as factories, vehicles, and military installations. The latter group includes industrial process control systems where temperature information may be gathered by sensors on tanks, boilers, or pipelines that may be spread over miles of facilities. That data may then be sent to a central processor to provide real-time process control. The digital control of steel mills, automated chemical production, and machine tools is carried out in this kind of hostile environment. The vulnerability of the data signals leads to the requirement for isolation and other techniques.

At the other end of the spectrum-laboratory applications, such as test systems for gathering information on gas chromatographs, mass spectrometers, and other sophisticated instruments, the designer's problems are concerned with the performing of sensitive measurements under favorable conditions rather than with the problem of protecting the integrity of collected data under hostile conditions.

Systems in hostile environments might require components for wide temperatures, shielding, common-mode noise reduction, conversion at an early stage, redundant circuits for critical measurements, and preprocessing of the digital data to test its reliability. Laboratory systems, on the other hand, will have narrower temperature ranges and less ambient noise. But the higher accuracies require sensitive devices, and a major effort may be necessary for the required signal/noise ratios.

The choice of configuration and components in data-acquisition design depends on consideration of a number of factors:
- Resolution and accuracy required in final format;
- Number of analog sensors to be monitored;
- Sampling rate desired;
- Signal-conditioning requirement due to environment and accuracy;
- Cost trade-offs.

Some of the choices for a basic data-acquisition configuration include:

(1) Single-channel techniques.
- Direct conversion;
- Preamplification and direct conversion;
- Sample-hold and conversion;
- Preamplification, sample-hold, and conversion;
- Preamplification, signal-conditioning, and direct conversion;
- Preamplification, signal-conditioning, sample-hold, and conversion.

(2) Multichannel techniques.
- Multiplexing the outputs of single-channel converters;
- Multiplexing the outputs of sample-holds;
- Multiplexing the inputs of sample-holds;
- Multiplexing low-level data;
- More than one tier of multiplexers.

(3) Signal-conditioning may include:
- Radiometric conversion techniques;
- Range biasing;
- Logarithmic compression;
- Analog filtering;
- Integrating converters;
- Digital data processing.

We shall consider these techniques later, but first we will examine some of the components used in these data-acquisition system configurations.

Words and Expressions

logger ['lɔgə] n. 记录器,注册器
mainframe computer 大型计算机
in binary or octal code 以二进制或八进制码形式
raw data values 原始数据
pre-set n. 预置
potential [pə'tenʃ(ə)l] a. 可能的,潜在的 n. 潜力,潜能;电位,电势
rejection capability 抑制能力
adjustable gain 可调增益,可变增益
monolithic IC 单块集成电路
potted modules 封装模块
transformer [træns'fɔːmə(r), trɑː-] n. 变压器
multiplexer ['mʌltiˌpleksə] n. 多路器
refresh [ri'freʃ] v. 刷新
shaft encoder 轴端编码盘,计数鼓,转轴编码器,轴角编码器
come down 降落;贬抑

for concern   关注,关切
real-time process control   实时过程控制
vulnerability [ˌvʌlnərəˈbilətɪ] *n*. 易受伤,易受责难,弱点;(计算机)漏洞
chromatograph [ˈkrəumətəɡrɑːf] *n*. 色谱;色谱仪
gas chromatograph   气相色谱仪
mass spectrometer   质谱仪
trade-off [ˈtreidɔf,-ɔːf] *n*. 物物交换,以物易物,换取,交换;权衡;平衡

Notes

1. The conventional hardwired data loggers, without any programming facilities, simply record the instantaneous values of transducer outputs at a regular sampling interval.

(1) The conventional hardwired data loggers:常规数据记录仪

(2) at a regular sampling interval:以常规的采样间隔

(3) 全句可翻译为:不带编程装置的常规数据记录仪仅以常规的采样间隔记录传感器输出的瞬时值。

2. Prior to the availability of programmable data loggers, this function was usually carried out in the off-line mode on a mini-or mainframe computer.

(1) prior *ad*. 在前,居先

(2) off-line *a*. 脱机的,离线的

(3) 全句可翻译为:在可编程数据记录仪出现之前,该功能一般利用脱机模式的小型或巨型计算机实现。

3. If the analog data must be transmitted over any distance, differences in ground potential between the signal source and final location can add noise in the interface design.

(1) ground potential:地电势,地电位

(2) 全句可翻译为:如果要在任意距离内传递模拟数据,那么,信号源和目的地间的地电势的不同会在接口处引入噪声。

4. The changes in this signal level during the conversion process can result in errors since the conversion period can be completed some time after the conversion command.

全句可翻译为:因为转换指令发出后一段时间转换过程才能完成,所以转换过程中信号电平的变化会使转换结果产生误差。

5. These devices, which range from IC chips to rack-mounted instruments, convert analog input data, usually voltage, into an equivalent digital form.

全句可翻译为:这些仪器把模拟输入数据(通常是电压)转换为等效的数字量,仪器结构可以是IC芯片型也可以是机架上安装型。

Reading Material

Data Acquisition Systems

1) Introduction to Data Acquisition Systems

Data acquisition systems, as the name implies, are products and/or processes used to collect information to document or analyze some phenomena. In the simplest form, a technician logging the temperature of an oven on a piece of paper is performing data acquisition. As technology has progressed, this type of process has been simplified and made more accurate, versatile, and reliable through electronic equipment. Equipment ranges from simple recorders to sophisticated computer systems. Data acquisition products serve as a focal point in a system, tying together a wide variety of products, such as sensors that indicate temperature, flow, level, or pressure. Some common data acquistion terms are shown below:

(1) Analog-to-Digital Converter (ADC).

An electronic device that converts analog signals to an equivalent digital form. The analog-to-digital converter is the heart of most data acquisition systems.

(2) Digital-to-Analog Converter (D/A).

An electronic component found in many data acquistion devices that produce an analog output signal.

(3) Digital Input/Output (DIO).

Digital Input/Output (DIO) refers to a type of data acquistion signal. Digital I/O signals are discrete signals which are either one of two states. These states may be on/off, high/low, 1/0, etc. Digital I/O is also referred to as binary I/O.

(4) Differential Input.

It refers to the way a signal is wired to a data acquisition device. Differential inputs have a unique high and unique low connection for each channel. Data acquisition devices have either single-ended or differential inputs, many devices support both configurations.

(5) General Purpose Interface Bus (GPIB).

Synonymous with HPIB (for Hewlett-Packard), the standard bus used for controlling electronic instruments with a computer. Also called IEEE 488 in reference to defining ANSI/IEEE standards.

(6) Resolution.

The smallest signal increment that can be detected by a data acquisition system. Resolution can be expressed in bits, in proportions, or in percent of full scale. For example, a system has 12-bit resolution, one part in 4 096 resolution, and 0.024 4 percent of full scale.

(7) RS232.

A standard for serial communications found in many data acquistion systems. RS232 is the most common serial communication, however, it is somewhat limited in that it only supports communication to one device connected to the bus at a time and it only supports transmission distances up to 50 feet.

(8) RS485.

A standard for serial communications found in many data acquistion systems. RS485 is not as popular as RS232, however, it is more flexible in that it supports communication to more than one device on the bus at a time and supports transmission distances of approximately 5 000 feet.

(9) Sample Rate.

The speed at which a data acquisition system collects data. The speed is normally expressed in samples per second. For multi-channel data acquisition devices the sample rate is typically given as the speed of the analog-to-digital converter(A/D). To obtain individual channel sample rate, you need to divide the speed of the A/D by the number of channels being sampled.

(10) Single-Ended Input (SE).

It refers to the way a signal is wired to a data acquisition device. In single-ended wiring, each analog input has a unique high connection but all channels share a common ground connection. Data acquisition devices have either single-ended or differential inputs. Many support both configurations.

2) Types of Data Acquistion Systems

(1) Serial Communication Data Acquistion Systems.

Serial communcation data acquistion systems are a good choice when the measurement needs to be made at a location which is distant from the computer. There are several different communication standards, RS232 is the most common but only supports tranmission distances up to 50 feet. RS485 is superior to RS232 and supports transmission distances to 5 000 feet.

(2) USB Data Acquistion Systems.

The Universal Serial Bus (USB) is a new standard for connecting PCs to peripheral devices such as printers, monitors, modems and data acquisition devices. USB offers several advantages over conventional serial and parallel connections, including higher bandwidth (up to 12 Mbits/s) and the ability to provide power to the peripheral device. USB is ideal for data acquisition applications. Since USB connections supply power, only one cable is required to link the data acquisition device to the PC, which most likely has at least one USB port.

(3) Data Acquisition Plug-in Boards.

Computer data acquisition boards plug directly into the computer bus. Advantages of using boards are speed (because they are connected directly to the bus) and cost (because the overhead of packaging and power is provided by the computer). Boards offered are primarily for IBM PC and compatible computers. Features provided by the cards can vary due to the number and type of inputs (voltage, thermocouple, on/off), outputs, speed and other functions provided. Each board installed in the computer is addressed at a unique Input/Output map location. The I/O map in the computer provides the address locations the processor uses to gain access to the specific device as required by its program.

(4) Parallel Port Data Acquistion Systems.

The standard parallel port on a computer which is commonly used for a printer connection can also be used to connect to a data acquistion device. Parallel port systems often support very high sample rates, although the distance between the computer and the data acquistion device is limited to a few feet.

Lesson 2 Operational Amplifier

1. Introduction

The operational amplifier was first introduced in the early 1940s. Primary usage of these vacuum tube forerunners of the ideal gain block was in computational circuits. They were fed back in such a way as to accomplish addition, subtraction, and other mathematical functions.

Expensive and extremely bulky, the operational amplifier found limited use until new technology brought about the integrated version, solving both size and cost drawbacks.

Volumes upon volumes have been and could be written on the subject of op amps. In the interest of brevity, this application note will cover the basic op amp as it is defined, along with test methods and suggestive applications. Also, included is a basic coverage of the feedback theory from which all configurations can be analyzed.

2. The Perfect Amplifier

The ideal operational amplifier possesses several unique characteristics. Since the device will be used as a gain block, the ideal amplifier should have infinite gain. By definition also, the gain block should have an infinite input impedance in order not to draw any power from the driving source. Additionally, the output impedance would be zero in order to supply infinite current to the load being driven. These ideal definitions are illustrated by the ideal amplifier model of Figure 4.2.

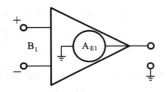

Figure 4.2 An ideal operational amplifier

Further desirable attributes would include infinite bandwidth, zero offset voltage, and complete insensitivity to temperature, power supply variations, and common-mode input signals.

Keeping these parameters in mind, further contemplation produces two very powerful analysis tools. Since the input impedance is infinite, there will be no current flowing at the amplifier input nodes. In addition, when feedback is employed, the different input voltage reduces to zero. These two statements are used universally as beginning points for any network analysis and will be explored in detail later on.

3. The Practical Amplifier

Tremendous strides have been made by modern technology with respect to the ideal amplifier. Integrated circuits are coming closer and closer to the ideal gain block. In bipolar devices, for instance, input bias currents are in the pA range for FET input amplifiers while offset voltages have been reduced to less than 1mV in many cases.

Any device has limitations however, and the integrated circuit is no exception. Modern op amps have both voltage and current limitations. Peak-to-peak output voltage, for instance, is generally limited to one or two base-emitter voltage drops below the supply voltage, while output current is internally limited to approximately 25 mA. Other limitations such as bandwidth and slew rates are also present, although each generation of devices improves over the previous one.

4. Definition of Terms

Earlier, the ideal operational amplifier was defined. No circuit is ideal, of course, so practical realizations contain some sources of error. Most sources of error are very small and therefore can usually be ignored. It should be noted that some applications require special attention to specific sources of error.

Before the internal circuitry of the op amp is further explored, it would be beneficial to define those parameters commonly referenced.

1) Input Offset Voltage

Ideal amplifiers produce 0 V out for 0 V input. But, since the practical case is not perfect, a small DC voltage will appear at the output, even though no differential voltage is applied. This DC voltage is called the input offset voltage, with the majority of its magnitude being generated by the differential input stage pictured in Figure 4.3.

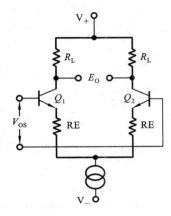

Figure 4.3 Differential input stage

An operational amplifier's performance is, in large part, dependent upon the first stage. It is the very high gain of the first stage that amplifies small signal levels to drive remaining circuitry. Coincidentally, the input current, a function of beta, must be as small as possible. Collector current levels are thus made very low in the input stage in order to gain low bias currents. It is this input stage which also determines DC parameters such as offset voltage, since the amplified output of this stage is of sufficient voltage levels to eclipse most subsequent error terms added by the remaining circuitry. Under balanced conditions, the collector currents of Q1 and Q2 are perfectly matched, hence we may say:

$$E_{OS} = I_{C2}R_L - I_{C1}R_L = 0$$

In practice, small differences in geometries of the base-emitter regions of Q1 and Q2 will cause E_{OS} not to equal 0. Thus, for balance to be restored, a small DC voltage must be added to one V_{BE} or

$$V_{OS} = V_{BE1} - V_{BE2}$$

where the V_{BE} of the transistor is found by

$$V_{BE} = \frac{kT}{q} I_n \left(\frac{I_E}{I_S} \right)$$

Reference is made to the input when talking of offset voltage. Thus, the classic definition of input offset voltage is "that differential DC voltage required between inputs of an amplifier to force its output to zero volts."

Offset voltage becomes a very useful quantity for the designer because many other sources of error can be expressed in terms of V_{OS}. For instance, the error contribution of input bias current can be expressed as offset voltages appearing across the input resistors.

2) Input Offset Voltage Drift

Another related parameter to offset voltage is V_{OS} drift with temperature. Present-day amplifiers usually possess V_{OS} drift levels in the range of 5 V/C to 40 V/C. The magnitude of V_{OS} drift is directly related to the initial offset voltage at room temperature.

Amplifiers exhibiting larger initial offset voltages will also possess higher drift rates with temperature. A rule of thumb often applied is that the drift per C will be 3.3 V for each millivolt of initial offset. Thus, for tighter control of thermal drift, a low offset amplifier would be selected.

3) Input Bias Current

Referring to Figure 4.4, it is apparent that the input pins of this op amp are base inputs. They must, therefore, possess a DC current path to ground in order for the input to function. Input bias current, then, is the DC current required by the inputs of the amplifier to properly drive the first stage.

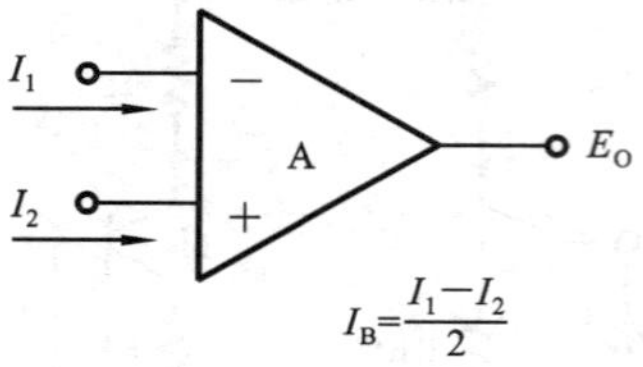

Figure 4.4 Input bias current

The magnitude of I_{BIAS} is calculated as the average of both currents flowing into the inputs and is calculated from

$$I_B = \frac{I_1 - I_2}{2}$$

Bias current requirements are made as small as possible by using high beta input transistors and very low collector currents in the first stage. The trade-off for bias current is lower stage gain due to low collector current levels and lower slew rates. The effect upon slew rate is covered in detail under the compensation section.

4) Input Offset Current

The ideal case of the differential amplifier and its associated bias current does not possess an input offset current. Circuit realizations always have a small difference in bias currents from one input to the other, however. This difference is called the input offset current.

Actual magnitudes of offset current are usually at least an order of magnitude below the bias current. For many applications this offset may be ignored but very high gain, high input impedance amplifiers should possess as little I_{OS} as possible because the difference in currents flowing across large impedances develops substantial offset voltages. Output voltage offset due to I_{OS} can be calculated by

$$V_{OUT} = A_{Cl}(I_{OS}R_S)$$

Hence, high gain and high input impedances magnify directly to the output, the error created by offset current. Circuits capable of nulling the input voltage and current errors are available and will be covered later in this chapter.

5) Input Offset Current Drift

Of considerable importance is the temperature coefficient of input offset current. Even though the effects of offset are nulled at room temperature, the output will drift due to changes in offset current over temperature. Many popular models now include a typical specification for I_{OS} drift with values ranging in the 0.5 nA/C area.

Obviously, those applications requiring low input offset currents also require low drift with temperature.

6) Input Impedance

Differential and common-mode impedances looking into the input are often specified for integrated op amps. The differential impedance is the total resistance looking from one input to the other, while common-mode is the common impedance as measured to ground. Differential impedances are calculated by measuring the change of bias current caused by a change in the input voltage.

7) Common-Mode Range

All input structures have limitations as to the range of voltages over which they will operate properly. This range of voltages impressed upon both inputs which will not cause the output to misbehave is called the common-mode range. Most amplifiers possess common-mode ranges of 12 V with supplies of 15 V.

8) Common-Mode Rejection Ratio

The ideal operational amplifier should have no gain for an input signal common to both inputs. Practical amplifiers do have some gain to common-mode signals. The classic definition for common-mode rejection ratio of an amplifier is the ratio of the differential signal gain to the common-mode signal gain expressed in dB as shown in the following equation.

$$C_{MRR}(dB) = 20\log \frac{e_O e_{CM}}{e_O e_I}$$

The measurement CMRR requires 2 sets of measurements. However, note that if e_O is held constant, CMRR becomes:

$$C_{MRR}(dB) = 20\log \frac{e_{CM}}{e_I}$$

A new alternate definition of C_{MRR} is the ratio of the change of input offset voltage to the input common-mode voltage change producing it.

Figure 4.5 illustrates the application of the equivalent common-mode error generator to the voltage-follower circuit.

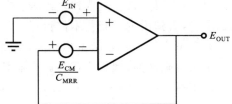

Figure 4.5 Effects of CMRR on voltage-follower

Words and Expressions

vacuum tube 电子管,真空管
bulky ['bʌlki] *a.* 庞大的
drawback ['drɔːbæk] *n.* 欠缺,短处,缺点,瑕疵
unique [juːˈniːk] *a.* 独一无二的,独特的,稀罕的
infinite gain 无限大增益
impedance [imˈpidns] *n.* 阻抗

zero offset voltage 零偏移电压
insensitivity [in,sensə'tiviti] n. 钝性(不灵敏性,不敏感;昏迷)
differential input 差分输入
peak-to-peak 峰峰
base-emitter voltage drops 基极-发射基压降
input offset voltage 输入补偿电压
eclipse [i'klips] n. 日蚀,月蚀,衰落 v. 引起日蚀,引起月蚀,使……黯然失色
drift [drift] n. 漂移;漂流物;观望;漂流;吹积物;趋势 v. 漂移,漂流,吹积覆盖
rule of thumb 经验法则,根据经验
offset voltage 失调电压
beta ['beitə] n. 本文指电流放大倍数
null [nʌl] vt. 使……无效
common-mode rejection ratio 共模抑制比

Notes

1. Primary usage of these vacuum tube forerunners of the ideal gain block was in computational circuits. They were fed back in such a way as to accomplish addition, subtraction, and other mathematical functions.

（1）fed back：反馈

（2）全句可翻译为：理想增益模块出现之前先出现了真空管,该元件主要用于计算电路,利用反馈方式实现加、减,以及其他数学运算。

2. Expensive and extremely bulky, the operational amplifier found limited use until new technology brought about the integrated version, solving both size and cost drawbacks.

全句可翻译为：在集成技术出现之前,运算放大器由于价格昂贵、体积又笨又大而使应用受到限制,直到出现了新技术使得运算放大器集成化才解决了其体积和价格的缺点。

3. The ideal operational amplifier possesses several unique characteristics.

全句可翻译为：理想的运算放大器具有几个独特(有)的特性。

4. Peak-to-peak output voltage, for instance, is generally limited to one or two base-emitter voltage drops below the supply voltage, while output current is internally limited to approximately 25mA.

全句可翻译为：例如,当输出电流限制在 25 mA 附近时,峰峰输出电压一般比电源电压低一到两个基极-发射基压降。

5. Collector current levels are thus made very low in the input stage in order to gain low bias currents.

全句可翻译为：这样使输入级集电极电流很小,从而使偏置电流较低。

6. It is this input stage which also determines DC parameters such as offset voltage, since the amplified output of this stage is of sufficient voltage levels to eclipse most subsequent error terms added by the remaining circuitry.

全句可翻译为：正是这个输入级确定了如偏移电压等直流参数,因为该级的放大输出电平要足够高,以抑制其余电路引入的大部分误差。

7. They must, therefore, possess a DC current path to ground in order for the input to function. Input bias current, then, is the DC current required by the inputs of the amplifier to properly drive the first stage.

全句可翻译为：因此，必须有和地联通的直流通路已实现输入功能，输入的偏(压)置电流就是放大器输入端所需的用于驱动输入级的直流电流。

8. Actual magnitudes of offset current are usually at least an order of magnitude below the bias current.

全句可翻译为：通常，实际的漂移电流至少比偏置电流低一个数量级。

Reading Material

Amplifier

Amplifiers are necessary in many types of electronic equipment such as radios, oscilloscopes and record players. Often it is a small alternating voltage that has to be amplified.

The operational amplifier is the most important basic building block of all linear circuits. It has a wide range of applications in such fields as audio power amplifiers, timer, voltage regulators, sensitive measuring circuits, etc.

The term "operational amplifier" was originally applied to high gain amplifiers operating down to zero frequency which were used in analogue computers to perform certain mathematical operations. These high gain amplifiers are now used for a wide variety of applications, but the name "operational amplifier" or "op-amp" is normally used even though no mathematical operations are involved. The early operational amplifiers employed discrete components, but it is now much more convenient to employ an integrated circuit (IC). The circuit designers are not generally interested in the internal components of an integrated circuit, but only in the performance of the unit as a whole. Therefore, the symbol in Figure 4.6 is used to denote the operational amplifier. It can be seen that there are two inputs, one output and connections to the positive and negative supply lines.

If the inverting input is made slightly more positive, the output will become more negative, this is why the name "inverting" is given to this input. If, however, the non inverting input is made more positive, the output will also become more positive.

Type 741 device is one of the best known general purpose operational amplifiers and is also one of the cheapest of all linear integrated circuits. The device is actually available in a number of different packages. Readers will usually find the type of 741 shown in Figure 4.7 the most convenient to use, this type of package is known as the 8 pin dual-in-line. The gain

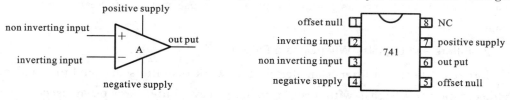

Figure 4.6 Basic symbol for an operational amplifier   Figure 4.7 741 in an 8 pin dual-in line package

of the 741 at zero frequency is quoted as being typically 2×10^5 in most manufacturer's datasheets, with a minimum for any one device of 2×10^4 or 2.5×10^4 and no maximum value quoted. The value of R_1 shown in Figure 4.8 should be about 50 kΩ when the 741 has a gain near to the minimum value of 2×10^4, but a value of 2 MΩ is more suitable for 741 devices which have a high gain. When R_1 has a value of 50 kΩ, the potential at the junction of R_1 and R_2 will be about 400 mV, if this is amplified 20 000 times, a convenient reading of about 8 V on the output meter is optional. It will be found that the gain of a 741 device falls off quite rapidly at frequencies above about 5Hz, this variation of gain with frequency is shown in Figure 4.9 for a typical 741 device. It may be noted that the gain falls to zero at a frequency of the order of 1 MHz.

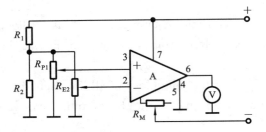 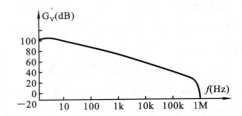

Figure 4.8 A practical operational amplifier   Figure 4.9 The variation of gain with frequency

When a suitable amount of negative feedback is employed, the differences between integrated circuit operational amplifiers of the same type number can be made negligible for all practical purposes.

Lesson 3   Filters

1. Introduction

Filters of some sort are essential to the operation of most electronic circuits. It is therefore in the interest of anyone involved in electronic circuit design to have the ability to develop filter circuits capable of meeting a given set of specifications. Unfortunately, many in the electronics field are uncomfortable with the subject, whether due to a lack of familiarity with it, or a reluctance to grapple with the mathematics involved in a complex filter design.

This application note is intended to serve as a very basic introduction to some of the fundamental concepts and terms associated with filters. It will not turn a novice into a filter designer, but it can serve as a starting point for those wishing to learn more about filter design.

2. Filters and Signals: What Does a Filter Do?

In circuit theory, a filter is an electrical network that alters the amplitude and/or phase characteristics of a signal with respect to frequency. Filters are often used in electronic systems to emphasize signals in certain frequency ranges and reject signals in other frequency ranges. Such a filter has a gain which is dependent on signal frequency. As an example, consider a situation where a useful signal at frequency f_1 has been contaminated with an unwanted signal at f_2. If the contaminated signal is passed through a circuit (See Figure 4.10) that has very low gain at f_2 compared to f_1, the undesired signal can be removed, and the useful signal will remain. Note that in this case we are not concerned with the gain of the filter at any frequency other than f_1 and f_2. As long as f_2 is sufficiently attenuated relative to f_1, the performance of this filter will be satisfactory. In general, however, a filter's gain may be specified at several different frequencies, or over a band of frequencies. Since filters are defined by their frequency-domain effects on signals, it makes sense that the most useful analytical and graphical descriptions of filters also fall into the frequency domain.

Thus, curves of gain vs frequency and phase vs frequency are commonly used to illustrate filter characteristics, and the most widely-used mathematical tools are based in the frequency domain.

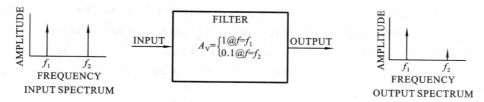

Figure 4.10 Using a filter to reduce the effect of an undesired signal

The frequency-domain behavior of a filter is described mathematically in terms of its transfer function or network function. This is the ratio of the Laplace transforms of its output and input signals. The voltage transfer function $H(s)$ of a filter can therefore be written as:

$$H_{LP}(s) = \frac{V_{OUT}(s)}{V_{IN}(s)}$$

Where $V_{IN}(s)$ and $V_{OUT}(s)$ are the input and output signal voltages and s is the complex frequency variable.

The transfer function defines the filter's response to any arbitrary input signal, but we are most often concerned with its effect on continuous sine waves. Especially important is the magnitude of the transfer function as a function of frequency, which indicates the effect of the filter on the amplitudes of sinusoidal signals at various frequencies. Knowing the transfer function magnitude (or gain) at each frequency allows us to determine how well the filter can distinguish between signals at different frequencies. The transfer function magnitude versus frequency is called the amplitude response or sometimes, especially in audio applications, the frequency response.

Similarly, the phase response of the filter gives the amount of phase shift introduced in sinusoidal signals as a function of frequency. Since a change in phase of a signal also represents a change in time, the phase characteristics of a filter become especially important when dealing with complex signals where the time relationships between signal components at different frequencies are critical. By replacing the variable s in (1) with $j\omega$, where j is equal to $\sqrt{-1}$, and ω is the radian frequency, we can find the filter's effect on the magnitude and phase of the input signal. The magnitude is:

$$|H(j\omega)| = \left|\frac{V_{OUT}(j\omega)}{V_{IN}(j\omega)}\right|$$

and the phase is:

$$\arg H(j\omega) = \arg \frac{V_{OUT}(j\omega)}{V_{IN}(j\omega)}$$

3. The Basic Filter Types-Bandpass

There are five basic filter types (bandpass, notch, low-pass, high-pass, and all-pass). Several examples of bandpass amplitude response curves are shown in Figure 4.11. The curve in (a) is what might be called an "ideal" bandpass response, with absolutely constant gain within the passband, zero gain outside the passband, and an abrupt boundary between the two. This response characteristic is impossible to realize in practice, but it can be approximated to varying degrees of accuracy by real filters. Curves from (b) to (f) are examples of a few bandpass amplitude response curves that approximate the ideal curves with varying degrees of accuracy. Note that while some bandpass responses are very smooth, other have ripple (gain variations in their passbands). Other have ripple in their stopbands as well.

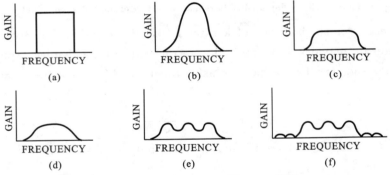

Figure 4.11 Examples of bandpass filter amplitude response

Just as it is difficult to determine by observation exactly where the passband ends, the boundary of the stopband is also seldom obvious. Consequently, the frequency at which a stopband begins is usually defined by the requirements of a given system. For example, a system specification might require that the signal must be attenuated at least 35 dB at 1.5 kHz. This would define the beginning of a stopband at 1.5 kHz.

The rate of change of attenuation between the passband and the stopband also differs from one filter to the other. The slope of the curve in this region depends strongly on the order of the filter, with higher-order filters having steeper cutoff slopes. The attenuation slope is usually expressed in dB/octave (an octave is a factor of 2 in frequency) or dB/decade (a decade is a factor of 10 in frequency).

Bandpass filters are used in electronic systems to separate a signal at one frequency or within a band of frequencies from signals at other frequencies.

4. The Basic Filter Types—Notch or Band-Reject

A filter with effectively the opposite function of the bandpass is the band-reject or notch filter. As an example, the notch filter of Figure 4.12 has the transfer function

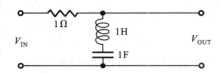

Figure 4.12 An example of a simple notch filter

$$H_N(s) = \frac{V_{OUT}(s)}{V_{IN}(s)} = \frac{s^2 + 1}{s^2 + s + 1}$$

The amplitude and phase curves for this circuit are shown in Figure 4.13. As can be seen from the curves, the quantities f_c, f_l, and f_h used to describe the behavior of the bandpass filter are also appropriate for the notch filter. A number of notch filter amplitude response curves are shown in Figure 4.14.

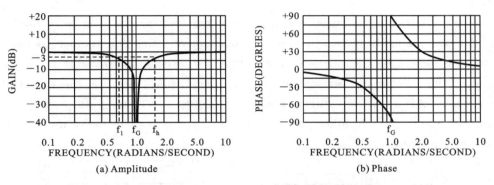

Figure 4.13 Response curves for example notch filter

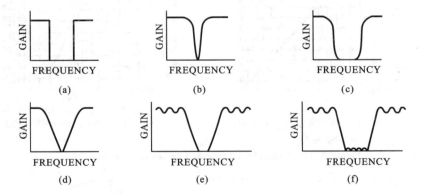

Figure 4.14 Examples of notch filter amplitude responses

Notch filters are used to remove an unwanted frequency from a signal, while affecting all other frequencies as little as possible. An example of the use of a notch filter is with an audio program that has been contaminated by 60 Hz powerline hum. A notch filter with a center frequency of 60 Hz can remove the hum while having little effect on the audio signals.

5. The Basic Filter Types—Low-Pass

A third filter type is the low-pass. A low-pass filter passes low frequency signals, and rejects signals at frequencies above the filter's cutoff frequency. If the components of

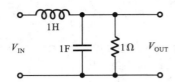

Figure 4.15 Example of a simple low-pass filter

our example circuit are rearranged as in Figure 4.15, the resultant transfer function is:

$$H_{LP}(s) = \frac{V_{OUT}(s)}{V_{IN}(s)} = \frac{1}{s^2 + s + 1}$$

It is easy to see by inspection that this transfer function has more gain at low frequencies than at high frequencies. As ω approaches 0, H_{LP} approaches 1; as ω approaches infinity, H_{LP} approaches 0.

Amplitude and phase response curves are shown in Figure 4.16, with an assortment of possible amplitude response curves in Figure 4.17. Note that the various approximations to the unrealizable ideal low-pass amplitude characteristics take different forms, some being monotonic (always having a negative slope), and others having ripple in the passband and/or stopband.

Low-pass filters are used whenever high frequency components must be removed from a signal. An example might be in a light-sensing instrument using a photodiode. If light levels are low, the output of the photodiode could be very small, allowing it to be partially obscured by the noise of the sensor and its amplifier, whose spectrum can extend to very high frequencies. If a low-pass filter is placed at the output of the amplifier, and if its cutoff frequency is high enough to allow the desired signal frequencies to pass, the overall noise level can be reduced.

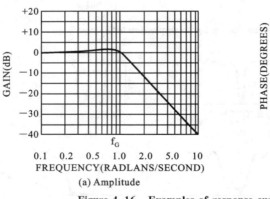
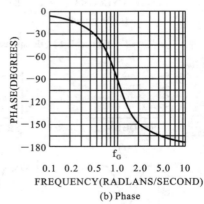

Figure 4.16 Examples of response curves for low-pass filter

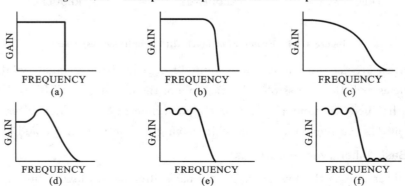

Figure 4.17 Examples of low-pass filter amplitude response curves

Words and Expressions

reluctance [ri'lʌktəns] n. 不愿意,勉强;厌恶
grapple ['græpl] v. 抓住;设法解决 n. 抓斗(钩竿)
novice ['nɔvis] n. 新手,初学者
reject [ri'dʒekt] n. 被拒之人;不合格品;不及格者 v. 拒绝,驳回;丢弃
contaminate [kən'tæmineit] v. 污染
phase shift 相移
progressively [prə'gresivli] ad. 渐进地,逐渐地
radian ['reidjən] n. 弧度
interchangeable [intə'tʃeindʒəb(ə)l] a. 可互换的
fall off 跌落
passband ['pɑːsbænd] n. 通频带
attenuation [ə,tenju'eiʃən] n. 衰减
weight [weit] n. 重量,体重;重担;权重
decibel ['desibel] n. 分贝
notch [nɔtʃ] n. 刻痕;等级 v. 刻凹痕,用刻痕计算;得分。在此指的是带阻滤波器。
stopband ['stɔpbænd] n. 抑止频带(阻带,不透明带)
powerline ['pauəlain] n. 输电线(电源线)
hum [hʌm] n. 嗡嗡声,哼声,杂声 v. 发低哼声,闭口哼歌,嗡嗡叫 int. 哼,嗯
cutoff frequency 截止频率
assortment [ə'sɔːtmənt] n. 分类,分配合;花色品种
monotonic [mɔnəu'tɔnik] a. 单调的
light-sensing instrument 感光仪器
photodiode [fəutəu'daiəud] n. 光电二极管

Notes

1. Similarly, the phase response of the filter gives the amount of phase shift introduced in sinusoidal signals as a function of frequency.

全句可翻译为:同样地,正弦信号输入的滤波器的相位响应给出了相移量,该量是频率的函数。(注意与正文上一段"continuous sine waves"对应)

2. This response characteristic is impossible to realize in practice, but it can be approximated to varying degrees of accuracy by real filters.

全句可翻译为:这种响应特性在实际中是不可能实现的,但可以通过实际滤波器以不同程度的精度来近似。

3. Note that while some bandpass responses are very smooth, other have ripple (gain variations in their passbands).

全句可翻译为:注意到某些通频带响应非常平滑,其他则有(褶皱)波纹(在相应的通频带增益有变化)。

4. An example of the use of a notch filter is with an audio program that has been

contaminated by 60 Hz powerline hum. A notch filter with a center frequency of 60 Hz can remove the hum while having little effect on the audio signals.

全句可翻译为：带阻滤波器的一个应用实例是处理带 60 Hz 电源噪声的（声）音频程序。将带阻滤波器的中心频率设为 60 Hz 就可以去除声音中的嗡嗡声，而对（声）音频信号的影响很小。

Reading Material

Filter

1) Introduction

Linear filters form a class of system which is of crucial importance in signal processing. Although in its most general sense the term "filter" implies any frequency selective device or processor, in practice it is generally reserved for a system which transmits a certain range of frequencies, and rejects other; such frequency ranges are called "passbands" and "stopbands" respectively. We shall see later that the ideal filter, which would introduce no attenuation of input signals falling within the passband, and infinite an attenuation of signals in the stopband, is not attainable in practice.

Historically, both the theory and practical application of filters have been very much tied up with electronic communications. For example, a radio receiver is required to discriminate in favour of just one of the many incoming signals picked up by its aerial; it does this on the basis of their different frequency bands, by use of a highly selective filter. Such a filter processes continuous signals and is therefore an example of what we have previously called a "continuous" linear system; it is also widely referred to as an "analogue" filter. Analogue filters are invariably constructed from linear electrical circuit components, and their detailed design falls outside the scope of this book; on the other hand we are in a position to discuss the overall performance of certain well-known types of analogue filter, and this is done in section.

Although a knowledge of electrical network theory is needed for the design of analogue filters, the same is fortunately not true of filters for sampled-data signals. Sampled-data filters, generally known as "digital" filters, may be realized by suitable programming of a digital computer which is fed with a sampled version of the input signal. The increasing interest in digital filters is largely a reflection of the availability of the digital computer as a research tool in all branches of science and technology. But before getting involved in detail, we first investigate some general aspects of filter performance in time and frequency domains.

2) Filter categories

Apart from the division of linear filters into the two broad categories of analogue and digital filters, they may be further classified according to the frequency ranges which they transmit or reject, as shown in Figure 4.18.

A "low-pass" filter has a passband in the low-frequency region, whereas a "high-pass" filter transmits only high-frequency input signals; "band-pass" and "band-stop" filters are

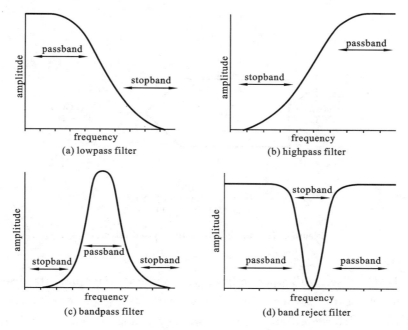

Figure 4.18 Four common filter types

defined by their ability to discriminate in favor of, or against, particular frequency bands. The actual frequency at which the transition from passband to stopband occurs varies from case to case. And is clearly an important parameter of filter design.

Since the frequency response of a linear sampled-data system is always a periodic function of ω, it follows that the terms low-pass, high-pass, band-pass and band-stop have to be interpreted slightly differently in the case of digital filters. Sampling with an interval of T seconds allows faithful representation of a continuous signal having frequency components up to $\omega(=\pi/T)$ radians/second. A digital filter is therefore classified according to its effect on frequency components in the range $-\pi/T < \omega < \pi/T$, which is the maximum range occupied by any adequately-sampled input signal.

Lesson 4   DAC and ADC

1. An Introduction to DAC

Those unfamiliar with DACs regard them simply as devices with digital input and analog output. But the analog output depends on the presence of that analog input known as the reference, and the accuracy of the reference is almost always the limiting factor on the absolute accuracy of a DAC. We shall consider the various architectures of DACs, and the forms which the reference may take, later in this section.

Some DACs use external references (See Figure 4.19) and have a reference input terminal, while others have an output from an internal reference.

If a DAC has an internal reference, the overall accuracy of the DAC is specified when

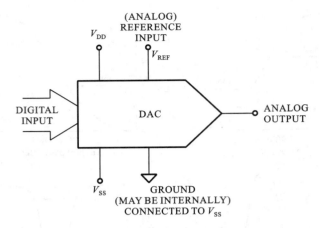

Figure 4.19 Basic DAC with external reference

using that reference.

If such a DAC is used with a perfectly accurate external reference, its absolute accuracy may actually be worse than when it is operated with its own internal reference. This is because it is trimmed for absolute accuracy when working with its own actual reference voltage, not with the nominal value. Twenty years ago it was common for converter references to have accuracies as poor as ±5% since these references were trimmed for low temperature coefficient rather than absolute accuracy, and the inaccuracy of the reference was compensated in the gain trim of the DAC itself. Today the problem is much less severe, but it is still important to check for possible loss of absolute accuracy when using an external reference with a DAC with one that is built-in.

DACs that have reference terminals must, of course, specify their behavior and parameters. If there is a reference input, the first specification will be the reference input voltage—and of course this has two values, the absolute maximum rating, and the range of voltages over which the DAC performs correctly.

Most DACs require that their reference voltage be within quite a narrow range whose maximum value is less than or equal to the DAC's VDD, but some DACs, called multiplying DACs (or "MDACs"), will work over a wide range of reference voltages that may go well outside their power supplies. The AD7943 multiplying DAC, for example, has an absolute maximum rating on its VDD terminal of +6 V but a rating of ±15 V on its reference input, and it works perfectly well with positive, negative, or ac references. MDACs that work with ac references have a "reference bandwidth" specification which defines the maximum practical frequency at the reference input.

The reference input terminal of a DAC may be buffered as shown in Figure 4.20, in which case it has input impedance (usually high) and bias current (usually low) specifications, or it may connect directly to the DAC. In this case the input impedance specification may become more complicated since some DAC structures have an input impedance that varies substantially with the digital code applied to the DAC. In such cases the (usually simplified) structure of the DAC is shown on the data sheet, and the nominal values of resistance are given.

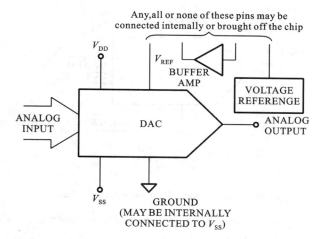

Figure 4.20 DAC with reference and buffer

Surprisingly for such an accurate circuit, the reference input impedance of a resistive DAC network is rarely very well defined. For example, the AD7943 has a nominal input impedance of 9 kΩ, but the data sheet limits are 6 kΩ and 12 kΩ, a variation of $\pm 33\%$.

Where a DAC has a reference output terminal, it will carry a defined reference voltage, with a specified accuracy. There may also be specifications of temperature coefficient and long-term stability.

The reference output (if available) may be buffered or unbuffered. If it is buffered the maximum output current will be specified. In general such a buffer will have a unidirectional output stage which sources current but does not allow current to flow into the output terminal. If the buffer does have a push-pull output stage, the output current will probably be defined as $\pm$(SOME VALUE) mA. If the reference output is unbuffered, the output impedance may be specified, or the data sheet may simply advise the use of a high input impedance external buffer.

2. An Introduction to ADC

As in the case of DACs, the relationship between the digital output and the analog input of an ADC depends on the value of the reference, and the accuracy of the reference is almost always the limiting factor on the absolute accuracy of an ADC.

Similar to DACs, many ADCs use external references (See Figure 4.21) and have a reference input terminal, while others have an output from an internal reference. The simplest ADCs, of course, have neither—the reference is on the ADC chip and has no external connections.

If an ADC has an internal reference, its overall accuracy is specified when using that reference. If such an ADC is used with a perfectly accurate external reference, its absolute accuracy may actually be worse than when it is operated with its own internal reference. This is because it is trimmed for absolute accuracy when working with its own actual reference voltage, not with the nominal value. Twenty years ago it was common for converter

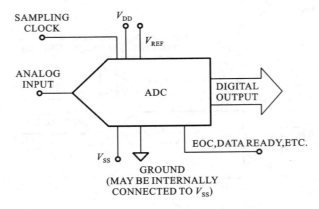

Figure 4.21 Basic ADC with external reference

references to have accuracies as poor as ±5% since these references were trimmed for low temperature coefficient rather than absolute accuracy, and the inaccuracy of the reference was compensated in the gain trim of the ADC itself. Though today the problem is much less severe, it is still important to check for possible loss of absolute accuracy when using an external reference with an ADC that has a built-in one.

ADCs that have reference terminals must, of course, specify their behavior and parameters. If there is a reference input the first specification will be the reference input voltage—and of course this has two values, the absolute maximum rating, and the range of voltages over which the ADC performs correctly. Most ADCs require that their reference voltage is within quite a narrow range whose maximum value is less than or equal to the ADC's VDD.

The reference input terminal of an ADC may be buffered as shown in Figure 4.22, in which case it has input impedance (usually high) and bias current (usually low) specifications, or it may connect directly to the ADC. In either case, the transient currents developed on the reference input due to the internal conversion process need good decoupling with external low inductance capacitors. Most ADC data sheets recommend appropriate

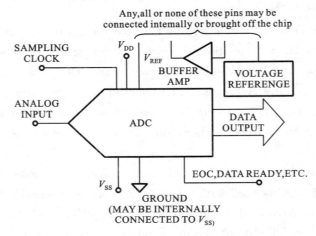

Figure 4.22 ADC with reference and buffer

decoupling networks.

Where an ADC has an internal reference, it will carry a defined reference voltage, with a specified accuracy.

The reference input may be buffered or unbuffered. If it is buffered, the maximum output current will probably be specified. In general such a buffer will have a unidirectional output stage which sources current but does not allow current to flow into the output terminal. If the buffer does have a push-pull output stage, the output current will probably be defined as $\pm$(SOME VALUE) mA. If the reference output is unbuffered, the output impedance may be specified, or the data sheet may simply advise the use of a high input impedance external buffer.

The sampling clock input (sometimes called convert-start or encode command) is a critical function in an ADC and a source of some confusion. Many of the early integrated circuit ADCs (such as the industry-standard AD574) did not have a built-in sample-and-hold function, and were known simply as encoders. These converters require an external clock to begin the conversion process. In the case of the AD574, the application of the external clock initiated an internal high-speed clock oscillator which in turn controll the actual conversion process.

Most modern ADCs have the sample-and-hold function on-chip and require an external sampling clock to initiate the conversion. In some ADCs, only a single sampling clock is required; in others, both a high frequency clock as well as a lower speed sampling clock are required. Regardless of the ADC, it is extremely important to read the data sheet and determine exactly what the external clock requirements are because they can vary widely from one ADC to another, since there is no standard.

At some point after the assertion of the sampling clock, the output data is valid. This data may be in parallel or serial format depending upon the ADC. Early successive approximation ADCs such as the AD574 simply provid a STATUS output (STS) which went high during the conversion, and return to the low state when the output data is valid. In other ADCs, this line is variously called busy, end-of-conversion (EOC), data ready, etc. Regardless of the ADC, there must be some method of knowing when the output data is valid—and again, the data sheet is where this information can always be found.

There are one or two other practical points worth remembering about the logic of ADCs. On power-up, many ADCs do not have logic reset circuitry and may enter an anomalous logical state. One or two conversions may be necessary to restore their logic to proper operation so: (a) the first and second conversions after power-up should never be trusted, and (b) control outputs (EOC, data ready, etc.) may behave in unexpected ways at this time (and not necessarily in the same way at each power-up), and (c) care should be taken to ensure that such anomalous behavior cannot cause system latch-up.

Some low power ADCs now have power-saving modes of operation variously called standby, power-down, sleep, etc. When an ADC comes out of one of these low power modes, there is a certain recovery time required before the ADC can operate at its full specified performance.

Another detail that can cause trouble is the difference between EOC and DRDY (data ready). EOC indicates that conversion has finished, DRDY data is available at the output. In some ADCs, EOC functions as DRDY; in others, data is not valid until several tens of nanoseconds after the EOC has become valid, and if EOC is used as a data strobe, the results will be unreliable.

For more detail, it is important to read the whole data sheet before using an ADC since there are innumerable small logic variations from type to type.

Words and Expressions

trim [trim] n. 整齐;装饰;修剪 a. 整齐的 v. 整理;修剪
trimmed [trimd] a. 平衡的;纵倾的
nominal value　标称值
gain trim　增益归整,增益控制
severe [si'viə] a. 剧烈的,严重的;严峻的,严厉的,严格的
absolute maximum rating　最大绝对额定值
buffer ['bʌfə] n. 缓冲;缓冲区
data sheet　数据表,这里指生产厂家提供的元件参数表
unidirectional [,ju:nidi'rekʃənəl, -dai-] a. 单向的
a unidirectional output stage　单向输出级
push-pull ['puʃ'pul] n. [电子]推挽式的
overall accuracy　总准确度,总精度
built-in ['bilt'in] n. 内部,内置 a. 嵌入的,内装的
confusion [kən'fju:ʒən] n. 混乱,混淆;干扰
sample-and-hold　采样保持电路
encoder [in'kəudə] n. 编码器
at some point　在某一时刻
power-up　升高
anomalous behavior　反常行为
latch-up　封闭
power-saving mode　省电模式
nanosecond ['nænəu,sekənd] n. 纳秒
data strobe　数据选通
unreliable ['ʌnri'laiəbl] a. 不可靠的

Notes

1. If a DAC has an internal reference, the overall accuracy of the DAC is specified when using that reference.

全句可翻译为:如果 DAC 有内部参考电压,则当使用该参考电压时 DAC 的总精度就确定了。

2. This is because it is trimmed for absolute accuracy when working with its own actual reference voltage, not with the nominal value.

全句可翻译为：因为自带的实际参考电压和标称电压值不同，所以绝对精度降低了。

3. In either case, the transient currents developed on the reference input due to the internal conversion process need good decoupling with external low inductance capacitors.

全句可翻译为：无论哪种情况，由于内部转换过程而在参考输入端建立的瞬时电流都需要用外部低电感器件和电容器件进行良好(解)去耦。

4. The sampling clock input (sometimes called convert-start or encode command) is a critical function in an ADC and a source of some confusion.

全句可翻译为：采样时钟输入(有时称为转换启动或解码指令)是 ADC 的重要功能，同时也是干扰源。

5. Most modern ADCs have the sample-and-hold function on-chip and require an external sampling clock to initiate the conversion.

全句可翻译为：绝大多数现代的 ADC 都带有在片的采样保持功能，需要外部采样时钟启动转换。

6. Regardless of the ADC, it is extremely important to read the data sheet and determine exactly what the external clock requirements are because they can vary widely from one ADC to another, since there is no standard.

全句可翻译为：不论是什么类型的 ADC，仔细阅读说明书并确定所需的外部时钟极为重要，因为不同 ADC 器件时钟变化较大，没有标准值。

Reading Material

Analog to Digital (A/D) Converters

Analog-to-digital converters (ADCs) are used to interface analog signals with digital circuits or computers. Various approaches are used, depending on the accuracy and the speed required, to convert an analog signal into its digital equivalent. Three such approaches are successes approximation, integrating, and the parallel (flash) types. A/D conversion is essentially a quantizing process, whereby an analog signal is represented by discrete states. These states can be assigned appropriate codes such as straight binary, BCD, or two's complement.

1) Transfer Function

Figure 4.23 (a) shows a 3-bit A/D converter. Its transfer function, with 1 V full-scale input, is provided in Figure 4.23 (b). A 3-bit converter has eight (2^3) discrete output states, 000_2 to 111_2 corresponding to eight segments (1/8 V each) of the analog input. In examining the ideal transfer function of Figure 4.23 (b), note that:

The 3-bit A/D converter has $2^n = 2^3 = 8$ output states where n is the number of output bits. The value of the first discrete level, or LSB, is obtained by dividing the full-scale input voltage into the number of discrete states. The analog input values shown (0.125 V, 0.25 V, and so on) represent the center points of the analog values for each output word, with transition points LSB from the center points.

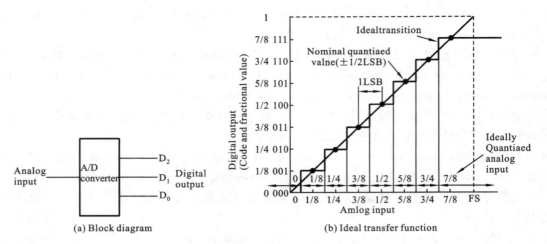

Figure 4.23 A 3-bit A/D converter

The MSB $(100)_2$ output corresponds to 0.5 V, which is half of the input full-scale voltage. The largest output word 111_2 corresponds to 7/8 V and not the full-scale voltage.

These points are summarized in Table 4.1 and are further clarified in the following example.

Table 4.1 Analog input and binary output for a 3-bit A/D converter

Analog input (normalized fraction)	Analog input (V) (10 V full scale)	Binary digital output
0	0	000
1/8	1.25	001
1/4	2.50	010
3/8	3.75	011
1/2	5.00	100
5/8	6.25	101
3/4	7.50	110
7/8	8.75	111

Example calculate analog voltages corresponding to the LSB, and the maximum output for an 8-bit A/D converter (straight binary code) if the input range is 0 to 10 V.

2) Procedure

(1) For 8 bits, $2^8 = 256$ output states.

(2) Because the full-scale input voltage is 10 V, the LSB voltage $V_{LSB} = 10 \text{ V}/256 = 39 \text{ mV}$.

(3) The voltage corresponding to the maximum output word V_{max} = Full-Scale, the LSB voltage $V_{LSB} = 10 \text{ V} - 0.039 \text{ V} = 9.961 \text{ V}$.

3) Sampling Concepts

An A/D converter requires a certain amount of time, called conversion time, to change an analog signal into the corresponding digital signal. If the analog signal changes during the conversion time, the converter output may be in error. To prevent this, a sample-and-hold circuit is used to sense the analog signal at the start of conversion, and store it on a capacitor furring the remaining conversion time.

Figure 4.24 shows a simplified schematic of a sample-and-hold circuit. Amplifier A_1 is an input buffer with a high-input impedance and A_2 is an output amplifier with a low-output impedance. Switch S is generally a rapidly switching FET circuit. When S is closed, capacitor C charges rapidly to the input voltage. When S opens, the initial voltage is maintained. However, if a sampling rate is much slower than changes in the analog signal, information will be lost. Therefore, the minimum sampling rate, as defined by sampling theory, should be 2 f_e samples/s, where f_e is the highest frequency component in the analog signal.

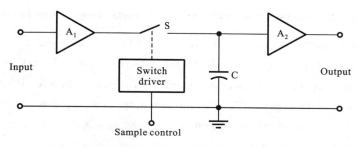

Figure 4.24 A basic sample-and-hold circuit

Lesson 5 Instrumentation and Ground

1. The Two-Ground Problem

The basic analog problem is to condition a signal associated with one ground reference potential and transport this signal without adding interference to a second ground reference potential. Consider the arrangement in Figure 4.25. The input and output circuits have been separated so that the input common grounds at the source of signal and the output common grounds at the termination of the output signal are not connected. This unbalanced signal source represents the most difficult problem in instrumentation. The ground potential difference between the two enclosures causes current to flow in the unbalanced source resistor R_1 and the impedance Z_1 in enclosure 2. The current is limited by the value of Z_1.

Input signal conductors should be guarded right up to the input base or gate of the input amplifier. The guard shield in this arrangement is not a circuit conductor. It is an electrostatic shield. On a circuit board, added traces can be used to guard the signal instead of a shielded cable.

In this approach the second enclosure has a high input impedance differential amplifier that provides all the needed gain. There is circuitry between the input leads and the amplifier input. This circuitry is really a part of the input enclosure so it must be well guarded. It includes diode clamps, high-impedance conductive paths for gate or base currents, and any input filters. The detailed treatment of the input circuit is not shown.

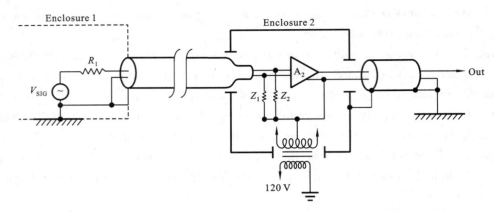

Figure 4.25 The two-circuit enclosures used to transport signals between grounds

Consider instrumentation in Figure 4.25, where the gain is 1 000 and the input unbalanced resistance R_1 is 1 000 ohms. If the output error limit is 10 mV and the input error is 10 μV, the current in the unbalanced resistance is limited to 10 nA. If the common-mode voltage is 10 μV, the impedance Z limiting common-mode current flow must be 1 000 megohms. General-purpose instrumentation is designed to have an input impedance of 1 000 megohms on both inputs. In this way the unbalanced resistance can be on either input connection.

The ability to reject a common-mode signal is called the common-mode rejection ratio (CMRR). If a common-mode signal is 10 V and the resulting output signal is 10 mV, the rejection ratio is 1 000 to one or 60 dB. If the amplifier gain is 100, the error signal at the input is 0.1 mV. The ratio of 0.1 mV to 10 V output is 100 000 to one or 100 dB. This figure is the CMRR referred to the input (rti). In the previous example, the CMRR referred to the input is a million to one or 120 dB measured at 60 Hz with a 1 000-ohm input line unbalance.

At 60 Hz a capacitance of 2 pF has a reactance of about 1 000 megohms. To maintain this, same reactance at 600 Hz the leakage capacitance would have to be held to 0.2 pF. These numbers show how difficult it is to reject higher frequency common-mode signals using this type of circuitry.

The input guard shield is necessary in areas where there are nearby conductors that are not at the input ground potential. In Figure 4.25 the guarding near R_1 may not be needed as all nearby conductors are at the input reference potential. Inside enclosure 2, most of the conductors are referenced to the output common. In this area, the input guard shield must surround the input signal line. Any leakage capacitance is a part of the impedance Z_1 or Z_2.

The technique we have just discussed uses a differential amplifier that is located a distance from the transducer. When amplification is provided at the transducer then several different approaches are possible:

(1) Provide an rf link using a modulator and demodulator (analog or digital).

(2) Provide optical coupling using a digital data link.

(3) Use a current loop to couple to a remote differential amplifier.

The first two methods raise the isolating impedance Z to infinity. These methods can be used to transport signals from an aircraft to earth or between two buildings or between computers. Current-transmitting loops are used in many industrial applications. The differential method shown in Figure 4.25 is often used in general-purpose test bays. When all of the electronics is located in the test bay, it is convenient to reconfigure the testing by moving transducers. Providing electronics at each transducer or at groups of transducers is more complicated.

Amplifying the signal near each transducer can solve the common-mode interference problem. If the full-scale signal level is increased to 100 mV or greater and the new signal source impedance is below a few ohms, the new common-mode interference problem is not difficult to solve.

If an input signal is preamplified inside the guard shield enclosure and carried by cable to a second amplifier in this enclosure, the CMRR requirement in the second amplifier is reduced by the preamplifier gain. In this case the impedance at the interface between the two amplifiers can be quite low. If the pre-gain is 100, then the CMRR in the second amplifier may only have to be 10^3. This approach is practical when there is no need for signal conditioning at the transducer. Any reduction in the required CMRR does not change the requirement for a high Z in the common-mode path. This impedance is needed to limit the common-mode current flow just as before.

2. Strain-Gauge Instrumentation

Strain-gauge instrumentation is a two-enclosure problem as shown in Figure 4.26. The signal source is a symmetric Wheatstone bridge. The input enclosure contains the gauge resistors as well as the source of transducer excitation. In this diagram all four bridge arms are active, which means they are mounted on the structure being tested. In many applications only one arm of the bridge is active and the remaining arms are located near the source of excitation. All bridge arms must be inside the input guard enclosure. If the

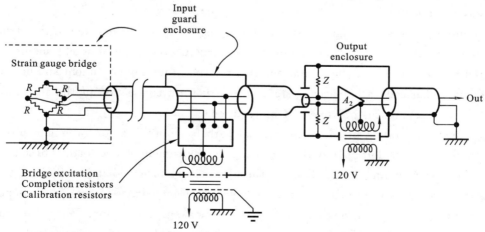

Figure 4.26 The basic strain-gauge circuit

excitation source is centertapped, then only two bridge resistors are required.

The capacitance from a conducting surface to a gauge element can be several hundred picofarads. It is safe to assume that there will be a potential difference between the surface under test and the instrumentation output ground. If the gauge is not grounded to the surface under test, this potential difference will add signal to the input circuit. If there is only one active arm, the interference will be the greatest. The best protection against this type of interference is to ground the bridge at the structure and connect the guard shield to this ground.

A strain-gauge bridge can require up to 10 signal conductors. These conductors provide for excitation, remote excitation sensing, calibration, signal and the guard shield. One conductor group is required for each signal. The guard shield should be carried through any interface without a break. Connecting all the guard shields together at an intermediate point can defeat the purpose of the guard shield.

When the gauge elements of the bridge undergo stress or strain the unbalanced resistance can be as high as 50 ohms. If the interference error limit is 10 μV, the interference current flow is limited to 0.2 μA. If the common-mode voltage is 10 V, the impedance Z allowing common-mode current flow must be 5 MΩ. This is the reactance of 3 pF at 10 kHz. This mode of interference coupling is maximum for a full-scale signal. In effect the stress or strain modulates the interference. This problem can be resolved only by limiting common-mode current flow in the gauge arms.

3. The Floating Strain Gauge

An electrical connection from a strain gauge to the structure is not always convenient. If the structure is not used as the reference conductor, then there can be current flow from the structure through leakage capacitance through the gauge elements to the input cable shield. If the coupling is symmetrical, then this current flow creates a common-mode signal that is rejected by the amplifier. If one arm of the gauge is active, then the reactive coupling is definitely unbalanced and any coupled interference will be normal mode. This signal is amplified, not rejected.

The input guard shield and one side of the signal are shown connected to the structure, in Figure 4.26. If there is no connection to the structure, the guard shield should still be connected to the low side of the excitation. In a relatively quiet environment and because the strain gauge is basically a balanced system, the structural connection of the shield and the signal as shown in Figure 4.26 may not be required.

Most instrumentation provides an internal path for input base or gates currents. This allows the inputs to be left open without causing the instrument to overload. These paths are often in the 100-megohm range. Even if these paths are provided it is still best to avoid making measurements where the input leads have a high-impedance to ground. It is possible for the inputs to saturate through a high impedance leakage connection. When this happens the inputs are in overload, but because of feedback the problem may go unnoticed.

Making measurements on a floating structure is also not recommended. If possible, a grounding strap should be used so that the potential difference is controlled.

It is very difficult to mount a gauge and control the coupling capacitance to the structure. If one gauge element is mounted closer to the structure than another, the reactive current flowing in the gauge resistances will not be symmetrical. In a noisy environment this lack of symmetry will introduce a normal-mode signal. This interference can be rejected only by limiting the bandwidth of the system.

In applications where it is difficult to ground the gauge and guard shield to the structure under test, one central point can be used as a ground for a cluster of gauges. This works when the interference field in the space near the transducers is not intense.

There are two common-mode signals that must be rejected by the input amplifier. We have just discussed the ground potential difference mode. The second common-mode signal is one-half of the excitation supply. If the excitation level is 10 V, then this common-mode signal is 5.0 V. The CMRR for this signal should also be 120 dB. As an example, if the excitation level is 10 V, the error signal or offset that is introduced should be less than 5 μV. This requirement is usually not mentioned in a list of specifications. Since the excitation level is constant this is a static specifications.

Words and Expressions

right up to 直到
electrostatic shield 静电屏蔽
diode clamp 钳位二极管
common-mode voltage 共模电压
megohm ['megəum] n. 百万欧姆,兆欧(姆)
common-mode rejection ratio (CMRR) 共模抑制比
reactance [ri'æktəns] n. 电抗,诱导抵抗,感应抵抗
leakage capacitance 泄漏电容
test bay 测试室,试验间
pre-gain 前置放大器增益
strain-gauge instrumentation 应变仪设备
Wheatstone bridge ['(h)wi:tstəunˌbridʒ] n. [电]惠斯通电桥,单臂电桥
centertapped a. 中心抽头的
picofarad [ˌpikə'færəd] n. 微微法(拉)
interference error limit 干扰误差极限
mode of interference coupling 干扰耦合模式

Notes

1. The basic analog problem is to condition a signal associated with one ground reference potential and transport this signal without adding interference to a second ground reference potential.

全句可翻译为:模拟信号的基本问题是调理和地参考电势相联系的信号,并将该信号不附

加任何干扰地传输到另一个地参考电势。

2. Input signal conductors should be guarded right up to the input base or gate of the input amplifier.

全句可翻译为：对输入信号线的保护应直至输入放大器的输入处或门的输入端。

3. Amplifying the signal near each transducer can solve the common-mode interference problem.

全句可翻译为：对传感器信号就近放大可以解决共模干扰问题。

4. The capacitance from a conducting surface to a gauge element can be several hundred picofarads.

全句可翻译为：从导体表面到测量元件的电容有几百微微法（拉）。

5. When the gauge elements of the bridge undergo stress or strain the unbalanced resistance can be as high as 50 ohms.

全句可翻译为：如果电桥的测量元件承受应力或应变，不平衡电阻会高达 50 欧姆。

6. The input guard shield and one side of the signal are shown connected to the structure, in Figure 4.26.

全句可翻译为：输入保护屏蔽罩和信号的一段连接到结构上，如图 4.26 所示。

Reading Material

The Basic Low-Gain Differential Amplifier

A simple low-gain differential amplifier is shown in Figure 4.27. This type of amplifier can be applied when the input signal has a low source impedance and signal levels are above 0.1 V full scale. The circuit has inputs labeled V_{IN1} and V_{IN2}. The gain from V_{IN1} to the output is $+R_2/R_1$. The gain from V_{IN2} is $-R_2/R_1$. If the same signal is applied to the two inputs, the gain is near zero. If a difference signal V_{DIFF} is applied between the two inputs, the output signal is $V_{DIFF} R_2/R_1$. This circuit provides gain to a difference signal and rejects the average or common-mode signal. If either input is at zero volts (grounded), the gain to the other input is the ratio of resistors R_2/R_1. The sign of the gain is plus or minus depending on which input is used.

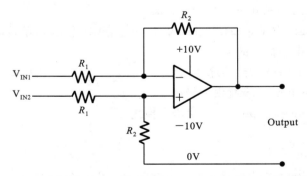

Figure 4.27　The basic low gain differential amplifier

The differential amplifier can be used as the input circuit for the second enclosure as shown in Figure 4.28. The added differential amplifier uses the power supplies available in the second enclosure. If the output common of the second enclosure is taken as the reference conductor, then the input ground potential of the first enclosure becomes the common-mode signal. Ideally the gain for the common-mode component of the signal should be zero. In this application the differential amplifier is called a forward-referencing amplifier. This amplifier re-references the signal found in the first enclosure to the signal common found in the second enclosure.

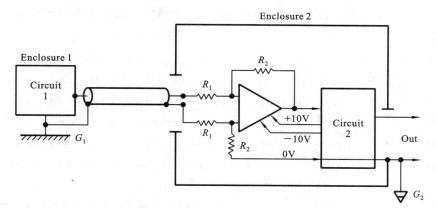

Figure 4.28 The basic low gain differential amplifier applied to the two-ground problem

The common-mode rejection of the circuit in Figure 4.27 depends mainly on the ratio of feedback resistors. If the resistors are equal and their ratios are matched to 1%, the CMRR will be about 100 : 1. This means a 1-volt common-mode signal at 60 Hz will generate a 10 mV error. This is a 0.1% error compared to a 10 V output. Typical resistor values might be 10 kΩ. This same circuit can be applied to isolating video signals if the integrated circuit amplifier has adequate bandwidth. In this application the feedback resistors should be about 1 kΩ. In video applications the signal is usually limited to 2 volts peak-to-peak.

The gain of the differential amplifier in the above example is unity. If gain is provided by the differential amplifier or by circuits that follow, a higher CMRR should be provided. For example, if the gain in the amplifier is 10, the CMRR should be 1 000 : 1 to limit the signal error to 0.1% of full scale.

A CMRR depends on the feedback factor (loop gain) of the integrated circuit. At frequencies above a few kHz the CMRR will generally fall off proportional to gain. It is good design practice to verify the CMRR at high frequencies if this performance is needed.

The resistances R_1 and R_2 in Figure 4.27 limit the amount of common-mode current that flows in the input common conductor. If this value is 10 kΩ and the common-mode voltage is 1 volt, the current in R_1 is 0.2 mA. If the input common lead has a resistance of 1 ohm, the interference coupling is 0.2 mV. This coupling has no relationship to the CMRR of the forward referencing amplifier. If the feedback resistors are 100 kΩ, the current flow would be reduced by another factor of 10.

Common-mode rejection does not reduce coupling from the power transformer. To limit this coupling, shielding can be added to the power transformer.

PART FIVE   Control

Lesson 1   An Introduction to Automatic Control

1. Introduction

Engineering is concerned with understanding and controlling the materials and forces of nature for the benefit of humankind. Control system engineers are concerned with understanding and controlling segments of their environment, to provide useful products for society. Control engineering is based on the foundations of feedback theory and linear system analysis. It is not limited to any engineering discipline but is equally applicable to aeronautical, chemical, mechanical, environmental, civil, and electrical engineering.

A control system is an interconnection of components forming a system configuration that will provide a desired system response. The study of control systems involves not so much the development of new engineering components or machines, but taking combinations of existing hardware to achieve a predetermined goal. Control systems operate in almost every aspect of human activity, including walking, talking, and handling objects. In addition, control systems exist that require no human interaction, such as aircraft automatic pilots and automobile cruise control systems.

In dealing with control systems, particularly engineering control systems, we will deal with a variety of components, indicating that the subject is an interdisciplinary one. The control engineer needs a working knowledge of mechanics, electronics, electrical machines, fluid mechanics, thermodynamics, structures, material properties, and so on. Obviously not every control system contains elements from more than one discipline.

The basis for analysis of a system is the foundation provided by linear system theory, which assumes a cause-effect relationship for the components of a system. Control system analysis involves the uniform treatment of different engineering components. What this means is that we try to represent the system elements in a common format and identify the connections between the elements in a similar way. When we do this, most control systems look the same in schematic form and lend themselves to common methods of analysis.

2. History of Automatic Control

The use of feedback to control a system has had a fascinating history. The first applications of feedback control appeared in the development of float regulator mechanisms in Greece in the period 300 to 1 B. C. The first feedback system invented in modern Europe is the temperature regulator of Cornelis Drebbel (1572—1633) of Holland. The first automatic feedback controller used in an industrial process is generally agreed to be James Watt's flyball governor, developed in 1769 for controlling the speed of a steam engine. The all-mechanical device, shown in Figure 5.1, measures the speed of the output shaft and utilizes the movement of the flyball with speed to control the valve and therefore the amount of steam entering the engine. As the speed increases, the ball weights rise and move away from the shaft axis, thus closing the valve. The flyweights require power from the engine to turn and therefore cause the speed measurement to be less accurate.

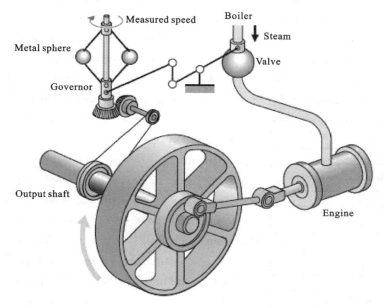

Figure 5.1　Watt's flyball governor

A large impetus to the history and practice of automatic control occurred during World War Ⅱ when it became necessary to design and construct automatic airplane pilots, gun-positioning systems, radar antenna control systems, and other military systems based on the feedback control approach. The complexity and expected performance of these military systems necessitated an extension of the available control techniques and fostered interest in control systems and the development of new insights and methods.

Frequency-domain techniques continued to dominate the field of control following World War Ⅱ with the increased use of the Laplace transform and the complex frequency plane. During the 1950s, the emphasis in control engineering theory was on the development and use of the s-plane methods and, particularly, the root locus approach. Furthermore, during the 1980s, the utilization of digital computers for control components became routine. The technology of these new control elements to perform accurate and rapid calculations was formerly unavailable to control engineers.

With the advent of Sputnik and the space age, another new impetus was imparted to control engineering. It became necessary to design complex, highly accurate control systems for missiles and space probes. Furthermore, the necessity to minimize the weight of satellites and to control them very accurately has spawned the important field of optimal control. Due to these requirements, the time-domain methods developed by Liapunov, Minorsky, and others have met with great interest in the last two decades.

3. Control System Design

The design of control systems is a specific example of engineering design. Again, the goal of control engineering design is to obtain the configuration, specifications, and identification of the key parameters of a proposed system to meet an actual need.

The first step in the design process consists of establishing the system goals. For example, we may state that our goal is to control the velocity of a motor accurately. The second step is to identify the variables that we desire to control. The third step is to write the specifications in terms of the accuracy we must attain. This required accuracy of control will then lead to the identification of a sensor to measure the controlled variable.

As designers, we proceed to the first attempt to configure a system that will result in the desired control performance. This system configuration will normally consist of a sensor, the process under control, an actuator, and a controller, as shown in Figure 5.2. The next step consists of identifying a candidate for the actuator. This will, of course, depend on the process, but the actuation chosen must be capable of effectively adjusting the performance of the process. The next step is the selection of a controller, which often consists of a summing amplifier that will compare the desired response with the actual response and then forward this error-measurement signal to an amplifier. The final step in the design process is the adjustment of the parameters of the system in order to achieve the desired performance. If we can achieve the desired performance by adjusting the parameters, we will finalize the design and proceed to document the results. If not, we will need to establish an improved system configuration and

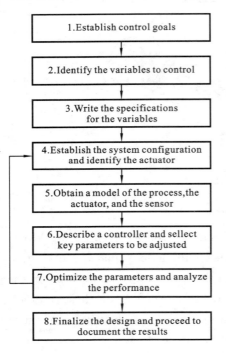

Figure 5.2 The control system design process

perhaps select an enhanced actuator and sensor. Then we will repeat the design steps until we are able to meet the specifications, or until we decide the specifications are too demanding and should be relaxed.

In summary, the controller design problem is as follows: Given a model of the system to be controlled (including its sensors and actuators) and a set of design goals, find a suitable controller, or determine that none exists.

Words and Expressions

aeronautical [ˌɛərəˈnɔːtikəl] *a.* 航空的（航空导航用的）

civil [ˈsivl] *a.* 国内的；公民的；民用的；民事的

predetermined [ˌpriːdiˈtəːmind] a. 预先约定的,预定的,预设的
interdisciplinary [ˌintə(ː)ˈdisiplinəri] a. 各学科间的
thermodynamics [ˈθəːmoudaiˈnæmiks] n. 热力学
cause-effect　因果关系
fascinating [ˈfæsineitiŋ] a. 迷人的
flyball governor　飞球调速器
impetus [ˈimpitəs] n. 动力;推动力
antenna [ænˈtenə] n. 触角;天线
foster [ˈfɔstə] a. 收养的,养育的 v. 养育,抚育,培养
frequency-domain　频域
Laplace transform　拉普拉斯变换
s-plane　复平面
root locus　根轨迹
impart [imˈpɑːt] vt. 给予(尤指抽象事物);传授;告知;透露
probe [prəub] n. 探针;调查;探测针
spawn [spɔːn] vt. 使产卵;使出生;产生
optimal [ˈɔptiməl] a. 最佳的,最理想的
actuator [ˈæktjueitə] n. 执行机构

Notes

1. The study of control systems involves not so much the development of new engineering components or machines, but taking combinations of existing hardware to achieve a predetermined goal.

(1) not so much... but...:与其说是……倒不如说是……,其中的并列连词 but 可用 as 或 rather 替换。

(2) 全句可翻译为:对控制系统的研究,与其说是开发新的工程部件或装置,倒不如说是组合现有的部件来达到预设的目标。

2. In dealing with control systems, particularly engineering control systems, we will deal with a variety of components, indicating that the subject is an interdisciplinary one.

(1) 句中的 indicating 是现在分词作状语,它在句子中作一个伴随状语。that 引导的是一个宾语从句,作 indicating 的宾语。

(2) 全句可翻译为:在研究控制系统,尤其是工程控制系统时,会涉及到各种不同的学科,这表明控制学科是一个交叉学科。

3. A large impetus to the history and practice of automatic control occurred during World War Ⅱ when it became necessary to design and construct automatic airplane pilots, gun-positioning systems, radar antenna control systems, and other military systems based on the feedback control approach.

(1) 句中 when 作从属连词,引导状语从句;it 是先行代词,作形式主语。

(2) 全句可翻译为:在第二次世界大战期间,当用基于反馈控制方法来设计和构建自动飞机驾驶系统、枪定位系统、雷达天线控制系统及其他军事系统变得必不可少时,推动自动控制

的历史和实践的巨大变革发生了。

Reading Material

What is Adaptive Control

In everyday language, "to adapt" means to change a behavior to conform to new circumstances. Intuitively, an adaptive controller is thus a controller that can modify its behavior in response to changes in the dynamics of the process and the character of the disturbances. Since ordinary feedback also attempts to reduce the effects of disturbances and plant uncertainty, the question of the difference between feedback control and adaptive control immediately arises. Over the years there have been many attempts to define adaptive control formally. At an early symposium in 1961 a long discussion ended with the following suggestion: "An adaptive system is any physical system that has been designed with an adaptive viewpoint." A renewed attempt was made by an IEEE committee in 1973. It proposed a new vocabulary based on notions like self-organizing control system (SOC), parameter-adaptive SOC, performance-adaptive SOC, and learning control system. However, these efforts were not widely accepted. A meaningful definition of adaptive control, which would make it possible to look at a controller hardware and software and decide whether or not it is adaptive, is still lacking. However, there appears to be a consensus that a constant-gain feedback system is not an adaptive system.

An adaptive controller is a controller with adjustable parameters and a mechanism for adjusting the parameters. The controller becomes nonlinear because of the parameter adjustment mechanism. It has, however, a very special structure. Since general nonlinear systems are difficult to deal with, it makes sense to consider special classes of nonlinear systems. An adaptive control system can be thought of as having two loops. One loop is a normal feedback with the process and the controller. The other loop is the parameter adjustment loop.

A control engineer should know about adaptive systems because they have useful properties, which can be profitably used to design control systems with improved performance and functionality.

There have been many experiments on adaptive control in laboratories and industry. The rapid progress in microelectronics is a strong stimulation. Interaction between theory and experimentation resulted in a vigorous development of the field. As a result, adaptive controllers started to appear commercially in the early 1980s. This development is now accelerating. One result is that virtually all single-loop controllers that are commercially available today allow adaptive techniques of some forms. The primary reason for introducing adaptive control was to obtain controllers that could adapt to changes in process dynamics and disturbance characteristics. It has been found that adaptive techniques can also be used to provide automatic tuning of controllers.

Lesson 2 Open-Loop and Closed-Loop Control

1. Introduction

Control systems are broadly classified as either open-loop or closed-loop. An open-loop system (Figure 5.3(a)) is a system whose input $u(t)$ does not depend on the output $y(t)$, i.e., $u(t)$ is not a function of $y(t)$. A closed-loop system (Figure 5.3(b)) is a system whose input $u(t)$ depends on the output $y(t)$, i.e., $u(t)$ is a function of $y(t)$.

In control systems, the control signal $u(t)$ is not the output of a signal generator, but the output of another new additional component that we add to the system under control. This new component is called controller (and in special cases regulator or compensator). Furthermore, in control systems, the controller is excited by an external signal $r(t)$, which is called the reference or command signal. This reference signal $r(t)$ specifies the desired performance (i.e., the desired output $y(t)$) of the open- or closed-loop system. That is, in control systems, we aim to design an appropriate controller such that the output $y(t)$ follows the command signal $r(t)$ as close as possible. In particular, in open-loop systems (See Figure 5.3(a)) the controller is excited only by the reference signal $r(t)$ and it is designed such that its output $u(t)$ is the appropriate input signal to the system under control, which in turn will produce the desired output $y(t)$. In closed-loop systems (See Figure 5.3(b)), the controller is excited not only by reference signal $r(t)$, but also by the output $y(t)$. In this case the control signal $u(t)$ depends on both $r(t)$ and $y(t)$. To facilitate better understanding of the operation of open-loop and closed-loop systems we present the following introductory examples.

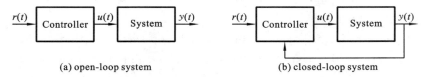

(a) open-loop system   (b) closed-loop system

Figure 5.3 Two types of systems

2. Open-Loop System

A characteristic of the open-loop control system is that it does not use feedback to determine if its input has achieved the desired goal. This means that the system does not observe the output of the processes that it is controlling. Consequently, a true open-loop system can not engage in machine learning and also cannot correct any errors that it makes. It also may not compensate for disturbances in the system.

An open-loop controller is often used in simple processes because of its simplicity and low-cost, especially in systems where feedback is not critical.

A very simple introductory example of an open-loop system is that of the clothes washing machine (See Figure 5.4). Here, the reference signal $r(t)$ designates the various operating conditions that we set on the "programmer", such as water temperature, duration

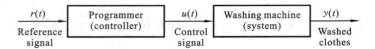

Figure 5.4 The clothes washing machine as an open-loop system

of various washing cycles, duration of clothes wringing, etc. These operating conditions are carefully chosen so as to achieve satisfactory clothes washing. The controller is the "programmer", whose output $u(t)$ is the control signal. This control signal is the input to the washing machine and forces the washing machine to execute the desired operations preassigned in the reference signal $r(t)$, i. e., water heating, water changing, clothes wringing, etc. The output of the system $y(t)$ is the "quality" of washing, i. e., how well the clothes have been washed. It is well known that during the operation of the washing machine, the output (i. e., whether the clothes are well washed or not) it not taken into consideration. The washing machine performs only a series of operations contained in $u(t)$ without being influenced at all by $y(t)$. It is clear that here $u(t)$ in not a function of $y(t)$ and, therefore, the washing machine is a typical example of an open-loop system. Other examples of open-loop systems are the electric stove, the alarm clock, the elevator, the traffic lights, the worldwide telephone communication system, the computer, and the Internet.

3. Closed-Loop System

A closed-loop system also is called a feedback control system. A feedback control system often uses a function of a prescribed relationship between the output and reference input to control the system. Often the difference between the output of the system under control and the reference input is amplified and used to control the system so that the difference is continually reduced.

A very simple introductory example of a closed-loop system is that of the water heater (See Figure 5.5). Here, the system is the water heater and the output $y(t)$ is the water temperature. Let this desired temperature lie in the range from 65 ℃ to 70 ℃. In this example, the water is heated by electric power, i. e., by a resistor that is supplied by an electric current. The controller of the system is a thermostat, which works as a switch as follows: when the temperature of the water reaches 70 ℃, the switch opens and the electric supply is interrupted. As a result, the water temperature starts falling and when it reaches 65 ℃, the switch closes and the electric supply is back on again. Subsequently, the water temperature rises again to 70 ℃, the switch opens again, and so on. This procedure is continuously repeated, keeping the temperature of the water in the desired temperature range, i. e., between 65 ℃ to 70 ℃. A careful examination of the water heater example shows that the controller provides the appropriate input to the water heater. Clearly, this input is decisively affected by the output, i. e., $u(t)$ is a function of not only of $r(t)$ but also $y(t)$. Therefore, here we have a typical example of a closed-loop system.

Other examples of closed-loop systems are the refrigerator, the voltage control system,

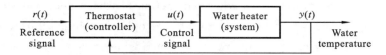

Figure 5.5 The water heater as a closed-loop system

the liquid-level control system, the position regulator, the speed regulator, the nuclear reactor control system, the robot, and the guided aircraft. All these closed-loop systems operate by the same principles as the water heater presented above.

4. Comparison of Open-Loop System and Closed-Loop System

From the above examples it is obvious that closed-loop systems differ from open-loop systems, the difference being whether or not information concerning the system's output is fed back to the system's input. Indeed, it is of paramount importance to point out that in open-loop systems, if the performance of the system is not satisfactory, the controller does nothing to improve it. On the contrary, in closed-loop systems the controller acts in such a way as to keep the performance of the system within satisfactory limits.

Closed-loop systems are mostly used when the control specifications are highly demanding, while open-loop systems are used in simple control problems. Closed-loop systems are, in almost all cases, more difficult to design and implement than open-loop systems.

The complexity in implementing controllers for open- or closed-loop systems increases as the design requirements increase. We can have simple controllers, e.g., thermostats or programmers, but we can also have more complex controllers like an amplifier and/or an RC or RL network to control a system or process, a computer to control an airplane, or even a number of computers to control the landing of a spacecraft on Mars. Furthermore, depending mainly upon the design requirements and the nature of the system under control, a controller may be electronic, electrical, mechanical, pneumatic, or hydraulic, or a combination of two or more of these types of controllers.

5. Practical Control Examples

Here we describe several well-known practical control examples. These examples give an overall picture of the wide use of control systems in modern technology. Furthermore, some of these examples show how the principles of control can be used to understand and solve control problems in other fields, such as economics, medicine, politics, and sociology.

Remote robot control A remote control system can control, from the earth, the motion of a robot arm on the surface of the moon. The operator at earth station watches the robot on the moon through a TV monitor. The system's output is the position of the robot's arm and the input is the position of the control stick. The operator compares the desired and the real position of the robot's arm, by looking at the position of the robot's arm on the monitor and decides on how to move the control stick so that the position of the robot arm is the desired one.

Laser eye surgery control system Laser can be used to "weld" the retina of the eye in its proper position inside the eye in cases where the retina has been detached from its original place. The control scheme is of great assistance to the ophthalmologist during surgery, since the controller continuously monitors the retina (using a wide-angle video camera system) and controls the laser's position so that each lesion of the retina is placed in its proper position.

Teaching The proper procedure for teaching has the structure of a closed-loop system. Let the students be the system, the teaching material presented by the teacher the input, and the "degree" of understanding of this material by the students the output. The system's output, i.e., the degree of understanding by students of the material taught, is fed back to the input, i.e., to the teacher. Indeed, an experienced teacher should be able to "sense" if the students understood the material taught. Subsequently, the teacher will either go on teaching with new material, if the students understood the material taught, or repeat the same material, if they did not. Therefore, proper teaching has indeed the structure of a closed-loop system. Clearly, if teachers keep on teaching with new material without checking whether or not the students understand what they are saying, this is not proper teaching.

Words and Expressions

generator ['dʒenəreitə] n. 发电机,发生器
controller [kən'trəulə] n. 控制器;管理者
regulator ['regjuleitə] n. 调整器;调整者
compensator ['kɔmpenseitə] n. 补整器,补偿器
reference signal　参考信号
facilitate [fə'siliteit] v. 帮助;使……容易;促进
feedback ['fi:dbæk] n. 反馈
engage [in'geidʒ] v. 从事,参加;忙于;卷入(in)
designate ['dezigneit] v. 指定,标示
preassign ['pri:ə'sain] v. 预先指定,预先分配
stove [stəuv] n. 炉子,火炉
resistor [ri'zistə] n. 电阻器
thermostat ['θə:məstæt] n. 恒温器
paramount ['pærəmaunt] a. 最高的;至上的;首要的;卓越的
surgery ['sə:dʒəri] n. 外科;外科手术
retina ['retinə] n. 网膜
ophthalmologist [ˌɔfθæl'mɔlədʒist] n. 眼科医师
lesion ['li:ʒən] n. 损害,精神的伤害;障碍

Notes

1. Consequently, a true open-loop system can not engage in machine learning and also cannot correct any errors that it makes.

(1) engage in:从事;参加

例:He has engaged in farming for 20 years. 他从事耕作已有 20 年。

（2）句中 it 指代 open-loop system。

（3）全句可翻译为：因此，一个真正的开环系统既不能从事机器学习，也不能纠正系统产生的任何误差。

2. Often the difference between the output of the system under control and the reference input is amplified and used to control the system so that the difference is continually reduced.

（1）句中主语是 the difference，谓语是 is，so that 引导目的状语从句。

（2）全句可翻译为：通常对控制系统的输出与参考输入之间的差值进行放大并用于控制系统，以便不断减小差值。

3. Closed-loop systems are, in almost all cases, more difficult to design and implement than open-loop systems.

（1）in almost all cases：在大多数的情况下

（2）全句可翻译为：闭环控制系统的设计及应用在大多数情况下都比开环控制系统复杂。

Reading Material

Control System Examples

Control systems are all around us in the modern technological world. They maintain the environment, lighting, and power in our buildings and factories; they regulate the operation of our cars, consumer electronics, and manufacturing processes; they enable our transportation and communications systems; and they are critical elements in our military and space systems. For the most part, they are hidden view, buried within the code of processors, executing their functions accurately and reliably. Nevertheless, their existence is a major intellectual and engineering accomplishment that is still evolving and growing, promising ever more important consequences to society.

1) Early Examples

The proliferation of control in engineered systems has occurred primarily in the later half of the 20th century. There are some familiar exceptions, such as the centrifugal governor described earlier and the thermostat designed at the turn of the century to regulate the temperature of buildings. There are many other control system examples, of course, that have developed over the years with progressively increasing levels of sophistication and impact. An early system with broad public exposure was the "cruise control" option introduced on automobiles in 1958. In the industrial world, control systems have been key enabling technologies for everything from factory automation to process control in oil refineries and chemical plants, to integrated circuit manufacturing, to power generation and distribution. They now also play critical roles in the routing of messages across the Internet and in power management for wireless communication systems.

2) Aerospace Applications

Similarly, control systems have been critical enablers in the aerospace and military world. We are familiar, for example, with the saturation bombing campaigns of World War II, which dropped unguided explosives almost indiscriminately on population centers to destroy selected industrial or military targets. These have been replaced with precision guided weapons with uncanny accuracy, a single round for a single target. This is enabled by advanced control systems, combining inertial guidance sensors, radar and infrared homing seekers, satellite navigation updating from the global positioning system and sophisticated processing of the "feedback error", all combined in an affordably disposable package.

3) Flight Control

Another notable success story for control in the aerospace world comes from the control of flight. This example illustrates just how significant the intellectual and technological accomplishments of control have been and how important their continued evolution will be in the future. Control has played a key role in the development of aircraft from the very beginning. Indeed, the Wright brother's first powered flight is successful only because the aircraft included control surfaces that are adjusted continuously by the pilot to stabilize the flight. Today, we even entrust the very survival of aircraft to automation. Examples include the all-weather auto-land functions of commercial transports, in which safe go-around maneuvers are not available if failures occur at certain critical flight phases. Other examples include the F-16, B-2, and X-29 military aircraft. Finally, in modern flight systems there is a growing trend to automate more and more functions—all the way to removing the pilot entirely from the cockpit. This is already commonplace in certain military reconnaissance and surveillance missions and will soon be extended to more lethal ones, such as suppressing enemy air defenses with unmanned aerial vehicles.

Lesson 3 Discrete-Time Control

1. Introduction

The advances made in microprocessors, micro-computers and digital signal processors have accelerated the growth of digital control systems theory. The discrete-time systems are dynamic systems in which the system-variables are defined only at discrete instants of time.

The terms sampled-data control systems, discrete-time control systems and digital control systems have all been used interchangeably in the control-system literatures. Strictly speaking, sampled-data are pulse-amplitude modulated signals and are obtained by some means of sampling an analog signal. Digital signals are generated by means of digital transducers or digital computers, often in digitally coded form. The discrete-time systems, in broad sense, describe all systems having some form of digital or sampled signals.

Discrete-time systems differ from continuous-time systems in that the signals for discrete-time systems are in sampled-data form. In contrast to the continuous-time system, the operation of discrete-time systems are described by a set of difference-equations. The analysis and design of discrete-time systems may be effectively carried out by use of the z-transform which evolved from the Laplace transform as a special form.

2. Sampled-Data and Digital Control Systems

Figure 5.6(a) shows the block diagram of sampled data control systems. The continuous error signal $e(t)$ is sampled at an interval of time T by means of a sampler. The plant output is also a continuous-signal and it is due to the fact that a hold circuit proceeds the plant.

Figure 5.6(b) shows the block diagram of a digital control system. A digital control system uses digital signals and a digital computer to control a process. The continuous time error signals are converted from analog form to digital form by means of an A/D converter. In practice, the A/D converter itself contains the sampler. After processing the inputs, the digital computer provides an output in digital form. This output is then converted to analog form by means of a D/A converter. In practice, the D/A converter itself contains the hold-device.

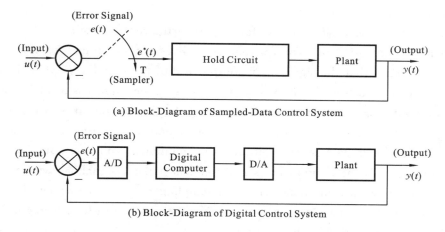

Figure 5.6 Sampled-Data and Digital Control Systems

The use of sampled-data in control systems enables time-sharing among different input signals using the same control equipments. Different input signals can be sampled periodically by staggering sampling time and thus, a number of inputs can be handled over the same control equipment.

Even in relatively simple control schemes, sampling may be warranted from other considerations. In fact sampling is a necessity wherever a high degree of accuracy is a prerequisite. This is the case in most automated machine tools. For example if it is required to move the table of a drilling machine within an accuracy of 0.01 mm over a total distance of 1 m, a resolution of 1 in 100 000 is needed which is impossible to measure using an analog type output transducer say a potentiometer. The problem can only be tackled by employing a digitally coded output sensor like an optical encoder.

Sampled data technique is most appropriate for control system requiring long distance data transmission. Pulse amplitude modulated (PAM) data is easily transmitted by means of a carrier over a transmission channel and the data reconstructed at the receiving end. It is well known that pulses may be transmitted with little loss of accuracy. Data in analog form may suffer considerable distortion in the transmission channel. Using sampled-data technique, a number of communication signals can be sequentially sampled and transmitted through a single transmission channel, thus, decreasing the cost of transmission installation. This technique is referred as time multiplexing.

Signal sampling reduces the power demand made on the signal and is therefore helpful for signals of weak power origin.

The examples cited above are those of systems in which the sampling operation is purposely introduced. However, there is a class of systems where the signals are available in sampled form only. For example in radar tracking system, the signal sent out and received is in form of pulse trains.

The circumstances that lead to the use of sampled-data control systems are:
- For using digital computer (or microprocessor) as part of the control loop;
- For time sharing of control components;
- Whenever a transmission channel forms part of the control loop;
- Whenever the output of a control component is essentially in discrete form.

Sampling implies that the signal at the output end of the sampler is available in form of short duration pulses each followed by a skip period when one signal is available so that the control system essentially operates open-loop during the skip period. It is intuitively obvious that if the sampling rate (or frequency) is too low, significant information contained in the input signal may be missed in the output. The minimum sampling rate has a definite relationship with the highest significant signal frequency (i.e., signal bandwidth). With the availability of high speed computers very high sampling rates can be achieved. In fact the sampling period in some cases may be so small that the system can for all practical purposes be approximated as a continuous time system.

Assuming sample width (time) as fixed, other forms of sampling are:

Multi-order sampling: A particular sampling pattern is repeated periodically.

Multi-rate sampling: In this case two simultaneous sampling operations with different time periods are carried out on the signal to produce the sampled output.

Random sampling: In this case the sampling instants are random with a particular kind of distribution.

3. Sampler

A sampler is the basic element of discrete-time control system, which converts a continuous-time signal into a train of pulses occurring at the sampling instants 0, T, 2T,..., where T is sampling period. It is to be noted that in between the sampling instants, the sampler dose not transmit any information.

Figure 5.7(a) shows a switch being used as a sampler. A continuous-time signal $f(t)$, as shown in Figure 5.7(b) is the input to the sampler. The switch is closed for a very short duration of time Δt, and then remains open for some duration of time.

The process is repeated with a time period T, called sampling time and the signal at the output end of the sampler is available in form of the pulses of very short duration Δt, each followed by a skip period when no output appears at the output end of the sampler. The continuous-time signal $f(t)$ is thus, sampled at a regular interval of time T, as shown in

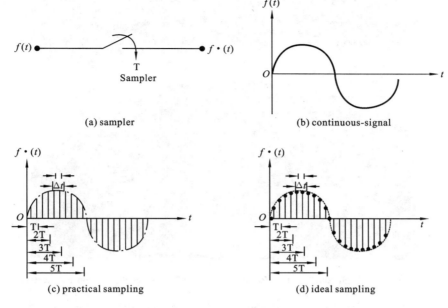

Figure 5.7 Uniform periodic sampling

Figure 5.7(c). The sampled signal is denoted as $f \cdot (t)$ which is obtained after sampling the continuous time input signal $f(t)$.

Figure 5.7(c) shows the signal-modulated pulse train having pulse-width Δt and is the case of practical-sampling. However, in the case of ideal-sampling, the pulse width Δt approaches to zero and therefore, the output $f \cdot (t)$ of an ideal sampler is the signal-modulated impulse train as shown in Figure 5.7(d).

4. Digital Control System Applications

The total number of computer control systems installed in industry has grown over the past three decades. Currently there are approximately 100 million control systems using computers, although the computer size and power may vary significantly. Improvements in computational capability have revolutionized the application of control theory and design in the modern-era. With the availability of fast, low-priced, and small-sized microprocessors, much of the control of industrial and commercial processes is moving toward the use of computers within the control system.

Digital control systems are used in many applications: for machine tools, metal-working processes, chemical processes, aircraft control, and automobile traffic control, among others. An example of a computer control system used in the aircraft industry is shown in Figure 5.8. Automatic computer-controlled systems are used for purposes as diverse as measuring the objective refraction of the human eye and controlling the engine spark timing or air-fuel ratio of automobile engines. The latter innovations are necessary to reduce automobile emissions and increase fuel economy.

The advantages of using digital control include improved measurement sensitivity; the use of digitally coded signals, digital sensors and transducers, and microprocessors; reduced

Figure 5.8 The flight dock of the Boeing 757 and 767 features digital control electronics

sensitivity to signal noise; and the capability to easily reconfigure the control algorithm in software. Improved sensitivity results from the low-energy signals required by digital sensors and devices. The used of digital coded signals permits the wide application of digital devices and communications. Digital sensors and transducers can effectively measure, transmit, and couple signals and devices. In addition many systems are inherently digital because they send out pulse signals. Examples of such a digital system are a radar tracking system and a space satellite.

Words and Expressions

microprocessor [ˌmaikrəu'prəusesə] n. 微处理器
sampled-data   采样数据
interchangeable [intə'tʃeindʒəb(ə)1] a. 可互换的
literature ['litəritʃə] n. 文学；文献
transducer [trænz'djuːsə] n. 转换器；传感器
difference-equations   差分方程
z-transform   z 变换
sampler ['sɑːmplə] n. 取样器, 采样器
hold circuit   保持电路
converter [kən'vəːtə(r)] n. 转换器
prerequisite ['priː'rekwizit] n. 先决条件
potentiometer [pəˌtenʃi'ɔmitə] n. 电位计, 分压计
tackle ['tækl] v. 处理, 解决
optical encoder   光学编码器
PAM   脉冲幅度放大调制
time multiplexing   时分多路复用

circumstance ['səːkəmstəns] n. 环境，状况，事件
intuitively [in'tjuːitivli] ad. 直觉地，直观地
impulse train 脉冲序列

Notes

1. The discrete-time systems, in broad sense, describe all systems having some form of digital or sampled signals.

(1) in broad sense：从广义上讲，广义而言

(2) 全句可翻译为：从广义上讲，离散时间控制系统描述具有某种形式的数字或采样信号的所有系统。

2. Different input signals can be sampled periodically by staggering sampling time and thus, a number of inputs can be handled over the same control equipment.

(1) staggering sampling time：交错的采样时间

(2) 全句可翻译为：不同的输入信号可以通过交错的采样时间进行周期性采样，因此大量的输入信号可以用同一个控制装置处理。

3. Automatic computer-controlled systems are used for purposes as diverse as measuring the objective refraction of the human eye and controlling the engine spark timing or air-fuel ratio of automobile engines.

(1) as diverse as：像……一样多种多样

(2) 全句可翻译为：全自动计算机控制系统可用于多种用途，如测量人眼的客观折射度和控制发动机点火正时或汽车发动机的空燃比。

Reading Material

Mechatronics Systems

A natural stage in the evolutionary process of modern engineering design is encompassed in the area known as mechatronics. The term mechatronics was coined in Japan in the 1970s. Mechatronics is the synergistic integration of mechanical, electrical, and computer systems and has evolved over the past 30 years, leading to a new breed of intelligent products. Feedback control is an integral aspect of modern mechatronic systems. One can understand the extent that mechatronics reaches into various disciplines by considering the components that make up mechatronics. The key elements of mechatronics are ①physical systems modeling, ②sensors and actuators, ③signals and systems, ④computers and logic systems, and ⑤software and data acquisition. Feedback control encompasses aspects of all five key elements of mechatronics, but is associated primarily with the element of signals and systems.

Advances in computer hardware and software technology coupled with the desire to increase the performance-to-cost-ratio have revolutionized engineering design. New products are being developed at the intersection of traditional disciplines of engineering, computer science, and the natural sciences. Advancements in traditional disciplines are fueling the growth of mechatronics systems by providing "enabling technologies". A critical enabling technology is the microprocessor which has a profound effect on the design of consumer products. We should expect continued advancements in cost effective microprocessors and microcontrollers, novel sensors and actuators enabled by advancements in applications of microelectromechanical systems (MEMS), advanced control methodologies and real time programming methods, networking and wireless technologies, and mature computer-aided engineering (CAE) technologies for advanced system modeling, virtual prototyping, and testing. The continued rapid development in these areas will only accelerate the pace of smart (that is, actively controlled) products.

An exciting area of future mechatronic system development in which control systems will play a significant role is the area of alternative energy production and usage. Hybrid fuel automobiles and efficient wind power generation are two examples of systems that can benefit from mechatronic design methods. In fact, the mechatronic design philosophy can be effectively illustrated with the example of the evolution of the modern automobile. Prior to the 1960s, the radio is the only significant electronic device in an automobile. Today, many automobiles have 30~60 microcontrollers, up to 100 electric motors, about 200 pounds of wiring, a multitude of sensors, and thousands of lines of software code. A modern automobile can no longer be classified as a strictly mechanical machine—it has been transformed into a comprehensive mechatronic system.

Lesson 4 Process Control

1. Process-Control Principles

Process Control is the active changing of the process based on the results of process monitoring. In process control, the basic objective is to regular the value of some quantity. To regulate means to maintain that quantity at some desired value regardless of external influences. The desired value is called the reference value or setpoint.

Figure 5.9 shows the process to be used for this discussion. Liquid is flowing into a tank at some rate Q_{in} and out of the tank at some rate Q_{out}. The liquid in the tank has some height or level h. It is known that the flow rate out varies as the square root of the height, so the higher the level the faster the liquid flows out. If the output flow rate is not exactly equal to the input flow rate, the tank will either empty, if $Q_{out} > Q_{in}$, or overflow, if $Q_{out} < Q_{in}$.

This process has a property called self-regulation. This means that for some input flow rate, the liquid height will rise until it reaches a height for which the output flow rate matches the input flow rate. A self-regulating system does not provide regulation of a variable to any particular reference value. In this example the liquid level will adopt some value for which input and output flow rates are the same and there it will stay. If the input flow rate changed, then the level would change also, so it is not regulated to a reference value.

Suppose we want to maintain the level at some particular value H in Figure 5.9, regardless of the input flow rate, then something more than self-regulation is needed.

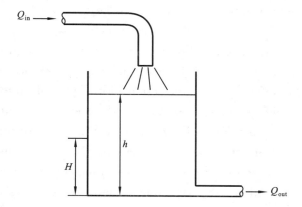

Figure 5.9 An example of process-control

Human-Aided Control Human-aided control shows a modification of the tank system to allow artificial regulation of the level by a human. To regulate the level so that it maintains the value H it will be necessary to employ a sensor to measure the level. This has been provided via a sight tube. The actual liquid level or height is called the controlled variable. In addition, a valve has been added so the output flow rate can be changed by the human. The output flow rate is called the manipulated variable or controlling variable.

Now the height can be regulated apart from the input flow rate using the following strategy: The person measures the height in the sight tube and compares the value to the setpoint. If the measured value is larger, the human opens the valve a little to let the flow out increase, and thus the level lowers toward the setpoint. If the measured value is smaller than the setpoint, the person closes the valve a little to decrease the flow out and allow the level to rise toward the setpoint.

By a succession of incremental opening and closing of the valve, the human can bring the level to the setpoint value H and maintain it there by continuous monitoring of the sight tube and adjustment of the valve.

Automatic Control To provide automatic control, the system is modified using machines, electronics, or computers to replace the operations of the human. An instrument called a sensor is added that is able to measure the value of the level and convert it into a proportional signal. The signal is provided as input to a machine, an electronic circuit, or a computer, called the controller. This performs the function of the human in evaluating the measurement and providing an output signal to change the valve setting via an actuator connected to the valve by a mechanical linkage.

2. Identification of Elements

The elements of a process-control system are defined in terms of separate functional parts of the system.

Process In general, a process can consist of a complex assembly of phenomena that relate to some manufacturing sequence. Many variables may be involved in such a process, and it may be desirable to control all these variables at the same time. There are single-variable processes, in which only one variable is to be controlled, as well as multivariable processes, in which many variables, perhaps interrelated, may require regulation.

Measurement   Clearly, to effect control of a variable in a process, we must have information on the variable itself. Such information is found by measuring the variable. In general, a measurement refers to the conversion of the variable into some corresponding analog of the variable, such as a pneumatic pressure, an electrical voltage, or a current. A sensor is a device that performs the initial measurement and energy conversion of a variable into analogous electrical or pneumatic information. Further transformation or signal conditioning may be required to complete the measurement function. The result of the measurement is a representation of the variable value in some forms required by the other elements in the process-control operation.

Controller   The next step in the process-control sequence is to examine the error and determine what action, if any, should be taken. This part of the control system has many names; however, controller is the most common. The evaluation may be performed by an operator, by electronic signal processing, by pneumatic signal processing, or by a computer. The controller requires an input of both a measured indication of the controlled variable and a representation of the reference value of the variable, expressed in the same terms as the measured value.

Control Element   The final element in the process-control operation is the device that exerts a direct influence on the process; that is, it provides those required changes in the controlled variable to bring it to the setpoint. This element accepts an input from the controller, which is then transformed into some proportional operation performed on the process.

3. Process-Control Block Diagram

To provide a practical, working description of process control, it is useful to describe the elements and operations involved in more generic terms. Such a description should be independent of a particular application and thus be applicable to all control situations. A model may be constructed using blocks to represent each distinctive element. The characteristics of control operation then may be developed from a consideration of the properties and interfacing of these elements. Figure 5.10 shows a general block diagram. The controlled variable in the process is denoted by c in this diagram, and the measured representation of the controlled variable is labeled b. The controlled variable setpoint is labeled r, for reference.

The error detector is a subtracting-summing point that outputs an error signal $e = r - b$ to the controller for comparison and action.

The purpose of a block diagram approach is to allow the process-control system to be analyzed as the interaction of smaller and simpler subsystems. If the characteristics of each element of the system can be determined, then the characteristics of the assembled system can be established by an analytical marriage of these subsystems. The historical development of the system approach in technology is dictated by this practical aspect: first, to specify the

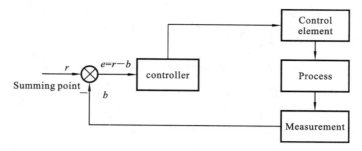

Figure 5.10　The block diagram of a control loop

characteristics desired of a total system and, then, to delegate the development of subsystems that provide the overall criteria.

4. Control System Evaluation

A process-control system is used to regulate the value of some process variable. When such a system is in use, it is natural to ask, "How well is it working?" This is not an easy question to answer, because it is possible to adjust a control system to provide different kinds of response to errors. This section discusses some methods for evaluating how well the system is working.

The variable used to measure the performance of the control system is the error, which is the difference between the constant setpoint or reference value r and the controlled variable $c(t)$.

$$e(t)=r-c(t)$$

Since the value of the controlled variable may vary in time, so may the error.

In principle, the objective of a control system is to make the error exactly zero, but the control system responds only to errors. Conversely, if the error were zero and stayed zero, the control system would be doing nothing and would not be needed in the first place. Therefore, this objective can never be perfectly achieved, and there will always be some errors. The question of evaluation becomes one of how large the error is and how it varies in time.

The purpose of the control system is to regulate the value of some variables. This requires that action be taken on the purpose itself in response to a measurement of the variable. If this is not done correctly, the control system can cause the process to become unstable. In fact, the more tightly we try to control the variable, the greater the possibility of an instability.

The first objective, then, simply means that the control system must be designed and adjusted so the system is stable. Typically, as the control system is adjusted to give better control, the likelihood of instability also increases.

Words and Expressions

setpoint ['setpɔint] $n.$ 设定值,控制点

property ['prɔpəti] $n.$ 财产,所有物,所有权;性质,特性

self-regulation ['self,regiu'leiʃn] n. 自动调节
pneumatic [nju(:)'mætik] a. 气动的(有空气的,气体学的)
analogous [ə'næləɡəs] a. 类似的
controller [kən'trəulə] n. 控制器;管理者;审计员
generic [dʒi'nerik] a. 一般的,普通的,共有的
distinctive [di'stiŋktiv] a. 有特色的,出众的
delegate ['deligit] vt. 委任(某人)为代表;代表
criteria [krai'tiəriə] n. 标准
likelihood ['laiklihud] n. 可能性

Notes

1. It is known that the flow rate out varies as the square root of the height, so the higher the level the faster the liquid flows out.

(1) It is known that...:众所周知……

(2) 全句可翻译为:众所周知,流出速率随着高度的平方根变化,因此液面越高,液体流出速率越大。

2. There are single-variable processes, in which only one variable is to be controlled, as well as multivariable processes, in which many variables, perhaps interrelated, may require regulation.

(1) as well as: conj. 以及,又

(2) single-variable processes:单变量过程
   multivariable processes:多变量过程

(3) 全句可翻译为:整个过程分为单变量过程和多变量过程。单变量过程中只有一个变量需要控制,而多变量过程中有许多可能相互关联的变量需要控制。

3. The controller requires an input of both a measured indication of the controlled variable and a representation of the reference value of the variable, expressed in the same terms as the measured value.

(1) in the same terms as:在同样的条件下

(2) 全句可翻译为:控制器要求输入控制变量的测量值和变量的参考值,表示为相同的条件下的测量值。

Reading Material

Statistical Process Control (SPC)

Statistical Process Control (SPC) is an effective method of monitoring a process through the use of control chart. Control charts enable the use of objective criteria for distinguishing background variation from events of significance based on statistical techniques. Much of its power lies in the ability to monitor both process center and its variation about that center. By collecting data from samples at various points within the process, variations in the process that may affect the quality of the end product or service can be detected and corrected, thus reducing waste as well as the likelihood that problems will be passed on to the customer.

With its emphasis on early detection and prevention of problems, SPC has a distinct advantage over quality methods, such as inspection, that apply resources to detecting and correcting problems in the end product or service.

In addition to reducing waste, SPC can lead to a reduction in the time required to produce the product or service from end to end. This is partially due to a diminished likelihood that the final product will have to be reworked, but it may also result from using SPC data to identify bottlenecks, wait times, and other sources of delays within the process. Process cycle time reductions coupled with improvements in yield have made SPC a valuable tool from both a cost reduction and a customer satisfaction standpoint.

In mass-manufacturing, the quality of the finished article is traditionally achieved through post-manufacturing inspection of the product; accepting or rejecting each article (or samples from a production lot) based on how well it met its design specifications. In contrast, statistical process control uses statistical tools to observe the performance of the production process to predict significant deviations that may later result in rejected product.

Two kinds of variation occur in all manufacturing processes, both these types of process variation cause subsequent variation in the final product. The first is known as natural or common cause variation and may be variation in temperature, properties of raw materials, strength of an electrical current etc. This variation is small, the observed values generally being quite close to the average value. The pattern of variation will be similar to those found in nature, and the distribution forms the bell-shaped normal distribution curve. The second kind of variation is known as special cause variation, and happens less frequently than the first.

For example, a breakfast cereal packaging line may be designed to fill each cereal box with 500 grams of product, but some boxes will have slightly more than 500 grams, and some will have slightly less, in accordance with a distribution of net weights. If the production process, its inputs, or its environment changes (for example, the machines doing the manufacture begin to wear) this distribution can change. For example, as its cams and pulleys wear out, the cereal filling machine may start putting more cereal into each box than specified. If this change is allowed to continue unchecked, more and more product will be produced that fall outside the tolerances of the manufacturer or consumer, resulting in waste. While in this case, the waste is in the form of "free" product for the consumer, typically waste consists of rework or scrap.

By observing at the right time what happened in the process that led to a change, the quality engineer or any member of the team responsible for the production line can troubleshoot the root cause of the variation that has crept in to the process and correct the problem.

SPC indicates when an action should be taken in a process, but it also indicates when NO action should be taken. An example is a person who would like to maintain a constant body weight and takes weight measurements weekly. A person who does not understand SPC concepts might start dieting every time his or her weight increased, or eat more every time his or her weight decreased. This type of action could be harmful and possibly generate even more variation in body weight. SPC would account for normal weight variation and better indicate when the person is in fact gaining or losing weight.

Lesson 5 PID Controller

1. Introduction

PID control is a name commonly given to three-term control. The mnemonic PID refers to the first letters of the names of the individual terms that make up the standard three-term controller. These are "P" for the proportional term, "I" for the integral term and "D" for the derivative term in the controller.

Three-term or PID controllers are probably the most widely used industrial controller. Even complex industrial control systems may comprise a control network whose main control building block is a PID control module. The three-term PID controller has had a long history of use and has survived the changes of technology from the analogue era into the digital computer control system age quite satisfactorily. It is the first controller to be mass produced for the high-volume market that existed in the process industries.

The introduction of the Laplace transform to study the performance of feedback control systems supports its technological success in the engineering community. The theoretical basis for analyzing the performance of PID control is considerably aided by the simple representation of an integrator by the Laplace transform $[1/s]$ and a differentiator using $[s]$. Conceptually, the PID controller is quite sophisticated and three different representations can be given. First, there is a symbolic representation (Figure 5.11(a)), where each of the three terms can be selected to achieve different control actions. Secondly, there is a time domain operator form (Figure 5.11(b)), and finally, there is a Laplace transform version of the PID controller (Figure 5.11(c)). This gives the controller an s-domain operator interpretation and allows the link between the time domain and the frequency domain to enter the discussion of PID controller performance. The PID algorithm is packaged in the form of standard regulators for process control and is also the basis of many tailor-made control systems. The final form of the PID algorithm is:

$$u_c(t) = K_P e(t) + K_I \int_0^t e(\tau) d\tau + K_D \frac{de(t)}{dt}$$

and the tuning parameters are:

1) Proportional gain, K_P

Larger values typically mean faster response since the larger the error, the larger the proportional term compensation. An excessively large proportional gain will lead to process instability and oscillation.

2) Integral gain, K_I

Larger values imply steady state errors are eliminated more quickly. The trade-off is larger overshoot: any negative error integrated during transient response must be integrated away by positive error before we reach steady state.

3) Derivative gain, K_D

Larger values decrease overshoot, but slow down transient response and may lead to instability due to signal noise amplification in the differentiation of the error.

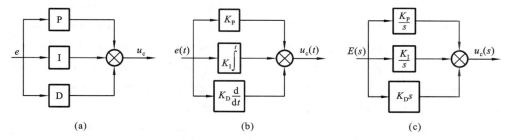

Figure 5.11　PID controller representations

2. Loop Tuning

If the PID controller parameters (the gains of the proportional, integral and derivative terms) are chosen incorrectly, the controlled process input can be unstable, i. e. its output diverges, with or without oscillation, and is limited only by saturation or mechanical breakage. Tuning a control loop is the adjustment of its control parameters (gain/proportional band, integral gain/reset, derivative gain/rate) to the optimum values for the desired control response.

The optimum behavior on a process change or setpoint change varies depending on the application. Some processes must not allow an overshoot of the process variable beyond the setpoint if, for example, this would be unsafe. Other processes must minimize the energy expended in reaching a new setpoint. Generally, stability of response (the reverse of instability) is required and the process must not oscillate for any combination of process conditions and setpoints. Some processes have a degree of non-linearity and so parameters that work well at full-load conditions don't work when the process is starting up from no-load. This section describes some traditional manual methods for loop tuning.

There are several methods for tuning a PID loop. The most effective methods generally involve the development of some form of process model, then choosing P, I, and D based on the dynamic model parameters. Manual tuning methods can be relatively inefficient.

The choice of method will depend largely on whether or not the loop can be taken "offline" for tuning, and the response time of the system. If the system can be taken offline, the best tuning method often involves subjecting the system to a step change in input, measuring the output as a function of time, and using this response to determine the control parameters.

3. Limitations of PID Control

While PID controllers are applicable to many control problems, they can perform poorly in some applications.

PID controllers, when used alone, can give poor performance when the PID loop gains must be reduced so that the control system does not overshoot, oscillate or hunt about the control setpoint value. The control system performance can be improved by combining the feedback (or closed-loop) control of a PID controller with feed-forward (or open-loop) control. Knowledge about the system (such as the desired acceleration and inertia) can be fed forward and combined with the PID output to improve the overall system performance. The feed-forward value alone can often provide the major portion of the controller output. The PID controller can then be used primarily to respond to whatever difference or error remains between the setpoint (SP) and the actual value of the process variable (PV). Since the feed-forward output is not affected by the process feedback, it can never cause the control system to oscillate, thus improving the system response and stability.

For example, in most motion control systems, in order to accelerate a mechanical load under control, more force or torque is required from the prime mover, motor, or actuator. If a velocity loop PID controller is being used to control the speed of the load and command the force or torque being applied by the prime mover, then it is beneficial to take the instantaneous acceleration desired for the load, scale that value appropriately and add it to the output of the PID velocity loop controller. This means that whenever the load is being accelerated or decelerated, a proportional amount of force is commanded from the prime mover regardless of the feedback value. The PID loop in this situation uses the feedback information to affect any increase or decrease of the combined output in order to reduce the remaining difference between the process setpoint and the feedback value. Working together, the combined open-loop feed-forward controller and closed-loop PID controller can provide a more responsive, stable and reliable control system.

Another problem faced with PID controllers is that they are linear. Thus, performance of PID controllers in non-linear systems (such as HVAC systems) is variable. Often PID controllers are enhanced through methods such as PID gain scheduling or fuzzy logic. Further practical application issues can arise from instrumentation connected to the controller. A high enough sampling rate, measurement precision, and measurement accuracy are required to achieve adequate control performance.

A problem with the derivative term is that small amounts of measurement or process noise can cause large amounts of change in the output. It is often helpful to filter the measurements with a low-pass filter in order to remove higher-frequency noise components. However, low-pass filtering and derivative control can cancel each other out, so reducing noise by instrumentation means is a much better choice. Alternatively, the differential band can be turned off in many systems with little loss of control. This is equivalent to using the PID controller as a PI controller.

Words and Expressions

mnemonic [ni(:)'mɔnik] *a.* 帮助记忆的；记忆的
proportional [prə'pɔ:ʃənl] *a.* 成比例的，(与……)相称的
integral ['intigrəl] *a.* 积分的；与积分有关的

derivative [di'rivətiv] *a.* 微分的
module ['mɔdju:l] *n.* 模块；组件
representation [,reprizen'teiʃən] *n.* 表示法；表现；陈述
differentiator [,difə'renʃi,eitə] *n.* 微分器
s-domain   复频域
algorithm ['ælgəriðəm] *n.* 算法
tuning ['tju:niŋ] *a.* 调整
compensation [,kɔmpen'seiʃən] *n.* 补偿；赔偿
oscillation [,ɔsi'leiʃən] *n.* 振动；动摇
steady state   稳态
trade-off   妥协；平衡；协调
overshoot ['əuvə'ʃu:t] *n.* 过调量，过冲量
diverge [dai'və:dʒ] *v.* 离题；偏离；背离，背驰
saturation [,sætʃə'reiʃən] *n.* 饱和
inertia [i'nə:ʃjə] *n.* 惯性，惰性
prime mover   原动力，发动者
fuzzy logic   模糊逻辑

Notes

1. The introduction of the Laplace transform to study the performance of feedback control systems supports its technological success in the engineering community.

（1）句中主语为 the introduction of the Laplace transform，谓语为 supports，不定式用作状语表目的。

（2）全句可翻译为：为了研究反馈控制系统的性能引入了拉氏变换，在工程界取得了技术上的成功。

2. The choice of method will depend largely on whether or not the loop can be taken "offline" for tuning, and the response time of the system.

（1）句中 whether or not 引导宾语从句，作"是否，会不会"解。

（2）全句可翻译为：方法的选择很大程度上取决于控制回路能否离线调整及系统的响应时间。

3. PID controllers, when used alone, can give poor performance when the PID loop gains must be reduced so that the control system does not overshoot, oscillate or hunt about the control setpoint value.

（1）句中第一个 when 引导时间状语从句，第二个 when 引导原因状语从句。

（2）全句可翻译为：当 PID 控制器单独使用时，会表现不佳的性能，因为 PID 回路的增益要不断减小以防止控制系统产生超调、振荡或偏离控制系统的参考值。

Reading Material

Basic Industrial Control

As can be seen from the typical industrial control loop structuregiven in Figure 5.12, even simple process loops comprise more than four engineering components.

The main components can be grouped according to the following loop operations:

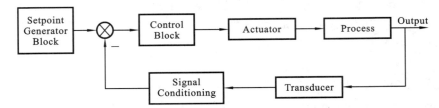

Figure 5.12 Components in a typical industrial control loop

Process: this is the actual system for which some specific physical variables are to be controlled or regulated. Typical process industry examples are boilers, kilns, furnaces and distillation towers.

Actuation: the actuator is a process unit that supplies material or power input to the process. The actuator can be considered to act through amplification. For example, the control signal could be a small movement on a valve stem controlling a large flow of natural gas into a gas-fired industrial boiler.

Measurement: the common adage is that without measurement there will be no control. Typically, the measurement process incorporates a transducer and associated signal processing components. The transducer will comprise a sensor to detect a specific physical property (such as temperature) and will output a representation of the property in a different physical form (such as voltage). It is quite possible that the measured output will be a noisy signal and that some of that noise will still manage to pass through the signal conditioning component of the measurement device into the control loop.

Control: the controller is the unit designed to create a stable closed-loop system and also achieve some pre-specified dynamic and static process performance requirements. The input to the controller unit is usually an error signal based on the difference between a desired setpoint or reference signal and the actual measured output.

Communications: the above units and components in the control loop are all linked together. In small local loops, the control system is usually hardwired, but in spatially distributed processes with distant operational control rooms, computer communication components (networks, transmitters and receivers) will possibly be needed. This aspect of control engineering is not often discussed; however, the presence of communication delays in the loop may be an important obstacle to good control system performance.

To specify the controller, the performance objectives of the loop must be considered carefully, but in many situations it is after the loop has been commissioned and in use for a longer period of production activity that new and unforeseen process problems are identified. Consequently industrial control engineering often has two stages of activity: ①control design and commissioning and ②post-commissioning control redesign.

It is in constructing the first control design that explicit process modeling is likely to be used. Almost all physical processes are nonlinear in operation, but fortunately, many industrial processes run in conditions of steady operation to try to maximize throughput. This makes linearization of the nonlinear process dynamics about steady state system operation a feasible analysis route for many processes. Subsequently, nonlinearity at different operating conditions can be overcome by gain scheduling or adaptation techniques. Although linearity is the route to simple model construction, even a straightforward loop can lead to a complicated model if all the components are considered, and the result could be a block diagram model.

Lesson 6   PLC

1. Introduction

A programmable logic controller (PLC) is a special form of micro-processor-based controller that uses a programmable memory to store instructions and to implement functions such as logic, sequencing, timing, counting and arithmetic to control machines and processes and is designed to be operated by engineers with perhaps a limited knowledge of computers and computing languages, shown in Figure 5.13. PLCs are used in many different industries and machines such as packaging and semiconductor machines. Unlike general-purpose computers, the PLC is designed for multiple inputs and output arrangements, extended temperature ranges, immunity to electrical noise, and resistance to vibration and impact.

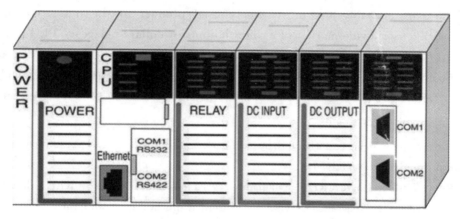

Figure 5.13   A programmable logic controller

PLCs have the great advantage that the same basic controller can be used with a wide range of control systems. To modify a control system and the rules that are to be sued, all that is necessary for an operator to key in a different set of instructions. There is no need to rewire. The result is a flexible, cost effective system which can be used with control systems which vary quite widely in their nature and complexity.

PLCs are similar to computers whereas computers are optimized for calculation and display tasks, PLCs are optimized for control tasks and the industrial environment. Thus PLCs are

(1) Rugged and designed to withstand vibrations, temperature, humidity and noise.

(2) Have interfacing for inputs and outputs already inside the controller.

(3) Are easily programmed and have an easily understood programming language which is primarily concerned with logic and switching operations.

2. History

The PLCs first hit the scene in the late 1960s. The primary reason for designing such a device is eliminating the large cost involved in replacing the complicated relay based machine control systems for major U.S. car manufacturers.

Before the PLC, control, sequencing, and safety interlock logic for manufacturing automobiles was accomplished using hundreds or thousands of relays, cam timers, and drum sequencers and dedicated closed-loop controllers. The process for updating such facilities for the yearly model change-over was very time consuming and expensive, as the relay systems needed to be rewired by skilled electricians.

Early PLCs are designed to replace relay logic systems. These PLCs are programmed in "ladder logic", which strongly resembles a schematic diagram of relay logic. Since then, a slow steady growth has allowed the manufacturing and process control industries to take advantage of PLC applications—oriented software-programmable language. Modern PLCs can be programmed in a variety of ways, from ladder logic to more traditional programming languages such as BASIC and C. Another method is state logic, a very high level programming language designed to program PLCs based on state transition diagrams.

Today, it is arguably the most widely used product in the industrial automation business, with a worldwide market of several billions of dollars per year. PLC products are available from hundreds of different sources, in many different form-factors (including embedded controllers), and with prices ranging from tens of thousands of dollars (for triple redundant, failure-proof systems) to commodity products at less than a hundred bucks.

3. Programming Languages

PLC programs can be constructed by using various methods of representation. Some of the common ones are described below.

The Relay Ladder Logic (RLL) Diagram A Relay Ladder Logic (RLL) diagram, also referred to as a Ladder diagram is a visual and logical method of displaying the control logic, which based on the inputs determine the outputs of the program. The ladder is made up of a series of "rungs" of logical expressions expressed graphically as series and parallel circuits of relay logic elements such as contacts, timers etc. Each rung consist of a set of inputs on the left end of the rung and a single output at the right end of each rung.

For the programs of small PLC systems, RLL programming technique has been regarded as the best choice because a programmer can understand the relations of the contacts and coils intuitively. Additionally, a maintenance engineer can easily monitor the operation of the RLL program on its graphical representation because most PLC manufacturers provide an animated display that clearly identifies the states of the contacts and coils. Although RLL is still an important language, as the memory size of today's PLC systems increases, a large-sized RLL program brings some significant problems because RLL is not particularly suitable for the well-structured programming: It is difficult to structure an RLL program hierarchically.

The Statement List (STL) The statement list is made up of series of assembly language like statements each one of which represents a logic control statement executable by the processor of the programmable controller. The statement list is the most unrestricted of all the methods of representation. Individual statements are made up of mnemonics, which represent the function to be executed. This method of representation is favored by those who have already had experience in programming microprocessors or computers.

4. Hardware

Typically a PLC system has five basic components. These are the processor unit, memory, the power supply unit, input/output interface section and the programming device. Figure 5.14 shows the basic arrangement.

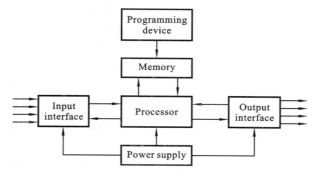

Figure 5.14 The PLC system

(1) The processor unit or central processing unit (CPU) is the unit containing the microprocessor and this interprets the input signals and carries out the control actions, according to the program stored in its memory, communicating the decisions as action signals to the outputs.

(2) The power supply unit in needed to convert the mains AC voltage to the low DC voltage (5V) necessary for the processor and the circuits in the input and output interface modules.

(3) The programming device is used to enter the required program into the memory of the processor. The program is developed in the device and then transferred to the memory unit of the PLC.

(4) The memory unit is where the program is stored that it to be used for the control actions to be exercised by the microprocessor.

(5) The input and output sections are where the processor receives information from external devices and communicates information to external devices. The inputs might thus be from switches, or other sensors such as photoelectric cells, temperature sensors, or flow sensors, etc. The outputs might be to motor starter coils, solenoid valves, etc.

5. Mechanical Design of PLC Systems

There are three common types of mechanical design for PLC systems, a single box, the modular and rack types. The single box type is commonly used for small programmable controllers and is supplied as an integral compact package complete with power supply, processor, memory, and input/output units. Typically such a PLC might have 40 input/output points and a memory which can store some 300 to 1 000 instructions. The modular type consists of separate modules for power supply, processor etc., which are often mounted on rails within a metal cabinet. The rack type can be used for all sizes of programmable controllers and has the various functional units packaged in individual modules which can be plugged into sockets in a base rack. The mix of modules required for a particular purpose is decided by the user and the appropriate ones then plugged into the rack. Thus it is comparatively easy to expand the number of input/output connections by just adding more input/output modules or to expand the memory by adding more memory units.

Programs are entered into a PLC's memory by using a program device which is usually not permanently connected to a particular PLC and can be moved from one controller to the next without disturbing operations. For the operation of the PLC it is not necessary for the programming device to be connected to the PLC since it transfers the program to the PLC memory.

Programming devices can be a hand-held device, a desktop console or a computer. Hand-held systems incorporate a small keyboard and liquid crystal display. Desktop devices are likely to have a visual display unit with a full keyboard and screen display. Personal computers are widely configured as program development workstations. Some PLCs only require the computer to have appropriate software, others special communication cards to interface with the PLC. A major advantage of using a computer is that the program can be stored on the hard disk or a floppy disk and copies easily made. The disadvantage is that the programming often tends to be not so user-friendly. Hand-held programming consoles will normally contain enough memory to allow the unit to retain programs while being carried from one place to another. Only when the program has been designed on the programming device and is ready is it transferred to the memory unit of the PLC.

Words and Expressions

programmable logic controller (PLC) n. 可编程逻辑控制器
instruction [in'strʌkʃən] n. 指令；说明
packing ['pækiŋ] n. 包装
semiconductor ['semikən'dʌktə] n. 半导体
immunity [i'mju:niti] n. 免疫，免疫性；免除
sue [sju:, su:] v. 要求，请求；控告 vi. 控告，控诉；提出诉讼
rugged ['rʌgid] a. 坚固的
relay ['ri:lei] n. 继电器；转播；备用品；替换人员
interlock [ˌintə'lɔk] v. 连结，连锁 n. ['intə(:)lɔk] 连结；联锁(装置)

cam timers   凸轮定时器
drum sequencers   鼓形定序器
ladder logic   梯形逻辑
triple redundant   三重冗余
buck [bʌk] n. [美国俚语]美元
solenoid ['səulinɔid] n. 螺线形电导管
hand-held a. (三角架、摄像机等)手提式的,便携的,手持的
console [kən'səul] n. 控制台,操纵台
floppy disk   软盘

Notes

1. A programmable logic controller (PLC) is a special form of micro-processor-based controller that uses a programmable memory to store instructions and to implement functions such as logic, sequencing, timing, counting and arithmetic to control machines and processes and is designed to be operated by engineers with perhaps a limited knowledge of computers and computing languages, shown in Figure 5.13.

(1) 句中的主语是 A programmable logic controller (PLC), is a special form... 和 and is designed to... 是谓语部分。

(2) 全句可翻译为:如图 5.13 所示,可编程控制器是一种基于微处理器的特殊形式的控制器。为了控制机器和过程,利用可编程的存储器来存储指令及完成逻辑、排序、定时、计数和算术等功能。可编程控制器的设计便于只掌握了有限的计算机及计算语言方面知识的工程师操作使用。

2. The input and output sections are where the processor receives information from external devices and communicates information to external devices.

(1) 句中 where 引导的从句作表语。

(2) 全句可翻译为:输入输出部分是指处理器从外部设备接收信息和与外部设备交流信息的部分。

3. Only when the program has been designed on the programming device and is ready is it transferred to the memory unit of the PLC.

(1) 句中 only 修饰句子的状语位于句首时,句子要用部分倒装,it 是句子的主语,指代 program。

(2) 全句可翻译为:只有当程序在编程器上设计好并准备好,才传送到可编程控制器的存储单元。

Reading Material

Relay Sequencers

One way to provide a discrete-state controller is to use physical relays to put together a circuit that satisfies the requirements of the ladder diagram. Such a control system is called a relay sequencer or a relay logic panel. In the early days of industrial control processes, this is the only way to provide control. It is still used in many applications today, although modern computer-based controllers have replaced many relay-based systems.

The ladder diagram technique of describing discrete-state control systems originated from relay logic systems, which is why the diagram contains so many relay-related terms and symbols. The ladder diagram continues to be used today because it has evolved into an efficient method of defining the event sequence required in a discrete-state control system.

It is important to realize that with relay control each rung of the ladder is evaluated simultaneously and continuously, because the switches and relays are all hardwired to AC power. If any switch anywhere in the ladder diagram changes state, the consequences are immediate.

Special Functions　　To build a relay-based control system, it is necessary to provide certain kinds of special functions not normally associated with relays. These functions are often provide using analog and digital electronic techniques included in the special functions are such features as time-delay relays, up/down counters, and real-time clocks.

Hardwired Programming　　When a relay panel has been wired to implement a ladder diagram, we say that it has been programmed to satisfy the ladder diagram; that is, the event sequence required and described by the ladder diagram will be provided by the relay system when power is applied. Thus, the program has been wired into the relays that make up the relay logic panel.

If the event sequence is to be changed, it is necessary to rewrite all or part of the panel. It may even be necessary to add more relays to the system or the use more relays than in the previous program.

Obviously, such a task is quite troublesome and time consuming. A number of ingenious methods are used to ease some of the problems of changing the relay program. One is the use of patch panels for the programming. In these systems all relay contacts and coil are brought to an array of sockets. Cords with plugs in each end are then used to patch the required coils, contacts, inputs, and outputs together in the manner required by the ladder diagram.

The patch panel acts like a memory in which the program is placed. With the development of reliable computers, it is an easy decision to replace relay logic-based systems with computer-controlled systems.

PART SIX Computer

Lesson 1 Computer Hardware and Software

Computer is an electronic equipment which can make arithmetic and logical calculation, process information rapidly and automatically. A computer system consists of both hardware and software systems.

1. Hardware

By and large, once you switch the machine on, you will have enough to do working out how Windows™ or the various programs work. This is the software side of the computer, and it makes sense for you to concentrate on these initially, because without them the physical (hardware) bits and pieces of the machine are incapable of achieving anything useful. It is the software, not the hardware that allows you to write letters, send emails, process pictures, play games, etc. and you, the user, can largely ignore the clever electronics and precise engineering of the hardware that does as it is told by the software.

So why are we asking you to spend some time reading this brief introduction to computer hardware? The reason is that many of the frustrations that new users of computers experience are due to a lack of understanding of how the hardware works. It's little use having digital cameras and sophisticated scanners and printers if you are unsure how they connect to your computer (or the things you should check first when they go wrong). A brief introduction to the primary parts of a hardware system is given below(See Figure 6. 1).

These components can usually be put together with little knowledge to build a computer. The motherboard is a main part of a computer that connects all devices together. The memory card (s), graphics card and processor are mounted directly onto the motherboard (the processor in a socket and the memory and graphics cards in expansion slots). The mass storage is connected to it with cables and can be installed in the computer case or in a separate case. This is the same for the keyboard and mouse, except that they are external and connect to the I/O panel on the back of the computer. The monitor is also connected to the I/O panel, either through an onboard port on the motherboard, or a port on the graphics card.

Several functions (implemented by chipsets) can be integrated into the motherboard, typically USB and network, but also graphics and sound. Even if these are present, a separate card can be added if what is available isn't sufficient. The graphics and sound cards can have a break out box to keep the analog parts away from the electromagnetic radiation inside the computer case. For really large amounts of data, a tape drive can be used or (extra) hard disks can be put together in an external case.

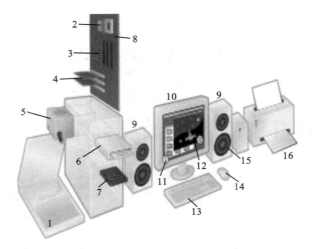

Figure 6.1 An exploded view of a modern personal computer and peripherals
1—Scanner; 2—CPU(Microprocessor); 3—Primary storage (RAM); 4—Expansion cards;
5—Power supply; 6—Optical disc drive; 7—Secondary storage; 8—Motherboard; 9—Speakers;
10—Monitor; 11—System software; 12—Application software; 13—Keyboard; 14—Mouse;
15—External hard disk; 16—Printer

The hardware capabilities of personal computers can sometimes be extended by the addition of expansion cards connected via an expansion bus. Some standard peripheral buses often used for adding expansion cards in personal computers as of 2005 are PCI, AGP (a high-speed PCI bus dedicated to graphics adapters), and PCI Express. Most personal computers as of 2005 have multiple physical PCI expansion slots. Many also include an AGP bus and expansion slot or a PCI Express bus and one or more expansion slots, but few PCs contain both buses.

1) Central processing unit (CPU)

The central processing unit is the essential component of a computer because it executes the programs and controls the operation of all the hardware. Powerful computers may have several processors handling different tasks, although there will need to be one central processing unit controlling the flow of instructions and data through the subsidiary processors.

In older computers this circuitry is formerly on several printed circuit boards, but in PCs a single integrated circuit. Nearly all PCs contain a type of CPU known as a microprocessor. The microprocessor often plugs into the motherboard using one of many different types of sockets. IBM PC compatible computers use an x86-compatible processor, usually made by Intel, AMD, VIA Technologies or Transmeta. Apple Macintosh computers are initially built with the Motorola 680x0 family of processors, then switch to the PowerPC series (a RISC architecture jointly developed by Apple Computer, IBM and Motorola), but as of 2006, Apple switch again, this time to x86-compatible processors by Intel. Modern CPUs are equipped with a fan attached via heat sink.

2) Storage

A storage is the part that stores programs, original data and intermediary results. Its basic function is to put in (write in) or to take out (read out) information into or from the given place. It stores information primarily by recording the electric pulse being on or off. It's divided into internal and external storages.

Internal storage The internal storage (also called main memory) is a fast storage linked to ALU and controller to access information electrically. There are two internal storages in all computers: RAM (random access memory) and ROM (read only memory). When data and programs are written into or read out from storage through computers, RAM will change its status. However, ROM is designed to be read only and remain unchangeable. Information can't be written into ROM.

External storage External storages are those components that are put outside mainframe with great capacity and slow access speed. As a supplementary unit to internal storages, they are designed to exchange information in batches rather than with CPU. Examples of external storages are disks (floppy and rigid disk) and CDs.

3) Peripherals

Peripherals refer to all the other devices attached to computers that handle input and output. Input devices include keyboards, mice, trackballs, digitizers, disk drives. Output devices include screens, printers and plotters.

2. Software

Computer software is often regarded as anything but hardware, meaning that the "hard" are the parts that are tangible while the "soft" part is the intangible objects inside the computer. Software encompasses an extremely wide array of products and technologies developed using different techniques like programming languages, scripting languages or even microcode or a FPGA state. The types of software include web pages developed by technologies like HTML, PHP, Perl, JSP, ASP.NET, XML, and desktop applications like Microsoft Word, OpenOffice developed by technologies like C, C++, Java, C# etc. Software usually runs on underlying software operating systems such as the Microsoft Windows or Linux. Software also includes video games and the logic systems of modern consumer devices such as automobiles, televisions, toasters etc.

1) Relationship to computer hardware

Computer software is so called to distinguish it from computer hardware, which encompasses the physical interconnections and devices required to store and execute (or run) the software. At the lowest level, software consists of a machine language specific to an individual processor. A machine language consists of groups of binary values signifying processor instructions which change the state of the computer from its preceding state. Software is an ordered sequence of instructions for changing the state of the computer hardware in a particular sequence. It is usually written in high-level programming languages that are easier and more efficient for humans to use (closer to natural language) than machine language. High-level languages are compiled or interpreted into machine language object code. Software may also be written in an assembly language, essentially, a mnemonic representation of a machine language using a natural language alphabet. Assembly language must be assembled into object code via an assembler.

The term "software" is first used in this sense by John W. Tukey in 1958. In computer science and software engineering, computer software is all computer programs.

2) Types of software

Practical computer systems divide software systems into three major classes: system software, programming software and application software, although the distinction is arbitrary, and often blurred.

(1) System software.

System software helps run the computer hardware and computer system. It includes device drivers, operating systems, servers, utilities, Faraware and windowing systems.

The purpose of system software is to unburden the applications programmer from the details of the particular computer complex being used, including such accessory devices as communications, printers, readers, displays, keyboards etc. And also to partition the computer's resources such as memory and processor time in a safe and stable manner.

(2) Programming software.

Programming software usually provides tools to assist a programmer in writing computer programs, and software using different programming languages in a more convenient way. The tools include compilers, debuggers, interpreters, linkers and text editors.

An Integrated Development Environment (IDE) is a single application that attempts to manage all these functions.

(3) Application software.

Application software allows end users to accomplish one or more specific (not directly computer development related) tasks. Typical applications include industrial automation, business software, computer games, telecommunications, databases, educational software and medical software.

Application software exists for and has impacted a wide variety of topics.

3) Software architecture

Users often see things differently than programmers. People who use modern general purpose computers (as opposed to embedded systems, analog computers, supercomputers etc.) usually see three layers of software performing a variety of tasks: platform, application, and user software.

Platform software: Platform includes the firmware, device drivers, an operating system, and typically a graphical user interface which, in total, allow a user to interact with the computer and its peripherals (associated equipment). Platform software often comes bundled with the computer. On a PC you will usually have the ability to change the platform software.

Application software: Application software or applications are what most people think of when they think of software. Typical examples include office suites and video games. Application software is often purchased separately from computer hardware. Sometimes applications are bundled with the computer, but that does not change the fact that they run as independent applications. Applications are almost always independent programs from the operating system, though they are often tailored for specific platforms. Most users think of compilers, databases, and other "system software" as applications.

User-written software: End-user development tailors systems to meet users' specific needs. User software includes spreadsheet templates, word processor macros, scientific simulations, and scripts for graphics and animations. Even email filters are a kind of user software. Users create this software themselves and often overlook how important it is. Depending on how competently the user-written software has been integrated into default application packages, many users may not be aware of the distinction between the original packages, and what has been added by co-workers.

Words and Expressions

electronic [ilek'trɔnik] a. 电子的 n. [-s] 电子学;电子设备
case [keis] n. 情形,情况;箱;案例
central ['sentrəl] a. 中心的,中央的
Central Processing Unit(CPU)　中央处理器
socket ['sɔkit] n. 插座,插口
compatible [kəm'pætəbl] a. 能共处的,可并立的,适合的;[计算机]互相兼容的
sink [siŋk] n. 接收端;沟渠;污水槽 v. 下沉,使……低落,陷于
motherboard ['mʌðəbɔːd] n. 母板
main memory　主存储器
RAM (random access memory)　随机存储器
ROM (read only memory)　只读存储器
interface ['intə(ː)ˌfeis] n. 接触面;[计算机]界面,接口
mass [mæs] n. 块;大多数;质量 a. 群众的,大规模的 v. 使……集合
assembler [ə'semblə] n. 汇编程序
compiler [kəm'pailə] n. 编译器;编译程序
interpreter [in'təːpritə] n. 译码机,翻译机,解释[翻译]程序
linker ['liŋkə] n. [计算机]链接器
server ['səːvə] n. 服伺者,服勤者;[计算机]伺服器
utilities pl. 城市管理服务行业;公用工程
firmware ['fəːmˌwɛə] n. 固件
animation [æni'meiʃən] n. 活泼;卡通制作

Notes

1. The central processing unit is the essential component of a computer because it is the part that executes the programs and controls the operation of all the hardware.

(1) 这里 that 引导的定语从句,作 the part 的定语。

(2) 全句可翻译为:中央处理单元是计算机的基本组成部分,因为它是执行程序和控制所

有硬件运行的部分。

2. Even if these are present, a separate card can be added if what is available isn't sufficient.

(1) 这里"these"指的是 several functions。

(2) 全句可翻译为：即使上述功能都有，如果有功能不能满足的话，可以加一个单独的卡。

3. Computer software is so called to distinguish it from computer hardware, which encompasses the physical interconnections and devices required to store and execute (or run) the software.

(1) 这里 so called 翻译成"如此叫做……"、"如此称谓……"，"which"这里指 computer hardware。

(2) 全句可翻译为：计算机软件如此称谓是为了与计算机硬件区分开来，计算机硬件包括用于存储以及执行（或运行）软件所必需的物理互联连接和设备。

Reading Material

Personal Computer Hardware

The newspaper adverts scream out prices, and include seemingly meaningless abbreviations such as MHz, ATA-100, DDR, XGA. Do you know what these buzzwords really mean? Does anyone?

The PC may be the single most important tool for many workers, but because it is often purchased in a high street camera store or even a supermarket, it is often treated as a commodity item, almost a "white good" such as a fridge, freezer or microwave.

First the good news: There are no bad Personal Computer systems. The least powerful system available today is better than the most expensive system of a few years ago. High quality components are produced in such large numbers at such low prices, that there is no profit building substandard systems.

The bad news is that the process doesn't stop, and the most expensive or most powerful system you buy today will be (practically) obsolete next year.

If you want to know how a PC works and what all the jargon means, this section will attempt to answer your questions. No technical background is assumed, and even very complex issues will be explained in terms that everyone can understand.

Who Made It?

Your computer wasn't made by the company from which you bought it. If you buy a car from Ford, you expect the frame, engine, transmission, generator, and other parts to come from Ford or at least be built to Ford specifications. That isn't how the computer industry works. The companies that sell computers and whose names you know, such as Dell, Gateway, IBM, and Compaq, don't make any of the important parts. Instead, they assemble a computer from parts made by other companies.

Your computer was really made by companies such as Asus, Abit, ATI, and AMD. This is really an international business with companies scattered around the world. But they are not scattered uniformly. For reasons that are not clear, different countries and regions seem to specialize in particular parts. The US companies build the CPU (Intel, AMD). The motherboard comes from Taiwan (Asus, Abit, Shuttle, MSI). Disks come from Singapore or Indonesia (Seagate, Western Digital, IBM, Maxtor). Memory most often comes from Korea. The external case and the power supply come from any of a dozen Mainland China companies.

You can buy the components from any number of sites on the internet and assemble a computer yourself, but you won't save any money this way. The big computer makers buy parts in lots of a thousand, packaged in bulk to save packing and shipping. Twelve screws attach the motherboard to the mounts on the case. Four screws attach the disk to the disk bay. Then the cables all plug into sockets. An unskilled worker can be quickly trained to assemble a computer every few minutes.

The advanced technology is in the manufacture of the chips, not the final assembly of the finished product. A CPU chip is constructed in a plant that costs billions. The building is on shock absorbers because the vibration generated by passing trucks would disturb the process! People wear spacesuits not to protect them from the environment, but to protect the chips from flakes of loose skin or the particles we exhale.

Then the chip is packaged in plastic and shipped out. There is a socket on the motherboard and a mark to line up the corners of the chip to the corresponding corners of the socket. Lift a lever on the side of the socket and the chip simply drops into place. Lower the lever and the chip is locked in place. It is harder to tie a shoelace than to install a CPU chip on a motherboard. Plugging in the other components is only marginally more difficult.

Computers can be assembled from interchangeable components made by dozens of different vendors because the plugs, sockets and cables that connect the components are standardized. More frequently, however, the first company to build something creates a de facto standard. Standards last for a long time, but not forever.

The round connectors on the motherboard for the keyboard and mouse are called "PS2" ports because they were introduced by IBM in 1987 with its PS/2 line of computers (no, this has nothing to do with "PS2" in the sense of the Sony PlayStation 2 game console). For the next 15 years they have served as a simple low speed interface for these two serial input devices. However, the collection of standard "legacy" connectors in the back of every computer has now become obsolete. Instead of PS2, serial and parallel ports, the keyboard, mouse, printer, and scanner can all be connected to a computer through the new standard, smaller, and more flexible USB ports. Unfortunately, consumers still expect the old connectors to be present.

In 1987 IBM also introduced a new 15 pin interface between the video card and CRT monitor. (CRT stands for Cathode Ray Tube and is the same basic mechanism for providing images on the monitor screen as is inside the domestic television). It is called the "VGA" port. This standard interface has survived because it is flexible enough to adapt to much higher resolutions and refresh rates used in modern monitors. Today, however, if you use a flat LCD display panel, you will get a sharper picture and more accurate colors using the new larger digital DVI connector.

Lesson 2 Microprocessor

1. The Architecture of Microprocessor

The architecture of Microprocessor is shown in Figure 6.2. The term microprocessor typically refers to the central processing unit (CPU) of a microcomputer, containing the arithmetic logic unit (ALU) and the control units. It is typically implemented on a single LSI chip. This separates the "brains" of the operation from the other units of the computer.

The microprocessor contains the arithmetic logic unit (ALU) and the control unit for a microcomputer. It is connected to memory and I/O by buses which carry information between the units.

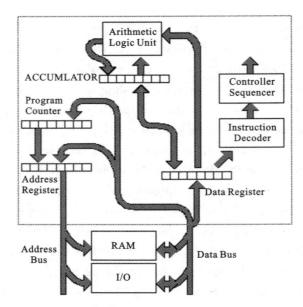

Figure 6.2 An example of microprocessor architecture

1) Arithmetic Logic Unit

All the arithmetic operations of a microprocessor take place in the arithmetic logic unit (ALU). Figure 6.3 shows an arithmetic logic unit. Using a combination of gates and flip-flops, numbers can be added in less than a microsecond, even in small personal computers. The operation to be performed is specified by signals from the control unit. The data upon which operations are performed can come from memory or an external input. The data may be combined in some way with the contents of the accumulator and the results are typically placed in the accumulator. From there they may be transferred to memory or to an output unit.

2) The Accumulator

The accumulator is the principal register of the arithmetic logic unit of a microprocessor. Registers are sets of flip-flops which can hold data. The accumulator typically holds the first

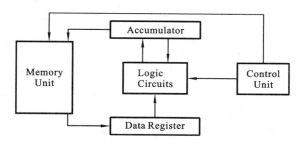

Figure 6.3 An arithmetic logic unit

piece of data for a calculation. If a number from memory is added to that date, the sum replaces the original data in the accumulator. It is the repository for successive results of arithmetic operations, which may then be transferred to memory, to an output device, etc.

3) Buses: The exchange of information(See Figure 6.4)

Information is transferred between units of the microcomputer by collections of conductors called buses.

There will be one conductor for each bit of information to be passed, e. g. , 16 lines for a 16 bit address bus. There will be address, control, and data buses.

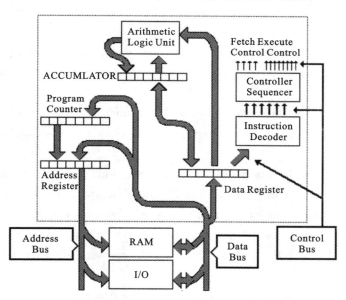

Figure 6.4 The exchange of information

4) Control Unit of Microprocessor

The control unit of a microprocessor directs the operation of the other units by providing timing and control signals. It is the function of the microcomputer to execute programs which are stored in memory in the form of instructions and data. The control unit contains the necessary logic to interpret instructions and to generate the signals necessary for the execution of those instructions. The descriptive words "fetch" and "execute" are used to describe the actions of the control unit. It fetches an instruction by sending an address and a read command to the memory unit. The instruction at that memory address is transferred to the control unit for decoding. It then generates the necessary signals to execute the instruction.

The computer you are using to read this page uses a microprocessor to do its work. The microprocessor is the heart of any normal computer, whether it is a desktop machine, a server or a laptop. The microprocessor you are using might be a Pentium, a K6, a PowerPC, a Sparc or any of the many other brands and types of microprocessors, but they all do approximately the same thing in approximately the same way.

2. Microprocessor Logic

To understand how a microprocessor works, it ishelpful to look inside and learn about the logic used to create one. In the process you can also learn about assembly language—the native language of a microprocessor—and many of the things that engineers can do to boost the speed of a processor.

A microprocessor executes a collection of machine instructions that tell the processor what to do. Based on the instructions, a microprocessor does three basic things:

Using its ALU (Arithmetic Logic Unit), a microprocessor can perform mathematical operations like addition, subtraction, multiplication and division. Modern microprocessors contain complete floating point processors that can perform extremely sophisticated operations on large floating point numbers.

A microprocessor can move data from one memory location to another.

A microprocessor can make decisions and jump to a new set of instructions based on those decisions.

There may be very sophisticated things that a microprocessor does, but those are its three basic activities. Figure 6.5 shows an extremely simple microprocessor capable of doing those three things.

This is about as simple as a microprocessor gets. This microprocessor has:

- an address bus (that may be 8, 16 or 32 bits wide) that sends an address to memory;
- a data bus (that may be 8, 16 or 32 bits wide) that can send data to memory or receive data from memory;
- an RD (read) and WR (write) line to tell the memory whether it wants to set or get the addressed location;
- a clock line that lets a clock pulse sequence the processor;
- a reset line that resets the program counter to zero (or whatever) and restarts execution.

Let's assume that both the address and data buses are 8 bits wide in this example. Here are the components of this simple microprocessor:

Registers A, B and C are simply latches made out of flip-flops.

The address latch is just like Registers A, B and C.

The program counter is a latch with the extra ability to increment by 1 when told to do so, and also to reset to zero when told to do so.

The ALU could be as simple as an 8-bit adder, or it might be able to add, subtract,

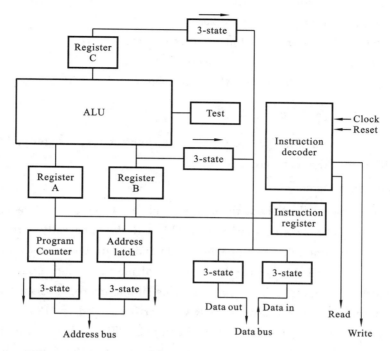

Figure 6.5 The diagram of an extremely simple microprocessor

multiply and divide 8-bit values. Let's assume the latter here.

The test register is a special latch that can hold values from comparisons performed in the ALU. An ALU can normally compare two numbers and determine if they are equal, if one is greater than the other, etc. The test register can also normally hold a carry bit from the last stage of the adder. It stores these values in flip-flops and then the instruction decoder can use the values to make decisions.

There are six boxes marked "3-State" in the diagram. These are tri-state buffers. A tri-state buffer can pass a 1, a 0 or it can essentially disconnect its output (imagine a switch that totally disconnects the output line from the wire that the output is heading toward). A tri-state buffer allows multiple outputs to connect to a wire, but only one of them to actually drive a 1 or a 0 onto the line.

The instruction register and instruction decoder are responsible for controlling all of the other components.

Although they are not shown in this diagram, there would be control lines from the instruction decoder that would:

- tell register A to latch the value currently on the data bus;
- tell register B to latch the value currently on the data bus;
- tell register C to latch the value currently output by the ALU;
- tell the program counter register to latch the value currently on the data bus;
- tell the address register to latch the value currently on the data bus;
- tell the instruction register to latch the value currently on the data bus;

- tell the program counter to increment;
- tell the program counter to reset to zero;
- activate any of the six tri-state buffers (six separate lines);
- tell the ALU what operation to perform;
- tell the test register to latch the ALU's test bits;
- activate the RD line;
- activate the WR line.

Coming into the instruction decoder are the bits from the test register and the clock line, as well as the bits from the instruction register.

3. Microprocessor Memory

The previous section talked about the address and data buses, as well as the RD and WR lines. These buses and lines connect either to RAM or ROM—generally both. In our sample microprocessor, we have an address bus 8 bits wide and a data bus 8 bits wide. That means that the microprocessor can address (2^8) 256 bytes of memory, and it can read or write 8 bits of the memory at a time. Let's assume that this simple microprocessor has 128 bytes of ROM starting at address 0 and 128 bytes of RAM starting at address 128.

ROM stands for read-only memory. A ROM chip(See Figure 6.6) is programmed with a permanent collection of pre-set bytes. The address bus tells the ROM chip which byte to get and place on the data bus. When the RD line changes state, the ROM chip presents the selected byte onto the data bus.

Figure 6.6　A ROM chip

Figure 6.7　A RAM chip

RAM stands for random-access memory. RAM contains bytes of information, and the microprocessor can read or write to those bytes depending on whether the RD or WR line is signaled. One problem with today's RAM chips (See Figure 6.7) is that they forget everything once the power goes off. That is why the computer needs ROM.

By the way, nearly all computers contain some amount of ROM (it is possible to create a simple computer that contains no RAM—many microcontrollers do this by placing a handful of RAM bytes on the processor chip itself—but generally impossible to create one that contains no ROM). On a PC, the ROM is called the BIOS (Basic Input/Output System). When the microprocessor starts, it begins executing instructions it finds in the BIOS. The BIOS instructions do things like test the hardware in the machine, and then it goes to the hard disk to fetch the boot sector. This boot sector is another small program, and the BIOS stores it in RAM after reading it off the disk. The microprocessor then begins executing the boot sector's instructions from RAM. The boot sector program will tell the microprocessor to fetch something else from the hard disk into RAM, which the microprocessor then executes, and so on. This is how the microprocessor loads and executes the entire operating system.

4. Microprocessor Instructions

Even the incredibly simple microprocessor shown in the previous example will have a fairly large set of instructions that it can perform. The collection of instructions is implemented as bit patterns, each one of which has a different meaning when loaded into the instruction register. Humans are not particularly good at remembering bit patterns, so a set of short words are defined to represent the different bit patterns. This collection of words is called the assembly language of the processor. An assembler can translate the words into their bit patterns very easily, and then the output of the assembler is placed in memory for the microprocessor to execute.

5. Microprocessor Performance and Trends

The number of transistors available has a huge effect on the performance of a processor. As seen earlier, a typical instruction in a processor like an 8088 took 15 clock cycles to execute. Because of the design of the multiplier, it took approximately 80 cycles just to do one 16-bit multiplication on the 8088. With more transistors, much more powerful multipliers capable of single-cycle speeds become possible.

More transistors also allow for a technology called pipelining. In a pipelined architecture, instruction execution overlaps. So even though it might take five clock cycles to execute each instruction, there can be five instructions in various stages of execution simultaneously. That way it looks like one instruction completes every clock cycle.

Many modern processors have multiple instruction decoders, each with its own pipeline. This allows for multiple instruction streams, which means that more than one instruction can complete during each clock cycle. This technique can be quite complex to implement, so it takes lots of transistors.

Trends The trend in processor design has primarily been toward full 32-bit ALUs with fast floating point processors built in and pipelined execution with multiple instruction streams. The newest thing in processor design is 64-bit ALUs, and people are expected to have these processors in their home PCs in the next decade. There has also been a tendency toward special instructions (like the MMX instructions) that make certain operations particularly efficient, and the addition of hardware virtual memory support and L1 caching on the processor chip. All of these trends push up the transistor count, leading to the multi-million transistor powerhouses available today. These processors can execute about one billion instructions per second!

Words and Expressions

microprocessor [maikrəuˈprəusesə] *n.* [计算机]微处理器
arithmetic logic unit   算术逻辑单元
accumulator [əˈkjuːmjuleitə] *n.* 累加器
opcode *n.* 作业码
assembly [əˈsembli] *n.* 集合；集会；装配
assembly language   汇编语言

Notes

1. All the arithmetic operations of a microprocessor take place in the arithmetic logic unit (ALU).

(1) take place in：在……发生，这里翻译成"进行"

(2) 全句可翻译为：所有微处理器的运算是在算术逻辑单元(ALU)进行的。

2. The accumulator typically holds the first piece of data for a calculation.

(1) 句中 hold 是"握住，拿着，持有"的意思，这里翻译成"锁定"。

(2) 全句可翻译为：累加器主要锁定第一条数据段用于计算。

3. The address bus tells the ROM chip which byte to get and place on the data bus.

(1) 句中 which 引导的是宾语从句，作 the ROM chip 的宾语补语。

(2) 全句可翻译为：地址总线告诉 ROM 芯片获取和放在数据总线的字节。

Reading Material

64-bit Microprocessors

Sixty-four-bit processors have been with us since 1992, and in the 21st century they have started to become mainstream. Both Intel and AMD (See Figure 6.8) have introduced 64-bit chips, and the Mac G5 sports a 64-bit processor. Sixty-four-bit processors have 64-bit ALUs, 64-bit registers, 64-bit buses and so on.

One reason why the world needs 64-bit processors is because of their enlarged address spaces. Thirty-two-bit chips are often constrained to a maximum of 2 GB or 4 GB of RAM access. That sounds like a lot, given that most home computers currently use only 256 MB to 512 MB of RAM. However, a 4-GB limit can be a severe problem for server machines and machines running large databases. And even home machines will start bumping up against the 2 GB or 4 GB limit pretty soon if current trends continue. A 64-bit chip has none of these constraints because a 64-bit RAM address space is essentially infinite for the foreseeable future—2^{64} bytes of RAM is something on the order of a billion gigabytes of RAM.

With a 64-bit address bus and wide, high-speed data buses on the motherboard, 64-bit machines also offer faster I/O (input/output) speeds to things like hard disk

Figure 6.8   Photo courtesy AMD

drives and video cards. These features can greatly increase system performance.

Servers can definitely benefit from 64 bits, but what about normal users? Beyond the RAM solution, it is not clear that a 64-bit chip offers "normal users" any real, tangible benefits at the moment. They can process data (very complex data features lots of real numbers) faster. People doing video editing and people doing photographic editing on very large images benefit from this kind of computing power. High-end games will also benefit, once they are re-coded to take advantage of 64-bit features. But the average user who is reading e-mail, browsing the Web and editing Word documents is not really using the processor in that way.

Lesson 3 Bus Network Technology

1. Introduction

A bus network topology is a network architecture in which a set of clients are connected via a shared communications line, called a bus shown in Figure 6.9. There are several common instances of the bus architecture, including one in the motherboard of most computers, and those in some versions of Ethernet networks.

Bus networks are the simplest way to connect multiple clients, but may have problems when two clients want to transmit at the same time on the same bus. Thus systems which use bus network architectures normally have some scheme of collision handling or collision avoidance for communication on the bus, quite often using Carrier Sense Multiple Access or the presence of a bus master which controls access to the shared bus resource.

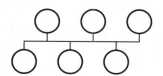

Figure 6.9 Image showing bus network layout

A true bus network is passive—the computers on the bus simply listen for a signal; they are not responsible for moving the signal along. However, many active architectures can also be described as a "bus", as they provide the same logical functions as a passive bus. For example, switched Ethernet can still be regarded as a logical bus network, if not a physical one. Indeed, the hardware may be abstracted away completely in the case of a software bus.

With the dominance of switched Ethernet over passive Ethernet, passive bus networks are uncommon in wired networks. However, almost all current wireless networks can be viewed as examples of passive bus networks, with radio propagation serving as the shared passive medium.

The bus topology makes the addition of new devices straightforward. The term used to describe clients is station or workstation in this type of network. Bus network topology uses a broadcast channel which means that all attached stations can hear every transmission and all stations have equal priority in using the network to transmit data.

2. Advantages and Disadvantages of A Bus Network

Advantages:

- easy to implement and extend;
- well suited for temporary or small networks not requiring high speeds (quick setup);
- cheaper than other topologies;
- cost effective as only a single cable is used;
- cable faults are easily identified.

Disadvantages:
- Limited cable length and number of stations;
- If there is a problem with the cable, the entire network goes down;
- Maintenance costs may be higher in the long run;
- Performance degrades as additional computers are added or on heavy traffic;
- Proper termination is required (loop must be in closed path);
- Significant Capacitive Load (each bus transaction must be able to stretch to most distant link);
- It works best with limited number of nodes;
- It is slower than the other topologies.

3. Fieldbus

There have emerged literally hundreds of fieldbuses developed by different companies and organisations all over the world. The term fieldbus covers many different industrial network protocols. Most fieldbus protocols have been developed and supported by specific PLC manufacturers. The accompanying table summarises some of the main ones.

At the lowest level are the sensor networks, which are originally designed primarily for digital (on/off) interface. These are fast and effective, but with only limited applications beyond relatively simple machine-control. ASI (actuator/sensor interface) is popular in Europe, while Seriplex is a US development. ASI—perhaps the simplest and least expensive fieldbus. ASI was developed by a consortium of European automation companies, which saw need for networking the simplest devices at the lowest level. ASI is easy to configure and low in cost. It is most often used for proximity sensors, photoeyes, limit switches, valves and indicators in applications like packaging machines and material handling systems. ASI is designed for small systems employing discrete I/O. It allows for up to 31 slaves, which can provide for up to four inputs and four outputs each for a total of 248 I/O.

Fieldbus was developed by GESPAC as a comprehensive remote I/O system, based on distributed intelligence and peer-to-peer communication. Firmware functions are built into each Fieldbus I/O module and allow basic capabilities such as pulse count, delay before action and sending/receiving messages to/from other modules on the network.

Bitbus was originally introduced by Intel as a way to add remote I/O capability to Multibus systems. This original fieldbus is one of the most mature and most broadly used networks today. Bitbus allows programs to be downloaded and executed in a remote node for truly distributed system configurations.

WorldFIP provides a deterministic and reliable scheme for communicating process variables (generated by sensors and executed by actuators) and messages (events, configuration commands) at up to 1Mbit per second on inexpensive twisted pairs cables. FIP uses an original mechanism where the bus arbitrator broadcasts a variable identifier to all nodes on the network, triggering the node producing that variable to place its value on the network. Once on the network, all modules which need that information "consume" it simultaneously. This concept results in a decentralised database of variables in the nodes and remarkable real-time characteristics. This feature eliminates the notion of node address and makes it possible to design truly distributed process control systems.

At the next level are the device buses, which provide analogue and digital support for more complex instruments and products. DeviceNet interfaces very well with programmable controllers. However, it is still only a local, device-level network, operating typically with up to 64 points within about 300 m. Profibus DP and Interbus are somewhat comparable to DeviceNet and are excellent general-purpose device-level networks.

Profibus is a fieldbus network designed for deterministic communication between computers and PLCs. It is the most widely accepted international networking standard. Nearly universal in Europe and also popular in North America, South America and parts of Africa and Asia, Profibus can handle large amounts of data at high speed and serve the needs of large installations. Based on a real-time capable asynchronous token bus principle, Profibus defines multi-master and master-slave communication relations, with cyclic or acyclic access, allowing transfer rates of up to 500 kbit/s. The physical layer (two-wire RS485), the data link layer 2 and the application layer are all standardised. Profibus distinguishes between confirmed and unconfirmed services, allowing process communication, broadcast and multi-tasking. Profibus DP is a master/slave polling network with the ability to upload/download configuration data and precisely synchronise multiple devices on the network. Multiple masters are possible in Profibus, but the outputs of any device can only be assigned to one master. There is no power on the bus.

Interbus is one of the very first Fieldbuses to achieve widespread popularity. It continues to be popular because of its versatility, speed, diagnostic and auto-addressing capabilities. Physically, it has the appearance of being a typical line-and-drop based network, but in reality it is a serial ring shift register. Each slave node has two connectors, one which receives data and one which passes data onto the next slave.

Controller Area Network (CAN) is a fast serial bus that is designed to provide an efficient, reliable and very economical link between sensors and actuators. CAN uses a twisted pair cable to communicate at speeds up to 1 Mbit/s with up to 40 devices. Originally developed to simplify the wiring in automobiles, its use has spread in machine and factory automation products. CAN provides standardised communication objects for process data, service data, network management, synchronisation, time-stamping and emergency messages. It is the basis of several sensor buses, such as DeviceNet (Allen-Bradley), Honeywell's SDS or Can Application Layer (CAL) from CAN in Automation, group of international users and manufacturers, which is over 300 companies strong. CANOpen is a family of profiles based on CAN which was developed within the CAN in Automation group.

The extensive error detection and correction features of CAN can easily withstand the harsh physical and electrical environment presented by a car. SDS was developed by Bosch for networking most of the distributed electrical devices throughout an automobile, initially for eliminating the large and expensive wiring harnesses in Mercedes.

DeviceNet is a manifestation of CAN adapted for critical factory networking purposes. At the next level are the "control" networks, which include ControlNet, developed by Allen-Bradley and utilised by Honeywell, overlapping with some of the functionality intended to be provided by Profibus-FMS and Fieldbus SP-50—Profibus FMS uses the same physical layer as Profibus DP but allows multi-master, asynchronous, peer-to-peer communication. FMS and DP can operate simultaneously on the same network. ControlNet was conceived as the ultimate high-level fieldbus network and was designed to meet several high performance automation and process control criteria. Of primary importance is the ability to communicate with each other with 100% determinism, while achieving faster response than traditional master/slave poll/strobe networks.

LONWorks operates over greater distances and is a practical peer-to-peer network, extensible to many thousands of points, though it can be comparatively slow and more complex. Profibus PA is a specification for using Profibus in intrinsically safe applications. It provides improved performance at the fieldbus level, for instruments and controls, replacing the features and functions which are provided by HART, originally developed for transmitter calibration and diagnostics. The primary differences are in speed, complexity and distance. LONWorks also extends into this realm.

Foundation Fieldbus is a sophisticated, object-oriented protocol that uses multiple messaging formats and allows a controller to recognize a rich set of configuration and parameter information ("device description") from devices that have been plugged into the bus. Foundation Fieldbus even allows a device to transmit parameters relating to the estimated reliability of a particular piece of data. Foundation Fieldbus uses a scheduler to guarantee the delivery of messages, so issues of determinism and repeatability are solidly addressed (determinism means knowing absolute worst-case response times with 100% certainty). Each segment of the network contains one scheduler.

In the United States, DeviceNet, Profibus DP, and Foundation Fieldbus H1 have taken their places as the dominant open systems for connecting industrial devices. DeviceNet is the leader in automotive, materials handling, and semiconductor applications, while Foundation Fieldbus is taking the lead in process control. Profibus is strong in both realms, as well as being the dominant technology in Europe.

Since its introduction, DeviceNet has grown rapidly in the UK and, according to DeviceNet UK Chairman Richard McLaughlin, now boasts more than 320 companies worldwide actively developing compatible products within the Open DeviceNet Vendor Association (ODVA). These include sensors, actuators and smart devices.

Against this backdrop, frustrating for many, came the re-emergence of the Ethernet. Ten years ago, no serious design engineer would have suggested using Ethernet for networking factory floor devices. Ethernet, the technology for office automation, was developed more than 20 years ago as a high-speed serial data-transfer network. It has become a worldwide standard and is now the most widely used Local Area Network (LAN) in existence. More than 85% of all installed network connections in the world are Ethernet. But it was deliberately ignored for industrial applications, and for good reasons; its lack of determinism and robustness made it a feeble, unpredictable companion for the shop floor. Yet today, the scene has almost reversed. Why such a radical change? Over the past few years there have been many enhancements to the Ethernet standard, especially in areas of determinism, speed, and message prioritisation. So there is no longer any reason why Ethernet cannot be used to build deterministic fieldbus networks that are cost-effective and open. And since Ethernet is already the network choice for business computing, its presence at the control level will make sensor-to-boardroom integration a reality. Another good reason manufacturers are looking at Ethernet is the coming explosion of factory floor data traffic. As smart sensors and various devices on the plant floor eat up the available bandwidth over the next four years, manufacturing plant information generated by PLCs and control systems is expected to increase from 10 to 30 times the current level. Ethernet, with its Internet-friendly TCP/IP protocol, is ideally positioned. It is popular, plummeting in price and being propelled by sheer market demand.

So Ethernet is poised to penetrate deep into the factory network hierarchy, down to the I/O level. That makes some programmable controller (PLC) manufacturers uncomfortable. Even the recently arrived fieldbus systems are beginning to feel the impact-some say threat-of Ethernet. Furthermore, the DeviceNet, Profibus and Foundation Fieldbus protocols are all available or in development as application layers for Ethernet. And most PLCs now offer Ethernet as a standard networking option in addition to their fieldbus of choice. High Speed Ethernet (HSE) is a 100 Mbit Ethernet standard that uses the same protocol and objects as Foundation Fieldbus H1, on TCP/IP. The next generation of Ethernet is called Gigabit Ethernet, which is capable of 1 Gbits/sec. This will bridge the gap between the necessity of industrially hardened wiring capability and the growing need for process data via business LANs and the Internet. Most firms cannot afford to have a DeviceNet or Profibus specialist on staff who thoroughly understands the network protocol. Even if a company could afford such a person, it is unlikely fieldbus would be their specialty. However, almost every company has a network administrator who is well versed and specialises in Ethernet protocol, making Ethernet all the more attractive for industrial control.

Words and Expressions

Ethernet   以太网
client ['klaiənt] *n.* 顾客;委托人;客户
collision [kə'liʒən] *n.* 碰撞,冲突
carrier ['kæriə] *n.* 运送者;媒介物;带菌者
dominance ['dɔminəns] *n.* 支配(控制,统治,权威,优势)

fieldbus　现场总线，同 field bus
Fieldbus Foundation　现场总线基金会
ASI　空速指示器。此处的 ASI 是 actuator/sensor interface 的缩略词，为执行机构及传感器接口
interbus [ˈintəbʌs] n. 联络母线
Bitbus　位总线网
controller area network　控域网，控制局域网
Lonworks　局部操作网络
prioritization　优先级
protocol [ˈprəutəkɔl] n. 草案，协议；礼仪 vt. 拟订议定书
High Speed Ethernet(HSE)　高速以太网
CANOpen　CAN 总线中的一族
DeviceNet　一种底层设备现场总线

Notes

1. Honeywell 霍尼韦尔国际（财富 500 强公司之一，总部所在地美国，主要经营航空航天产品）。

2. Allen-Bradley 艾伦－布拉德利是罗克韦尔公司旗下的一个世界知名品牌，其主要产品包括标准和中压变频器。

3. Open DeviceNet Vendor Association（开放式设备网络供货商协会），1995 年 6 月成立，简称 ODVA。2000 年 7 月正式成立中国电器工业协会现场总线委员会（ODVA CHINA）。

4. However, almost every company has a network administrator who is well versed and specialises in Ethernet protocol, making Ethernet all the more attractive for industrial control.

（1）句中 who 引导定语从句，making 现在分词作状语，它在句子中作一个目的状语。

（2）全句可翻译为：但是，几乎每家公司有一名网络管理员，他们熟悉和擅长以太网协议，这使以太网在工业控制方面更具吸引力。

Reading Material

Introduction to the Controller Area Network (CAN)

1) Introduction

The CAN bus is developed by BOSCH as a multi-master, message broadcast system that specifies a maximum signaling rate of 1 megabit per second (bps). Unlike a traditional network such as USB or Ethernet, CAN does not send large blocks of data point-to-point from node A to node B under the supervision of a central bus master. In a CAN network, many short messages like temperature or RPM are broadcast to the entire network, which provides for data consistency in every node of the system. Once CAN basics such as message format, message identifiers, and bit-wise arbitration—a major benefit of the CAN signaling scheme are explained, a CAN bus implementation is examined, typical waveforms presented, and transceiver features examined.

2) The CAN Standard

CAN is an International Standardization Organization (ISO) defined serial communications bus originally developed for the automotive industry to replace the complex wiring harness with a two-wire bus. The specification calls for high immunity to electrical interference and the ability to self-diagnose and repair data errors. These features have led to CAN's popularity in a variety of industries including building automation, medical, and manufacturing.

The CAN communications protocol, ISO-11898: 2003, describes how information is passed between devices on a network and conforms to the Open Systems Interconnection (OSI) model that is defined in terms of layers. Actual communication between devices connected by the physical medium is defined by the physical layer of the model. The ISO 11898 architecture defines the lowest two layers of the seven layer OSI/ISO model as the data-link layer and physical layer in Figure 6.10.

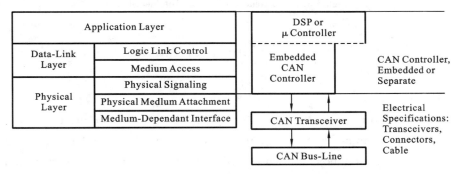

Figure 6.10 The Layered ISO 11898 Standard Architecture

In Figure 6.10, the application layer establishes the communication link to an upper-level application specific protocol such as the vendor-independent CANopen™ protocol. This protocol is supported by the international users and manufacturers group, CAN in Automation (CiA). Additional CAN information is located at the CiA Web site, can-cia.de. Many protocols are dedicated to particular applications like industrial automation, diesel engines, or aviation. Other examples of industry-standard, CAN-based protocols are KVASER's CAN Kingdom and Rockwell Automation's DeviceNet™.

3) Standard CAN or Extended CAN

The CAN communication protocol is a carrier-sense, multiple-access protocol with collision detection and arbitration on message priority (CSMA/CD+AMP). CSMA means that each node on a bus must wait for a prescribed period of inactivity before attempting to send a message. CD+AMP means that collisions are resolved through a bit-wise arbitration, based on a preprogrammed priority of each message in the identifier field of a message. The higher priority identifier always wins bus access. That is, the last logic-high in the identifier keeps on transmitting because it is the highest priority. Since every node on a bus takes part in writing every bit "as it is being written," an arbitrating node knows if it placed the logic-high bit on the bus. The ISO-11898:2003 Standard, with the standard 11-bit identifier, provides for signaling rates from 125 kbps to 1 Mbps. The standard was later amended with the "extended" 29-bit identifier. The standard 11-bit identifier field in Figure 6.11 provides for 2^{11}, or 2048 different message identifiers, whereas the extended 29-bit identifier in Figure 6.12 provides for 2^{29}, or 537 million identifiers.

Figure 6.11　Standard CAN: 11-Bit Identifier

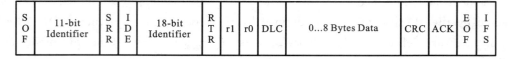

Figure 6.12　Extended CAN: 29-Bit Identifier

Lesson 4　Computer Network

1. Introduction

A computer network is a collection of computers and devices connected to each other. The network allows computers to communicate with each other and share resources and information. Networks may be classified according to a wide variety of characteristics. This section provides a general overview of some types and categories and also presents the basic components of a network.

2. Network Classification

The following list presents categories used for classifying networks.

1) Connection method

Computer networks can also be classified according to the hardware and software technology that is used to interconnect the individual devices in the network, such as Optical Fiber, Ethernet, Wireless LAN, HomePNA, Power line communication.

Ethernet uses physical wiring to connect devices. Frequently deployed devices include hubs, switches, bridges and/or routers.

Wireless LAN technology is designed to connect devices without wiring. These devices use radio waves or infrared signals as a transmission medium.

ITU-T technology uses existing home wiring (coaxial cable, phone lines and power lines) to create a high-speed (up to 1 Giga bit/s) local area network.

2) Scale

Networks are often classified as Local Area Network (LAN), Wide Area Network (WAN), Metropolitan Area Network (MAN), Personal Area Network (PAN), Virtual

Private Network (VPN), Campus Area Network (CAN), Storage Area Network (SAN), etc. depending on their scale, scope and purpose. Usage, trust levels and access rights often differ between these types of network—for example, LANs tend to be designed for internal use by an organization's internal systems and employees in individual physical locations (such as a building), while WANs may connect physically separate parts of an organization to each other and may include connections to third parties.

3) Functional relationship (network architecture)

Computer networks may be classified according to the functional relationships which exist among the elements of the network, e.g., Active Networking, Client-server and Peer-to-peer (workgroup) architecture.

4) Network topology

Computer networks may be classified according to the network topology upon which the network is based, such as bus network, star network, ring network, mesh network, star-bus network, tree or hierarchical topology network. Network topology signifies the way in which devices in the network see their logical relations to one another. The use of the term "logical" here is significant. That is, network topology is independent of the "physical" layout of the network. Even if networked computers are physically placed in a linear arrangement, if they are connected via a hub, the network has a star topology, rather than a bus topology. In this regard the visual and operational characteristics of a network are distinct; the logical network topology is not necessarily the same as the physical layout. Networks may be classified based on the method of data used to convey the data, these include digital and analog networks.

3. Types of Networks

Computer networks are often classified as Local Area Network (LAN), Wide Area Network (WAN), Metropolitan Area Network (MAN), Personal Area Network (PAN), Virtual Private Network (VPN), Campus Area Network (CAN), Storage Area Network (SAN), etc. depending on their scale, scope and purpose.

1) Personal Area Network

A personal area network (PAN) is a computer network used for communication among computer devices close to one person. Some examples of devices that are used in a PAN are printers, fax machines, telephones, PDAs and scanners. The reach of a PAN is typically about 20 ~ 30 feet (approximately 6 ~ 9 meters), but this is expected to increase with technology improvements.

2) Local area network

A local area network (LAN) is a computer network covering a small physical area, like a family, an office, or a small group of buildings, such as a school, or an airport. Current wired LANs are most likely to be based on Ethernet technology, although new standards like ITU-T also provide a way to create a wired LAN by using existing home wires (coaxial cables, phone lines and power lines).

For example, a library may have a wired or wireless LAN for users to interconnect local devices (e. g. , printers and servers) and to connect to the internet. On a wired LAN, PCs in the library are typically connected by category 5 (Cat 5) cable, running the IEEE 802. 3 protocol through a system of interconnected devices and eventually connect to the Internet. The cables to the servers are typically on Cat 5 enhanced cable, which will support IEEE 802. 3 at 1 G bit/s. A wireless LAN may exist using a different IEEE protocol, 802. 11b, 802. 11g or possibly 802. 11n. The staff computers (left part in the Figure 6. 13) can get to the color printer, checkout records, and the academic network and the Internet. All user computers can get to the Internet and the card catalog. Each workgroup can get to its local printer. Note that the printers are not accessible from outside their workgroup.

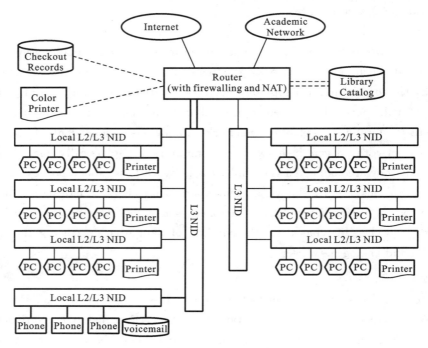

Figure 6. 13   Typical library network, in a branching tree topology and controlled access to resources

All interconnected devices must understand the network layer (layer 3), because they are handling multiple subnets (the different colors). Those inside the library, which have only 10/100 M bit/s Ethernet connections to the user device and a Gigabit Ethernet connection to the central router, could be called "layer 3 switches" because they only have Ethernet interfaces and must understand IP. It would be more correct to call them access routers, where the router at the top is a distribution router that connects to the Internet and academic networks' customer access routers.

The defining characteristics of LANs, in contrast to WANs (wide area networks), include their higher data transfer rates, smaller geographic range, and lack of a need for leased telecommunication lines. Current Ethernet or other IEEE 802. 3 LAN technologies operate at speeds up to 10 G bit/s. This is the data transfer rate. IEEE has projects investigating the standardization of 100 G bit/s, and possibly 400 G bit/s.

3) Campus area network

A campus area network (CAN) is a computer network made up of an interconnection of local area networks (LANs) within a limited geographical area. It can be considered one form of a metropolitan area network, specific to an academic setting.

In thecase of a university campus-based campus area network, the network is likely to link a variety of campus buildings including academic departments, university libraries and student residence halls. A campus area network is larger than a local area network but smaller than a wide area network (WAN) (in some cases).

The main aim of a campus area network is to facilitate students accessing internet and university resources. This is a network that connects two or more LANs but that is limited to a specific and contiguous geographical area such as a college campus, industrial complex, office building, or a military base. A CAN may be considered a type of MAN (metropolitan area network), but is generally limited to a smaller area than a typical MAN. This term is most often used to discuss the implementation of networks for a contiguous area. This should not be confused with a Controller Area Network. A LAN connects network devices over a relatively short distance. A networked office building, school, or home usually contains a single LAN, though sometimes one building will contain a few small LANs (perhaps one per room), and occasionally a LAN will span a group of nearby buildings. In TCP/IP networking, a LAN is often but not always implemented as a single IP subnet.

4) Metropolitan area network

A metropolitan area network (MAN) is a network that connects two or more local area networks or campus area networks together but does not extend beyond the boundaries of the immediate town/city. Routers, switches and hubs are connected to create a metropolitan area network.

5) Wide area network

A wide area network (WAN) is a computer network that covers a broad area (i. e. any network whose communications links cross metropolitan, regional, or national boundaries). Less formally, a WAN is a network that uses routers and public communications links. Contrast with personal area networks (PANs), local area networks (LANs), campus area networks (CANs), or metropolitan area networks (MANs), which are usually limited to a room, building, campus or specific metropolitan area (e. g., a city) respectively. The largest and most well-known example of a WAN is the Internet. A WAN is a data communications network that covers a relatively broad geographic area (i. e. one city to another city and one country to another country) and that often uses transmission facilities provided by common carriers, such as telephone companies. WAN technologies generally function at the lower three layers of the OSI reference model: the physical layer, the data link layer, and the network layer.

6) Global area network

A global area networks (GAN) specification is in development by several groups, and there is no common definition. In general, however, a GAN is a model for supporting mobile communications across an arbitrary number of wireless LANs, satellite coverage areas, etc. The key challenge in mobile communications is "handing off" the user communications from one local coverage area to the next. In IEEE Project 802, this involves a succession of terrestrial wireless local area networks (WLAN).

7) Virtual private network

A virtual private network (VPN) is a computer network in which some of the links between nodes are carried by open connections or virtual circuits in some larger network (e. g., the Internet) instead of by physical wires. The link-layer protocols of the virtual network are said to be tunneled through the larger network when this is the case. One common application is secure communications through the public Internet, but a VPN need not have explicit security features, such as authentification or content encryption. VPNs, for example, can be used to separate the traffic of different user communities over an underlying network with strong security features.

A VPN may have best-effort performance, or may have a defined service level agreement (SLA) between the VPN customer and the VPN service provider. Generally, a VPN has a topology more complex than point-to-point.

A VPN allows computer users to appear to be editing from an IP address location other than the one which connects the actual computer to the Internet.

8) Internetwork

Internetworking involves connecting two or more distinct computer networks or network segments via a common routing technology. The result is called an internetwork (often shortened to internet). Two or more networks or network segments connected using devices that operate at layer 3 (the "network" layer) of the OSI Basic Reference Model, such as a router. Any interconnection among or between public, private, commercial, industrial, or governmental networks may also be defined as an internetwork.

In modern practice, the interconnected networks use the Internet Protocol. There are at least three variants of internetwork, depending on who administers and who participates in them:

- Intranet
- Extranet
- Internet

Intranets and extranets may or may not have connections to the Internet. If connected to the Internet, the intranet or extranet is normally protected from being accessed from the Internet with proper authorization. The Internet is not considered to be a part of the intranet or extranet, although it may serve as a portal for access to portions of an extranet.

4. Basic Hardware Components

All networks are made up of basic hardware building blocks to interconnect network nodes, such as network interface cards (NICs), bridges, hubs, switches, and routers. In addition, some methods of connecting these building blocks is required, usually in the form of galvanic cable (most commonly Category 5 cable). Less common are microwave links (as in IEEE 802.12) or optical cable ("optical fiber"). An Ethernet card may also be required.

Words and Expressions

local area network (LAN)　局域网
Home PNA　家庭电话线联网联盟
power line communication　电力线通信
International Telecommunication Union (ITU)　联合国国际电信联盟
coaxial cable　同轴电缆
virtual private network (VPN)　虚拟专用网络
Storage Area Network (SAN)　存储区域网络
active network　有源网络
client-server　客户端,服务器
wide area network(WAN)　广布网络,广域网络,广域网
metropolitan area network(MAN)　城域网
personal area network(PAN)　个人区域网
ARPANET　阿帕网
service level agreement　服务水平协议
global area network(GAN)　全球区域网络
OSI(Open System Interconnection)　开放系统互连
Border Gateway Protocol(BGP)　边界网关协议
network interface card(NIC)　网络接口卡
DARPA　防御远景研究规划局
overemphasize [ˈəuvəˈemfəsaiz] v. 过分强调
Wireless local area networks (WLAN)　无线局域网
router [ˈruːtə(r), ˈrau-] n. 路由程序；路由器

Notes

1. Power Line Communication(电力线通信)是指以电力线为传输媒介进行数据传送和信息交换。随着调制技术、传输技术和信号处理技术的进步,电力线通信技术不断发展。

2. ITU(联合国国际电信联盟)是世界上最权威、最广泛的通信标准化组织。为了制定通信标准或协议,国际上许多通信组织都将标准作为其最重要的工作。ITU最突出的特点是标准制定过程比较公开、公正以及标准体系尽可能完整。

3. Coaxial Cable(同轴电缆)是计算机网络中使用广泛的一种线材；与电力电缆相比,由于直径小,外型细长,通常称为细缆。

4. SLA(服务水平协议)定义了服务类型、服务质量和客户付款等术语。

5. Many experienced network designers and operators recommend starting with the logic of devices dealing with only one protocol level, not all of which are covered by OSI.

(1) 句中 starting with 动名词,作 recommend 的宾语,翻译为"从……开始"。

(2) 全句可翻译为:许多经验丰富的网络设计者和操作员建议从只有一个协议层面的设备开始,并非所有这些都被开放系统互联覆盖。

Reading Material

Network Topology

Network topology is the study of the arrangement or mapping of the elements (links, nodes, etc.) of a network, especially the physical (real) and logical (virtual) interconnections between nodes. A local area network (LAN) is one example of a network that exhibits both a physical topology and a logical topology. Any given node in the LAN will have one or more links to one or more other nodes in the network and the mapping of these links and nodes onto a graph results in a geometrical shape that determines the physical topology of the network. Likewise, the mapping of the flow of data between the nodes in the network determines the logical topology of the network. The physical and logical topologies might be identical in any particular network but they also may be different.

Any particular network topology is determined only by the graphical mapping of the configuration of physical and/or logical connections between nodes. LAN Network Topology is, therefore, technically a part of graph theory. Distances between nodes, physical interconnections, transmission rates, and/or signal types may differ in two networks and yet their topologies may be identical. Figure 6.14 shows different network topologies.

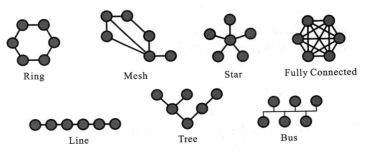

Figure 6.14 Diagram of different network topologies

There are also three basic categories of network topologies:

Physical topologies: The mapping of the nodes of a network and the physical connections between them—i.e., the layout of wiring, cables, the locations of nodes and the interconnections between the nodes and the cabling or wiring system.

Signal topologies: The mapping of the actual connections between the nodes of a network as evidenced by the path that the signals take when propagating between the nodes. The term "signal topology" is often used synonymously with the term "logical topology", however, some confusion may result from this practice in certain situations since, by definition, the term "logical topology" refers to the apparent path that the data takes between nodes in a network while the term "signal topology" generally refers to the actual path that the signals (e.g., optical, electrical, electromagnetic, etc.) take when propagating between nodes.

Logical topologies: The mapping of the apparent connections between the nodes of a network, as evidenced by the path that data appears to take when traveling between the nodes. The logical classification of network topologies generally follows the same classifications as those in the physical classifications of network topologies, the path that the data takes between nodes being used to determine the topology as opposed to the actual physical connections being used to determine the topology. The terms signal topology and logical topology are often used interchangeably even though there is a subtle difference between the two and the distinction is not often made between the two.

Lesson 5 Digital Signal Processing

1. Introduction

Digital signal processing (DSP) is concerned with the representation of the signals by a sequence of numbers or symbols and the processing of these signals. Digital signal processing and analog signal processing are subfields of signal processing. DSP includes subfields like audio and speech signal processing, sonar and radar signal processing, sensor array processing, spectral estimation, statistical signal processing, digital image processing, signal processing for communications, biomedical signal processing, seismic data processing, etc.

Since the goal of DSP is usually to measure or filter continuous real-world analog signals, the first step is usually to convert the signal from an analog to a digital form, by using an analog to digital converter. Often, the required output signal is another analog output signal, which requires a digital to analog converter. Even if this process is more complex than analog processing and has a discrete value range, the stability of digital signal processing thanks to error detection and correction and being less vulnerable to noise makes it advantageous over analog signal processing for many, though not all, applications.

DSP algorithms have long been run on standard computers, on specialized processors called digital signal processors (DSPs), or on purpose-built hardware such as application-specific integrated circuit (ASICs). Today there are additional technologies used for digital signal processing including more powerful general purpose microprocessors, field-programmable gate arrays (FPGAs), digital signal controllers (mostly for industrial applications such as motor control), and stream processors, among others.

In DSP, engineers usually study digital signals in one of the following domains: time domain (one-dimensional signals), spatial domain (multidimensional signals), frequency domain, autocorrelation domain, and wavelet domains. They choose the domain in which to process a signal by making an informed guess (or by trying different possibilities) as to which domain best represents the essential characteristics of the signal. A sequence of samples from a measuring device produces a time or spatial domain representation, whereas a discrete Fourier transform produces the frequency domain information that is the frequency spectrum. Autocorrelation is defined as the cross-correlation of the signal with itself over varying intervals of time or space.

2. Signal Sampling

With the increasing use of computers the usage of and need for digital signal processing has increased. In order to use an analog signal on a computer it must be digitized with an analog to digital converter (ADC). Sampling is usually carried out in two stages, discretization and quantization. In the discretization stage, the space of signals is partitioned into equivalence classes and quantization is carried out by replacing the signal with representative signal of the corresponding equivalence class. In the quantization stage, the representative signal values are approximated by values from a finite set.

The Nyquist-Shannon sampling theorem states that a signal can be exactly reconstructed from its samples if the sampling frequency is greater than twice the highest frequency of the signal. In practice, the sampling frequency is often significantly more than twice the required bandwidth.

A digital to analog converter (DAC) is used to convert the digital signal back to analog signal. The use of a digital computer is a key ingredient in digital control systems.

3. Time and Space Domains

The most common processing approach in the time or space domain is enhancement of the input signal through a method called filtering. Filtering generally consists of some transformation of a number of surrounding samples around the current sample of the input or output signal. There are various ways to characterize filters, for example:

A "linear" filter is a linear transformation of input samples; other filters are "non-linear." Linear filters satisfy the superposition condition, i.e. if an input is a weighted linear combination of different signals, the output is an equally weighted linear combination of the corresponding output signals.

A "causal" filter uses only previous samples of the input or output signals; while a "non-causal" filter uses future input samples. A non-causal filter can usually be changed into a causal filter by adding a delay to it.

A "time-invariant" filter has constant properties over time; other filters such as adaptive filters change in time.

Some filters are "stable", others are "unstable". A stable filter produces an output that converges to a constant value with time, or remains bounded within a finite interval. An unstable filter can produce an output that grows without bounds, with bounded or even zero input.

A "Finite Impulse Response" (FIR) filter uses only the input signal, while an "Infinite Impulse Response" filter (IIR) uses both the input signal and previous samples of the output signal. FIR filters are always stable, while IIR filters may be unstable.

Most filters can be described in Z-domain (a superset of the frequency domain) by their transfer functions. A filter may also be described as a difference equation, a collection of zeroes and poles or, if it is an FIR filter, an impulse response or step response. The output of an FIR filter to any given input may be calculated by convolving the input signal with the impulse response. Filters can also be represented by block diagrams which can then be used to derive a sample processing algorithm to implement the filter using hardware instructions.

4. Frequency Domain

Signals are converted from time or space domain to the frequency domain usually through the Fourier transform. The Fourier transform converts the signal information to a magnitude and phase component of each frequency. Often the Fourier transform is converted to the power spectrum, which is the magnitude of each frequency component squared.

The most common purpose for analysis of signals in the frequency domain is analysis of signal properties. The engineer can study the spectrum to determine which frequencies are present in the input signal and which are missing.

Filtering, particularly in non real-time work can also be achieved by converting to the frequency domain, applying the filter and then converting back to the time domain. This is a fast, $O(n\log^n)$ operation, and can give essentially any filter shape including excellent approximations to brickwall filters.

There are some commonly used frequency domain transformations. For example, the cepstrum converts a signal to the frequency domain through Fourier transform, takes the logarithm, then applies another Fourier transform. This emphasizes the frequency components with smaller magnitude while retaining the order of magnitudes of frequency components. Frequency domain analysis is also called spectrum or spectral analysis.

5. Signal Processing

Signals commonly need to be processed in a variety of ways. For example, the output signal from a transducer may well be contaminated with unwanted electrical "noise". The electrodes attached to a patient's chest when an ECG is taken measure tiny electrical voltage changes due to the activity of the heart and other muscles. The signal is often strongly affected by "mains pickup" due to electrical interference from the mains supply. Processing the signal using a filter circuit can remove or at least reduce the unwanted part of the signal. Increasingly nowadays, the filtering of signals to improve signal quality or to extract important information is done by DSP techniques rather than by analog electronics.

6. Development of DSP

The development of digital signal processing dates from the 1960's with the use of mainframe digital computers for number-crunching applications such as the Fast Fourier Transform (FFT), which allows the frequency spectrum of a signal to be computed rapidly. These techniques are not widely used at that time, because suitable computing equipment was generally available only in universities and other scientific research institutions.

7. Digital Signal Processors (DSPs)

The introduction of the microprocessor in the late 1970's and early 1980's made it possible for DSP techniques to be used in a much wider range of applications. However, general-purpose microprocessors such as the Intel x86 family are not ideally suited to the numerically-intensive requirements of DSP, and during the 1980's the increasing importance of DSP led several major electronics manufacturers (such as Texas Instruments, Analog Devices and Motorola) to develop Digital Signal Processor chips-specialised microprocessors with architectures designed specifically for the types of operations required in digital signal processing. (Note that the acronym DSP can variously mean Digital Signal Processing, the term used for a wide range of techniques for processing signals digitally, or Digital Signal Processor, a specialised type of microprocessor chip). Like a general-purpose microprocessor, a DSP is a programmable device, with its own native instruction code. DSP chips are capable of carrying out millions of floating point operations per second, and like their better-known general-purpose cousins, faster and more powerful versions are continually being introduced. DSPs can also be embedded within complex "system-on-chip" devices, often containing both analog and digital circuitry.

8. Applications of DSP

DSP technology is nowadays commonplace in such devices as mobile phones, multimedia computers, video recorders, CD players, hard disc drive controllers and modems, and will soon replace analog circuitry in TV sets and telephones. An important application of DSP is in signal compression and decompression. Signal compression is used in digital cellular phones to allow a greater number of calls to be handled simultaneously within each local "cell". DSP signal compression technology allows people not only to talk to one another but also to see one another on their computer screens, using small video cameras mounted on the computer monitors, with only a conventional telephone line linking them together. In audio CD systems, DSP technology is used to perform complex error detection and correction on the raw data as it is read from the CD.

Although some of the mathematical theory underlying DSP techniques, such as Fourier and Hilbert transforms, digital filter design and signal compression, can be fairly complex, the numerical operations required actually to implement these techniques are very simple, consisting mainly of operations that could be done on a cheap four-function calculator. The architecture of a DSP chip is designed to carry out such operations incredibly fast, processing hundreds of millions of samples every second, to provide real-time performance: that is, the ability to process a signal "live" as it is sampled and then output the processed signal, for example to a loudspeaker or video display. All of the practical examples of DSP applications mentioned earlier, such as hard disc drives and mobile phones, demand real-time operation.

The major electronics manufacturers have invested heavily in DSP technology. Because they now find application in mass-market products, DSP chips account for a substantial proportion of the world market for electronic devices. Sales amount to billions of dollars annually, and seem likely to continue to increase rapidly.

The main applications of DSP are audio signal processing, audio compression, digital image processing, video compression, speech processing, speech recognition, digital communications, RADAR, SONAR, seismology, and biomedicine. Specific examples are speech compression and transmission in digital mobile phones, room matching equalization of sound in hi-fi and sound reinforcement applications, weather forecasting, economic forecasting, seismic data processing, analysis and control of industrial processes, computer-generated animations in movies, medical imaging such as CAT scans and MRI, MP3 compression, image manipulation, high fidelity loudspeaker crossovers and equalization, and audio effects for use with electric guitar amplifiers.

9. Implementation

Digital signal processing is often implemented using specialised microprocessors such as the DSP56000, the TMS320, or the SHARC. These often process data using fixed-point arithmetic, although some versions are available which use floating point arithmetic and are more powerful. For faster applications FPGAs might be used. Beginning in 2007, multicore implementations of DSPs have started to emerge from companies including Freescale and startup Stream Processors Inc. For faster applications with vast usage, ASICs might be designed specifically. For slow applications, a traditional slower processor such as a microcontroller may be adequate.

Words and Expressions

autocorrelation [ˌɔːtəukɔriˈleiʃən] n. 自相关作用,自动交互作用
discrete Fourier transform 离散傅里叶变换
frequency spectrum 频谱
cross-correlation [ˈkrɔsˌkɔriˈleiʃən] n. 互相关联（关系）
discretization [disˌkriːtiˈzeiʃən] n. 离散化
quantization [ˌkwɔntaiˈzeiʃən] n. 量子化,数字化
equivalence classes 等价类
causal filter 因果滤波器
adaptive filter 自适应滤波器
finite impulse response 有限脉冲响应
step response 阶跃响应
cepstrum 倒频谱;对数逆谱;对数倒频谱
ECG 心电图
pickup [ˈpikʌp] n. 拾起;拾音器;传感器 a. 临时的,挑选的

Notes

1. A "finite impulse response" (FIR) filter uses only the input signal, while an "infinite impulse response" filter (IIR) uses both the input signal and previous samples of the output signal.

(1) 有限脉冲响应滤波器(finite impulse response filter)是数字滤波器的一种,简称 FIR 数字滤波器。这类滤波器对于脉冲输入信号的响应最终趋向于 0,因此是有限的。它是相对于无限脉冲响应(IIR)滤波器而言的。由于无限脉冲响应滤波器中存在反馈回路,因此对于脉冲输入信号的响应是无限延续的。

(2) 全句可翻译为:"有限脉冲响应"(FIR)滤波器只使用输入信号,而"无限脉冲响应"过滤器(IIR)同时使用输入信号和来自于输出信号的前次样本。

2. For example, the cepstrum converts a signal to the frequency domain through Fourier transform, takes the logarithm, then applies another Fourier transform.

（1）句中cepstrum为倒频谱，利用倒频谱可将回声的影响消除，得到接近无回声影响的真实功率谱，以便在频域里对噪声进行更好的分析。

（2）全句可翻译为：例如，倒频谱通过傅里叶变换将信号转换到频率域，取对数，然后用于其他傅里叶变换。

3. The signal is often strongly affected by "mains pickup" due to electrical interference from the mains supply.

（1）这里 be affected by 受……的作用，受……的影响。

（2）全句可翻译为：由于电网供电的电波干扰，信号受电源拾音器的影响很大。

Reading Material

Analog and Digital Filters

In signal processing, the function of a filter is to remove unwanted parts of the signal, such as random noise, or to extract useful parts of the signal, such as the components lying within a certain frequency range.

Figure 6.15 illustrates the basic idea.

Figure 6.15 The function diagram of a filter

There are two main kinds of filters, analog and digital. They are quite different in their physical makeup and in how they work.

An analog filter uses analog electronic circuits made up from components such as resistors, capacitors and op amps to produce the required filtering effect. Such filter circuits are widely used in such applications as noise reduction, video signal enhancement, graphic equalizers in hi-fi systems, and many other areas.

There are well-established standard techniques for designing an analog filter circuit for a given requirement. At all stages, the signal being filtered is an electrical voltage or current which is the direct analogue of the physical quantity (e.g. a sound or video signal or transducer output) involved.

A digital filter uses a digital processor to perform numerical calculations on sampled values of the signal. The processor may be a general-purpose computer such as a PC, or a specialized DSP (Digital Signal Processor) chip.

The analog input signal must first be sampled and digitized using an ADC (analog to digital converter). The resulting binary numbers, representing successive sampled values of the input signal, are transferred to the processor, which carries out numerical calculations on them. These calculations typically involve multiplying the input values by constants and adding the products together. If necessary, the results of these calculations, which now represent sampled values of the filtered signal, are output through a DAC (digital to analog converter) to convert the signal back to analog form.

Note that in a digital filter, the signal is represented by a sequence of numbers, rather than a voltage or current. Figure 6.16 shows the basic setup of such a system.

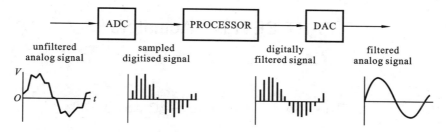

Figure 6.16 The basic setup of a digital filter system

PART SEVEN Actuators

Lesson 1 Electric Actuators

1. Definition of Actuators and Actuation System

Automatic control of valves requires an actuator, which is defined as any device mounted on a valve that, in response to a signal, automatically moves the valve to the required position by using an outside power source. The addition of an actuator to a throttling valve, which has the ability to adjust to a signal, is called a control valve. Some say that by the pure definition of actuator, a manual operator is an actuator. However, when most people associated with valves discuss the term actuator, they are referring to a power-actuated operator using an outside signal and power source rather than a human being. Typical classification of actuators includes pneumatic actuators (diaphragm, piston cylinder, vane, etc.), electric motor actuators, and hydraulic actuators. Actuation systems are special actuators that are commonly mounted on manually operated valves and can be used either on-off or throttling applications.

Actuators are critical elements in the control loop, which consist of a sensing device, controller, and an actuator mounted on a valve. With a control loop, a sensing device in the process system—such as a temperature sensor or a flow meter—is installed downstream from the control valve and is set to measure a particular variable in the process. The sensor reports its finding to a controller, which compares the actual data against the predetermined value required by the process. If the measured value is different from the predetermined value, the controller sends a correction signal to control valve's actuator. This signal can be sent using one of three methods: increasing or decreasing air pressure, varying electric voltage, or increasing or decreasing hydraulic pressure. The actuator receives this signal and moves accordingly to vary the position of the closure element until the controller determines that the measured value is equal to the predetermined value. At that point, the signal increase or decrease stops, and the actuator—and subsequently, the closure element—holds its position.

Not only must the actuator have the ability to adjust to a changing signal, but it must also have enough power to overcome the internal forces of the process, the effects of gravity, and friction in the valve itself. The majority of applications requiring actuators today require the use of compressed air, with nine out of ten actuators pneumatically driven. Air is by far the preferred power medium, since it is relatively cheap and is available in nearly all plants. In addition, it does not contaminate the environment and can be regulated easily. Typical plant compressed air supply is generally between 60 and 150 psi (between 4 and 10 bar), which is sufficient to run a large portion of the pneumatic actuators available today. When a valve must overcome exceptionally high pressures or when the valve must stroke quickly, bottled nitrogen is often used, allowing pressures up to 2 200 psi (150 bar). Not only does a bottle allow for high pressures of nitrogen, it also relatively moisture-free and extremely free of particulates and other foreign material. In general, the disadvantage of air-driven actuators is that, because of the comprehensibility of gases, some exactness is lost through that medium.

Other power sources can include electrical (both ac and dc power) as well as hydraulics (and to a far lesser extent, steam). Although electromechanical and electrohydraulic actuators are more expensive than pneumatic actuators, they do have the advantages of extremely good accuracy and the ability to operate in environments experiencing low temperatures (where typical air lines can freeze from condensed water) or when high thrusts are required.

Actuators are described as either single or double acting. A single-acting actuator uses a design in which the power source is applied to only one side of an actuator barrier and the opposite is not opposed by the power sources. A spring may be added to the opposite side to counteract the single action. A related term is the direct-acting actuator, which refers to a design in which the power source is applied to extend the stem. On the other hand, a reverse-acting actuator refers to an actuator where the power source causes the actuator stem to react. Double-acting actuator is a term used for actuators that have power supplied to both sides of an actuator barrier. By varying the pressure on either side of the actuator barrier, the barrier moves up or down.

2. Electric Valve Actuators

Electric motors installed on process valves were one of the first types of actuators used in the process industry. Such electric actuators have been used since the 1920s, although the designs have improved dramatically since those early days, especially in terms of performance, reliability, and size. In basic terms, the electric actuator consists of a reversible electric motor, control box, gearbox, limit switches, and other controls (such as a potentiometer to show valve position).

The chief applications for electric actuators are in the power and nuclear power industries, where high-pressure water systems require smooth, stable, and slow valve stroking. The main advantages of electric actuators are the high degree of stability and constant thrust available to the user. In general, the thrust capability of the electric actuator is dependent on the size of the electric motor and the gearing involved. The largest electric actuators are capable of producing torque values as high as 500 000 lb (225 000 kgf) of linear thrust. The only other comparable actuator with such thrust capabilities is the electrohydraulic actuator, although the electric actuator is much less costly.

The disadvantagies of electric actuators is their relative expensive cost when compared to the more commonly applied pneumatic actuators. Also, they are much more complex—involving an electric motor, electrical controls, and a gearbox—therefore much more can go wrong. An electric motor is not conducive to flammable atmospheres unless stringent explosion-proof requirements are met. When high amounts of torque or thrust are required for a particular valve application, an electric actuator can be quite large and heavy, making it more difficult to remove from the valve. Depending upon the gear ratios involved and the pressures involved with the process, an electric actuator can be quite slow, when compared to electrohydraulic actuators or even pneumatic actuators. It can also generate heat, which may be an issue in enclosed spaces. If the torque or limit switches are not set correctly, the force of the actuator can easily destroy the regulating element of the valve.

Based on the thrust requirements, electric actuators are available in compact, self-contained packages (See Figure 7.1), as well as larger units with direct-drive handwheels (See Figure 7.2). The basic design of the electric actuator consists of the electric motor, the gearbox or gearing, the electrical controls, limit or torque switches, and the positioning device. By design, electric motors are more efficient at their maximum speed; therefore, most electric actuators use some types of mechanical devices, such as a hammer blow yoke nut, to engage the load after the motor has achieved its full speed. This is especially important since the largest amount of thrust or torque is required at the opening or closing of the valve. For the actuator to operate in both directions, the motor must be reversible to open and close the valve. For efficiency reasons, electric motors operate best at high revolutions per minute (1 000 to 3 600 r/min). Therefore, gearing is used to reduce the stroking speed for use with valves. The gearbox uses worm gearing to make the reduction and is totally encased in an oil bath for maximum life of the gears.

Figure 7.1 Compact electric actuator　　　Figure 7.2 Electric actuator with direct-drive handwheel

Because of the exceptional stiffness and torque associated with electric actuators, the valve can overstroke if the actuator is not adjusted correctly—and possibly damage or destroy the regulating element or limit the stroke of the valve. To avoid overtravel, limit switches are used to shut off the motor when the open or closed position is reached. Torque switches can also be used to shut off the motor when the torque resistance increases as the closed or open positions are reached. The added benefit of the torque switch is that if an object is caught in the regulating element or if the valve is binding, the actuator will shut off rather than apply thrust to reach the closed position and further damage the valve. Ideally, torque switches are best used with valves that have floating seats (such as ball or wedge gate valves), while limit switches are best used with valves with fixed seats (such as globe or butterfly valves).

The electrical controls can be accessed on the valve itself or controlled at a remote location using extended electrical lines. Either handlevers or buttons are provided to operate the electric motor. With the handlever, turning the lever clockwise extends the actuator stem, while counterclockwise retracts the stem. Placing the handlever in the middle position shuts off the motor and maintains that particular valve position. With button controls, three buttons are used in the normal configuration: one to extend the actuator stem, one to retract, and another to stop the motor. When manual operation or manual override is needed, most electric actuators allow for the electric motor to be disengaged. A declutchable handwheel can then be used to position the valve manually. Because of the complex electrical and mechanical nature of electric actuators, most calibration adjustments and recommended servicing are made at the manufacturer's factory or an authorized service center.

Words and Expressions

actuator [ˈæktjueitə] n. 执行器
throttling valve 节流阀
pneumatic [nju(ː)ˈmætik] a. 气动的;有空气的;气体学的
diaphragm [ˈdaiəfræm] n. 横隔膜;控光装置
vane [vein] n. (风车、叶轮机、抽水机等的)翼,叶片;轮叶
downstream [ˈdaunˈstriːm] ad. 顺流地;在(往)下游
contaminate [kənˈtæmineit] v. 弄脏,污染
nitrogen [ˈnaitrədʒən] n. 氮
moisture [ˈmɔistʃə] n. 潮湿;湿气
counteract [ˌkauntəˈrækt] v. 抵消;阻碍;中和
gearbox [ˈgiəbɔks] n. 齿轮箱,变速箱
thrust [θrʌst] n. 推力,刺,力推
conducive [kənˈdjuːsiv] a. 有助于……的
flammable [ˈflæməbl] a. 易燃的,可燃性的
stringent [ˈstrindʒənt] a. 迫切的;严厉的
handwheel [ˈhændwiːl] n. 驾驶盘,操纵轮,手轮
yoke nut 阀杆螺母
encase [inˈkeis] v. 包围;装入箱内
butterfly valve 蝶形阀
declutchable [ˌdiːˈklʌtʃəbl] a. 离合式的

Notes

1. Automatic control of valves requires an actuator, which is defined as any device mounted on a valve that, in response to a signal, automatically moves the valve to the required position by using an outside power source.

（1）句中 which 引导一个定语从句,在从句中作主语,指代前面的 actuator。

（2）句中 that 引导一个定语从句,在从句中作主语,指代前面的 device。

（3）全句可翻译为:阀的自动控制需要执行机构,它被定义为一种安装在阀上的装置,在信号的作用下,能利用外在的动力源自动地将阀移到所需的位置上。

2. The sensor reports its finding to a controller, which compares the actual data against the predetermined value required by the process.

（1）句中 which 引导一个定语从句,在从句中作主语,指代前面的 controller。

（2）全句可翻译为:传感器将它的发现反馈给控制器,控制器将实际数据与过程所需的预定值进行比较。

3. Depending upon the gear ratios involved and the pressures involved with the process, an electric actuator can be quite slow, when compared to electrohydraulic actuators or even pneumatic actuators.

（1）句中 depending upon 是现在分词作状语,它在句子中作一个方式状语,类似用法如下:We'll decide whether to hold the sports meet depending on the weather.

（2）全句可翻译为:相对于电液执行机构甚至气动执行机构,通过调节控制过程中的齿轮比和压力,电动执行机构的速度可以相当慢。

Reading Material

Electric Motor

1) AC Motor

The AC induction motor is the major converter of electrical energy into mechanical and other useable forms. For this purpose, about two thirds of the electrical energy produced is fed to motors. Much of the power that is consumed by AC motors goes into the operation of fans, blowers and pumps. It has been estimated that approximately 50% of the motors in use are for these types of loads. These particular loads—fans, blowers and pumps, are particularly attractive to look at for energy savings. Several alternate methods of control for fans and pumps have been advanced recently that show substantial energy savings over traditional methods. Newer methods include direct variable speed control of the fan or pump motor. This method produces a more efficient means of flow control than the existing methods. In addition, adjustable frequency drives offer a distinct advantage over other forms of variable speed control.

2) Step Motor

Step motors (often referred as stepper motors) are different from all other types of electrical drives in the sense that they operate on discrete control pulses received and rotate in discrete steps. On the other hand ordinary electrical AC and DC drives are analog in nature and rotate continuously depending on magnitude and polarity of the control signal received. The discrete nature of operation of a step motor makes it suitable for directly interfacing with a computer and direct computer control. These motors are widely employed in industrial control, specifically for CNC machines, where open loop control in discrete steps are acceptable. These motors can also be adapted for continuous rotation.

3) DC Motor

While AC motors have replaced DC motors in most of the adjustable speed drive applications. For servo drive applications, DC motors are still used, although they are also being replaced by BLDC motors. Direct current servomotors are used as feed actuators in many machine tool industries. These motors are generally of the permanent magnet (PM) type in which the stator magnetic flux remains essentially constant at all levels of the armature current and the speed-torque relationship is linear.

4) Brushless DC motor

Brushless DC motor, rather surprisingly, is a kind of permanent magnate synchronous motor. Permanent magnet synchronous motors are classified on the basis of the wave shape of their induce emf, i. e, sinusoidal and trapezoidal. The sinusoidal type is known as permanent magnet synchronous motor; the trapezoidal type goes under the name of PM Brushless DC (BLDC) machine. Permanent magnet (PM) DC brushed and brushless motors incorporate a combination of PM and electromagnetic fields to produce torque (or force) resulting in motion. This is done in the DC motor by a PM stator and a wound armature or rotor. Current in the DC motor is automatically switched to different windings by means of a commutator and brushes to create continuous motion. In a brushless motor, the rotor incorporates the magnets, and the stator contains the windings. As the name suggests brushes are absent and hence in this case, commutation is implemented electronically with a drive amplifier that uses semiconductor switches to change current in the windings based on rotor position feedback.

Lesson 2   Hydraulic Actuators

1. Introduction

Hydraulic actuators, as used in industrial process control, employ hydraulic pressure to drive an output member. These are used where high speed and large forces are required. The fluid used in hydraulic actuator is highly incompressible so that pressure applied can be transmitted instantaneously to the member attached to it.

It was not, however, until the 17th century that the branch of hydraulics with which we are to be concerned first came into use. Based on a principle discovered by the French scientist Pascal, it relates to the use of confined fluids in transmitting power, multiplying force and modifying motions.

Then, in the early stages of the industrial revolution, a British mechanic named Joseph Bramah utilized Pascal's discovery in developing a hydraulic press. Bramah decided that, if a small force on a small area would create a proportionally larger force on a larger area, the only limit to the force a machine can exert is the area to which the pressure is applied.

2. Actuators (Cylinders, Motors)

Actuators have either a linear output (cylinders, rams or jacks) or rotary output (rotary actuators or motors). Motors very closely resemble hydraulic pumps in their construction. Indeed, many pumps can also be used as motors. Instead of pushing fluid into the system as pumps do, motors are pushed by the fluid and thus they develop torque and continuous rotary motion.

Linear actuators may be further sub-divided into those in which hydraulic pressure is applied to one side of the piston only (single acting) and are capable of movement only in one direction, and those in which pressure is applied to both sides of the piston (double acting) and are therefore capable of controlled movement in both directions.

Linear actuators may also be classified as single-ended type, in which the piston has an extension rod on one end only, or the double-ended type which has rods on both ends. Single-ended actuators are useful in space constrained applications, but unequal areas on each side of the piston results in asymmetrical flow gain which can complicate the control problem. Double-ended actuators have the advantage that they naturally produce equal force and speed in both directions, and for this reason are sometimes called symmetric or synchronizing cylinders. Hydraulic motors are a separate class of actuator, in which the speed and direction of a rotating output shaft is regulated by the flow control valve.

One of the classical components of hydraulic systems is the linear actuator, commonly known as the hydraulic cylinder. Cylinders are used to convert hydraulic power into linear mechanical force or motion. Many types of linear actuator exist. Single-acting actuators permit the application of hydraulic force in one direction only (See Figure 7.3). Double-acting actuators allow hydraulic force in both directions to be applied. Double-ended actuators with rods on both actuator ends, also termed symmetric or synchronizing cylinders, are used where the force developed must be equal in both directions (extension and retraction). Since the voids to be filled with hydraulic fluid are equal for extension and retraction, the resulting piston speeds are also equal for both strokes. Synchronizing cylinders have greater overall length and are more expensive than double-acting cylinders, thus, in practice, double-acting cylinders with one rod, also referred to as asymmetric or differential cylinders, are widely used. They have the advantage that the space needed for the cylinder is considerably smaller, because there is only one piston rod.

3. Advantages of Hydraulic Actuation Systems

Hydraulics refers to the means and mechanisms of transmitting power through liquids. The original power source for the hydraulic system is a prime mover such as an electric motor or an engine which drives the pump. However, the mechanical equipment cannot be coupled directly to the prime mover because the required control over the motion, necessary for industrial operations cannot be achieved. In terms of these Hydraulic Actuation Systems

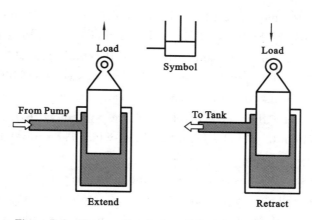

Figure 7.3 Cross sectional view of single-acting cylinder

offer unique advantages, as given below.

Variable Speed and Direction Most large electric motors run at adjustable, but constant speeds. It is also the case for engines. The actuator (linear or rotary) of a hydraulic system, however, can be driven at speeds that vary by large amounts and fast, by varying the pump delivery or using a flow control valve. In addition, a hydraulic actuator can be reversed instantly while in full motion without damage. This is not possible for most other prime movers.

Power-to-Weight Ratio Hydraulic components, because of their high speed and pressure capabilities, can provide high power output with very small weight and size, say, in comparison to electric system components. Note that in electric components, the size of equipment is mostly limited by the magnetic saturation limit of the iron. It is one of the reasons that hydraulic equipment finds wide usage in aircrafts, where dead-weight must be reduced to a minimum.

Stall Condition and Overload Protection A hydraulic actuator can be stalled without damage when overloaded, and will start up immediately when the load is reduced. The pressure relief valve in a hydraulic system protects it from overload damage. During stall, or when the load pressure exceeds the valve setting, pump delivery is directed to tank with definite limits to torque or force output. The only loss encountered is in terms of pump energy. On the contrary, stalling an electric motor is likely to cause damage. Likewise, engines cannot be stalled without the necessity for restarting.

4. Components of Hydraulic Actuation Systems

Hydraulic Fluid Hydraulic fluid must be essentially non-compressible to be able to transmit power instantaneously from one part of the system to another. At the same time, it should lubricate the moving parts to reduce friction loss and cool the components so that the heat generated does not lead to fire hazards. It also helps in removing the contaminants to filter. The most common liquid used in hydraulic systems is petroleum oil because it is only very slightly compressible. The other desirable property of oil is its lubricating ability. Finally, often, the fluid also acts as a seal against leakage inside a hydraulic component. The degree of closeness of the mechanical fit and the oil viscosity determines leakage rate.

Reservoir   It holds the hydraulic fluid to be circulated and allows air entrapped in the fluid to escape. This is an important feature as the bulk modulus of the oil, which determines the stiffness of hydraulic system, deteriorates considerably in the presence of entrapped air bubbles. It also helps in dissipating heat.

Filter   The hydraulic fluid is kept clean in the system with the help of filters and strainers. It removes minute particles from the fluid, which can cause blocking of the orifices of servo-valves or cause jamming of spools.

Fittings and Seals   Various additional components are needed to join pipe or tube sections, create bends and also to prevent internal and external leakage in hydraulic systems. Although some amount of internal leakage is built-in, to provide lubrication, excessive internal leakage causes loss of pump power since high pressure fluid returns to the tank, without doing useful work. External leakage, on the other hand, causes loss of fluid and can create fire hazards, as well as fluid contamination. Various kinds of sealing components are employed in hydraulic systems to prevent leakage.

Hydraulic Pumps   The pump converts the mechanical energy of its prime-mover to hydraulic energy by delivering a given quantity of hydraulic fluid at high pressure into the system. Generically, all pumps are divided into two categories, namely, hydrodynamic or non-positive displacement and hydrostatic or positive displacement. Hydraulic systems generally employ positive displacement pumps only. The symbol for a pump, is shown in Figure 7.4.

Pump

Reversible

Figure 7.4   The graphical symbol for pumps

Motors   Motors work exactly on the reverse principle of pumps. In motors fluid is forced into the motor from pump outlets at high pressure. This fluid pressure creates the motion of the motor shaft and finally goes out through the motor outlet port and returns to tank. All three variants of motors, already described for pumps, namely Gear motors, Vane motors and Piston motors are in use.

Accumulators   Unlike gases the fluids used in hydraulic systems cannot be compressed and stored to cater to sudden demands of high flow rates that cannot be supplied by the pump. An accumulator in a hydraulic system provides a means of storing these incompressible fluids under pressure created either by a spring, or a compressed gas. Any tendency for pressure to drop at the inlet causes the spring or the gas to force the fluid back out, supplying the demand for flow rate.

Words and Expressions

incompressible [ˌinkəmˈpresəbl] *a.* 不能压缩的
mechanic [miˈkænik] *n.* 技工, 机修工
hydraulic press   液压机; 水压机
symmetric [siˈmetrik] *a.* 对称的

synchronizing ['siŋkrənaiziŋ] *a.* 同步的
asymmetric [ˌeisi'metrik] *a.* 不对称的
differential cylinder 差动缸
saturation [ˌsætʃə'reiʃən] *n.* 饱和
contaminant [kən'tæminənt] *n.* 杂质,污染物质
viscosity [vi'skɔsəti] *n.* 黏(滞)性;黏滞度;黏性物质
entrap [in'træp] *v.* 骗入;诱捕;使陷入
bulk modulus 体积弹性模量
deteriorate [di'tiəriəreit] *v.* 恶化
dissipate ['disipeit] *v.* 使……消散(耗散);浪费;消耗
orifice ['ɔrifis] *n.* 孔口
spool [spu:l] *n.* 线轴,线管
outlet ['autlet, -lit] *n.* 出口,出路,通风口;批发商店
accumulator [ə'kju:mjuleitə] *n.* 储能器

Notes

1. Hydraulic actuators, as used in industrial process control, employ hydraulic pressure to drive an output member.

(1) 句中 as 引导非限制性定语从句,修饰 hydraulic actuators,通常用逗号将其与主句隔开。这时,as 可译为"正如"、"正像"。

(2) 全句可翻译为:正如在工业过程控制中的应用,液压执行机构采用液体压力驱动输出部件。

2. It was not, however, until the 17th century that the branch of hydraulics with which we are to be concerned first came into use.

(1) 本句为"It is (was) not until ＋ 时间状语(从句)＋ that＋主句"的强调结构,其中 it 指代 that 引导的主句。

例:It was not until yesterday that I remembered it. 直到昨天我才记起这事。

(2) 全句可翻译为:直到 17 世纪,我们所关注的这个液压分支才开始使用。

3. This is an important feature as the bulk modulus of the oil, which determines the stiffness of hydraulic system, deteriorates considerably in the presence of entrapped air bubbles.

(1) 句中 as 引导原因状语从句,which 引导非限定性定语从句修饰 bulk modulus。

(2) in the presence of:在……存在下

(3) 全句可翻译为:这是一个重要的特性,因为决定液压系统刚度的液压油的体积弹性模数会因残留空气的存在而严重恶化。

Reading Material

Control Valves

1) Introduction

The control action in any control loop system, is executed by the final control element.

The most common type of final control element used in chemical and other process control is the control valve. A control valve is normally driven by a diaphragm type pneumatic actuator that throttles the flow of the manipulating variable for obtaining the desired control action. A control valve essentially consists of a plug and a stem. The stem can be raised or lowered by air pressure and the plug changes the effective area of an orifice in the flow path.

2) Classifications

Control valves are available in different types and shapes. They can be classified in different ways: based on: (a) action, (b) number of plugs, and (c) flow characteristics.

Action Control valves operated through pneumatic actuators can be either (i) air to open, or (ii) air to close. They are designed such that if the air supply fails, the control valve will be either fully open, or fully closed, depending on the safety requirement of the process. For example, if the valve is used to control steam or fuel flow, the valve should be shut off completely in case of air failure. On the other hand, if the valve is handling cooling water to a reactor, the flow should be maximum in case of emergency.

Number of plugs Control valves can also be characterized in terms of the number of plugs present, as single-seated valve and double-seated valve.

In single-seated valve, only one plug is present in the control valve, so it is single-seated valve. The advantage of this type of valve is that, it can be fully closed and flow variation from 0 to 100% can be achieved. But due to the pressure drop across the orifice a large upward force is present in the orifice area, and as a result, the force required to move the valve against this upward thrust is also large. Thus this type of valves is more suitable for small flow rates. On the other hand, there are two plugs in a double-seated valve; flow moves upward in one orifice area, and downward in the other orifice. The resultant upward or downward thrust is almost zero. As a result, the force required to move a double-seated valve is comparatively much less.

But the double-seated valve suffers from one disadvantage. The flow cannot be shut off completely because of the differential temperature expansion of the stem and the valve seat. If one plug is tightly closed, there is usually a small gap between the other plug and its seat. Thus, single-seated valves are recommended when the valves are required to be shut off completely. But there are many processes, where the valve used is not expected to operate near shut off position. For this condition, double-seated valves are recommended.

Flow Characteristics It describes how the flow rate changes with the movement or lift of the stem. The shape of the plug primarily decides the flow characteristics. However, the design of the shape of a control valve and its shape requires further discussions. The flow characteristic of a valve is normally defined in terms of (a) inherent characteristics and (b) effective characteristics. An inherent characteristic is the ideal flow characteristics of a control valve and is decided by the shape and size of the plug. On the other hand, when the valve is connected to a pipeline, its overall performance is decided by its effective characteristic.

Lesson 3 Pneumatic Actuators

1. Introduction

Pneumatic actuators are devices in which energy of compressed air is utilized for carrying out mechanical work like linear, rotary, and oscillatory movement. The most commonly applied actuator is the pneumatically driven actuator, because the power source—compressed air—is relatively inexpensive compared to electrical or hydraulic power sources. For that reason, approximately 90 percent of all actuators in service today are driven by compressed air. When compared to the cost of electromechanical and electrohydraulic actuators, pneumatic actuators are relatively inexpensive as well as easy to understand and maintain. Most are available as standard off-the-shelf products in a number of predetermined sizes corresponding to maximum thrust. Only in special services are special-engineered actuators produced, such as those applications requiring exceptionally long strokes, high stroking speeds, or severe temperatures. From a maintenance standpoint, pneumatic actuators are more easily serviced and calibrated than other types of actuators. Some pneumatic actuators are designed to be field-reversible, meaning that they can be converted from air-to-extend to air-to-retract (or visa versa) in the field without special tools or maintenance procedures.

2. Features of Pneumatic Actuators

In general, essential systems for power transmission in machineries are pneumatic, hydraulic, electric, and mechanical. By making comparisons with these systems, the features of the pneumatic actuators can be enumerated as below:

(1) Compared to hydraulic systems, pneumatic systems are more suitable for light and medium loads. In reciprocating air compressors, since the discharge pressure at the first and the end stage are 600~700 kPa and 1 200~1 400 kPa respectively, the air pressure mostly utilized is below 1 000 kPa. As pressures higher than this, the efficiency suffers, and its use become difficult as the system has to conform to the applicable rule requirements for high-pressure gas.

(2) The best feature of compressed air is that, by utilizing the compressibility characteristics of air, energy can be stored in the form of pressure in air tanks. This can be used for high-speed operations or emergency operations during power failures.

In addition, during the momentary air consumption of the pneumatic machine, even if it exceeds the discharge volume of the air compressor, work greater than the capacity of the air compressor can be done with the provision of air tanks etc provided that the average air consumption (value obtained by dividing the total consumed by the sum of the operating and idling time of the air compressor) is not exceeded.

(3) Control of position and speed is difficult due to the compressibility characteristics of air.

(4) Due to various losses involved, the overall efficiency of the pneumatic actuator, in

comparison with the other systems is low. In an air compressor, theoretical work is done in adiabatic compression but the volume gets reduced when the compressed air is cooled. Moreover, there is pressure loss when compressed air is sent to the pipings and the control valves and form the air tank and in addition if it is assumed that there are leakages on the way then there is reduction in its volume by the time it reaches the pneumatic actuator. If the pneumatic actuator is of the complete-expansion type, the work done can be effectively used in a non-expansion type, this degree of advantages is further reduced.

(5) Due to the compressibility characteristics of air, no surge pressure similar to that which occurs in the hydraulic system is generated which obvious the necessity of overload prevention device in the system, and also the mutual interference between the machines due to the surge pressure is low.

Furthermore, as the output in the pneumatic actuator does not exceed the theoretical output, it is safe. This allows the theoretical output to be calculated from the useable air pressure only without taking into account the surge pressure.

(6) Piping is easier than in the hydraulic system and has no environmental pollution problem or fire risk due to external leakages.

(7) Pressure loss is small, because inertia and viscosity of the air are small compared to the hydraulic fluid. Air can be piped to each and every part of the factory and used readily. The maintenance is also easy.

(8) It has a large range of practical application because it can be adopted for wide range of temperature, vibration and combustion environments.

The useable temperature is rather wide, -40 ℃ to 200 ℃ and thus especially suitable where consideration in the specification must be given to prevent freezing of moisture contents and use of seals and electrical parts at low temperatures.

(9) Pneumatic actuators have no fire hazards and are made of explosion proof construction.

(10) It is easy to convert electrical signals to pneumatic, pneumatic to hydraulic, and pneumatic to electrical signals. As opposed to the response in electrical signal systems, it is inferior for the control elements in the pneumatic systems.

3. Two Kinds of Pneumatic Actuators

The most commonly applied pneumatic actuator over the past 40 years has been the diaphragm actuator (See Figure 7.5). Most diaphragm actuators are designed for linear motion, although some rotary-motion designs exist. By definition, a typical diaphragm actuator is a single-acting actuator that provides air pressure to one side of an elastomeric barrier (called the diaphragm) to extend or retract the actuator stem, which is connected to the closure element. The diaphragm is sandwiched between upper and lower casings, either of which can be used to hold air pressure, depending on the style of the actuator.

Diaphragm actuators have both direct-acting and reverse-acting designs. With the direct-acting design, air pressure is sent to the actuator, which extends the actuator stem and allows the valve to close. This also means that the actuator will retract its stem upon loss of air, allowing the valve to open and remain open. With the reverse-acting design, as the air pressure is sent to the actuator, the stem retracts and the valve opens. If the supply or signal air pressure is interrupted, the actuator moves to the extended position, allowing the valve to close.

The chief advantage of diaphragm actuators is that they are relatively inexpensive to produce and are commonly seen through the entire process industry. Although limited in high-thrust requirements, they are well suited to a good portion of applications in lower-pressure ranges, where thrust requirements are not so demanding. On the other hand, diaphragm actuators— because of the limitations of the diaphragm—do not provide exceptional stiffness and therefore have problems with fluctuations in the process flow. They also experience problems when throttling close to the seat, not having enough power to prevent the closure element from being pulled into the seat. The stiffness value of a diaphragm actuator is usually constant throughout the entire stroke. When the closure element is close to the seat, a sudden change or fluctuation in the process flow can cause the valve to slam shut, causing water-hammer effects.

Figure 7.5　Single-acting diaphragm actuator

From a maintenance standpoint, the life of diaphragm actuators is somewhat limited by the life of the diaphragm. If the diaphragm develops even a minor failure, the actuator is inoperable. Since the two casings are bolted together with numerous bolts, disassembly can be somewhat laborious and time consuming. Diaphragm actuators are not field-reversible, because different parts are required for the direct and reserve-acting designs. Diaphragm actuators have about one-third more parts than other types of pneumatic actuators, which increases their cost somewhat.

Although the diaphragm actuator is the most common pneumatic actuator, the piston cylinder actuator (See Figure 7.6) is gaining widespread acceptance, especially as processes become more advanced and demanding. The piston cylinder actuator uses a sliding sealed plate (called the piston) inside a pressure-retaining cylinder to provide double-acting operation. With the double-acting design, air is supplied to both sides of the piston by a positioner. As with all double-acting actuators, a positioner must be used to take the pneumatic or electric signal from the controller and send air to one side of the piston while bleeding the opposite side until the correction position is reached. An opposing range spring is not necessary with the piston cylinder actuator, although a spring may be included inside the cylinder to act as a fail-safe mechanism.

Like diaphragm actuator designs, piston cylinder actuators can be used with either linear or rotary valves. Linear designs are the most efficient since the entire movement of the actuator stem is transferred directly to the valve stem. On the other hand, the rotary design

Figure 7.6　Piston cylinder actuator with canister assembly and integral positioner

must use some type of linear- to rotary-motion linkage. This can create some hysteresis and dead band because of the lost motion caused by the use of linkages or slotted levers.

The primary advantage of cylinder actuators is the higher thrust capability, size for size, over comparable diaphragm actuators. Because the cylinder actuator with a positioner does not need to use air supply as a signal, the plant's full air-supply pressure can be used to power the actuator. The piston with its sliding O-ring seal is much more capable of handling greater air pressure than the diaphragm. Piston actuators, which have smaller chambers to fill with higher pressures of air, have faster stroking speeds than diaphragm actuators, which must fill larger chambers with lower pressures of air. Piston cylinder actuators are much more compact, being smaller in height and weight, than diaphragm actuators—an important consideration with installation, maintenance, and seismic requirements.

Piston cylinder actuators have some drawbacks. First, if the actuator remains in a static position for some time, some breakout force may be necessary to move the piston when a signal is eventually sent. When considering the added thrust and response associated with piston cylinder actuators, this breakout torque may not be noticeable. The requirement of a positioner does add expense to the actuator—although with less parts, the actuator itself is less expensive than a diaphragm actuator. A positioner also requires calibration.

Words and Expressions

pneumatic [nju(:)'mætik] *a.* 气动的；有空气的；气体学的
off-the-shelf *a.* & *ad.* 现成的(地)
thrust [θrʌst] *n.* 推力，刺，力推
compressibility [kəmˌpresi'biliti] *n.* 压缩的可能性，压缩性，压缩率
surge pressure　波动压力；峰值压力；冲击压力
moisture ['mɔistʃə] *n.* 潮湿；湿气
hazard ['hæzəd] *n.* 冒险，危险，危害
elastomeric [iˌlæstə'merik] *a.* 弹性材料的
stiffness ['stifnis] *n.* 刚度
fluctuation [ˌflʌktju'eiʃən] *n.* 波动，起伏
throttle ['θrɔtl] *n.* 节流阀；节气阀；喉咙
inoperable [in'ɔpərəbl] *a.* 不能实行的，行不通的；不能操作的
slotted lever　连杆；摇杆

drawback ['drɔːˌbæk] n. 毛病，缺点；不利因素

Notes

1. Only in special services are special-engineered actuators produced, such as those applications requiring exceptionally long strokes, high stroking speeds, or severe temperatures.

（1）句中 only 修饰句子的状语位于句首，句子要用部分倒装。

（2）全句可翻译为：只有在一些特殊的设备中才会使用专业工程执行机构，比如那些需要特别长的行程、高的行程速度或恶劣的温度的情况。

2. The best feature of compressed air is that, by utilizing the compressibility characteristics of air, energy can be stored in the form of pressure in air tanks.

（1）句中 by 是介词，后面接名词或动词 ing 形式，作方式状语。

（2）全句可翻译为：利用空气的可压缩性特征，压缩空气的最大特点就是能以压力的形式储存在空气罐中。

3. With the direct-acting design, air pressure is sent to the actuator, which extends the actuator stem and allows the valve to close.

（1）句中 which 引导的定语从句修饰 air pressure。

（2）全句可翻译为：在直接作用型的设计中，空气压力被传送到执行机构，执行机构的输出杆伸出，阀门关闭。

Reading Material

Introduction to Pneumatics

Fluid power in the form of compressed air fulfilled the need for an energy transmission system with muscle, which could easily be customized as per the needs of automated machinery. Tremendous amount of compressed air is used throughout industry due to its versatility and simplicity in application. Many unique characteristics of air make it more suitable to fulfill various needs of industrial applications than other energy media.

The "pneumatic muscle" power has managed to find its place between low-cost automatic and high-tech applications, affirming its innovative capability. Pneumatics not only includes the cylinder and directional control valves, it also encompasses a wide range of diversified components such as sensors, processors, various types of actuators, and extensive accessories and auxiliary components.

1) Pneumatics definition

The study of pneumatics deals with systems operated with air or other gaseous media to impact power or to control power. The term "pneumatics" is derived from the Greek word *pneuma*, meaning wind or breath. Hence pneumatics may be defined as the study of the movement of air. Pneumatic power is the power that is transmitted by pressurized air. It may be used to power machines or to control or regulate machines.

2) Compressed air for transmitting power

In industry, the pneumatic medium usually employed for transmitting power is the highly compressible air. Since gaseous substances are compressible in the ratio of decrease in volume to increase in pressure, a compressor is used as an energy source. The compressed air is then prepared or treated in several stages to remove undesirable contaminants present in it and stored in a tank called receiver tank. Other issues of concern at this stage are the distribution of compressed air, regulation of pressure and introduction of fine mist of lubricating oil in the compressed air.

The compressed air medium is subsequently used to do work in a controlled manner by allowing it to expand back to the atmospheric pressure. The work done in this expansion is transmitted to a load surface such as a piston or a vane, which will be moved by the expanding air with a force equal to the product of the air pressure acting on the piston and area of the piston.

The function of a pneumatic system can be simply summed up as follows: apply a force to a gaseous fluid like air and transmit pneumatic pressure all through the fluid, and then convert the stored energy back into mechanical force before work could be done.

3) Historical review

The use of fluid power predates the Christian era, and it is in all probability as old as civilization. There are many ancient, historical descriptions of the use of air to power vessels for almost as long as man has been embarking on the waters of the world. The economic exploitation of compressed air as a source of energy has been practiced at least for the last 100 years. Modern pneumatics with its capacity to perform work and various control functions has been developed only since the 1960s.

PART EIGHT New Technology

Lesson 1 An Introduction to Robotics Technology

The word "robot" originates from the Czech word for forced labor, or serf. It is introduced by playwright Karel Capek, whose fictional robotic inventions are much like Dr. Frankenstein's monster—creatures created by chemical and biological, rather than mechanical, methods. But the current mechanical robots of popular culture are not much different from these fictional biological creations. Basically a robot consists of:

(1) A mechanical device, such as a wheeled platform, arm, or other construction, capable of interacting with its environment.

(2) Sensors on or around the device that are able to sense the environment and give useful feedback to the device.

(3) Systems that process sensory input in the context of the device's current situation and instruct the device to perform actions in response to the situation.

Here is the definition of "robot" (from the Robot Institute of America, 1979): A re-programmable, multifunctional manipulator designed to move material, parts, tools, or specialized devices through various programmed motions for the performance of a variety of tasks. Figure 8.1 shows an example of a robot.

Figure 8.1 An example of a robot

1. Mechanical Platforms—The Hardware Base

A robot consists of two main parts: the robot body and some form of Artificial Intelligence (AI) system. Many different body parts can be called a robot. Articulated arms are used in welding and painting; gantry and conveyor systems move parts in factories; and giant robotic machines move earth deep inside mines. One of the most interesting aspects of robots in general is their behavior, which requires a form of intelligence. The simplest behavior of a robot is locomotion. Typically, wheels are used as the underlying mechanism to make a robot move from one point to the next. And some force such as electricity is required to make the wheels turn under command.

1) Motors

A variety of electric motors provide power to robots, allowing them to move material, parts, tools, or specialized devices with various programmed motions. The efficiency rating of a motor describes how much of the electricity consumed is converted to mechanical energy.

Let's take a look at some of the mechanical devices that are currently being used in modern robotics technology.

DC motors: Permanent-Magnet, Direct-Current (PMDC) motors require only two leads, and use an arrangement of fixed-and electro-magnets (stator and rotor) and switches. These form a commutator to create motion through a spinning magnetic field.

AC motors: AC motors cycle the power at the input-leads, to continuously move the field. Given a signal, AC and DC motors perform their action to the best of their ability.

Stepper motors: Stepper motors are like a brushless DC or AC motor. They move the rotor by applying power to different magnets in the motor in sequence (stepped). Steppers are designed for fine control and will not only spin on command, but can spin at any number of steps-per-second (up to their maximum speed).

Servomotors: Servomotors are closed-loop devices. Given a signal, they adjust themselves until they match the signal. Servos are used in radio control airplanes and cars. They are simple DC motors with gearing and a feedback control system.

2) Driving mechanisms

Gears and chains: Gears and chains are mechanical platforms that provide a strong and accurate way to transmit rotary motion from one place to another, possibly changing it along the way. The speed change between two gears depends on the number of teeth on each gear. When a powered gear goes through a full rotation, it pulls the chain by the number of teeth on that gear.

Pulleys and belts: Pulleys and belts, two other types of mechanical platforms used in robots, work the same way as gears and chains. Pulleys are wheels with a groove around the edge, and belts are the rubber loops that fit in that groove.

Gearboxes: A gearbox operates on the same principles as the gear and chain, without the chain. Gearboxes require closer tolerances, since instead of using a large loose chain to transfer force and adjust for misalignments, the gears mesh directly with each other. Examples of gearboxes can be found on the transmission in a car, the timing mechanism in a grandfather clock, and the paper-feed of your printer.

3) Power supplies

Power supplies are generally provided by two types of battery. Primary batteries are used once and then discarded; secondary batteries operate from a (mostly) reversible chemical reaction and can be recharged many times. Primary batteries have higher density and a lower self-discharge rate. Secondary (rechargeable) batteries have less energy than primary batteries, but can be recharged up to a thousand times depending on their chemistry and environment. Typically the first use of a rechargeable battery gives almost 4 hours of continuous operation in an application or robot.

There are literally hundreds of types and styles of batteries available for use in robots. Batteries are categorized by their chemistry and size, and rated by their voltage and capacity. The voltage of a battery is determined by the chemistry of the cell, and the capacity by both the chemistry and size. See Table 8.1 for battery sizes.

Table 8.1 Power supplies

Size	NEDA	IEC	Description
AAA	24A	LR03	smallest of the command sizes
AA	15A	LR6	most popular small battery, typically used in packs of 2 or 4
C	14A	LR14	small flashlight battery, large toys
D	13A	LR20	largest common battery
9V	1604A	6L-R61	rectangular with clip-on connector

The robot platform runs off of two separate battery packs, which share only a ground. In this way, the motor may dirty up one power source while the electronics can run off of the other. The electronics and the motors can also operate from different voltages.

4) Electronic control

In a robot, there are two major hardware platforms: The mechanical platform of unregulated voltages, power and back-EMF (ElectroMotive Force) spikes, and the electronic platform of clean power and 5-volt signals. These two platforms need to be bridged in order for digital logic to control mechanical systems. The classical component for this is a bridge relay. A control signal generates a magnetic field in the relay's coil that physically closes a switch. MOSFETs (Metallic Oxide Semiconductor Field Effect Transistors), for example, are highly efficient silicon switches, available in many sizes like the transistor that can operate as a solid state relay to control the mechanical systems.

On the other hand, larger size robots may require a PMDC motor, in which the decrease of the value of the MOSFETs "on" resistance, results in great increases in the heat dissipation of the chip, thereby significantly reducing the chip's heat temperature. Junction temperatures within the MOSFET and the coefficients of conduction of the MOSFET package and heat sink are other important characteristics of PMDC motors.

There are two broad families of transistors: Bipolar Junction Transistors (BJT) and Field-Effect Transistors (FET). In BJT devices, a small current flow at the base moderates a much larger current between the emitter and collector. In FET devices, the presence of an electrical field at the gate moderates the flow between the source and drain.

5) Sensors

Robots react according to a basic temporal measurement, requiring different kinds of sensors.

In most systems a sense of time is built-in through the circuits and programming. For this to be productive in practice, a robot has to have perceptual hardware and software, which updates quickly. Regardless of sensor hardware or software, sensing and sensors can be thought of as interacting with external events (in other words, the outside world). The sensor measures some attribute of the world. The term transducer is often used interchangeably with sensor. A transducer is the mechanism, or element, of the sensor that transforms the energy associated with what is being measured into another form of energy. A sensor receives energy and transmits a signal to a display or computer. Sensors use transducers to change the input signal (sound, light, pressure, temperature etc.) into an analog or digital form capable of being used by a robot.

Logical sensors: One powerful abstraction of a sensor is a logical sensor, which is a unit of sensing or module that supplies a particular percept. It consists of the signal processing, from the physical sensor, and the software processing needed to extract the percept.

Proprioceptive sensors: Proprioception is dead reckoning, where the robot measures a signal originating within itself.

Proximity sensors: A proximity sensor measures the relative distance between the sensor and objects in the environment.

InfraRed (IR) sensors: Another type of active proximity sensor is an infrared sensor. It emits near-infrared energy and measures whether any significant amount of the IR light is returned.

Bump and feeler sensors: Another popular class of robotic sensing is tactile, or touch-based, done with a bump and feeler sensor. Feelers or whiskers are constructed from sturdy wires. A bump sensor is usually a protruding ring around the robot consisting of two layers.

2. Microcontroller systems

Microcontrollers (MCUs) are intelligent electronic devices used inside robots. They deliver functions similar to those performed by a microprocessor (Central Processing Unit, or CPU) inside a personal computer. MCUs are slower and can address less memory than CPUs, but are designed for real-world control problems. One of the major differences between CPUs and MCUs is the number of external components needed to operate them. MCUs can often run with zero external part, and typically need only an external crystal or oscillator.

There are four basic aspects of a microcontroller: speed, size, memory, and other. Speed is designated in clock cycles, and is usually measured in millions of cycles per second (MegaHertz, MHz). The use of the cycles varies in different MCUs, affecting the usable speed of the processor. Size specifies the number of bits of information the MCU can process in one step—the size of its natural cluster of information. MCUs come in 4-, 8-, 16-, and 32-bits, with 8-bit MCUs being the most common size. MCUs count most of their ROM in thousands of bytes (KB) and RAM (Random Access Memory) in single bytes. Many MCUs use the Harvard architecture, in which the program is kept in one section of memory (usually the internal or external SRAM). This in turn allows the processor to access the separate memories more efficiently.

The fourth aspect of microcontrollers, referred to as "other", includes features such as a dedicated input device that often (but not always) has a small LED or LCD display for output. A microcontroller also takes input from the device and controls it by sending signals to different components in the device. Also the program counter keeps track of which command is to be executed by the microcontroller.

R/C Servos: Servomotors, used in radio-controlled models (cars, planes, etc.) are useful in many kinds of smaller robots, because they are compact and quite inexpensive. The servomotors themselves have built-in motor, gearbox, position-feedback mechanisms and controlling electronics. Standard radio control servomotors which are used in model airplanes, cars and boats are useful for making arms, legs and other mechanical appendages which move back and forth rather than rotating in circles.

Pneumatics: Pneumatics is the name for fluid power used in a large number of commercial robots. Pneumatics is also used in a variety of anthropomorphic systems that fall under the category of fluid power. A better known branch of fluid power is hydraulics. Visit the pneumatics website for additional information.

3. Summary

The field of robotics has created a large class of robots with basic physical and navigational competencies. At the same time, society has begun to move towards incorporating robots into everyday life, from entertainment to health care. Moreover, robots could free a large number of people from hazardous situations, essentially allowing them to be used as replacements for human beings. Many of the applications being pursued by AI robotics researchers are already fulfilling that potential. In addition, robots can be used for more commonplace tasks such as janitorial work. Whereas robots were initially developed for dirty, dull, and dangerous applications, they are now being considered as personal assistants. Regardless of application, robots will require more rather than less intelligence, and will thereby have a significant impact on our society in the future as technology expands to new horizons.

Words and Expressions

serf [sə:f] n. 农奴；奴隶
articulated [ɑ:'tikjulitid] a. 铰接式(的)，枢接(的)，有关节的
gantry ['gæntri] n. 构台；桶架
permanent-magnet n. [物]永久磁铁
commutator ['kɔmjuteitə] n. 换向器，转接器
servomotor ['sə:vəu,məutə] n. 伺服电动机[马达]
pulley ['puli] n. 滑车，滑轮
gearbox ['giəbɔks] n. 变速箱
grandfather clock 有摆的落地大座钟
EMF (Electromotive Force) 电动势
MOSFET (Metallic Oxide Semiconductor Field Effect Transistor) 金属氧化物半导体场效应晶体管
BJT (Bipolar Junction Transistor) 双极结晶体管
proprioceptive [,prəupriəu'septiv] a. [生理]本体感受的
dead reckoning 推测，猜想；推算
proximity sensor 接近传感器
bump and feeler sensor 凹凸触角传感器

anthropomorphic [ˌænθrəpəuˈmɔːfik] a. 神与人或动物同形[同性]论的

Notes

1\. A re-programmable, multifunctional manipulator designed to move material, parts, tools, or specialized devices through various programmed motions for the performance of a variety of tasks.

（1）这不是一个完整的句子，是用来解释什么是机器人的，designed to…都是用来说明 a re-programmable, multifunctional manipulator 的。

（2）全句可翻译为：（机器人是）一种可以重复编程的、多功能的操作装置，通过不同的程序，它可以移动材料、零件、工具或特殊装备，最终完成各种各样的任务。

2\. On the other hand, larger size robots may require a PMDC motor, in which the decrease of the value of the MOSFETs "on" resistance, results in great increases in the heat dissipation of the chip, thereby significantly reducing the chip's heat temperature.

（1）句中 in which 所引导的从句是对 PMDC motor 作进一步的说明。

（2）全句可翻译为：另一方面，大尺寸的机器人可能需要一个永磁直流电机，其中金属氧化物半导体场效应晶体管的通态电阻的降低，会极大地增加芯片的热散失，从而大大地降低芯片的温度。

3\. Standard radio control servomotors which are used in model airplanes, cars and boats are useful for making arms, legs and other mechanical appendages which move back and forth rather than rotating in circles.

（1）句中前一个 which 指代 standard radio control servomotors，后一个 which 指代 other mechanical appendages。

（2）全句可翻译为：飞机、汽车和轮船模型中所使用的标准无线电控制伺服电机，对于加工胳膊、腿以及其他一些只作来回运动（而不是圆周运动）的机械附属肢体是很有用的。

Reading Material

Bioloid Humanoid (or Non-Humanoid) Robotics Kit

As shown in Figure 8.1, Bioloid features 18 servo motors, an amazing range of movement, and versatile modular construction. The Bioloid Humanoid Robotics Kit is truly a KIT. This means you can assemble the Bioloid's modules together to form any one of dozens of different robotic creatures. This really sets it apart from other humanoid robot kits and lesser toys.

The sensor array is impressive: an IrDA receiver, three proximity sensors that can measure distance and luminosity, and a microphone for sound detection and a piezoelectric speaker that can be used to play musical or beeps. This is a robot aware of its surroundings—another big plus.

Using the included motion editor software and visual programming environment, you can make the Bioloid interact with its surroundings and perform complex movements. Motions are built up frame-by-frame like a story board in an animation sequence. This allows quite complicated movements to be programmed. Once a motion has been defined it can then be downloaded into the Bioloid's memory and called from the Behaviour Control Program. The Bioloid comes with several example programs to make it walk, avoid obstacles and interact with sound.

This is an impressive platform for robotics allowing for many configurations, many ways to sense the environment, and a well-developed system for programming actions.

Take a look at the extensive documentation (including the manual and screen shots of the programming interface) on the Bioloid Humanoid Robotics Kit.

Lesson 2 Advanced Control Technologies in DCS

1. An Introduction

Higher productivity, strict environmental restrictions, increasing global competition is the current situation the elemental material process industries have been faced with. To copy with these situations the plant operation control system are hierarchically constructed illustrated in Figure 8.2. But the problem is that the current control system is not being used up to their full potential.

The lowest level in Figure 8.2 is the regulatory control. The main concern in this level is as follows:

(1) Process outputs come properly from sensors/process inputs and transfers to actuators.

(2) The controllers in the lower level (mainly PID) are tuned properly.

(3) The process variables are maintained at the current setpoint values.

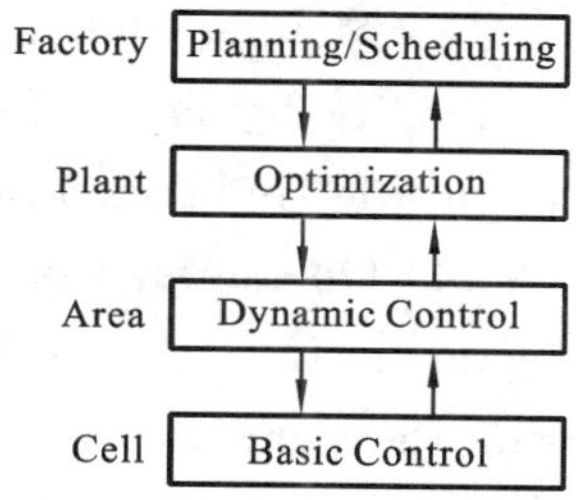

As more than 90% of control loops are located in the level, it is essential for each control variable to keep the items described above. Feedforward control, deadtime compensation and gain scheduling techniques et al. are available to supplement PID (Proportional-Integral-Differential) control.

Figure 8.2 Hierarchy of plant operation system

The second level of the hierarchy is dynamic control. MIMO (Multi-Input Multi-Output) control and constraint control are effective in this level. The variations of each control variables are minimized and the controller consistently pushes the plant outputs toward the optimum operating points to maximize the operating profits. The optimum operating points such as setpoints of control variables and constraints are given from the upper level. In order to make it easy to design MIMO control, some kind of design tools such as process modeling, controller definition and simulation are also required.

The third level is optimization. The optimum operating points of the plant are successfully computed using the rigorous optimization model. Some kinds of operation supporting systems are also required in this level for advanced alarming, plant diagnosis and operator training. These systems are effective to help the advanced control to work effectively and vice versa.

The top level is planning. The production scheduling has planned in order to achieve plant economy and satisfying the changing market demands.

2. Functional Requirements to Implementation

The regulatory control functions and some part of advanced control functions are implemented on the FCS (Field Control Station). MIMO control is implemented on the field-proven ACS (Advanced Control Station) and APWS (Advanced Process Work Station), which depends on the required reliability and each algorithm's portability. Advanced operation supporting systems and other engineering tools are implemented on APS. In implementation the following items are required.

(1) Continuity: In the FCS level, advanced control functions have the same functions as in the conventional controllers, e.g., input filtering, alarm processing, output limiter and bumpless auto/manual transfer and so on. The same structure enables to realize more complex control by cooperation of standard control functions.

(2) Expandability: The number of input, output and controller is configurable to cope with a wide range of customers' application. Operator interface is also preferred to be configurable to meet customers' individuality.

(3) Maintainability: Control configuration and operator interface are easy to maintain and modify by nonprofessional engineers. Engineering supporting tools are preferable to expand the application field of each control.

(4) Openness: Control variables and parameters are read and written from other control functions. Upper level control application can access the data of lower level control functions using the same access protocols.

(5) Operability: Operator interface part has no difference from those of conventional controllers—e.g., advanced control functions are displayed on the same operation windows and make it possible to operate without giving any confusion to operators.

(6) Portability: Control algorithm part does not depend on the hardware environment to adapt to the recent rapid progress of Large Scale Integrated (LSI) circuits and computer technologies.

(7) Profitability: Advantages of each control algorithm adaptation should be made clear. Not only controllability but also other advantages compared to the investments are made certain before and after implementation.

Various kinds of advanced control algorithms have been implemented on DCS (Distributed Control System) for commercial use and have been running in the real processes. In order to adapt the above functional requirements, original and individual techniques are developed and implemented.

3. Self Tuning Control

Many different type of self-tuning controller have been available in the industrial market. However some of them need oscillation of process output, while some need long duration of process perturbation et al. The features of our controller are as follows:

Only a single small step change in the setpoint or control output is applied under the closed loop condition to estimate a process model. This feature enables to follow up the changes of plant dynamics without disturbing plant operations.

The optimal PID parameters are computed when the certainty of the identified model is large enough to avoid ill-tuning.

The estimated model is displayed and utilized to detect if the process dynamic has changed.

Figure 8.3 shows the basic concept of the self-tuning controllers. The self-tuning controller always observes and collects the process input and output data. When the controller detects the process output move and becomes larger than the specified level after removing noise, signal trend and sensor failure, it starts the identification computing using the acquired process data. The key technology is how to estimate the process model rapidly by using a short duration of operating data in the closed loop condition. At first the noise and disturbance are removed to make a model in the neighborhood of the specified frequency domain. Secondly the process model is identified by using the obtained process input and output data iteratively as well as one kind of nonlinear programming technique. Thirdly the concept of "model certainty" is adopted to take into modeling errors. The identified model is adopted only when the model certainty is large enough. Process behavior is observed every monitoring period to trigger the identification again.

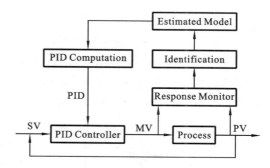

Figure 8.3 Basic concept of self-tuning controller

4. Fuzzy Control

Fuzzy control is a heuristic, nonlinear control function. If the process modeling is difficult but the operation procedure is obtained by operators and engineers, it makes concrete their knowledge by using if-then-else rules and fuzzy computation algorithm. It can also compensate for process nonlinearity and handle multi-input multi-output control.

In order to realize the fuzzy computation algorithm on DCS, the requirements to fuzzy control specifications have been investigated based on the application results. As a result the specification has been decided as follows: 12 inputs, 3 outputs, 7 labels for each input and output, 60 inference rules and so on. Input data is converted to an antecedent fuzzy variable using the membership function. The shape of an antecedent membership function should be a triangle or trapezoid. Each edge of one label is set as the vertex of triangle or the edge of the upper side of trapezoid of the adjacent label. Minimum values are computed for each fuzzy control rule. The computed outputs are converted to an actual value using the corresponding consequent variable. Each consequent variable has 13 labels and be set to one position. The fuzzy-output is obtained by computing the weighted mean of all data from the consequences.

Analyzing and tuning functions of fuzzy control is indispensable because of heuristic characteristics of fuzzy control. The inference status display windows and knowledge base builder windows are prepared for these purposes. The knowledge base editor defines the input and output membership functions and fuzzy inference rules. Real-time trend display and inference status display windows are enabled to monitor the inference processing of fuzzy control. Historical windows help to analyze the history of the inference processing. Simulation functions are effective after changing the input data and fuzzy rules.

5. Model Predictive Control and Internal Model Control

Model predictive control is one of the most popular and effective control technique in the industrial processes especially refinery and chemical processes. The model predictive control predicts the future behavior of the controlled process output using the embedded process models. It makes easy to stabilize the process with long dead time or integral process, and compensates the disturbances using the embedded feedforward function.

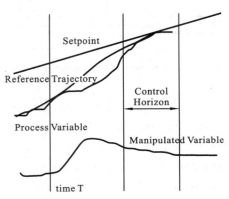

Figure 8.4 Basic scheme of model predictive control

Figure 8.4 shows the basic scheme of predictive control. General purpose predictive control needs the iterative computation to have the best coincidence between the predicted model behavior and the reference trajectory during the specified coincidence horizon on-line. In order to implement the model predictive control algorithm in DCS without losing its advantages, specifications are limited as follows: three input one output control, impulse response model, constant future input. When one output and constant future input, it is possible to obtain the solution without iterative computation even in the case of multiple inputs and integral process.

For model predictive control tuning three parameters are important: reference trajectory, coincidence horizon and future MV (Manipulated Variable) type, which are correspondent to dynamic response, robustness and control accuracy respectively. Reference trajectory starts from the current value of the process variable which tends towards to the future trajectory. The desired time response is selected to be equal to the time response of reference trajectory. The coincidence horizon mainly affects the robustness, which is generally selected to start after "non-well-behaved" period of the open loop time response and need not go further than the closed loop time response. The future MV time series is computed using a procedure which contains iteration, constraints, optimization, and so on. When the MV series are assumed to be constant, or to be a linear combination of state variables and so on, it is possible to simplify the future MV computation with the tradeoff with control accuracy.

One of the most simplified model predictive controls is IMC (Internal Model Control) which is also available on DCS. Generally speaking, this model is a first-order lag with delay, control horizon is one, and feedforward function is realized outside the controller using the combination of other calculation function blocks. Simple implementation is because of following reasons. A complex model leads to complex operation and time-consuming algorithms. As modeling error are bound to occur, successful applications are characterized by its capability to withstand these errors without serious deterioration of a closed loop behavior.

Not only gain and time constant of the model but also the delay parameter are changeable using other control functions according to the process dynamics changes. Model input is changeable to other input instead of control output according to the control loop configuration, which practically improves the performance and robustness of the controller.

6. Multivariable Model Predictive Control

Two of the most known MIMO predictive controls (MPC) in the world are now available in DCS level to obtain safety and easy to use. The multi-variable predictive control has more functions beyond MIMO control.

(1) Priority control: The operator carries out plant operation taking the actuator's operating range, plant's operating limits, product quality, etc. into consideration. MPC can add various constraint conditions to the manipulated variables and control variables based on the operators' knowledge base by prioritizing the constraint conditions.

(2) Optimization: MPC implements a sub-optimization function using the difference of the number of control variables and manipulated variables. If the number of control variables is larger than that of manipulated variable, MPC minimize the weighted sums of the offsets according to the plant operation. If the number of manipulated variables is larger than that of control variables, an economic indicator such as minimum utility cost, maximum throughput etc. can be optimized.

(3) Controllability monitoring: A multi-variable process is not always controllable which can be checked by using a gain matrix. Even if the inverse gain matrix exists, there is no assurance to obtain a good control performance because of ill-conditions of process such as MV saturation, operator's switching-off actions of MV, etc. In that case a practical solution is to control a subset of control variables instead of all control variables. Controllability monitoring analyzes on-line to decide which subset is effective to control.

In the implementation of MPC on DCS, the following items are taken into consideration realizing the seamless connection with conventional DCS functions:

(1) Input-output expansion: number of input/output is changeable according to applications.

(2) Signal compensation: input signal processing, alarm processing.

(3) Operator interface: the same interface to DCS's standard functions for use.

(4) Engineering: control loop configuration, initial parameter tuning.

Words and Expressions

DCS (Distributed Control System)　分布式控制系统

PID (Proportional-Integral-Differential)　［数］比例积分微分

setpoint['setpɔint] n. 设定点
feedforward [ˌfiːd'fɔːwəd] n. [电子]前馈
deadtime['dedtaim] n. 停工时间，无效时间
MIMO (Multi-Input Multi-Output) 多输入多输出
FCS (Field Control Station) 现场控制台
ACS (Advanced Control Station) 先进控制站
APS (Advanced Process Work Station) 先进过程工作站
heuristic [hjuə'ristik] a. 启发式的
trapezoid ['træpizɔid] n. [数]梯形，不等边四边形
IMC (Internal Model Control) 内模控制
prioritize [prai'ɔritaiz] vt. 把……区分优先次序

Notes

1. In the FCS level, advanced control functions have the same functions as in the conventional controllers—e. g. input filtering, alarm processing, output limiter and bumpless auto/manual transfer and so on.

(1) 整句主体结构为"…+advanced control functions+have+the same functions+…"。

(2) 全句可翻译为：在现场控制级中，先进控制与传统控制具有相同的功能，例如输入滤波、报警处理、输出限幅和自动/手动无扰切换等。

2. In order to implement the model predictive control algorithm in DCS without losing its advantages, specifications are limited as follows: three input one output control, impulse response model, constant future input.

(1) In order to 引导的是状语从句，表示目的。

(2) 全句可翻译为：为了在 DCS 中实现模型预测控制算法而不丢失其优点，需要制定以下规范：3 个输入/1 个输出控制，脉冲响应模型，常量输入。

3. Even if the inverse gain matrix exists, there is no assurance to obtain a good control performance because of ill-conditions of process such as MV saturation, operator's switching-off actions of MV, etc.

(1) Even if 引导的是条件状语从句，有转折的意思。

(2) 全句可翻译为：即使存在可逆增益矩阵，由于受控变量饱和、运算符号屏蔽受控变量等可能产生病态过程矩阵，因此也无法确保能够得到很好的控制性能。

Reading Material

Advanced Control Supporting Functions

Advanced control supporting functions are indispensable to promote advanced control implementation. These functions as follows are discussed with:

(1) Process modeling: To make process models using input/output operating data, modeling, controller building and simulation package are available on PC. In multi-variable control the determination of control specifications is as important as the model setting. Even the same controller operates in an entirely different manner if the MV rate-of-change values

changes.

(2) Training simulator: Training simulator, using a rigorous dynamic model and the DCS stations, is effective for the plant operation training including plant startup, shutdown, and emergency operation. It is also applicable to the evaluation of advanced control, better understanding of the plant behavior, and improve operator's skills.

(3) Advanced alarm: A flood of alarms is one of the matters of customers' concern for alarm redirection. Instead of simple loop alarm, to detect the process events is requested such as detection of weeping in the distillation column, decoding time in the furnace. Expert system, neural network, macro area monitoring are effective for these purposes.

(4) Plant operation support system: A plant operation support system is required to help operator's judgement, pattern recognition. On-line rigorous dynamic models and simulation technologies have become more and more important.

Recent progress in computer and network communication technologies has enabled to promote advanced control in industry automation field. Advanced control is not difficult to discuss with on the desk but it is not so easy to implement on the commercially feasible environments. Recent development of DCS has enabled to offer a variety of advanced control to customers with their satisfactions.

Lesson 3 Remote Sensing Technology

Remote sensing is the small or large-scale acquisition of information of an object or phenomenon, by the use of either recording or real-time sensing device(s) that is not in physical or intimate contact with the object (such as by way of aircraft, spacecraft, satellite, buoy, or ship). In practice, remote sensing is the stand-off collection through the use of a variety of devices for gathering information on a given object or area. Thus, Earth observation or weather satellite collection platforms, ocean and atmospheric observing weather buoy platforms, monitoring of a pregnancy via ultrasound, Magnetic Resonance Imaging (MRI), Positron Emission Tomography (PET), and space probes are all examples of remote sensing. In modern usage, the term generally refers to the use of imaging sensor technologies including but not limited to the use of instruments aboard aircraft and spacecraft, and is distinct from other imaging-related fields such as medical imaging.

There are two kinds of remote sensing. Passive sensors detect natural radiation that is emitted or reflected by the object or surrounding area being observed. Reflected sunlight is the most common source of radiation measured by passive sensors. Examples of passive remote sensors include film photography, infra-red, charge coupled devices, and radiometers. Active collection, on the other hand, emits energy to scan objects and areas whereupon a passive sensor then detects and measures the radiation that is reflected or backscattered from the target. RADAR is an example of active remote sensing where the time delay between emission and return is measured, establishing the location, height, speed and direction of an object(See Figure 8.5).

Remote sensing makes it possible to collect data on dangerous or inaccessible areas. Remote sensing applications include monitoring deforestation in areas such as the Amazon Basin, the effects of climate change on glaciers and Arctic and Antarctic regions, and depth sounding of coastal and ocean depths. Military collection during the cold war made use of stand-off collection of data about dangerous border areas. Remote sensing also replaces costly and slow data collection on the ground, ensuring in the process that areas or objects are not disturbed.

Orbital platforms collect and transmit data from different parts of the electromagnetic spectrum, which in conjunction with larger scale aerial or ground-based sensing and analysis, provide researchers with enough information to monitor trends such as El Niño and other natural long and short term phenomena. Other uses include different areas of the earth sciences such as natural resource management, agricultural fields such as land usage and conservation, and national security and overhead, ground-based and stand-off collection on border areas.

Figure 8.5 Synthetic aperture radar image of Death Valley colored using polarimetry

1. Data Acquisition Techniques

The basis for multi-spectral collection and analysis is that of examined areas or objects that reflect or emit radiation that stand out from surrounding areas.

1) Applications of Remote Sensing data

(1) Radar Conventional radar is mostly associated with aerial traffic control, early warning, and certain large scale meterological data. Doppler radar is used by local law enforcements' monitoring of speed limits and in enhanced meteorological collection such as wind speed and direction within weather systems. Other types of active collection include plasmas in the ionosphere. Interferometric synthetic aperture radar is used to produce precise digital elevation models of large scale terrain.

(2) Laser and radar altimeters on satellites have provided a wide range of data. By measuring the bulges of water caused by gravity, they map features on the seafloor to a resolution of a mile or so. By measuring the height and wave-length of ocean waves, the altimeters measure wind speeds and direction, and surface ocean currents and directions.

(3) LIDAR (Light Detection And Ranging) is well known in the examples of weapon ranging, laser illuminated homing of projectiles. LIDAR is used to detect and measure the concentration of various chemicals in the atmosphere, while airborne LIDAR can be used to measure heights of objects and features on the ground more accurately than with radar technology.

(4) Radiometers and photometers are the most common instrument in use, collecting

reflected and emitted radiation in a wide range of frequencies. The most common are visible and infrared sensors, followed by microwave, gamma ray and rarely, ultraviolet. They may also be used to detect the emission spectra of various chemicals, providing data on chemical concentrations in the atmosphere.

(5) Stereographic pairs of aerial photographs have often been used to make Topographic maps by Imagery Analysts, Terrain Analysts in trafficability and highway departments for potential routes.

(6) Simultaneous multi-spectral platforms such as Landsat have been in use since 1970s. These thematic mappers take images in multiple wavelengths of electro-magnetic radiation (multi-spectral) and are usually found on earth observation satellites, including (for example) the Landsat program or the IKONOS satellite. Maps of land cover and land use from thematic mapping can be used to prospect for minerals, detect or monitor land usage, deforestation, and examine the health of indigenous plants and crops, including entire farming regions or forests.

2) Geodetic

Overhead geodetic collection is first used in aerial submarine detection and gravitational data in military maps. This data reveal minute perturbations in the Earth's gravitational field (geodesy) may be used to determine changes in the mass distribution of the Earth, which in turn may be used for geological or hydrological studies.

3) Acoustic and near-acoustic

(1) Passive: Sonar is used for detecting, ranging and measuring underwater objects and terrain.

(2) Seismograms taken at different locations can locate and measure earthquakes (after they occur) by comparing the relative intensity and precise timing.

(3) Active: pulses are used by geologists to detect oil fields.

To coordinate a series of large-scale observations, most sensing systems depend on the following: platform location, what time it is, and the rotation and orientation of the sensor. High-end instruments now often use positional information from satellite navigation systems. The rotation and orientation is often provided within a degree or two with electronic compasses. Compasses can measure not just azimuth (i.e. degrees to magnetic north), but also altitude (degrees above the horizon), since the magnetic field curves into the Earth at different angles at different latitudes. More exact orientations require gyroscopic-aided orientation, periodically realigned by different methods including navigation from stars or known benchmarks.

Resolution impacts collection and is best explained with the following relationship: less resolution = less detail & larger coverage, more resolution = more detail & less coverage. The skilled management of collection results in cost-effective collection and avoids situations such as the use of multiple high resolution data tending to clog transmission and storage infrastructure.

2. Data Processing

Generally speaking, remote sensing works on the principle of the inverse problem. While the object or phenomenon of interest (the state) may not be directly measured, there exists some other variable that can be detected and measured (the observation), which may be related to the object of interest through the use of a data-derived computer model. The common analogy given to describe this is trying to determine the type of animal from its footprints. For example, while it is impossible to directly measure temperatures in the upper atmosphere, it is possible to measure the spectral emissions from a known chemical species (such as carbon dioxide) in that region. The frequency of the emission may then be related to the temperature in that region via various thermodynamic relations.

The quality of remote sensing data consists of its spatial, spectral, radiometric and temporal resolutions.

Spatial resolution: The size of a pixel that is recorded in a raster image—typically pixels may correspond to square areas ranging in side length from 1 to 1 000 meters (3 3 to 3 280 ft).

Spectral resolution: The number of different frequency bands recorded—usually, this is equivalent to the number of sensors carried by the platform(s). Current landsat collection is that of seven bands, including several in the infra-red spectrum. The MODIS satellites are the highest resolving at 31 bands.

Radiometric resolution: The number of different intensities of radiation the sensor is able to distinguish. Typically, this ranges from 8 to 14 bits, corresponding to 256 levels of the gray scale and up to 16 384 intensities or "shades" of color, in each band.

Temporal resolution: The frequency of flyovers by the satellite or plane, and is only relevant in time-series studies or those requiring an averaged or mosaic image as in deforesting monitoring. This is first used by the intelligence community where repeated coverage revealed changes in infrastructure, the deployment of units or the modification/introduction of equipment. Cloud cover over a given area or object makes it necessary to repeat the collection of said location.

Economic resolution: The cost-effective way to manage the collection of data.

In order to create sensor-based maps, most remote sensing systems expect to extrapolate sensor data in relation to a reference point including distances between known points on the ground. This depends on the type of sensor used. For example, in conventional photographs, distances are accurate in the center of the image, with the distortion of measurements increasing the farther you get from the center. Another factor is that of the platen against which the film is pressed can cause severe errors when photographs are used to measure ground distances. The step in which this problem is resolved is called georeferencing, and involves computer-aided matching up of points in the image (typically 30 or more points per image) which is extrapolated with the use of an established benchmark, "warping" the image to produce accurate spatial data. As of the early 1990s, most satellite images are sold fully georeferenced.

In addition, images may need to be radiometrically and atmospherically corrected.

Radiometric correction: Gives a scale to the pixel values, e. g. the monochromatic scale of 0 to 255 will be converted to actual radiance values.

Atmospheric correction: Eliminates atmospheric haze by rescaling each frequency band so that its minimum value (usually realized in water bodies) corresponds to a pixel value of 0. The digitizing of data also make is possible to manipulate the data by changing gray-scale values.

Interpretation is the critical process of making sense of the data. The first application is that of aerial photographic collection using the following process: spatial measurement through the use of a light table in both conventional single or stereographic coverage, added skills such as the use of photogrammetry, the use of photomosaics, repeat coverage, making use of objects' known dimensions in order to detect modifications. Image Analysis is the recently developed automated computer-aided application which is in increasing use.

Object-Based Image Analysis (OBIA) is a sub-discipline of GIScience devoted to partitioning remote sensing(RS) imagery into meaningful image-objects, and assessing their characteristics through spatial, spectral and temporal scale.

Old data from remote sensing is often valuable because it may provide the only long-term data for a large extent of geography. At the same time, the data is often complex to interpret, and bulky to store. Modern systems tend to store the data digitally, often with lossless compression. The difficulty with this approach is that the data is fragile, the format may be archaic, and the data may be easy to falsify. One of the best systems for archiving data series is as computer-generated machine-readable ultrafiche, usually in typefonts such as OCR-B, or as digitized half-tone images. Ultrafiches survive well in standard libraries, with lifetimes of several centuries. They can be created, copied, filed and retrieved by automated systems. They are about as compact as archival magnetic media, and yet can be read by human beings with minimal, standardized equipment.

Words and Expressions

MRI (magnetic resonance imaging)　核磁共振成像
positron ['pɔzitrɔn] n. 正电子,阳电子
tomography [tə'mɔgrəfi] n. [医]X线断层摄影术
CCD (charge coupled device)　电荷耦合装置
radiometer [ˌreidi'ɔmitə] n. 辐射计,放射计
backscatter ['bæk'skætə] n. 反向散射
deforestation [diˌfɔris'teiʃən] n. 砍伐森林
ionosphere [ai'ɔnəsfiə] n. 电离层
interferometric ['intəˌferəu'metrik] a. [物]干涉测量(法)的,干涉仪的,用干涉仪测量的
synthetic aperture radar　合成孔径雷达
altimeter ['æltimiːtə] n. 高度计
LIDAR ['laidə] n. 激光雷达
stereographic [ˌstiəriəu'græfik] a. 立体画法的,立体照相的

landsat [ˈlændsæt] n. （美国）地球资源（探测）卫星
thematic mapper   专题制图仪
indigenous plant   乡土植物,本地生植物
geodesy [dʒiːˈɔdisi] n. 大地测量学
seismogram [ˈsaizməgræm] n. 震动图
azimuth [ˈæziməθ] n. 方位,方位角
gyroscopic [ˌdʒairəsˈkɔpik] a. 回转仪的
mosaic [məˈzeiik] n. 镶嵌；镶嵌图案；镶嵌工艺 a. 嵌花式的,拼成的
extrapolate [eksˈtræpəleit] v. 推断；[数]外推
falsify [ˈfɔːlsiˌfai] v. 伪造
ultrafiche [ˈʌltrəˌfiːʃ] n. 超缩微平片,超缩微胶片

Notes

1. Orbital platforms collect and transmit data from different parts of the electromagnetic spectrum, which in conjunction with larger scale aerial or ground-based sensing and analysis, provide researchers with enough information to monitor trends such as El Niño and other natural long and short term phenomena.

(1) 整句主体结构为"Orbital platforms＋collect and transmit＋data＋..."。

(2) 全句可翻译为：轨道平台收集和传送来自电磁波频谱不同频段的数据，再通过大量基于航空和地面的传感和分析，就可以为研究者提供足够的信息来监测像厄尔尼诺和其他一些长期和短期自然现象的变化趋势。

2. Maps of land cover and land use from thematic mapping can be used to prospect for minerals, detect or monitor land usage, deforestation, and examine the health of indigenous plants and crops, including entire farming regions or forests.

(1) 整句主体结构为"Maps of land cover and land use＋...＋can be used＋..."。

(2) 全句可翻译为：关于土地覆盖和土地使用的专题地图可以用来勘探矿物，检测土地使用和森林砍伐状况，检查本土植物和庄稼的健康情况，甚至可以包括所有的农区或森林。

3. While the object or phenomenon of interest (the state) may not be directly measured, there exists some other variable that can be detected and measured (the observation), which may be related to the object of interest through the use of a data-derived computer model.

(1) 整句主体结构为"...＋there＋exists＋some other variable＋..."。

(2) 全句可翻译为：当我们所感兴趣的对象或现象（状态）不能被直接测量时，通过计算机数据模型，一定能够找到其他一些与之相关联的、能够被直接检测（观测）的变量。

Reading Material

History of Remote Sensing

Beyond the primitive methods of remote sensing our earliest ancestors used (eg. standing on a high cliff or tree to view the landscape), the modern discipline arose with the development of flight. The balloonist G. Tournachon (alias Nadar) made photographs of Paris from his balloon in 1858. The first tactical use is during the civil war. Messenger pigeons, kites, rockets and unmanned balloons are also used for early images. With the exception of balloons, these first, individual images are not particularly useful for map making or for scientific purposes.

Systematic aerial photography is developed for military surveillance and reconnaissance purposes beginning in World War I and reaching a climax during the cold war with the use of modified combat aircraft such as the P-51, P-38, RB-66, F4-C and the SR-71 or specifically designed collection platforms such as the U2/TR-1, A-5 and the OV-1 series both in overhead and stand-off collection. A more recent development is that of increasingly smaller sensor pods such as those used by law enforcement and the military, in both manned and unmanned platforms. The advantage of this approach is that this requires minimal modification to a given airframe. Later imaging technologies would include infra-red, conventional, doppler and synthetic aperture radar.

The development of artificial satellites in the latter half of the 20th century allows remote sensing to progress to a global scale as of the end of the cold war. Instrumentation aboard various Earth observing and weather satellites such as Landsat, the Nimbus and more recent missions such as RADARSAT and UARS provided global measurements of various data for civil, research, and military purposes. Space probes to other planets have also provided the opportunity to conduct remote sensing studies in extraterrestrial environments, synthetic aperture radar aboard the Magellan spacecraft provided detailed topographic maps of Venus, while instruments aboard SOHO allowed studies to be performed on the Sun and the solar wind, just to name a few examples.

Recent developments include, beginning in the 1960s and 1970s with the development of image processing of satellite imagery. Several research groups in Silicon Valley including NASA Ames Research Center, GTE and ESL Inc. developed Fourier transform techniques leading to the first notable enhancement of imagery data.

The introduction of online web services for easy access to remote sensing data in the 21st century (mainly low/medium-resolution images), like Google Earth, has made remote sensing more familiar to the big public and has popularized the science.

Lesson 4 Machine Vision in Brief

1. What is Machine Vision?

"Machine Vision (MV)" is a field of study and technology whose goal is to endow machines with the ability to perceive selective aspects of the world using visual means.

This sounds like a circular definition. One can easily get lost in a particular concept or technology when trying to define machine vision. Perhaps it's best to start with a more ostensible definition, then. Those of us fortunate enough to have functional eyes have an incredible ability to perceive and understand the world through them. Engineers have long sought to endow machines with this capability. It's easy to assume that this just means duplicating the mechanisms people use in machines, but that's not all there is to it. Some techniques involve projecting and reflecting laser beams off distant targets, for example, which is very different from how you and I work. Some systems can read and understand information in bar codes or other special constructs that are difficult for humans to deal with.

Most importantly, few techniques being researched or in use today really resemble the awesome complexity and flexibility available to humans. MV researchers have their own bag of tricks. It may be that some day, they bring all those tricks together and find they can make machines "see" as well as or even better than humans do.

All practical machine vision systems in use today exist for their own specific purposes. Some are used to ensure that parts coming off assembly lines are manufactured correctly. Some are used to detect the lines in a road for the benefit of cars that drive themselves. Though some interested parties claim otherwise, there are no general purpose vision systems, either in laboratories or on the market.

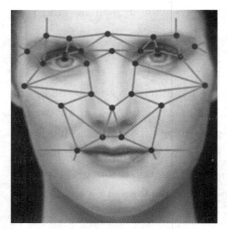

Figure 8.6 Facial measures used in a biometrics vision system

If it sounds like it's difficult to define machine vision, don't fret. The point is that the field of machine vision is not simply interested in duplicating human vision. What is essential is the basic goal of visual perception, i.e., the ability to "understand" the world visually, sufficiently for moving about in and interacting with a complex, ever-changing world and discerning information in the environment. Figure 8.6 shows facial measures used in a biometrics vision system.

2. General-Purpose Vision

As mentioned above, all practical machine vision end products available now are for specific purposes.

Human vision is general purpose. In our everyday experiences, we see a plenty of panoply things in all sorts of lighting conditions. We are able to operate well in almost any circumstance in which there's even a modest amount of light entering our eyes and which isn't damaging them.

Merely being able to see light is nearly useless, though. The best video cameras today are still just recording or transmission devices; they don't do anything else practical with it. By contrast, we are poor recording and transmission devices. It's our faculties for visual perception that distinguish us. So let's talk about what we do with the visual information we can see.

We can recognize the boundaries between objects. We can recognize objects. We can recognize the repetitions that compose both simple and rich textures. We can intuit the nature and location of light sources without seeing them directly. We can recognize the three dimensional nature of the things we see. We can see how things are connected together and how larger objects are subdivided into smaller ones. We can recognize that the two halves of a car on either side of a telephone pole are actually parts of a single car that is behind the pole. We can tell how far away things are. We can detect the motion of objects we see. We can recognize complex mechanisms with lots of moving parts as components of single larger objects and distinguish them from the backdrop of the rest of the world. We can even recognize a silver pitcher amidst a noisy background, though we only see the reflections of that background.

Perhaps the most interesting feature of human vision that distinguishes it from most machine vision techniques crafted to date is that we can deal very well with novel situations. A new car you've never seen before is still obviously a car because it looks like a car. You instantly catalog novel objects and register essential differences.

How does one distill all this down into a clear definition, then? What is the general purpose of machine vision? I think it's best to define it in terms of a set of core goals. A machine can be said to have general purpose machine vision if it can:

(1) construct a 3D model of the open space within its visual field sufficient for movement within that space and interaction with the objects within it;

(2) distinguish most any whole object, especially a complex moving one, from the rest of a visual field;

(3) recognize arbitrarily complex textures as continuous surfaces and objects;

(4) have a hierarchical way of characterizing all the objects within a scene and their relative positional and connectivity relationships to one another;

(5) characterize a novel object using a three dimensional animated model composed of simpler primitives and be able to recognize that object in most any orientation;

(6) be able to recognize and separate objects in a wide variety of lighting conditions, including complex arrangements of shadows;

(7) be able to separate and recognize objects that are transparent, translucent, or reflective, given sufficient visual cues.

There are probably other milestones one could add to this, but it seems a pretty lofty set for now.

Words and Expressions

endow [in'dau] v. 捐赠；赋予
ostensible [ɔs'tensəbl] a. 可公开的；(指理由等)表面的，虚假的
fret [fret] v. (使)烦恼；(使)焦急；(使)腐蚀；(使)磨损
panoply ['pænəpli] n. 全套甲胄；华丽服饰
intuit [in'tju(:)it] v. 由直觉知道
backdrop ['bækdrɔp] n. 背景幕；(事件等的)背景
craft [krɑ:ft] n. 工艺，手艺 vt. 手工制作；构思
distill [di'stil] vt. 蒸馏，提取 vi. 滴下
hierarchical [ˌhaiə'rɑ:kikəl] a. 分等级的
translucent [trænz'lju:snt] a. 半透明的，透明的

lofty ['lɔ(:)fti] a. 高高的;崇高的;高傲的;高级的

Notes

1. What is essential is the basic goal of visual perception, i. e., the ability to "understand" the world visually, sufficiently for moving about in and interacting with a complex, ever-changing world and discerning information in the environment.

(1) 整句主体结构为"What is essential+is+the basic goal of visual perception+..."。

(2) 全句可翻译为:机器视觉最本质的地方在于实现视觉最基本的目标,也就是说,能够可视地、充分地认识外界环境——在一个复杂的、不断变化的环境中自由地走动,并且能够辨识外界各种信息。

2. We can even recognize a silver pitcher amidst a noisy background, though we only see the reflections of that background.

(1) 整句主体结构为"We+can even recognize+a silver pitcher amidst a noisy background"。

(2) 全句可翻译为:我们甚至可以从一个充满噪声的背景图像中辨认出一个银色大水罐,尽管只是看到其倒影。

3. Perhaps the most interesting feature of human vision that distinguishes it from most machine vision techniques crafted to date is that we can deal very well with novel situations.

(1) 整句主体结构为"...+the most interesting feature of human vision+...+is+that we can deal very well with novel situations"。

(2) 全句可翻译为:或许,人类视觉之所以能够区别于迄今为止制作最精巧的机器视觉,其最有趣的特征在于人类能够很好地适应新的环境。

Reading Material

The Basics of CCD

A Charge Coupled Device (CCD) is a highly sensitive photon detector. The CCD is divided up into a large number of light-sensitive small areas (known as pixels) which can be used to build up an image of the scene of interest. A photon of light which falls within the area defined by one of the pixels will be converted into one (or more) electrons and the number of electrons collected will be directly proportional to the intensity of the scene at each pixel. When the CCD is clocked out, the number of electrons in each pixel is measured and the scene can be reconstructed.

The CCD is primarily made of silicon and the structure has been altered so that some of the silicon atoms have been replaced with impurity atoms.

In fact, the pixels in a CCD are defined by the position of electrodes above the CCD. If a positive voltage is applied to the electrode, then this positive potential will attract all of the negatively charged electrons close to the area under the electrode. In addition, any positively charged holes will be repulsed from the area around the electrode. Consequently a "potential well" will form in which all the electrons produced by incoming photons will be stored.

As more and more light falls onto the CCD, the potential well surrounding this electrode will attract more and more electrons until the potential well is full (the amount of electrons that can be stored under a pixel is known as the full well capacity). To prevent this, the light must be prevented from falling onto the CCD, for example, by using a shutter as in a camera. Thus, an image can be made of an object by opening the shutter, "integrating" for a length of time to fill up most of the electrons in the potential well, and then closing the shutter to ensure that the full well capacity is not exceeded.

An actual CCD will consist of a large number of pixels (i. e., potential wells), arranged horizontally in rows and vertically in columns. The number of rows and columns defines the CCD size, and typical sizes are 1024 pixels high by 1 024 pixels wide. The resolution of the CCD is defined by the size of the pixels, also by their separation (the pixel pitch). In most astronomical CCDs the pixels are touching each other and so the CCD resolution will be defined by the pixel size, typically 10—20 μm. Thus, a 1 024×1 024 sized CCD would have a physical area image size of about 10 mm×10 mm.

Lesson 5 Aeronautical Technologies for the 21st Century

1. Introduction

Throughout the latter half of this century the U. S. aeronautics industry has been one of the undisputed success stories in global competitiveness. From the end of World War II into the last decade, U. S. aircrafts, engines, and parts have been among the leaders of, and in most cases have dominated, both the domestic and the foreign markets for subsonic transports, general aviation, commuter, and military aircraft. The buildup of the global transportation infrastructure (i. e., airports and air traffic management systems) has also been driven by U. S. technology and products. The aeronautics industry is the largest positive industrial contributor to the U. S. balance of trade, plays a vital role in maintaining the safety and convenience of air travel throughout the world, and provides important contributions to the defense of U. S. interests. Further, U. S. aircrafts are flown in even the most remote parts of the world, engendering national pride and international prestige.

The importance that foreign governments ascribe to developing their domestic aeronautics industries is evidence of the perceived benefits from a strong aircraft industry. Europe and the Pacific rim countries have spawned numerous government and industry consortia aimed at producing aircraft and components across the entire range of the market. The European consortium, Airbus Industries, has moved into second place in the market for commercial transport aircraft, while the emerging Asian aircraft industries have begun to forge alliances with the two dominant U. S. companies, Boeing and McDonnell Douglas. Foreign interests dominate the commuter aircraft industry and are making roads into the general aviation market. European and Far Eastern nations have begun to apply significant effort toward developing the technological base needed to compete even more effectively over the next several decades. The inference is obvious—these nations believe it is in their national interest to maintain a healthy, broad-based domestic aircraft industry.

In keeping with the charter of the National Aeronautics and Space Administration

(NASA) to preserve "the role of the United States as a leader in aeronautical technology," NASA's Office of Aeronautics and Space Technology asked the Aeronautics and Space Engineering Board of the National Research Council to assist in assessing the current status of aeronautics in the United States and to help identify the technology advances necessary to meet the challenges of the next several decades. The Aeronautics and Space Engineering Board established the Committee on Aeronautical Technologies, which defined an approach to helping NASA determine the appropriate level and focus of its near-term technology development efforts to maintain a leadership role in the years 2000—2020.

The Committee discussed the transportation infrastructure that would likely exist in 2020. From this, an estimate was made of the types and capabilities of aircraft required to compete in the global market in the 2000—2020 time frame. Based on these projections, the Committee identified the high-leverage technologies that offer the most significant advances in aeronautics to ensure long-term competitiveness for U. S. aircrafts, engines, and components, and to enhance performance and safety in the total air transportation system.

2. The Technological Challenge

The fact that U. S. market share in aeronautics is eroding is well documented and is discussed in detail. The ultimate cause of eroding market share is that, for a variety of reasons, foreign competitors are able to market products that have lower total ownership costs than U. S. products. This can be achieved, for example, through implementation of new technologies that reduce long-term operating costs, or through products that enter the market with significantly lower purchase price. This presents a challenge to the industry and to the U. S. government. U. S. aircrafts, engines, and parts manufacturers must improve the quality, capability, and timeliness of their products, at reduced cost, to maintain or increase their market share.

Without advanced technology, market share will certainly be lost, but advanced technology cannot, by itself, ensure competitive products.

Foreign governments have undertaken determined, coordinated efforts to compete in all sectors of the market from general aviation through supersonic aircraft, and in most cases they have been successful. In terms of the current impact on the U. S. industry, this attack is most visible in the subsonic transport market that has historically been dominated by Boeing, Lockheed, and McDonnell Douglas. This segment of the market generates the highest revenues for aircrafts, engines, and parts manufacturers.

A long and successful history does not imply that there are no significant future gains to be realized. McDonnell Douglas and Boeing project a potential growth of 1 trillion passenger-miles each decade to 2 trillion in the year 2000, and 4 trillion by 2020, most of which will be carried on advanced subsonic transport aircraft. Such estimates indicate that technical advances resulting in increased range and safety, and reduced fuel consumption, noise, and emissions can have significant effects on the competitive posture of the nation that produces them.

Although increased research into advanced subsonic aircraft technologies is needed to bring about a near-term competitive advantage, without continued resources applied to the environmental and economic viability of supersonic aircraft, U. S. participation in that important future market may be forfeited.

Similarly, advances in the technology of the global air traffic management (ATM) system can reduce congestion both in the air and on the ground, and make traveling by air safer and easier for everyone.

3. Needs for the Future

The Committee identified seven needs that must be addressed by the U. S. aeronautics community, including NASA, the Federal Aviation Administration (FAA), aircraft manufacturers, and air carriers, if the United States is to maintain or increase its share of the global aircraft market: lower cost and greater convenience, greater capacity to handle passengers and cargo, reduced environmental impact, greater aircraft and ATM system safety, improved aircraft performance, more efficient technology transfer from NASA to industry, and reduced product development times. Neither the Committee's charter nor its makeup allowed detailed consideration of the latter two needs, so these are not discussed in detail. The remaining five are discussed below in terms of the needs of industry and the nation.

(1) Lower cost/greater convenience: Generally, people choose air travel over automobile, bus, ship, or rail because their desire for shorter trip times justifies the cost. Also, in many cases, air travel is the only choice, so that if the cost is excessive the potential traveler does not make the trip. To open new markets in developing nations and to expand current markets, the cost of the service must remain low enough to maintain that justification. Furthermore, the level of convenience of the service must not be compromised such that passengers in existing markets are driven to other forms of transportation. In short, advances in the speed, range, or payload of the various classes of aircraft must not be accompanied by large increases in cost or degradation of service. Thus, greater fuel efficiency and reduced operational costs must be vigorously pursued, and increases in airport and ATM system capacity must not come at the expense of convenience.

(2) Greater capacity to handle passengers and cargo: A major factor that may impose a ceiling on the ability of the aviation industry to respond to the growing demand for air travel is airport and ATM system capacity. Where local restrictions allow, it is simplest to build more airports and runways. However, this is not possible in most cases. Rather, to open up new markets or to expand existing markets, it is imperative that both the ATM system and the existing airports be capable of dealing with more people and packages flying on more and different kinds of aircraft. Safe reductions in aircraft separation, better real-time weather reporting, and facilities for a wide variety of long-and short-range aircraft all contribute to the ability to move more people and cargo through the system, and thus to the growth of both the industry and the economy.

(3) Reduced environmental impact: The impact of aircraft on the environment is a limiting factor on the growth of the industry. Aircraft noise restrictions limit the proximity

of airports to major population centers, the utility of rotorcraft within cities, and the potential for supersonic flight over land. In addition, a change in the ozone level that results from the emission of nitrogen oxide and hydrocarbons by aircraft is an area of growing concern that may, in the near future, limit the number and types of aircraft that fly over the United States and other environmentally conscious countries.

(4) Greater aircraft/ATM system safety: As more planes takeoff and land each year, it is vital that the rate of accidents continues to decrease to avoid the perception that air travel is unsafe.

(5) Improved aircraft performance: Advances in performance of conventional subsonic aircraft, rotorcraft, short takeoff and landing aircraft, and supersonic aircraft will enable more viable expansion into new markets and expansion of existing routes.

(6) The Committee grouped advanced aircraft into three classes, within which recommendations were prepared that cut across specific technologies:

advanced subsonic transport aircraft;

high-speed civil transports (HSCTs), the next generation of supersonic transports;

short-haul aircraft (commuters, rotorcraft, and general aviation aircraft).

Similarly, the Committee identified five generic disciplines that encompass the technologies that will provide the greatest overall benefit toward meeting future needs: ①aerodynamics, ② propulsion, ③ materials and structures, ④ avionics and controls, and ⑤cognitive engineering.

Words and Expressions

undisputed [ˈʌndisˈpjuːtid] a. 毫无疑问的,无争议的

subsonic [ˈsʌbˈsɔnik] a. [物]次音(速)的

spawn [spɔːn] n. (鱼等的)卵;(植物)菌丝;产物 v. 产卵

consortium [kənˈsɔːtjəm] n. 协会;联盟,(国际)财团,[律]配偶的权利,〈美〉大学联盟协定

erode [iˈrəud] vt. 侵蚀;腐蚀;使变化 vi. 受腐蚀,逐渐消蚀掉

forfeit [ˈfɔːfit] n. (因犯罪、过失、违约等而)丧失的事物,没收物,罚款 vt. 没收,丧失 a. 丧失了的;被没收了的

rotorcraft [ˈrəutəkrɑːft] n. 旋翼飞机

hydrocarbon [ˈhaidrəuˈkɑːbən] n. 烃,碳氢化合物

short-haul [ˈʃɔːtˈhɔːl] a. 短距离的,短程的

aerodynamics [ˌɛərəudaiˈnæmiks] n. 空气动力学,气体力学

avionics [ˌeiviˈɔniks] n. 航空电子工学;电子设备

Notes

1. From the end of World War II into the last decade, U.S. aircrafts, engines, and parts have been among the leaders of, and in most cases have dominated, both the domestic and the foreign markets for subsonic transports, general aviation, commuter, and military

aircraft.

(1) 整句主体结构为"…+U. S. aircrafts, engines, and parts+have been+…"。

(2) 全句可翻译为:从第二次世界大战结束到最近十年,美国的飞机、发动机及其零部件不论是在国内还是国外的亚音速运输、通用航空、往返运输以及军用飞机市场一直处于领先地位,而且大多数情况下是统治地位。

2. Although increased research into advanced subsonic aircraft technologies is needed to bring about a near-term competitive advantage, without continued resources applied to the environmental and economic viability of supersonic aircraft, U. S. participation in that important future market may be forfeited.

(1) although 和 without 所引导的均是从句,本句主语是 U. S. participation in that important future market,谓语是 may be forfeited。

(2) 全句可翻译为:尽管为了获得近期的竞争优势,必须要加强对先进亚音速飞机技术的研究,但如果没有为了保证其环境及经济生存能力的持续投入,那么在未来的市场上美国也将失去参与的机会。

3. The Committee identified seven needs that must be addressed by the U. S. aeronautics community, including NASA, the Federal Aviation Administration (FAA), aircraft manufacturers, and air carriers, if the United States is to maintain or increase its share of the global aircraft market: lower cost and greater convenience, greater capacity to handle passengers and cargo, reduced environmental impact, greater aircraft and ATM system safety, improved aircraft performance, more efficient technology transfer from NASA to industry, and reduced product development times.

(1) 这句话的主语是 The Committee,谓语是 identified,宾语是 seven needs that must be addressed。if 引导的是条件状语从句。

(2) 全句可翻译为:该委员会认为,如果美国政府要保住或增加它在全球飞机市场上的利益,那么美国航空协会(包括国家航空和宇宙航行局(NASA)、联邦航空局(FAA)、飞机制造商及航空公司)就必须要呼吁大家做到以下七个方面:更低的成本和更高的便利性,更大的载客量和载货量,减少环境影响,更高的飞机和 ATM 系统安全性,改善飞机性能,NASA 到工业更有效的技术转让,以及降低产品开发周期。

Reading Material

Forum on Aeronautical Engineering Science and Technology

On October 29th, 2002, Forum on Aeronautical Engineering Science and Technology sponsored by Division of Mechanical and Vehicle Engineering of CAE was convened in Beijing Science & Technology Hall. The theme is "Achievement and Prospectus of China's Aeronautical Engineering."

The forum was presided by Academician Gu Songfen and Liu Daxiang of CAE in turn. Academician Gu Songfen briefed the history of aeronautical engineering in nearly 100 years, praised the achievement of China's aeronautical engineering in recent years, and expounded the significance of this forum. Then, Researcher Ni Xianping and Yin Zeyong, Professor Fan Wei, Researcher Li Likun, Academician Zhang Yanzhong, Associate Professor Chen Yong,

Senior Engineer Su Muhuai, Professor Li Yinghong delivered speeches on "Development and Contemplation of Helicopter Technology", "Vigorously Strengthen the Development of Medium & Small Aero Engine Technology in China", "Latest Development of Research of New Concept Pulse Knocking Engine", "Status, Orientation and Strategy of Air-to-Air Missile", "Status of Research of Intelligent Structural System of Aircraft", "Research and Application of Human Factor of Civil Aviation", "Development of Tableland Aeronautical Engineering", etc.

In addition to the above-mentioned reports, the colloquium of the Forum also included "Summary of Development of Critical Technology of Fire Control System of Airborne Weapon" by Researcher Lu Guangshan, "From Automatic Fly to Independent Fly" by Researcher Zhang Xinguo, "Analysis of Key Points of Present Development of Advanced Composite Materials of Aviation" by Professor Yi Xiaosu, "Research of Maintainability and Service System of New Generation Fighter" by Research Gan Xiaohua and Senior Engineer Li Hanghang, totally 12 reports.

This Forum was financially supported by Shenyang Plane Research Institute and valuable assistance of other concerned organizations. Preparatory work was organized by Academician Gu Songfen, Li Ming, Zhang Yanzhong and Liu Daxiang of Division of Mechanical and Vehicle Engineering of CAE. Guided by leaders of CAE in charge of this forum, all documents of the Colloquium passed the examination by concerned Confidential Committee. Leaders of Academic Division and Comprehensive Department, General Office and other departments also offered assistance during preparatory and proceeding of this forum.

Related academicians of CAE attended this forum. Totally 200 delegates from State Economy & Trade Commission of, Ministry of Science & Technology, Ministry of Education, State Commission of Science, Technology and Industry for National Defense. China Aviation Industry Cooperation I, China Aviation Industry Cooperation, Space Research Institutes, related universities and colleges attended the forum, too.

PART NINE Translation and Writing

第一章　专业英语的特点

第一节　引　言

20世纪由于科学技术的飞速发展,各国技术情报资料大量涌现,国际上的学术交流日益频繁;随着科学技术不断发展,科学技术文献的数量与类型急剧增加,世界各国的科学技术出版物在种类、数量、出版速度、出版形式等方面都以飞跃的姿态向前推进。

据统计,从数量上来看,目前用各种语言出版的专业科技期刊约四万多种,并且,还在以每年一千多种的速度增加。在全世界范围内,发表论文400万篇/年,专利说明书40多万件/年(我国10万件/年(中国专利技术开发公司1999年数据)),技术标准总数20万件,国际会议录1万种以上/年,而新书,差不多是每分钟就有一本新书出版。真是形成了"文献的海洋"、"知识的海洋"了。在当今世界,特别是进入21世纪之后,要想"读遍天下文章"是根本不可能的了。

从出版类型上看,现代科技文献的种类也是繁多的,如科技图书(Book)、期刊论文(Journal Paper)、科技报告(Technique Report)、政府出版物(Government Publication)、专利文献(Patent)、技术标准(Technique Standard)、学位论文(Degree Dissertation)、产品样本(Sample Book)、说明书(Directions)和技术手册(Technique Manual)等。

在科技文献中,若以语种(语言种类)分,尤其以英语为最多。英语发展到今天,已经不仅成为了一种国际性的商业语言,在国际学术界,也成了一种重要的交流工具,而且,非英语系国家有些科技出版物也是用英文发表的,不少工程期刊都有英文版。例如,*Russian Engineering Journal* 是俄文版期刊 Вестник Машиностроения(《机械制造通报》)的英文版;*Precision Engineering* 是日文版《精密工程》的英文版期刊。

改革开放以来,在我国召开了大量的国际性学术会议,并出版了相当数量的英文专业杂志,有的在刊物中列有英文题录和摘要,如 ISTAI'2006(*Proceedings of the First International Symposium on Test Automation & Instrumentation*《第一届测试自动化和仪器国际研讨会论文集》)就是2006年由我国仪器仪表学会在北京主办的以英语作为交流语言的国际学术会议论文集。而 ISTAI'2008 则是第二届测试自动化和仪器国际研讨会的论文集。

《机械工程学报》、《仪器仪表学报》、《科学通报》、《数学通报》、《仪表技术与传感器》、《传感器世界》、《电子测量与仪器学报》、《测控技术》等刊物均列有英文题录和摘要。

而且,从来自美国科学基金会凯斯工学院基金委员会和日本国家统计局关于"一个科研人员从事一个科研项目各项研究过程所占时间的百分比"的统计数字表明,需用50.9%的时间用于查阅有关的科技文献资料(见表9-1)。

表 9-1　一名科研人员从事一个科研项目各项研究过程所占时间的百分比统计

各项研究过程	所占时间的百分比/(％)
一、开展思考计划	7.7
二、查阅有关的科技文献资料	50.9
三、进行科学实验	32.1
四、从事编写科研报告	9.3

从中我们可以体会到，学好外语，尤其是学好专业英语，对于科技人员吸收世界上最新的技术情报，从事科学研究，参与国际科学技术交流是非常重要的。而要掌握科技英语，必须在英语语法、翻译方法与科学技术三者上狠下工夫。

第二节　专业英语的特点

科学技术本身的性质要求专业外语与专业内容要相互配合、相互一致，专业英语也不例外。专业英语（English for Special Science and Technology）与普通英语（Common English or General English/Ordinary English）有很大的差异。专业英语的主要特点是它具有很强的专业性，需要有一定的专业基础知识，也就是说，对于专业英语的材料，有一定专业基础知识的人读起来，比不懂专业的人要得心应手得多。例如：Some operating clearance must exist between the piston and the cylinder wall. 此处的 clearance 不是"清除，清理"而应作为"间隙"理解。又如：lens stop 不是"透镜停止"，而应译成"透镜光阑"；stop nut 不是"停止坚果"，而是"防松螺母"；the light show screen 是"光显示屏"，而不是"轻快的表演银幕"，等等。

由此可见，应根据表达的内容所涉及的专业范畴选择恰当的词义进行翻译。

在专业英语中，都是用以表达科技概念的，或者是描述事实、叙述理论的，因此，要求专业英语注重客观事实和真理，逻辑性强，条理规范，表达准确、精练、正式。同时，要求数据无误、文字简练，尤其对定义、定律、公式、图表、结论等。

专业英语的特点可归纳为如下几点。

(1) 长句多。

例如：Factory will not buy machines unless they believe that the machines will produce goods that they are able to sell to consumers at a price that will cover all costs.

这是由一个主句和四个从句组成的复杂长句。

(2) 被动语态用得多。因为科技文章只是强调过程本身，注重做什么而不注重是谁做的。

例 1：Surface grinding machines *are designed* primarily for grinding flat surfaces. However, with special setups, angular and formed surfaces also *may be ground*.

Plain grinding machines *are designed* primarily for production grinding of external cylindrical surfaces. They *are used* for cylindrical grinding of straight surfaces, tapered surfaces, and shoulders. They also *may be used* for plunge grinding of formed surfaces which conform to the shape of the grinding wheel.

Universal grinding machines *are designed* to perform both external and internal cylindrical grinding operations. It can grind straight surfaces, tapered surfaces, shoulders, steep tapers, and face grinding. Also, straight fluted reamers and milling cutters *can be ground* on a universal grinder. The internal grinding machine *is used* for finishing cylindrical or tapered holes. It is a highly specialized machine which rarely *is found* in schools or small commercial shops. In such shops, internal grinding usually *is done* with a universal-grinding machine equipped with an internal grinding fixture.

The tool and cutter grinding machine *is designed* for grinding milling cutters, reamers, taps, and other precision cutting tools used on milling and drilling machines. When equipped with the appropriate accessories, tool and cutter grinding machines also *may be used* for accurately grinding single-point cutting tools.

上例短文由13个短句构成,其中有12句使用了被动语态。

例2:Laser can be used to measure distances with hitherto unimaginable convenience and accuracy. (参见本书第三部分第五课 Laser Technology)用的也是被动语态。

(3) 用虚拟语气表达假设与建议。

例1:It is necessary that the machine-tools of this workshop should be lubricated regularly.

例2:If computer were not used, our research work would be difficult.

(4) 名词性词组多。如:drinking water(饮用水), man-made satellites(人造卫星), developing countries(发展中国家), developed countries(发达国家)。

(5) 合成新词多。随着社会发展和科学技术的日新月异,新词新义不断涌现,据不完全统计,每年产生的新词有2 000个左右,如 mechantronics(mechanics+electronics)(机电一体化), electronography(电子摄像学,静电印刷学), biochip(生物硅片), sphygmomanometer(血压计), electroencephalograph(人脑电流示波器), electrocardiograph(心电图描记仪), electrooptics(电光学), diskcopy(磁盘拷贝), cyberzine(网络杂志), webcam(网络摄影机)等。

(6) 非限定动词(非谓语动词),尤其是分词使用频率高。

例1:The important step in *minimizing* costs of production is *choosing* the cheapest of the technical efficient alternatives. 降低生产成本的重要措施是选用最便宜、技术上有效的方法。

例2:The cathode ray is a stream of electrons *emitted by a heated wire called a cathode*. 阴极射线是由称为阴极的受热金属丝发射的电子流。

(7) 在说明书、使用手册(Manual)中广泛使用祈使句。

例如:Caution! When operating this equipment, please exercise extreme caution and use common sense. 警告! 操作这一设备时,请非常小心使用,并要有使用常识。

(8) 介词短语多。

例如:The change in the electrical resistance of the sensing element *brought about by* the resulting increase(or decrease)in the length of the sensor element is directly *proportional to* applied pressure.

(9) 常用 It... 句型结构。

例如:It is hoped that new easy-to-manage technique will help prevent further loses. 人们希望这种很容易操作的新技术有助于制止进一步的损失。

(10) 专用术语(term)多。

例如:Instruments used in medicine and biomedical research are just as varied as those in industry. Relatively simple medical instruments measure temperature, blood pressure (sphygmomanometer), or lung capacity(spirometer). More complex instruments include the familiar X-ray machines and electroencephalographs and electrocardiographs, which detect electrical signals generated by the brain and heart, respectively.（参见第三部分第一课 Reading Material）。

句中涉及一些医学和生物医学仪器的专用术语：sphygmomanometer（血压计）、spirometer（肺活量计）、electroencephalograph（人脑电流示波器）、electrocardiograph（心电图描记仪）等。

(11) 半技术词汇（semi-technical vocabulary）多。

从语汇上看，科技英语中虽然有大量专业技术词汇和专用术语，但其基本词汇都是普通英语中固有的。有关统计资料表明，一般科技英语书刊中的普通词汇（亦称半技术词汇）高达80%以上，由此可见普通词汇所占的比重之大。即使在专业性极强的科技文章中，普通词汇也远比专业词汇多。如不同专业都要经常使用这些通用词汇，如 frequency（频率）、energy（能量）、magnetism（磁性）等，这类词的词义比较单一，在科技英语中出现频率较高，数量也较多。在科技英语中还存在大量的普通词汇，它们除了本身的基本词义外，在不同的专业中又有不同的词义，如前面所说的 operate，再如 monkey 的普通词义是"猴子"，而在机械专业中有"活动扳手"、"打桩机"、"心轴"等词义。

(12) 缩略词（abbreviation）使用频繁。

如 CPU（central processing unit）（中央处理单元）、ULSI（ultra large scale integration）（超大规模集成电路）、VAL（virtual assembly language）（虚拟汇编语言）、VI（Visual Instrument 虚拟仪器）等。

(13) 插图、表格、公式、数字所占比例大。这样表达科技现象直观、简单、明了。

(14) 希腊词根和拉丁词根常出现。

如 e.g.（拉丁语 *egempli gratia* = for example，例如），etc.（拉丁语 *et cetera* = and so on, 等等），synchrotron（同步加速器）含有希腊词素 syn-（共同），aerospace（太空、宇宙空间）是由希腊词素 aero 和拉丁词素 space 构成的。

在阅读、翻译科技英语文献时要注意以上这些特点。

第三节　专业英语的语法特点

专业英语的语法特点可归纳总结为三个方面：客观（objectivity）、精练（conciseness）和准确（accuracy）。

一、客观（objectivity）

由于只注重客观，而在语法上的体现为多用被动语句和一般现在时。

有人统计过，在专业英语中，被动语态的句子约占 1/3～1/2，即使是主动语态，主语也常常是非动物的（inanimate subject）。这主要是因为在专业英语中，专业人员关心的是事实和行为，而不是行为者。同时，使用被动语态，可以使句子更短更简明；另外，由于将重要的信息放在句首，可以一下子就能抓住读者的注意力。

例1：（参见第二节被动语态用得多的例1）

在上例中，短文由 13 个短句构成，其中有 12 句使用了被动语态。以第一句为例，它并未指出是谁设计了平面磨床，而是为了介绍平面磨床的作用。

正因为如此，被动语态广泛用于表述规则、原理、过程、技术报告和说明书等。

而就时态而言,由于介绍科技文献所涉及的内容(如科学定义、定理、方程式或公式、图表等),一般没有特定的时间关系,所以,大部分都使用一般现在时。一般过去时、一般完成时也经常出现,这在科技报告、科技新闻、科技史料等中常常能看到。但过去将来时、完成进行时等时态,在专业英语中很少见。

二、精练(conciseness)

专业英语还要求精练,常常希望用尽可能少的单词来清晰地表达原意。为了精练,非限定动词、名词化单词或词组及其他简化形式广泛地得到使用。

(一) 动名词的运用

用动名词取代时间状语从句或简化时间陈述句。

例 1:Before you attempt to operate a lathe, you should become familiar with its principal parts, controls and accessories.

可运用动名词将上述例句精简为:

Before attempting to operate a lathe, you should become familiar with its principal parts, controls and accessories.

而在下一例句中,Heating 为动名词,用 Heating water 动名词短语作主语,将 change 作为句子的谓语。

例 2:Heating water does not change its chemical composition.

译为:把水加热并不会改变水的化学成分。

句中虽然有两个动词,仍很精练。

(二) 分词的运用

分词有过去分词和现在分词两种,用过去分词短语可取代被动语态关系从句,而用现在分词短语可取代主动语态关系从句。

例 1:The input is the desired temperature which is set for a room.

它可精练为:

The input is the desired temperature setting for a room.

在运用分词时要注意,现在分词含有主动和进行的意思,而过去分词含有被动和完成的意思。

例 2:The analyses and computations *made* number many millions.

译为:所作的分析和计算达到了几百万次。

此处的 made = that have been made。

(三) 不定式的运用

用不定式短语常可替换表示目的、功能的从句。

例如:We keep micrometers in boxes. Our object in doing this is to protect them from rust and dust.

它可精练为:

We keep micrometers in boxes to protect them from rust and dust.

译为:将千分尺放在盒子内以防生锈和尘土。

三、准确(accuracy)

专业英语的准确性主要表现在用词上。随着科学技术的发展,新术语、新概念、新理论和新产品不断涌现,还有新词、缩略语等不断产生。关于词汇的特点,以后再详细研究、讨论。在此,先举两个例子,说明用词的准确性。

mechatronics 是 mechanics 和 electronics 组合而成的一个新词,表示"机械电子学"或"机电一体化";Internet 是 inter-(表示"相互"的词头,当然也表示"在中间"、"在内")与 net(表示"网络,网状物,网格")的组合,表示"因特网"、"互联网络"。

这两个词虽然新,但构词较严密、准确。

专业英语的准确性还表现在语法结构上。如为了准确、详细地描述一个事物的过程,所用的句子都比较长,甚至一段就是一个句子。例如第二节中"长句多"中的例子。

长句反映了客观事物中复杂的关系,这并不是说它不精练。长句与精练并不矛盾,只是说明它包含的信息量大、准确性较高。

此外,还有许多其他的特点,如:通格名词作前置定语;虚拟语气使用频繁;分裂定语或定语从句较多;后置定语较多;名词及名词短语直接作状语的现象较普遍等等。

第四节　专业英语的词汇特点

词汇是语言发展的产物,在专业英语中,各类技术词汇随着专业领域的不同有着不同的含义。如 diaphragm,在光学领域,词义为"光阑,十字线片";在测量学中,词义为"挡板,(流量)孔板";而在力学中,词义为"膜片,膜盒"。

而且,在专业词汇中,缩略语也较多。根据所在领域的不同,也有着不同的含义。如 NC(no connection),词义为"不连接"(电工电子);NC(numerical control),词义为"数字控制"(机械加工);NC(network control),词义为"网络控制"(计算机)。又如 IT(information technology),词义为"信息产业"(信息);IT(immuity test),词义为"免疫"(医学类);IT(insulating transformer),词义为"隔离变压器"(电工电子)。再如查一下 VI,就有"可变间隔"(variable interval),"垂直间隔"(vertical interval),"黏度指数[指示器]"(viscosity index [indicator]),"视觉指示器"(visual indicator),"音量指示器"(volume indicator)和"虚拟仪器"(visual instrument)等词义。因此,在阅读时,需要弄清楚文章属于哪个学科领域,以便选用确切的专业词义。

专业英语中的词汇除了上面所述具有一定的专业性以外,还有如下一些特点。

一、词汇的构成比较复杂

词汇由技术词汇、次技术词汇(半技术词汇)、特用词和功能词等构成。

(一) 技术词汇(technical words)

这类词汇专业性很强,一般只在各自的专业范围内使用。而且这类词汇一般较长,由前后缀和一些单词组合而成,词越长,它的词义就越狭窄。它出现的频率一般不高。如 pneumonoultramicroscopicsilicovolcanoconiosis(硅酸盐沉着病,矽肺病)曾经是英语中最长的单词,由 45 个字母构成,但词义只有 1 个。冗长的词一般出现在化学、医学、生物学英语中,这种词虽然"难看"、"难读"、"难听",但含义确切,词义专一,构词有规律,对专业科技人员来说,并不难掌握。因此需要时科技人员从不回避使用它们。

又如 workhardening(加工硬化)、amplifier(放大器)、comparator(比较器)、superconductivity(超导性)、quadraphonics(四声道立体声)(quadr-[词头]四,平方)、ferroaluminium(铁铝合金)(ferro-[词头](亚、含、二价)铁的)。

（二）次技术词汇(sub-technical words)

这是在各专业中出现频率都很高的词。这类词往往在不同的专业中有不同的含义。如 conductor, energy, efficiency, field, force, load, operation, plant, power, reaction, revolution, register, solution, system, work 等。下面为其中一些词汇在不同的专业中有不同的含义的例子。

Reaction——在日常用语中,表示某人对某事的反应;在化学中,表示两种物质分子间的化学反应;在核物理中,表示原子核的链式反应;在土木工程中,表示反作用力。

Register——在电学中,表示"计数器,记录器";在乐器中,表示"音域,音区";在日常生活中,表示"登记簿,记录(员,表),挂号信"等;在计算机中,表示"寄存器"。

Solution——在数学中,表示"解法,解式";在化学中,表示"溶解"。

（三）特用词(big words)

在日常生活中,为使语言生动活泼,常用一些短小的词或词组。而在专业英语中,为了准确、正式、严谨、不与其他词义混淆,往往选用一些较长的特用词。这类词在非专业英语中极少使用,但却属于非专业英语。

例如:Then the light is turned on. 然后,把灯打开。

在专业英语中,为避免引起歧义,用 complete 表示接通,因为 complete 词义单一、准确。

The circuit is then *completed*. 然后接通电路。

而不用 The circuit is then *turned on*.

这是因为 turn on 的词义较多,除了表示"接通(入)"以外,还可表示如"(拧,旋)开,朝向,依靠(赖,据),攻击(sb)"等意义。

例如:The success of a pinic usually *turns on*（依赖）the weather.

The dog *turned on*（袭击） to me and bit me in the leg.

类似的词还有：

at once—immediately   a lot of—appreciable
enough—sufficient   find out—determine
go down—depress   keep—maintain
push in—insert   send—transmit
turn upside down—invert   used up—consume

（四）功能词(function words)

功能词包括介词、连词、冠词、代词等。它们在句子中提供十分重要的结构信号,对于理解专业内容十分重要。它们出现的频率极高。

有统计数据表明,在专业英语中出现频率最高的十个词都是功能词,它们是（按出现频率高低顺序排列）the, of, in, and, to, is, that, for, are, be。

例如:It simply means that tool have softened to the point where the movement of the tool in relation to the work makes the tool too soft for efficient cutting.

上述例句中 29 个词中就有 14 个功能词。

二、构词法(word building)的特点

专业英语中的词汇的构词法有如下特点：

(1) 大部分专业词汇来自拉丁语和希腊语;

(2) 前缀和后缀的出现频率比较高。

希腊语和拉丁语是现代科技英语词汇的基础,美国语言学专家 Oscar E. Nybaken 的统计结果表明,在 10 000 个普通词汇中大约有 46% 的词汇来源于拉丁语,7.2% 的词汇来源于希腊语。对于专业性强的词汇,这个比例就更高了。

对英语词汇进行分析,可以看到词汇的构词法大致有合成、转换和派生或词缀三种方式。

(一) 合成(composition)

由两个或更多的词合成一个词。合成词在英语中比较活跃。它由介词、名词、动词、副词、形容词等词组合而成。例如:

work+shop—workshop	名词+名词
in+put—input	介词+动词
feed+back—feedback	动词+副词
radio+photography—radiophotography	名词+名词
white+wash—whitewash	形容词+动词
hand+shake—handshake	名词+动词
hard+board—hardboard	形容词+名词
air+sick—airsick	名词+形容词
industrial distribution equipment	多词复合名词

(二) 转换(conversion)

and—to AND	$conj. \longrightarrow n.$
use—to use	$n. \longrightarrow v.$
extent—extend	$n. \longrightarrow v.$

转换时词形一般不变(有时发生重音变化或尾音变化),只是词类发生转换。

(三) 派生或词缀(derivation)

专业英语词汇大部分都是派生法构成的,即由词根(base)加上各种词缀(前缀(prefixes)和后缀(suffixes))来构成新词。如《英汉技术词典》(清华大学 1978 年编写,国防工业出版社 1978 年出版)中以 semi- 构成的词就有 283 个,以 auto- 构成的词有 260 多个,以 micro- 构成的词有 300 多个,以 thermo- 构成的词有 130 个。

了解并掌握一些常用的词缀,对学习是有益的。例如归纳一下常用的表示否定的前缀(negative prefixes)有下列 8 个:①a-(abnormal 异常的,asynchronous 异步的,asymmetric 不对称的);②dis-(disobey 不服从,dismount 拆除);③in-(injustice 不公正,inhomogeneous 不均匀的);④il-(illegal 非法的);⑤ir-(irrational 无理数,irrecognizable 不能辨认的);⑥im-(impossible 不可能的,imbalace 不稳定);⑦non-(noncontact 不接触,nondestructive 非破坏的);⑧un-(unwilling 不情愿的,unrenewable 不能回收的)。其中"un-"最常用。

常用的前缀和后缀多达上百个。作为专业科技人员,至少应掌握 50 个常用的前缀和后缀。常用的名词词缀、形容词词缀和动词词缀如下:

1. 名词词缀(24 个)

词 缀	词 例
auto-	automation(自动化),autoplotter(自动绘图仪)
inter—between, among	interalloy(中间合金),intergrinding(相互研磨)
counter—against	counteraction(反作用),countertorque(反力矩)
sub—beneath, less than	subway, submarine(潜水艇)

PART NINE Translation and Writing

词缀	词例
in-	intake(水、气等)入口, inlet(海湾,小港)
out-	outlet(河流)出口, output(产量,输出)
through-	throughput(生产量,(物料)通过量)
hyper—over	hyperbar(高气压), hyperpressure(超压), hyperplane(超平面)
di—two	diode(二极管), diphase(二相的)
tri—three	triangle(三角), triode(三极管)
tele—far away	telescope(望远镜), telemeter(遥测表)
photo—light	photoprocess(光学处理), photograph(照相)
micro—small	microwave(微波), micrometer(微米), microcomputer(微机)
ultra—excessive	ultrasonic(超声波), ultralimit(超极限)
super—to an unusually high degree	superhardness(超(级)硬度)
holo completely by oneself	holograph(全息照相), hololens(全息透镜)
-ics—subject	dynamics(动力学), statistics(统计学)
-cle—diminutive, small	particle(粒子)
-ism—an action	mechanism(机构)
-ist—a man	scientist(科学家), artist(艺术家)
-scope—see, observe	microscope(显微镜), telescope(望远镜)
-phone—sound	microphone(话筒)
-logy—subject	anthropology(人类学), technology(技术,工艺)
-ness	brightness(光亮), kindness(慈祥)

2. 形容词词缀(14 个)

词缀	词例
in—not	inadequate, insufficient(不适当的,不足的)
im—not	immaterial, impossible
ir—not	irrational, irresponsible(不负责任的)
un—not	unchanged, unstable
super—above, more than	superficial, supersonic(超声的)
-able, -ible	noticeable, negligible(可忽略的)
-ive	reactive, effective
-ent, -ant	convergent, sufficient(足够的)
-ing, -ed	cutting, compressed
-al	structural, critical(临界的)
-ar	circular, linear(直线的)
-ic	electronic, metallic(金属的)
-ous	synchronous(同步的), porous(多孔的)
-proof	fireproof, acid-proof, waterproof(防水)

3. 动词词缀(14个)

词缀	词例
re—again	reuse, rechange, recall
over—too much	overwork, overload
under—too little	under-load, underpay
dis—the opposite	disconnect, discharge
de—cause not to be	demagnetise(消磁), defreeze(解冻)
ab—being away from	abjure(誓绝), abstain(戒除,弃权)
con—together	confound(混淆,搞错)
ex—out	exit, external
ob—against	obstruct(阻塞,阻挡)
trans—across	transform(转换,变换)
-en—get, make, become	weaken, harden, shorten
-fy—make	electrify, purify
-ise	normalise, energise(激励,通电)
-ate	integrate, accelerate

三、词汇的缩略

(一)节略词(clipped words)

某些词汇在发展过程中,为方便起见,逐渐用它们的前几个字母来表示,这就是节略词。例如,maths(mathematics),ad(advertisement),lab(laboratory),kilo(kilogram),metro(metrology),dir(directory),del(delete),STB(Strobe)。

(二)缩写词(acronyms)

首字母缩写词,指由某些词的首字母所组成的新词。需按构成的新词拼读。例如:

radar	radio detecting and ranging
laser	light amplification by stimulated emission of radiation
ROM	Read-Only Memory
RAM	Random Access Memory
UNESCO	United Nations Educational, Scientific and Cultural Organization(联合国教科文组织)
MEMS	micro-electro-mechanical system(微电子机械系统)

(三)首字词(initials)

首字词与缩写词基本相同,区别在于首字词必须逐字母念出。例如:

CAD	computer-aided design(计算机辅助设计)
CAM	computer aided manufacturing(计算机辅助制造)
CPU	Central Process Unit(中央处理单元)
CIF	Cost Insurance and Freight(到岸价格(包括货价、保险费和运费))
ADC	Analog-to-Digital Converter(模数转换器)
ACB	Access Control Block(存取控制块)
ACE	Automatic Control Equipment(自动控制装置)
FOB	free on board(离岸价格)

IC	Integrated Circuit(集成电路)
IBM	International Business Machine(Corperation)(国际商用机器公司)
IT	Information Technology(信息技术)
OEM	Original Equipment Manufacturing(初始设备制造)
PCB	Printed Circuit Board(印制电路板)
EMC	Electromagnetic Compatibility(电磁兼容性)

（四）缩略词(abbreviations)

它并不一定像缩写词那样由某个词组的首字母组成。有些缩略词仅由一个单词变化而来，而且，大多数缩略词每个字母后都附有一个句点。这也是缩略词的特点。

专业英语中的缩略词数量很大，约有 2 万～3 万个。有些缩略词长达 9 个字母。例如：

Appx.	Appendix
Amp.	Amplifier
A. C.	Alternating Current，Aerodynamic Centre，Air Conditioning
et al.	and other
e. g.	exempli gratia
Fig.	Figure
M. S. E. E.	Master of Science in Electrical Engineering
M. S. E. M.	Master of Science in Electrical Mechanics
M. S. Nucl. Eng.	Master of Science in Nuclear Engineering
Ltd.	Limited
Sq.	square
vs.	Versus

第五节　符号、公式及其他

在专业英语中，为明确表达，还含有较多的符号、公式、方程、插图等。

一、符号

专业英语中常见的符号见表 9-2。

表 9-2　专业英语中常见的符号

符　号	意　义	符　号	意　义
$\because$	because	μp	microprocessor
$\therefore$	therefore	μc	microcomputer
$\not>$	is not greater than	$''$	seconds, inches
$\not<$	is not less than	$°, ℃$	Degree(Centigrade)
$\rightarrow$	result in, lead to, maps into	$\perp$	is perpendicular to
$\ll$	is much greater than	$//$	is parallel to
$\gg$	is much less than	@	print
&	and	$\iint$	double integral
$\equiv$	is identically equal to	$\iiint$	triple integral

续表

符　号	意　义	符　号	意　义
∽	is similar to	￥	yuan
£	pound	♯	number
∈	is member of set	$	dollar

二、常用希腊字母

常用希腊字母表如表 9-3 所示。

表 9-3　常用希腊字母表

字　母	英文读音	字　母	英文读音	字　母	英文读音
α	alpha	η	eta	ρ	rho
β	beta	θ	theta	σ	sigma
γ	gamma	λ	lambda	τ	tau
δ	delta	μ	mu	φ	phi
ε	epsilon	ν	nu	ψ	psi
ζ	zeta	π	pi	ω	omega

三、数学符号

（一）分数、小数及百分比

例如：

符号	读法
1/3	a third, or one third
2/9	two ninths
0.2	0 point two, or (nought, zero) point two
66.67	sixty six point-six seven
4.9̇	four point nine recurring（循环）
3.0326̈	three point nought three two six, two six recurring（循环）
0.3%	0 (nought, zero) point three per cent
8‰	eight per mille

（二）符号与方程

例如：

$a=b$	a equals b; a is equal to b; a is b
$a\neq b$	a is not equal to b; a is not b
$a\pm b$	a plus or minus b
$a\approx b$	a is approximately equal to b
$a\geq b$	a is greater than or equal to b
$a\leq b$	a is less than or equal to b
$a\gg b$	a is much greater than b
$a\ll b$	a is much less than b
$a\not< b$	a is not less than b

$a \not> b$	a is not greater than b
$a // b$	a is parallel to b
$a \perp b$	a is perpendicular to b
$a:b::c:d$	a is to b as c is to d
$a+b$	a and (plus) b
$a-b$	a minus b
$a \times b$	a times (multiplies) b
$a \div b (a/b)$	a over (divided by) b
x^2	x square; x squared; the second power of x
x^n	$x\{\sup n\}$; $x \cdot x \cdot x \cdots n$ factors; the n th power of x
y^3	y cube; y cubed; y to the third power
y^{-10}	y to the minus tenth (power)
a'	a prime
b''	b double (second, twice) prime
b_2	b sub two
b_m	b sub m
b_m''	b double prime sub m
Δx 或 δx	(the increment of x) delta x
dy/dx 或 $Dy(x)$	the differential coefficient of y with respect to x; the first derivative of y with respect to x
$d^2 y/dx^2$	the second derivative of y with respect to x
∇	del; nabla; vector differential operator
∇^n	n th del (nabla)
$20\,°C$	twenty degree centigrade
$38\,°F$	thirty-eight degree Fahrenheit
$\log_a b$	logarithm b to the base a
5×10^{-9}	five multiplied ten to the minus ninth (power), $5 \times 10\{\sup-9\}$
$M = P_1 x - Q_1(x-a_1)$	M is equal to P sub one multiplied by x minus Q sub one, round brackets opened x minus a sub one, round brackets closed
$R = \sqrt{(\sum Px)^2 + (\sum Py)^2}$	R equals the square root of sigma Px all squared, plus sigma Py all squared
$\int \dfrac{dy}{\sqrt{c^2 - y^2}}$	the integral of dy over (by) the square root of c square minus y square
$\int_a^b$	integral between limited a and b; integral of... from a to b
$12 > 8+3$	12 is greater than 8 plus 3
$x^2 + y^2 = 10$	x squared with y squared equals 10

第二章　专业英语翻译概论

第一节　翻译的过程、标准及对译者的要求

一、翻译的过程

由于世界上各国语言不尽相同，而随着世界各国科学技术与经济的不断发展，特别是全球化经济的发展趋势，国家间的交往在深度与广度上不断发展。要交流、交往，就要有语言（口头的或书面的）来表达，就需要通过翻译，用共同的语言来表达、沟通。

这儿讲的翻译，主要是指书面翻译。要想翻译好文章，不仅仅是能看懂就行了，还需要准确地表达，即用书面文字译成本国文字，如果只阅读而不译成文字，理解往往容易肤浅，浮于表面。只有通过翻译的反复实践，才能熟悉两种语言的对应和差别，深化对原文含义的领会和理解，并不断提高运用汉语表达外语（英语）原意的能力。

翻译的过程，可以分为理解、表达和校对三个阶段，或称作翻译的三步曲。

（一）理解阶段

理解原著是确切表达的前提。它是指通过对原著（原文）的语言现象理解原作的内容。理解包括理解语言现象、逻辑关系及原文所涉及的学科事物等。

1. 理解语言现象

为了正确理解原文，必须上、下有联系地、全面地理解原文的词汇含义、语法关系和修辞色彩，而不能孤立地看待一词一句，切忌"望词生义"，更不能堆砌文字。

在理解阶段，应当首先把全文阅读一遍，对全文的大意有个概括的了解，然后逐词逐句地推敲，再下笔翻译。

科技文献的翻译，理解阶段显得特别重要，尤其是对词义的理解。这在第一章第四节"专业英语的词汇特点"中已经讲过，次技术词汇往往在不同的专业中具有不同的含义。实际上，在其他语言中也都存在着一词多义的现象，如在汉语中：

（1）荷：荷花（莲），荷包（随身携带的小包）；荷：读音 hé。

（2）荷枪实弹（背或扛），荷重（负担），电荷。荷：读音 hè。

同样一个词或词组，在不同的上下文中、在不同的专业中、在不同的句法结构中就可能有不同的意义，因此，阅读理解不能脱离上下文，不能脱离全篇文献。

例如：dispersion 在数学方面作"离差，差量"解；在物理学方面（光学上）作"色散，弥散"解；在计算机方面，dispersion gate 即为"与非门"。

因此，先阅读全文，可了解它涉及的学科，是讨论数学方面、物理方面还是计算机方面的，以便于选用恰当的词义。

2. 理解逻辑关系

从逻辑上理解，有时可以帮助我们理解一些按原文语法关系所不能理解的问题，或发现译文中译错的词句。

这就需要仔细对原文的含义加以推敲，有时还要估计实际情况，并根据一些生活体验思考一下自己的理解是否合情合理，有无漏洞、不合逻辑的地方。

例如：第三部分第一课中的一句话：Such as radio waves from a distant star or the magnetic moment of a subatomic particle. 其中的"magnetic moment"不能译成"磁性片刻"，而应译为"**磁矩**"。

moment 有多种词义:在"Please wait for a moment"中解释为"片刻,瞬间";在"moment of inertia"中译成"惯性矩,转动惯量";在"moment of momentum"中则解释为"动量矩,角动量"。

3. 理解原文所涉及的学科事物

应特别注意某些特有事物、典故和专门术语所表示的概念。

例如:Damping slows down system response and avoids excessive overshoots or overcorrections.

overshoot 有"射(箭等)过头,作用(或动作)过度,超调(量),超越度"等词义。在这里原文是自动控制方面的内容,因此,应选用"**超调(量)**"的词义。

又如:The Egyptian cubit is generally recognized to have been the most widespread unit of linear measurement in the ancient world. 句中的 Egyptian cubit 是古代世界长度测量单位,应译为:**埃及库比特**。(参见第三部分第一课 Notes 8)

(二) 表达阶段

表达是理解的结果,表达就是把已完全理解了的原作内容,选择恰当的汉语重新表达出来。表达的好坏,通常取决于对原文理解的确切程度和对汉语的掌握程度。如只能正确理解原文而不能用通顺流畅的汉语文字表达出来,仍不能获得较好的译文,所以,理解正确是正确表达的前提,但不能代替正确表达。

例如:Matter is anything having weight and occupying space.

译文 1:物质是有重量和占据空间的任何东西。

译文 2:凡是物质,都有重量并占有空间。

从理解的角度来看,第 1 句译文表明译者已经理解了全句的语言、逻辑、语法关系和结构,having weight 和 occupying space 是 anything 的修饰语(定语)。但从表达的角度来看,第 2 句译文的语句显得要通顺流畅得多。

例 2:PAM is a method of cutting metal with a plasma-arc, or tungsten inert-gas-arc torch.

PAM 本是 plasma arc machining 的缩写词,其中 plasma 有不同的词义:〈解剖〉血浆,淋巴液;〈生〉原生质;〈物〉等离子(体);〈矿〉深绿玉髓。在这里,从上下文可以看出,属于物理学科领域,应选"等离子体"词义,而 PAM 则为"等离子(体)弧加工"的意思。但有的将 PAM 译成"用血浆弧加工";而将 tungsten inert-gas-arc 译成"钨丝内部的气体弧燃烧",可见在翻译时根本没有理解原句的意思。

可翻译为:等离子弧加工是用等离子弧焊枪或钨极惰性气体保护焊枪切割金属的一种方法。

(三) 校对阶段

校对,是理解和表达的进一步深化。校对,需对译文作两方面的检查:一是进一步核实原作的内容,看译文是否能转述原作的内容,是否忠实原文;二是进一步推敲译文的语言,看译文是否表达规范,语言通顺,读起来不感到费解。

对于科技文献的译文,由于科技文章(论文)要求高度精确,公式、数据又多,更不能有丝毫疏忽,更要仔细校对,不能有任何差错。

校对过程中,可以发现在理解阶段和表达阶段不够确切、不够完整的地方,从而对这些地方,仔细地加以修改,使译文质量有所提高。

校对阶段通常有初校、复校和完稿三个阶段：

(1) 初校：在初稿译出以后，对照原文进行校核，看是否有错译、漏译的地方；

(2) 复校：脱离原文，看译文是否符合本族语言的规范，是否通顺流畅；

(3) 完稿：在初校及复校的基础上，再次对照原文，进行一次仔细、认真的校核，如无其他问题，则可对译文定稿。

以上三个阶段在整个翻译过程中是互相联系、互相制约的，而正确地理解原文是一切翻译的基础。

总结以上过程可见，要搞好翻译，应按照下列程序进行工作：

(1) 通读原文，熟悉全文面貌，了解内容大意，清楚专业范围和体裁风格，然后开始翻译。在翻译科技文章时，往往会遇到新的科技术语和科学资料，这时最好能熟悉相关专业的中文知识，了解有关的社会背景，这对正式翻译是大有好处的。

(2) 应分章、分节、分段、逐句地精读和分析全文，彻底地弄懂每个词在具体句子中的含意、词义，彻底弄清句子的结构和语法关系。

(3) 遇到生词或不能理解的词组时，应根据上下文先分析判断，辨别它是专业用语还是普通用语。如果是专业用语，则应进一步分析确定是属于哪一个具体学科，再分类去查阅相关的专业词典或普通词典。如果在某个词典上查不到该词，则应多查阅几本词典；同时，应查阅有关资料，或从构词法方面进行分析，并结合上下文进行推测，决不能草率从事。

(4) 翻译时，不能逐词逐句死译，不要看一句译一句，更不能看一个词译一个词，而应看一小段（自然段）译一小段。这样，便于从上下文联系中辨别词义，也便于注意句与句之间的联系、段与段之间的逻辑关系和衔接情况，使译文前后连贯、通顺、流畅。可以避免译文成为一句句，甚至一个词一个词孤立的堆砌，更可避免逐词逐句死译的弊病。

例如：Measurement may be made by unaided human senses—in which case they are often called estimates—or, more usually, by the use of instruments, which may range in complexity from simple rules for measuring lengths to highly sophisticated systems designed to detect and measure quantities entirely beyond the capabilities of the senses, such as radio waves from a distant star or the magnetic moment of a subatomic particle.（参见第三部分第一课课文）

有人就译成：测量是不借助于人类的感觉，利用感觉是被称之为"估计"……

这在逻辑上就不合理，一会儿认为测量"不借助于感觉"，一会儿又认为要"利用感觉"，上下文矛盾。实际上，"估计"是测量的一种，是一种粗测量。

上句应译为：测量可以由人的感官独立完成，这时通常称作估测，而在更普通的情况下，测量是通过使用仪器来完成。……

又如：The number of control device added to an industrial plant may vary widely from plant to plant....

有人就译成：大量的控制装置补充至工业工厂，从一个工厂至另一个工厂变得广泛了。这是典型的死译！

应译为：工业工厂所添加的控制装置的数量，一个工厂可以与另一个工厂有很大的不同。

(5) 对科技文献的翻译，并不要求像翻译文艺作品那样要求语言形象、修辞严谨，甚至词句华丽，富有感情色彩。但要求译文概念清楚、术语定名正确，逻辑明确、文字简练、语句通顺易懂，公式或数据准确无误。

对译文中的用词造句,应绝对避免外国腔调,使读者在阅读(你所翻译的)译文时,如同阅读汉语作品(中文科技文献)一样。

二、翻译的标准

翻译是一种语言表达法,译者将原文作者的思想,用本国语言表达出来,这就要求译者必须准确地理解和掌握原文(原著)的内容,丝毫不可以离开原文而发挥译者个人的主观想法和推测(如发现原文有明显的表达错误或文字印刷错误,则可另外加上"译者注"加以说明)。在准确理解和掌握原著的基础上,译者还必须很好地运用本国语言将原文通顺流畅地表达出来。

什么样的译文能称得上好译文? 用什么标准来衡量译文的好坏? 对翻译的标准,历来提法较多。比较著名的有鲁迅先生的"信顺"原则,严复先生的"信达雅"三原则和英国翻译家泰特勒(Alexander Frase Tytler)的"翻译三原则"等标准。

伟大的文学家鲁迅(1881—1936年)不仅写了不少著作,还翻译了大量外国作品,并主编了《译文》杂志。在翻译过程中,他总结了许多宝贵的经验。他曾说过:"翻译必须兼顾两面,一则当然'求其易懂',一则保存原作的丰姿……。""保存原作的丰姿"就是忠实原著;"求其易懂",就是通顺流畅,符合本国语言的表达习惯。"忠实"原作,符合原著的内容是首要的,但不能逐词死译,甚至译文生硬欧化,一副外国腔调,这是要不得的;而单纯地追求通顺流畅而任意增删原作,也是切不可为的。

严复先生(1853—1921年)曾用文言文意译英国作家赫胥黎的《天演论》(*Evolution and Ethics and Other Essays*),将"物竞天择,适者生存"、"优胜劣汰"等进化观点介绍到中国,是近代中国著名的启蒙思想家。他翻译态度严谨、文字简朴,首次提出"信、达、雅"的翻译标准。严复先生说:"译事之难:信、达、雅。求其信已大难矣,顾信矣不达,虽译犹不译也,则达尚焉。"

鲁迅先生提出的"忠实",严复先生提出的"信",都是指掌握原作的思想内容问题,也就是要译者必须确切地理解和掌握原文的内容,不允许有丝毫曲解。鲁迅先生提出的译文"求其易懂"、通顺,严复先生强调译文要"达而雅",都是指汉语的表达方式。

这些,对今天的翻译人员来讲,仍具有重要的意义。

总而言之,我们可以把翻译标准归纳为以下三个方面:

(1) 译文必须忠实于原文,完整而准确地把原作的全部内容(包括思想、精神与风格)表达出来。不要任意增删、遗漏和篡改。但对于科技作品中毫不涉及技术内容的句子、段落和章节,或思想内容极端反动的内容应予以删节(可另以"[译者注]"的方式加以说明)。

(2) 译文语言必须规范标准,用词造句应符合本民族语言的表达习惯。要使用民族的、大众的、科学的语言,力求通顺易懂,不要逐词死译、生硬晦涩,不应有生搬硬套、文理不通的现象。

(3) 译文必须尽力保持原作的风格,包括民族风格、时代风格、语体风格和作者个人的语言风格等。不能以译者的爱好去代替原作的风格。

对于科技文献,由于主要是叙事说理,论证论点,它具有平铺直叙、结构严密、逻辑性强,公式、数据和专业术语繁多等特点,因此,要求翻译"明确"、"通顺"和"简练"。

明确——在技术内容上准确无误地表达原文的含义,做到概念清楚、逻辑正确、公式图表和数据准确无误。专业术语要符合专业(标准)要求,不要模糊不清、模棱两可。创造新译名,要能正确地表达出事物的真实含义。在同一篇文章、同一本书中,专业术语、名词译名前后必须统一。如果将概念和数据翻译不准,特别是单位换算方面(国际单位制和英美制等),将会带来严重后果,甚至造成巨大的经济损失,因此,不能掉以轻心。

例如：The liquid laser is not susceptible to such damage; the crystalline or glassy rod *is replaced by* a transparent cell containing a suitable liquid, such as *a solution of* neodymium oxide or chloride in selenium oxychloride.

在阅读时，应弄清楚谁代替谁；在所说溶液中，谁溶于谁。这样才能准确无误地表达。

通顺——不但选词造句要正确，而且译文的语气表达也应该正确无误。尤其要恰当地表达原文的语气、情态、语态、时态以及所强调的重点。

简练——译文要尽可能简短、精练，没有冗词、废字。在明确、通顺的基础上力求简洁明快、精练流畅。

三、对译者的要求

(1) 注意政治性和思想性。即以马列主义、毛泽东思想为指导，认清科技翻译在社会主义建设中的作用。对外国书刊中出现的不健康的东西，应自觉抵制，决不可随意引进。

(2) 要精通英文和汉语。在确切理解英语原文的前提下，能熟练地运用汉语表达原作的内容。精通原文语言是透彻理解的前提，熟练运用译文语言(汉语)是确切表达的条件，两者是统一的，无论缺少哪一方面，都会影响译文质量。

(3) 对所译科技作品应具有一定的专业知识，才能得心应手地翻译，否则会直接影响译文的质量，使读者难以理解，甚至会错误连篇，笑话百出。

前面的表达阶段的例2中将 plasma arc(等离子弧)译成血浆弧就是一例。

(4) 在实践的过程中不断地提高翻译理论知识水平和翻译技巧。不同类型的译文尽管各有特点，仍有共同的地方；同一类型的译文，更有共同之处。这些水平的提高，只有通过翻译的实践。因此，要多实践、多总结。

(5) 要学习广博的社会知识。科技文献涉及的知识，不仅限于科技领域，还涉及其他方面。社会知识越广博，译文的准确性与质量(可读性)就越有保证。

有时，一个常用单词有它的习惯用法和涵义，如有疏忽，也会闹出笑话。

例如：In practice, a rotor weighing about 10 tons and rotating at 3 000 r. p. m. may be so well balanced that the motion, except from sound, is *only just* perceptible.

〈误〉实际上，一根重达10吨、每分钟3 000转的转子可以平衡得非常好，以至于除了声音之外，运动<u>正好</u>察觉出来。

〈正〉实际上，一根重达10吨、每分钟3 000转的转子可以平衡得非常好，以至于除了声音之外，<u>勉勉强强</u>地察觉它在运动。

句中的 only just ＝ only almost not，just 用在 only 后，常作 almost not 解，如不加思索译作"正好"就错了，在这里是"刚刚才"的意思。

第二节　专业英语翻译的基本方法

在翻译过程中，面对的是整篇文章。但将它译成中文时，除了按照在第二章第一节中讲的分"理解、表达、校对"三个阶段外，下面就是"一口一口地""吃"了：将全文分成各个段、节，并将各个段、节分成句、词。

首先面临的是词。对词义的选择和处理、对词类的转换译法，对词类的处理，数词的译法，等等。

其次面临的是句。对句子成分的分析，对句子成分转变的译法等，特别要注意长句的译法。下面分别加以介绍。

一、词义的选择

英汉两种语言都有一词多类、一词多义的现象。所谓一词多类就是指一个词往往属于几个不同的词类(如名词、动词、形容词等),词类不同,词义也就不同。一词多义是指一个词在同一个词性中,往往有几个不同的词义。因此,在众多的词义中,选择一个最确切的词义是正确理解原文所表达的思想的基本环节,是成功翻译的基础。一般来说,词义的选择与确定可以从以下几个方面来考虑。

(一) 根据词类选择

根据词类选择词义的方法主要是针对一些兼类词,因为这些词在句中所承担的成分不同,其词类不同,词义也不同。因此,要选择正确的词义,首先要确定该词在句中属于哪一种词类,再进一步确定其词义。如:The thickness of a tooth measured along the pitch circle is one half the pitch. (沿节圆所测得的齿厚是周节的一半。) 句中 measure 是及物动词,意为"测量"。The earthquake measured 6.5 on the Richter scale. (这次地震震级为里氏 6.5 级。) 句中 measure 是系动词,意为"为"。This room measures 10 meters across. (这间房子宽 10 米。) measure 是不及物动词,作"有……宽(或长、高)"解。

(二) 根据上下文选择

英语中的同一个词、同一词类在不同场合往往有不同的含义,常常要求译者根据上下文的联系以及句型来确定某个词在特定场合下的词义。

例 1:Press the INV key and you can raise the constant e(2.7 182 818)to x powers.

按 INV 键便可得常数 e (2.71 828 18)的 x 次乘方。

例 2:The electronic microscope possesses very high resolving *power* compared with the optical microscope.

与光学显微镜相比,电子显微镜具有极高的分辨率。

例 3:Energy is the *power* to do work.

能量是指做功的能力。

例 4:*Power* can be transmitted over a long distance.

电能能长距离传输。

在这四句中,同一个"power",分别在数学中译为"乘方",在光学中译为"率",在力学中译为"能力",在电学中译为"电能"。

(三) 根据词的搭配选择

不同的搭配方式会产生不同的意思,如 large 在如下搭配中的意思就不相同。

large current 强电流;(2) a large amount of electric power 大量电力;(3) large growing 生长快的;(4) large capacity 高容量;(5) large scale integration 大规模集成电路。

二、词义的引申

英、汉两种语言在表达方式上差别较大。英语的一词多义现象又使得在翻译时,难以找到相对应的词义,有些词或词组无法直接搬用词典中的释义,若勉强按词典中的释义逐词死译,会使译文生硬晦涩,词不达意,很难让人看懂,甚至会造成误解。所以,要在弄清原文词义的基础上,根据上下文的逻辑关系和汉语的搭配习惯,对词义加以引申。若遇到有关专业方面的内容,必须选用专业方面的常用语。引申后的词义虽然同词典中的释义稍有不同,却能更确切地表达原文意义。

例1：There is no physical contact between tool and workpiece.

欠佳译法：在工具和工件之间没有有形的接触。

引申译法：工具和工件不直接接触。

例2：Public opinion is demanding more and more urgently that something must be done about noise.

欠佳译法：公众舆论越来越强烈地要求为消除噪声做某些事情。

引申译法：公众舆论越来越强烈地要求管一管噪声问题。

例3：There is a wide area of performance duplication between numerical control and automatics.

欠佳译法：在数控和自动化机床之间，有一个性能重复的广阔地带。

引申译法：数控和自动化机床有很多相同的性能。

例4：There are three steps which must be taken before we graduate from the integrated circuit technology.

欠佳译法：在我们从集成电路工艺那里毕业之前，必须采取三个步骤。

引申译法：我们要完全掌握集成电路工艺，必须采取三项措施。

三、词类的处理与转译

由于英汉两种语言结构与表达方式的不同，有些句子在译成汉语时不能逐词对译。为了更好地传达原文的思想内容，使译文更符合汉语的表达习惯，更加通顺自然，翻译时，常须对词类进行处理，将词类作适当的转换，即英语中的某一词类，并不一定译成汉语中的相应词类，而要作适当的转换。词类的转换主要有以下几种情况。

（一）转译为动词

与汉语相比，英语句子中往往只有一个谓语动词，而汉语句子中动词用得比较多，很可能有几个动词或动词性结构一起连用。

1. 将原文的名词转译为动词

Despite all the **improvements**, rubber still has a number of limitations.

尽管**改进**了很多，但合成橡胶仍有一些缺陷。

2. 将原文的形容词转译为动词

The circuits are connected in parallel in the interest of a **small** resistance.

将电路并联是为了**减小**电阻。

3. 将原文的副词转译为动词

When the switch is **off**, the circuit is open and electricity doesn't go through.

当开关**断开**时，电路就形成开路，电流不能通过。

4. 将原文的介词转译为动词

An analog computer manipulates data **by** analog means.

模拟计算机**采用**模拟方式处理数据。

（二）转译为名词

1. 将原文的动词转译为名词

Tests showed that the cooling air must **flow** at a rate of at least 17 m/s.

实验表明，冷空气的**流速**至少应为 17 m/s。

2. 代词转译为名词

代词转译为名词实际上就是将代词所代替的名词翻译出来。

This means the permittivity of oil is greater than **that** of air.

这就意味着油的介电系数大于空气的**介电系数**。

3. 形容词转译为名词

The diesel engine is highly **efficient**.

这种柴油机的**效率**很高。

4. 副词转译为名词

The device is shown **schematically** in Figure 2.

图 2 是这种装置的**简图**。

5. 将动词转译为名词，将副词转译为动词

Neutrons **act differently** from protons.

中子的**作用不同**于质子。（将动词 act 转译为名词，将副词 differently 转为动词）

（三）转译为形容词

1. 名词转译为形容词

Gene mutation is of great **importance** in breeding new varieties.

在新品种培育方面，基因突变是非常**重要的**。

2. 副词转译为形容词

Earthquakes are **closely** related to faulting.

地震与断层的作用有**密切的**关系。

3. 动词转译为形容词

Light waves **differ** in frequency just as sound waves do.

同声波一样，光波也有**不同的**频率。

（四）转译为副词

1. 形容词转译为副词

This experiment is an **absolute** necessity in determining the solubility.

对确定溶解度来说，这次试验是**绝对**必要的。

2. 动词转译为副词

Rapid evaporation **tends** to make the steam wet.

快速蒸发**往往**使蒸汽的湿度加大。

四、数词的译法

英语中的数词有基数词（表示数量的数字）、序数词（表示顺序）和分数词三大类。在科技文献中比较难处理的是表示数量的基数词。由于英语和汉语在数量的表达上有所不同，因此，翻译时应该特别谨慎，译后还要再次校核，使之准确无误。

（一）数字的译法

1. 直译

对于英语中数目不大的数字可采用直译。如温度、年代、数量、高度等。20℃（摄氏 20 度）；at 2008（在 2008 年）。英语的数词后面没有量词，所以，在英译汉时，一般在数字后面要加量词。例如：a factory（一家工厂）；two books（两本书）；a computer（一台计算机）等。

2. 换算

英语中没有"一万"这一单位,而用十个"千",因此,一些较大的数目汉译时可以换算,用汉语"万""亿"等词译出。

例如:Light travels at the rate of 300,000 kilometers per second.

光以每秒 30 万千米的速度传播。

(二) 不定数量的译法

不定数量是指表示若干、许多、大量、不少、成千上万等概念的词组。

1. 约定俗成的汉译

tens(数十个),hundreds(几百个),a hundred and one(许多,无数),dozens of(几十,几打),hundreds of thousands of(数十万,几十万),millions of(千千万万,数以百万计)。

2. 译为"超过"、"多达"等

The temperature in the furnace is not always above 1 000 ℃.

炉内的温度并不总是超过 1 000 ℃。

The machine tool yields were above last year's.

机床产量超过了去年。

(三) 倍数增减的译法

1. 倍数增加的译法

英语中说 increase by n times"增加了多少(n)倍",都是连基数也包括在内的,是表示增加后的结果;而在汉语里所谓"增加了多少倍",则表示纯粹增加的数量。所以,在翻译倍数的增加时,一定要注意所增加的倍数是否包含基数。如包含基数,通常可译为"增加到……n倍""增加为……n倍""是……n倍"等;而不包含基数表示净增时,则将 n 倍减一,可译为"增加了……(n−1)倍"。

例 1:Now the total installed capacity has increased by three times as compared with that of 2 000. 现在总装机容量比 2 000 年增加了 2 倍。(或:现在总装机容量是 2 000 年的 3 倍。)

但是,若采用 increase by twice 则表示纯粹增加的数量,应该照原数翻译而不减一。

例 2:This year the value of our industrial output has increased by twice as compared with that of last year. 今年我国的工业产值比去年增加了 2 倍。

2. 倍数比较的译法

英语中表示倍数比较的表达法有以下几种。

(1)"n times+larger than+被比较对象"。因为英语在倍数比较的表达上,其传统习惯是 larger than 等于 as large as,因此汉译时不能只从字面上理解,将其译为"比……大 n 倍",而应将其译为"其大小为……的 n 倍",或"比……大 n−1 倍"。例如:

This thermal power plant is four times larger than that one. 这个热电站比那个热电站大 3 倍。

(2)"n times+as+原级+as+被比较对象",译为"是……的 n 倍"。例如:

Iron is almost three times as heavy as aluminum. 铁的重量几乎是铝的 3 倍。

(3)"n times+that(或表示比较方面的词)of+被比较对象",译为"是……的 n 倍"。例如:

This reservoir is four times the size of that one. 这个水库是那个水库的 4 倍。

Sound travels nearly three times faster in copper than in lead. 声音在铜中传播的速度几

乎是在铅中的 3 倍。

3. 倍数减少的译法

英语中表示倍数减少的句型在汉译时应当把它译成"减少了或减少到几分之几,或减少了几倍"。英语表示倍数减少时的表达方式为:

(1) 表减少意义的词 reduce (decrease) by n times + 或 by a factor of n;

(2) n times + 表示减少意义的词的比较级如 less, shorter 等。如:

The length of the process was reduced to four times. 进度缩短了 1/4。

The automatic assembly line can shorten the assembling period (by) ten times. 自动装配线能够使装配期缩短 9/10。

The error probability of the new equipment was reduced eight times. 新设备的误差概率降低了 7/8。(或:新设备的误差概率降低为(原有的)1/8。)

(四)"每隔"与"每逢"的译法

英语形容词同数词 every 连用时,表示"每隔"与"每逢"的意思。例如:

every three days = every third day 每三天=每隔两天=每逢三天

注意在翻译成"每隔……"时,应把原数词减去一。

五、句子成分的分析

要做好翻译工作,必须从深刻理解原文入手,力求做到确切表达原文意思。原文是翻译的出发点和唯一依据,只有彻底理解原文含义,才有可能完成确切的翻译,才能达到上述翻译标准的要求。要深刻理解原文,首先要了解专业科技文献所特有的逻辑性、正确性、精密性和专业性等特点,力求从原文所包含的专业技术内容方面去加以理解。其次,要正确地分析句子的成分,根据原文的句子结构,弄清每句话的语法关系,采用分组归类的方法辨明主语、谓语、宾语及各种修饰语,并联系上下文来分析和理解句与句之间、主句与从句之间的关系。专业科技文献中长句、难句较多,各种短语和从句相互搭配、相互修饰,使人感到头绪纷繁,无所适从。在这种情况下更应该重视语法分析,突出句子骨架,采用分解归类,化繁为简,逐层推进理解的策略。

例如:The technical possibilities could well exist, therefore, of nation-wide integrated transmission network of high capacity, controlled by computers, interconnected globally by satellite and submarine cable, providing speedy and reliable communications throughout the world.

这句话看起来挺难理解,但若采用分解归类的语法分析方法则不难对付。首先,能够充当句子谓语的只能是 could well exist,而不可能是其他非限定动词,如 integrated, controlled, interconnected。接下来主语自然是 possibilities,由于 exist 是不及物动词,因此,不存在宾语。进一步分析将发现用作定语的介词短语 of nation-wide... cable 除了修饰 possibilities 以外没有其他名词可以承受,而分词短语 controlled... 和 interconnected... 又进一步修饰介词短语中的 network。至于 providing... the world 则显然是表示结果的状语。这样一来,句子的骨架就比较清楚了。本句之所以将定语和待修饰的词分开,是因为定语太长而谓语较短,将谓语提前有助于整个句子结构的平衡。经过这样的分析理解,再参照后面将介绍的翻译技巧,就可将该句译为:"因此,在技术上完全有可能实现全国性的集成发射网,这种网络容量大,可由计算机控制,并能通过卫星和海底电缆与全球相联系,成为全世界范围内高速、可靠的通讯工具。"

要深刻理解原文,还必须彻底辨明词义。否则,尽管语法结构已了解清楚,但因个别词的含义不能确定仍不能理解原文意思,更谈不上动手翻译表达了。辨明词义的方法除了多查几本词典外,还必须从全句的意思,从上下文的关系以及从专业内容上去体会。譬如,不能将专业用语 light show(光显示)错误理解为"轻快的表演",也不应将机械学中的 tratsmission(传动)误认为电学中的"发射"或医学中的"遗传"。

总之,在着手翻译之前要"吃透原文"。具体操作时可采用"多遍扫描法":第一遍,了解原文的大致内容及所属学科方向和内容;第二遍,分析篇章、段落结构及了解重点难点所在;第三遍,研读句子的语法结构,弄清句子骨架,并标注疑难生词;第四遍,查阅词典,弄清无法根据上下文关系和句子结构理解的单词,再从头仔细地、有重点地理解原文。

经过这几个步骤后,就可以动笔翻译了。

六、句子成分转变的译法

在英译汉时,除了依赖语法分析去处理译文,还必须充分考虑汉语的习惯及专业科技文献的逻辑性和严密性。这就要求在翻译过程中,视具体情况将句子的某一成分(主语、谓语、宾语、定语、表语、状语或补语)译成另一成分,或者将短语与短语、主句与从句、短语与从句进行转换。例如:

(1) The shortest distance between raw and a finished part is casting.

铸造是把原材料加工成成品的最简便方法。(表语译为主语)

(2) There is need for improvement in our designing.

我们的设计需要改进。(主语译为谓语)

(3) A coil of wire that moves in a magnetic field will have an e. m. f. induced in it.

当线圈在磁场中运动时,其内部会感应出一个电动势。(定语从句转为状语从句)

(4) Electronic computers must be programmed before they can work.

必须先为电子计算机编好程序,它才能工作。(从句译为主句)

(5) There is a large amount of energy wasted due to the fraction of commutator.

由于转换器的摩擦损耗了大量的能量。(主语译为宾语)

(6) Light beams can carry more information than radio ignals.

光束运载的信息比无线电信号运载的信息多。(宾语译为主语)

七、长句的译法

所谓长句,主要指语法结构复杂、修饰成分较多、内容层次在两个以上的复合句,亦可指带有修饰性短语(包括介词短语、不定式短语、分词短语、动名词短语和形容词短语)或附加成分(插入语、同位语和独立成分)的简单句或并列句。在科技英语中,大量使用长句可以严密、准确、客观地表达多重密切相关的概念。但由于英、汉两种语言连接句子的手段有别,表述概念、叙述事情和论述事理的逻辑不同,因此,在英汉互译的过程中要注重了解两者的差异,认真进行语法分析,不要拘泥于英语原文的形式,而应吃透句子所要表达的深层意思,并根据英汉表达的习惯,翻译出符合汉语表达习惯的句子。

(一) 英语长句的特点

在英语长句中,有的是含义丰富的简单句,它有一个主干,即有主语、谓语、宾语(表语),同时又有多个修饰成分与主干相连,相连的方式不同,诸如有单个形容词、形容词短语、介词短语、分词短语和不定式作定语;有的是复合句,它包括并列复合句、主从复合句或并列主从复合句:有层层包孕关系的定语从句修饰先行词,有原因、结果、让步、方式、条件、目的和时间状语从句,表示主从句之间的逻辑关系,还有副词、副词短语等所作的状语。但并非每个句子都包含所有类型。

(1) In a typical modern Hi-Fi system, the signals will come from a unit like a CD player, FM tuner, or a tape/minidisk unit.

分析:该句是简单句,其主要成分是 the signals(主语)+will come from(谓语)+a unit(宾语)。带有两个介词短语:In a typical modern Hi-Fi system 作状语,修饰整个句子,表示范围;

like a CD player, FM tuner, or a tape/minidisk unit 短语作宾语的后置定语,指具体设备。

翻译:在典型的现代高保真系统中,信号是来自于 CD 播放器、调频收音机或磁带/小型磁盘机等设备。

(2) The advent of jet and rocket propulsion, and of nuclear reactors, has shown that the materials which previously served for constructional purposes are no longer wholly satisfactory for the manufacture of equipment on which the efficient functioning of these new sources of power depends.

分析:该句是主从复合句,由 1 个主句和 4 个从句组成。其中 The advent(主语)...+has shown(谓语)+that clause(宾语)为主句的框架;of jet and rocket propulsion, and of nuclear reactors 作主语的后置定语;that 从句作句子的宾语;宾语从句里又套有两个由 which 引导的从句,直接跟在各自的先行词 the materials 和介词短语中的 equipment 之后,构成了层层推进的关系。

翻译:喷气式飞机、火箭助推器以及核反应堆的出现表明过去的建材再也不能令人满意地用来建造那些有效使用新能源的设备。

(二) 汉语长句的特点

汉语长句多以意合的方式组合在一起,缺少像英语中的关系代词或关系副词等标志逻辑关系的连接词。句子多以时间发生的先后顺序或动作之间的先后关系排列。

(三) 长句翻译的基本方法

对长句翻译的关键在于:一要对原文准确理解,把握好译文的要点,安排好译文的框架结构;二要恰如其分地表达,这在很大程度上取决于译者对外语和母语的驾驭能力以及对翻译技巧的灵活运用。在理解阶段,可分 3 个步骤进行:①扼要拟出全句的主要轮廓;②辨清该句的主从结构,并根据上下文领会全句的要旨;③找出句与句之间的从属关系,理清每句原文的意思。在表达阶段,可分为 2 个步骤进行:①将每个划开的单句逐一翻译;②将所译出的句子进行调整、组合,对译文进行加工润色。

对长句处理最常见的方法是化整为零,分散解决。一般用顺序译法、逆序译法、拆分译法和整合重组法等。

1. 顺序译法

当英语原句所表达的思想与意义在句型结构(如主谓结构、主谓宾结构、主系表和部分主谓状、主谓宾状结构)、时间顺序、句内逻辑顺序(如因果关系、对比转折关系、动宾关系和条件假设关系)上基本与汉语的语序一致时,或句子"同主多谓"、"同谓多宾时"常采用顺序译法,即按照英语原文的顺序进行翻译。但不能拘泥于词词对照,经常会有局部语序的变化。如:

The power amplifier has no way to "know in advance" what kind of loudspeaker you will use, so simply adopts the convention of asserting a voltage level to indicate the required signal level at each frequency in the signal and supplying whatever current the loudspeaker then requires.（句内逻辑顺序为因果关系，由 so 前后连接；且谓语 has 和 adopts 具有共同的主语）

功率放大器不可能预先知道将会使用的扬声器类型，因此就简单地按常规情况处理，提供一定大小的电压，表示信号中任意频率下所需信号的幅度，并提供扬声器所需要的电流。

2. 逆序译法

逆序译法主要指英汉对译的句子的时间顺序、句内逻辑顺序恰恰相反。这时就需要从原文的后面开始翻译，逆着原文的顺序翻译。如：

It is very interesting to note the differently chosen operating mechanism by the different manufacturers, in spite of the fact that the operating mechanism has a major influence on the reliability of the circuit-breakers.

尽管操作机构对断路器的可靠性具有较大的影响，但注意不同的制造厂按不同形式选择操作机构是非常有趣的。

3. 拆分译法

当英语长句中的主句与从句、或介词短语及分词短语、副词等所修饰的词与词之间的关系不是很密切时，可根据汉语一个小句表达一层意思的习惯，对原文的长句按意群进行分解（切分）为若干小句，再把长句中的短语或从句逐句翻译，译成独立的分句。拆分译法，又称切分法，它是翻译英语长句的最常见的一种方法。如：

On account of the accuracy and ease with which resistance measurements may be made and the well-known manner in which resistance varies with temperature, it is common to use this variation to indicate changes in temperature.

我们都知道，电阻的大小是随温度而变化的。用电阻进行测量既精确，又简单，因此通常都用电阻的变化来表示温度。

4. 整合重组法

当英汉长句不能按照上述 3 种方法进行翻译时，就要根据汉语的习惯，在把握原文意思的基础上，打破原文的结构，适当调整句子的顺序，准确反映句子的深层含义。如：

There is a great deal of difference in the ability of different substances to conduct or insulate and that decides which material is the best to use for a particular purpose.

不同物质的传导和绝缘的能力有很大的差别，这就决定了哪种材料最适用于某一特定的用途。

第三章　科技论文的写作方法

第一节　科技论文的结构

随着我国对外科技交流工作的不断深入，我国在国际科技界的地位日益提高，越来越多的科技工作者除了直接查阅和消化大量的国外英文专业科技文献外，还使用英文撰写出许多反映我国最新前沿科学技术水平及其发展动向的高质量的英语科技论文，并在国际性学术会议上宣读，或在国内外英文学术报刊上发表。因此，英语科技论文的写作对于加强国际间的科技交流，介绍我国创造性科学成果具有重要的意义。本章主要结合英语科技论文的特点，介绍一些实际写作过程中经常碰到的具体问题和写作要求。

一般来说,一篇科技论文的基本结构由以下几部份构成:
题目 Title
作者及作者单位与通信地址 Author and author's communication address
摘要 Abstract
关键词 Key words
正文 Text
致谢、附录及参考文献 Acknowledgments、Appendix and Reference

第二节 题目、摘要与关键词的写法

一、论文题目(Title)的写法

一篇科技论文首先必须有一个简明、具体、确切反映论文特定内容并能引人注目的题目。为使科技论文作为科技信息被广泛交流,即使在国内公开发行的一、二级中文刊物,也要求作者将论文题目译成英文,以便于编目检索。

论文英文题目应当具体地恰如其分地反映研究的范围和达到的深度。不宜使用过于笼统或泛指性很强的词汇。题目的特点是简短精练,概括性很强,能表达出核心内容及意义。一般应该控制在 12～15 个英文单词以内,同时单词的选择还必须有助于二次文献编制题录、索引、关键词,为文献检索提供有用的信息。英文题目经常使用动名词、名词短语、介词短语、动词不定式,或几种形式混合,也经常带有前置后置修饰语,也可用专有名词或专有名词的缩略语形式。例如:

(1) Research on test technique of orbit traffic signal machines

(2) Portable monitoring consistency of carbon monoxide device

(3) An Investigation on Diameter Measurement of Superthin Wire with Laser Diffraction

(4) An Overview of Modeling and Simulation of the Milling Process

(5) Motorola Motor Controller DSP56F807

(6) PROCESS CONTROL OF LASER GROOVING USING ACOUSTIC SENSING

关于英文题目的书写格式,各种杂志有不同的规定,但主要有三种形式:第一种形式是题目第一个词和每一个实词(如名词、动词、形容词、副词等)的第一个字母都用大写,虚词(如介词、连词等)则用小写,如上面的例(3)～(5)。第二种形式是全部用大写,如上面的例(6)。第三种形式是标题的第一个词的第一个字母用大写,其余均用小写,如上面的例(1)(2)。

论文的题目还可以采用主、副标题和破折号的形式。

二、作者(Author)及作者单位与通信地址(author's communication address)的写法

与题目相关的另一个问题是论文的作者(署名)。署名常位于题目之后,它不仅是作者辛勤劳动的体现和应得的荣誉,而且还表示作者对论文的全部内容负责。

论文作者姓名写在论文标题的正下方中央处。第一作者(担任论文主要工作、起决定作用的作者)的姓名排在最前面。如果有多名作者且不在同一单位,可以在姓名的右上角标上阿拉伯数字序号或标识符,以便下一步相应地标明单位和通信地址。所标注的单位和地址顺序要和作者名称一致。若某个单位是多层次的(如××大学××学院××系),则下一级单位排在上一级单位之前。中国作者英文译名的姓可写在名字的前面或后面,视具体要求而定;姓和名的首写字母都要大写;名字中的两个字(如果是双字结构的话)之间可以用破折号隔开,或直接

连写。各作者的姓名之间用逗号分开,每人的姓与名之间也空一格。例如:

Sensor Technology of the Building of Flexible Development Platform
for Modern Instrument Manufacture

LIANG Fu-ping [1,2], XU Xiao-li[2], ZHANG Fu-xue[2], SU Zhong[2], WU Guo-xing[2], HAN Qiu-shi[2]

(1. School of Optoelectronic Information & Telecommunication Engineering, Beijing Information & Science Technology University, Beijing 100192, China; 2. Beijing Key Laboratory: Measurement and Control of Mechanical and Electrical System, Beijing Information & Science Technology University, Beijing 100192, China)

三、摘要(abstract)的写法

(一)摘要的组成、特点及写作要点

摘要是论文中非常重要的部分,它应含有与论文同等量的主要信息。由于读者通常都是先读论文摘要,再决定有无通读全文的必要,一些文摘性刊物也仅收录论文摘要和出处。所以联合国教科文组织规定:"全世界公开发表的科技论文,不管用何种文字写成,都必须附有一篇短小精悍的英文摘要。"我国出版的大部分学术性刊物,也都在中文摘要之后加排英文摘要。由此可见,英文摘要质量的好坏,直接影响对外学术交流的效果和论文本身的科学价值,必须引起足够重视。

一篇好的论文摘要,具有概括性、完整性和独立性的特点。要求简短扼要,不仅能引人入胜,让读者不能不想通读全文,而且能独立使用,使同行读者即使只读文摘性索引刊物也能一目了然,得知论文的主要概念和研究成果。

摘要虽然放在正文的前面,却应该在整篇论文完成以后再进行写作,以便如实地摘取论文的要点。论文摘要一般应包括如下内容:

(1)研究的目的与意义。

(2)研究的方法与途径。

(3)研究的成果与结论。

由于研究内容和用途的差别,摘要一般分为指示性摘要和资料性摘要两种。指示性摘要主要给读者一个指示性的概括了解,介绍论文的论点和结论。资料性摘要除了介绍论文的论点、结论外,还要提供尽可能多的定量或定性的信息,如一些关键性数据,结果的比较等。二者的区别有时是不明显的。这里主要介绍科技期刊中常见的指示性摘要。

关于摘要的长度较难予以具体规定,因为这与论文的篇幅、性质和包含的信息量大小有关。一般来说,英文科技论文的摘要平均长度应为正文长度的3%~4%,大约150~200个单词。

(二)写作要点

为使英文摘要精练地表达论文的主要内容,在写作时要注意以下几点。

(1)摘要应具有独立的结构,一般不要引用正文中的图、表、公式或参考文献,也不要使用一些不常用的符号和缩略语,以保持摘要的完整性、独立性和可读性。

(2)摘要的时态大都使用一般现在时,个别使用一般过去时,但很少采用完成时态和其他时态。此外,还应注意摘要中时态的一致性及与正文时态的相对一致性。

(3)为使摘要包含更多的信息量,应避免在摘要中重复标题文字。

(4)由于科技论文侧重客观叙事和推理,读者感兴趣的是作者的研究方法、观点和结果,

而不是论文作者,因此,论文摘要应避免使用第一、第二人称代词 I,we,you,尽可能使用第三人称。然而,为使摘要亲切、自然、直截了当,近年来也有不少刊物的摘要较频繁地使用第一人称。

(三) 常用句型

英语摘要的开头、叙述和结尾都有一些较为固定的句型。掌握这些常用句型,对于提高写作能力是非常有用的。常用句型有:

(1) This paper (article) is concerned with...
 This paper (article) is aimed at...
 This paper (article) is limited to...
(2) This paper focuses on... (presents,describes,discusses, deals with,investigates)...
(3) (In this paper,)... is (are) described(presented, discussed, investigated, studied, reviewed, introduced,developed,proposed,considered,reported).
(4) The purpose (aim, objective) of this paper is to...
(5) It is the aim (intent,purpose) of this paper to discuss (present, describe)...
(6) (In this paper,)I (We) report (introduce, describe, present, consider)...
(7) The approach is based on...
(8) Conditions are considered for...
(9) The requirement for... is noted.
(10) The formula is derived for... according to...
(11) Test has been carried out to study...
(12) A procedure is described...
(13) The simulation is performed using...
(14) This result (fact, demonstration, illustration, classification, comparison, contrast, analyses) gives (shows)...
(15) The result of this study can be generalized for...
(16) Result for... are found to be close to the experimental data.

四、关键词(Key words)的写法

为了文献标引和检索,需要能集中反映本文的技术特点和理论的关键性技术术语、规范化单词作为关键词,另起一行排在摘要下方。单词、术语或词组一般要求选取 3~8 个。

例如:**Key words**:development platform;instrument;flexible;sensor

第三节 正文的写法

在正文中,包括引言(前言)、研究的内容、结论或总结。

一、前言的写法

前言(或引言、导言、绪论)是科技论文主体部分的开端。它以明快的语言向读者说明论文的主题和目的,研究背景和现状,研究所采用的方法以及所取得的成果等,以引导出正文的内容。前言的篇幅不宜过长,在内容取材和文字表达上也应反复推敲,以引起读者的兴趣。

前言的写作,在很大程度上取决于如何开头,怎样下笔。论文的开头是非常重要的。为了简洁清晰地揭示论文主题,通常可以用下述方法开头。

(1) 以叙述他人的研究工作开头,既交代了本论文的研究背景,又非常自然地引出了本文要解决的问题及其作用和意义。

例如:Since cutting temperatures strongly influence both tool life and cutting forces the thermal aspects of cutting have been widely studied for many years, and several steady-state models for calculating various temperatures have been proposed(Trigger and Chao, 1951; Barrow, 1973; Tay et al, 1974, 1976; Boothroyed, 1975; Trent, 1977; Weight et al., 1980; Smith and Armarego, 1980; Shaw, 1984; Venuvinod and Lau, 1986). Unfortunately the temperatures or temperature distributions predicted by these models traditionally could not... This paper compares calculations from four steady-state metal cutting temperature models with experimental results from the end turning of steel, aluminum...

(2) 以解释文中所涉及的主要概念开头,既补充了标题及摘要中对名词的说明,使读者容易理解,又便于后面的叙述(如使用缩略语等)。

例如:The purposeof an interrupt system is to let a peripheral asynchronously request the processor to attend to its requirements, and cause the processor to select the interrupt service routine (ISR) which relates specifically to that peripheral. The processor must leave its current task, execute the ISG and return to the point in the current task from which it left...

(3) 以所要论述的课题内容及范围开头,使读者一下子就弄清本文所述及的问题。

例如:Accurate models of the milling process are required both for analysis and for prediction of the quality of machining operations, many different models have been developed and used by researchers. This paper classifies and evaluates the various models currently being used according to the methods of force computation and of deflection feed back to the force, and to point to the strengths and weaknesses of the models.

(4) 以本文所要达到的目的开头,指出论文的主要内容,使读者心中有数。

例如:In an effort to maximize the metal removal rate in end milling while avoiding excessive cutter deflectionor breakage, both fixed gain and adaptive controllers have been implemented in this paper for on-line feedrate manipulation to maintain a constant cutting force...

(5) 以本课题研究中的主要问题开头,有针对性地提出解决问题的途径。

例如:The invention and dynamic development of modern digital computers have dramatically changed production methods and equipment over the last forty years. However, there are still areas of manufacturing where the potential of modern control and signal processing techniques have not been fully utilized. Two examples are Adaptive Control (Ac) and in-process Monitoring and Diagnosis(M&D)of machine tools and processes. A system presented in this paper...

(6) 以大家熟悉的事实开头,给读者一种亲切感。

例如:It is well-known that the roughness profile of a cut surface contains periodic compoments. The geometry of cutting action, namely, the tool geometry and cutting parameters are commonly presumed to be the main factors relating to the formation of the deterministic portion of the surface profile. ... The purpose of this paper is to develop a model which is capable of...

二、正文的组织和结构

科技论文的写作目的是介绍作者的科学研究成果,包括成果的基本内容、理论依据、实现方法、实验装置及方法、实验结果及分析等内容。而正文则是展现研究工作成果和学术水平的主体。一篇好的论文应该具有明确、鲜明、生动的特点,这就要求论文论点简明准确、论据充分、论证严密、层次清楚。要做到这一点,除进行大量的阅读练习和写作练习外,还必须掌握一些基本的写作规律。论文的写作,首先应明确中心内容并拟订一个写作提纲,把要用的材料和观点组织好。正文的组织,一方面是要将整个内容划分成几大部分,每部分既相对独立,又有机联系,服从于论文主题的要求;另一方面是对每一部分进行恰当分段,每段包括一个以上的句子,表达一个意思,讲明一个观点,围绕一个主题。

论文材料的组织,既可以按照时间顺序或空间顺序进行安排,也可以按照逻辑顺序进行安排。下面是一篇题为"Finite Element Modeling of Orthogonal Metal Cutting"的论文结构。

(1) Introduction
(2) Basic Aspects of Cutting and Problem Definition
(3) Finite Element Modeling Procedure
(4) Results and Discussion
(5) Conclusions
(6) Acknowledgments
(7) References

这篇论文主要是按逻辑顺序来组织的。在组织段落时,除了要注意各段落的相互衔接,还必须明确每一段落都是论文中心思想的一个环节,它只能表达一层意思,反映一个段落主题。根据这个要求,一个好的段落都应在段头或段中或段尾包含一个主题句。通常,推演段和辩论段的主题句放前面,归纳段的主题句放后面。

写作正文时,一般采用第三人称,以减少主观愿望的影响。通常采用一般现在时的时态,但对于某些特定内容,如介绍本研究之前所进行的工作用过去完成时;图表的描述用现在时;计划的工作和预期的结果用将来时。

三、结论或总结(Conclusion 或 Summary)的写法

结论或总结的宗旨一般是在理论分析和科学实验结果的基础上,向读者介绍所得到的富有创造性的成果,让读者对成果有一个全貌的了解。常常还要简单介绍该成果可以被推广到的重要领域,并可说明值得进一步探讨和解决的问题,或待改进的地方。

由于这种介绍是在读者已完成对全文了解的基础上进行的,因此,它比前面的摘要和引言要更高一层、更深一层,可以采用在正文中建立起来的专业性较强的术语。此外,还要注意与引言部分相互呼应、前后一致。

下面是一些表达结论的常用句型。

(1) It is clear from the forgoing discussion that...
(2) In conclusion (summary)...
(3) This demonstration (illustration, classification, comparison, contrast) shows...
(4) The above results (data, findings) leads us to a conclusion that...
(5) From the results we have obtained it and can be concluded that...

(6) On the basis of these results we conclude that...
(7) All these data confirm the previous assumption that...

第四节　致谢、附录及参考文献

一、致谢(Acknowledgments)的表达

当成果以论文形式发表时,应该对他人的劳动给予充分肯定,并表示谢意。致谢的对象通常是在研究工作或准备论文时提供经费、实验场所、实验仪器、图表、照片、数据、技术帮助或指导性意见的单位和个人。致谢的用词要恰如其分,不应过分夸张。

致谢通常放在论文之后,参考文献之前。

下面是致谢常用表达方法:

(1) The author is indebted to...for...and to...for...
(2) The authors would like to express their appreciation to...
(3) The authorwould like to thank...for...
(4) In particular we would like to acknowledge the contribution of...
(5) The author wishes to thank...for...
(6) This work was supported by...
(7) The authors are grateful to...for their fruitful discussion.

例如:

(1) The author wishes to thank Prof. ×× × and Dr. ×× × for their valuable discussions and useful suggestions.
(2) The author is very indebted to Prof. F. Jin for his encouragement and the colleagues and postgraduate students for their support.
(3) The authors would like to thank J. D. Minelly for his help with the fibre polishing technique.
(4) This work was supported by US Air Force RADC/DCLW.

二、附录(Appendix)的安排

附录置于文末,作为正文主体的补充。附录并不是必需的。一般仅在某些内容(如数学推导、定理证明、计算框图、计算结果、源程序清单、附图等)插入正文后有损论文的连贯性、条理性和完整性,或对一般读者价值不大,或引用他人工作不便于列入正文的情形下,才考虑作为附录处理,但在正文中必须提及附录及其作用。

三、参考文献(Reference)的要求

在科技论文中,凡是引用或参考他人文献的数据、材料、论点和研究成果,都应按照在正文中出现的先后顺序标明。列举参考文献,不仅是对他人劳动成果的尊重,而且反映了作者严肃的科学态度和研究工作的科学依据,同时还避免违反著作权法。参考文献还有一个非常重要的作用,即便于读者查找有关的原始文献,了解该领域中前人所做的工作。除了综述性论文之外,一般应引用最新、最直接、最重要的参考文献,切忌将与论文内容无关的或关系不大的文献罗列进去。

在正文中引用参考文献的标注方法一般都采用顺序编号体系,即在引用文献的著者姓名或成果叙述文字的右上角,用方括号标注阿拉伯数字,依正文出现的先后顺序编号。在文末罗

列参考文献时,也按此序号顺序排列。当引用同一著者或同一成果的多篇文献时,则应将各篇文献的顺序号之间用逗号分开,如 Hermans[1,2,5-7],其中5-7表示5,6,7。

按照国际标准化组织 ISO-690 和我国 GB/T7714-2005 文后参考文献著录规则标准,参考文献的著录项目应包括作者项、题名项和出版项3项内容。格式为:(1) 用阿拉伯数字表示索引顺序号;(2) 作者姓名;(3) 引用书籍名称(或论文题目);(4) 出版事项:论文则标注所在刊物名称、卷期号及页码;如是国际会议论文,则标注国际会议名称,开会地点和时间;如是书籍则标注出版社、出版地名称,出版时间,引用的页码。为便于资料检索,作者姓名一般姓在前名在后,中国作者用全拼音表示。文献题目一般第一个词的首字母用大写,也有些杂志规定每个实词首字母均用大写的。

第五节 专业术语和专有名词的译法

一、专业术语和专用名词或名称的翻译原则

专业术语和专用名词或名称的翻译一般遵循两个基本原则:一是"名从主人",二是"约定俗成"。

1. "名从主人"

"名从主人"的原则指的是在用音译法翻译专有名词或名称时,应以其所属国语言的发音为准,而不管该专有名词或名称是直接从原文翻译过来的,还是从其他文字转译的。例如:

Philip Prince(英国的)菲利普亲王;Philip IV(西班牙国王)腓力四世;Paris(法国首都)巴黎;Paris Mathew(英国编年史家)马修·帕里斯;Marxism-Leninism 马克思列宁主义。

翻译英语中的日本、朝鲜和越南的人名或地名时,遵守"名从主人"的原则就特别重要。由于历史的原因,这三个国家的文字中曾经或现在仍然借用大量的汉字。译成英语时,是按这些汉字在这三种语言中的读音翻译的,而译成汉语时,仍应以这三种语言中的汉字为准。这就造成相当大的翻译上的困难。例如:Hasegawa 长谷川(日本人姓名),Hiroshima 广岛(日本城市),Seoul 首尔(韩国首都),Hanoi 河内(越南首都)。假若我们将 Hiroshima 译为"赫洛希马",谁能猜得出它是指的什么地方呢?如将 Tokyo 译为"投科犹",也是不知道它是指日本的东京(城市)。

"名从主人"是翻译中一项很高的要求,当我们没有把握时,一定要查专用的辞书,例如,国内通用的《世界地名译名手册》、《英语姓名译名手册》、《日本人姓名译名手册》等。

2. "约定俗成"

有些人名、地名或组织机构的名称现在已有固定的译法,而按照现在的翻译标准来看有不妥甚至错误的地方,但由于原译名早已为大家所接受,也就不必再改了。这就叫"约定俗成"。例如:Greenwich 格林威治(伦敦东南小镇),Munich 慕尼黑(德国城市),Citibank 花旗银行(美国的一家老牌银行)等。以上三个词的译名虽有不妥之处,但已是"约定俗成"的译名。

二、专业术语和专用名词或名称的翻译方法

在专业翻译时,首先要注意的是区分词的一般意义和专业意义。翻译时,英语中有些词的一般意义与专业意义十分容易混淆。例如,现代新技术的词语很多是引用动物的名称来命名的。把动物的形态和习性引申应用到工程技术的专业术语上,以反映科技工具或机械的性能。这方面常用的一些词的一般意义与专业意义对照如表9-4所示。

表 9-4　常用词汇一般意义与专业意义对照表

英语词汇	一般意义	专业意义
cock	公鸡;头目	旋塞阀,水龙头,活栓,节气门,风向标,起重机
fly	苍蝇;飞行	飞轮,整速轮,摇臂轴
horse	马	(有脚的)支架,铁杆
monkey	猴子	(打桩)锤,心轴,活动扳手,起重机小车
pig	猪	生铁,(金属)锭
snail	蜗牛	蜗形轮
swallow	燕子	咽喉,食道,吸孔

翻译专业术语和专有名词或名称可采用音译、意译、形译或音意混译这四种基本方法。在没有把握而又无法查考原文的情况下,也可采用附注或照录原文这一临时办法。但切忌乱译,以免出现一人、一地或一组织机构名称由不同的人译成几个不同的译名,而造成混乱。

1. 音译法

人名和大部分地名的翻译一般都采用音译法。在科技术语中,如某些计量单位、科技发明及新型材料名称,某些字母缩略词以及一时尚未找到确切意译的词语,多采用音译法。如 Newton(牛顿,人名,力的单位),ohm(欧姆,电阻单位),London(伦敦,地名),radar(雷达,音字母缩略词),nylon(尼龙,新型材料)。

使用音译法应注意以下几点。

(1) 注意译音准确:译名既要符合该名所属国语言的标准发音,又要符合普通话的标准发音,不可按译者自己所操的方言来音译。

(2) 避免使用联想词:有人将磁通量单位 Maxwell(麦克斯韦)译为"墨克四喂";过去曾把非洲的一个国家 Mozambique(莫桑比克)译为"莫三鼻给"。这会造成贬意的联想,应避免使用。

(3) 音可省不可增:为了便于记忆,译名不宜过长,原文中不明显的音不必译。例如:Elizabeth 伊丽莎白,不必译为"伊丽莎贝思";Holland 荷兰,不必译为"荷兰德"。

2. 意译法

意译法一般不用于人名的翻译,而是用于某些地理名词的翻译。例如:Bay of Pigs 猪湾(古巴),Iceland 冰岛,Great Falls 大瀑布城(美国),Yellowstone National Park 黄石国家公园(美国),White Sea 白海,Red Sea 红海,White River 白河(美国),Red River 红河(越南)。

一些公司、厂家、金融机构以及政府部门的名称也常用意译法。例如:International Business Machine Corporation[IBM]国际商用机器公司(美),The Industrial and Commercial Bank of China 中国工商银行,Department of Housing and Urball Development 住房与城市发展部(美)。

科技方面的新词语,最好采用意译法。如 televisor(电视机),microelectronics(微电子学),holography(全息照相)。在意译时,术语中的前缀、后缀的意义,对术语的译名起着相当重要的作用。如 semiconductor(半导体)中的 semi-;microwave(微波)中的 micro-。因此掌握常见的前缀和后缀很重要。

3. 形译法

科技英语中有时用英文字母表示某种事物的外形,这时,可选用与这种字母形状相似的汉语词汇来表达。如 I-beam(工字铁),T-square(丁字尺),V-belt(三角皮带),O-ring(O形环),C-clamp(C形夹),U-steel(槽钢),twist drill(麻花钻)等。

4. 音意混译法

这种方法一般适用于某些地理名词以及科技材料和产品的翻译,即译名的一部分用音译,一部分用意译。例如:New Hampshire 新罕布什尔(美国州名),New Guinea 新几内亚,Fort Knox 诺克斯堡(美),Queen Maud Range 毛德王后山脉(南极)以及 covar(科伐合金),invar(殷钢),motor-car(摩托车),ampere-meter(安培表),Curie point(居里点),tractor(拖拉机),neon(霓虹灯),Doppler effect(多普勒效应),avalanche diode(雪崩二极管)等。

公司、厂家或其他机构的名称有时也可采用这种方法来翻译。例如:Foster United Parcel Service(福斯特联合包裹投递公司),Franklin antenna(富兰克林天线)。

三、附注与照录

附注是指在译者没有把握的情况下,在自译的译名后加注原文的翻译方法。例如:
After his defeat, Manco Inca lived for ten years as a fugitive ruler.
曼科·印加(Manco Inca)被打败后,作为流亡统治者又活了10年。

照录是指在未查到固定译名而又难以自译时,索性直接录用原文的翻译方法。例如:
One of the landmarks of library automation was the installation in 1942 of a prototype of the 357-type system in Montclair.
1942年,在 Montclair 安装了357型系统的样机,这是图书馆自动化的标志之一。

附注与照录是在翻译中万不得已采用的方法,不宜大量使用。表9-5所示为科技文稿中常见的拉丁缩写词。

表 9-5 科技文稿中常用的拉丁缩写词

拉 丁 词	缩 写	英 文 意 思	中 文 意 思
circa	ca.	about	大约;关于
et alii; et eliae	et al.	and others	及其他人
et cetera	etc.	and so on	等等(指物)
et cetera	&c.	and so forth	等等
exempli gratia	e. g.	for example	例如
ibidem	ibid.	in the same place	出处相同
id est	i. e.	that is (to say)	即;就是
idem quod	i. q.	the same is	与……同;同……
loca citato	loc. cit	in the place cited	引文处
Nota bone	N. B. (or) n. b.	observe carefully	注意
opera citato	op. cit.	In the work cited above	在上述引文中
quod vide	q. v.	which see	参阅
sic	sic	so; thus	原文如此
vice verse	v. v.	the other way round	反之亦然
vide licet	viz.	namely; that is	即;就是

References

[1] 刘宇.机电一体化专业英语[M].天津:天津大学出版社,2008.

[2] 赵运才,何法江.机电工程专业英语[M].北京:北京大学出版社,2006.

[3] 刘爱军,王斌.科技英语综合教程[M].北京:外语教学与研究出版社,2007.

[4] 钟华森.大学英语阅读与翻译教程[M].成都:电子科技大学出版社,1998.

[5] 韩建国,廖俊必.测控技术与仪器专业英语[M].北京:化学工业出版社,2002.

[6] 李国厚.自动化专业英语[M].北京:中国林业出版社,北京大学出版社,2006.

[7] 凌渭民.科技英语翻译教程[M].北京:高等教育出版社,1982.

[8] 彭蓉,李岁劳.测控技术与仪器科技英语[M].西安:西北工业大学出版社,2007.

[9] 施平.机械工程专业英语[M].5版.哈尔滨:哈尔滨工业大学出版社,2003.

[10] 卜玉坤.大学专业英语机械英语第一册[M].北京:外语教学与研究出版社,2001.

[11] 施平.机电工程专业英语阅读[M].修订版.哈尔滨:哈尔滨工业大学出版社,2004.

[12] 宋瑞苓,赵继永.机电工程专业英语[M].北京:化学工业出版社,2001.

[13] 陈统坚.机械工程英语[M].北京:机械工业出版社,2002.

[14] 刘镇昌.机械工程英语(上)[M].北京:机械工业出版社,2002.

[15] 周志雄,孙宗禹.机械设计制造及其自动化英语教程[M].长沙:湖南大学出版社,2000.

[16] 马玉录,刘东学.机械设计制造及其自动化专业英语[M].北京:化学工业出版社,2004.

[17] [美]多尔夫.现代控制系统(影印版)[M].北京:科学出版社,2002.

[18] [美]阿斯特罗姆.自适应控制(影印版)[M].北京:科学出版社,2003.

[19] Great Britain Encyclopedia[M/OL]. http://wordpedia.eb.com.

[20] Ralph Morrison. Grounding and Shielding: Circuits and Interference[M]. FIFTH EDITION. IEEE Computer Society Press,2007.

[21] P. N. Paraskevopoulos. Modern control engineering[M]. [s. l.]: CRC Press, 2002.

[22] Richard M Murray. Control in an information rich world: report of the Panel on Future Directions in Control, Dynamics, and Systems[M]. [s. l.]: SIAM, 2003.

[23] I. J. Nagrath, M. Gopal. Control systems engineering[M]. [s. l.]: New Age International, 2006.

[24] Saurabh Mani Tripathi. A course in modern control system[M]. [s. l.]: Laxmi Publications Pvt Ltd, 2007.

[25] Curtis D Johnson. Process Control Instrumentation Technology[M]. [s. l.]: Prentice-Hall, 2000.

[26] Michael A Johnson. PID Control: New Identification and Design Methods[M]. [s. l.]: Springer, 2005.

[27] Bolton. W. Programmable Logic Controllers[M]. [s. l.]: Newnes, 2006.

[28] Herbert E. Merritt. Hydraulic control systems [M]. [s. l.]: Wiley-Interscience, 1967.

[29] Mohieddine, Jelali, Andreas Kroll. Hydraulic servo-systems: modelling, identification, and 31. control Advances in industrial control[M]. Springer, 2003.

[30] Philip L. Skousen. Valve handbook[M]. [s. l.]: McGraw-Hill Professional, 2004.

[31] Joji P. pneumatic controls[M]. [s. l.]: Wiley India Pvt. Ltd. 2008.

[32] Hiroyasu Funakubo. Actuators for Control[M]. [s. l.]: CRC Press, 1991.

[33] David J. Maguire. Computers in Geography[M]. Longman Publishing Group, 1989.

[34] James D Broesch, Dag Stranneby, William Walker. Digital Signal Processing[M]. [s. l.]: Butterworth-heinemann, 2008.

[35] Dag Stranneby, William Walker. Digital Signal Processing and Applications [M]. 2nd ed. [s. l.]: Butterworth-heinemann, 2004.

[36] Calibration of Survey Instruments Used In Radiation Protection For The Assessment of Ionizing Radiation Fields and Radioactive Surface Contamination [R]. NCRP Report No. 112, 1991.

[37] William Putnam, R. Benjamin Knapp. Input/Data Acquisition System Design for Human Computer Interfacing[EB/OL]. 1996 [2009-12]. https://ccrma.stanford.edu/CCRMA/Courses/252/sensors/sensors.html.

[38] Jorn Bird. Electrical and Electronic Principles and Technology[M]. 3rd ed. [s. l.]: Elsevier Ltd. 2007.

[39] Nawrocki, Waldemar. Measurement Systems and Sensors [M]. Norwood, MA, USA: Artech House, Incorporated, 2005.

[40] M. J. Beesley. Laser and Their Applications[M]. [s. l.]: Taylor&Francis Ltd. 1976.

[41] Committee on Aeronautical Technologies, National Research Council. Aeronautical technologies for the twenty-first century [M]. Washington, D. C.: National Academy Press, 1992.

[42] Takatsu, H. Advanced control technologies in DCS [C]. Proceedings of the 1995 IEEE IECON 21st International Conference on Industrial Electronics, Control, and Instrumentation, 1995, 205-210.

[43] Philips. Application note AN165 integrated operational amplifier theory[EB/OL]. 1988. http://www.standardics.nxp.com/support/documents/interface/pdf/an165.pdf.

[44] Process Control[EB/OL]. From Wikipedia, the free encyclopedia[2009-11-5]http://en.wikipedia.org/wiki/process_control.

[45] Industrial automation control [EB/OL]. onlinefreeebooks.net [2008-6-15] http://www.onlinefreeebooks.net/engineering-ebooks/manufacture-mechanical-industrial-engineering/industrial-automation-control-pdf.html.

[46] Darrick Addison. Introduction to robotics technology [EB/OL]. [2001-09-01]. http://www.ibm.com/developerworks/opensource/library/l-rob.html.

[47] Dug North. Bioloid humanoid (or non-humanoid) robotics kit [EB/OL]. [2008-04-

[48] Wikipedia. The Free Encyclopedia. Remote sensing [EB/OL]. [2009-12-06]. http://en.wikipedia.org/wiki/Remote_sensing.

[49] Introduction to machine vision [EB/OL]. The Library of Alexandria, [2005-08-14]. http://www.alexandria.nu/ai/machine_vision/introduction.

[50] Chris McFee. An introduction to CCD operation [EB/OL]. http://www.mssl.ucl.ac.uk/www_detector/ccdgroup/optheory/ccdoperation.html.

[51] Forum on aeronautical engineering science and technology [EB/OL]. [2002-10-30]. http://www.cae.cn/swordcms/html/forumonengineeringandtechnology/419036.htm.

[52] Shanghai Jiao Tong University Mathematics and Applied Mathematics Bachelor's Degree Programs: Measurement & Control Technology and Instruments [EB/OL]. http://www2.sjtu.edu.cn/newweb/english/admission/programs/m01.htm.

[53] Arlene Garrison, Bruce Johnson. Process measurement and control: industrial needs [R/OL]. National institute of standards and technology, New Orleans Sheraton, 1998. http://www.chemicalvision2020.org/pdfs/workshop_processmanagement.pdf.

[54] Wikipedia, the free encyclopedia. Computer hardware and software [EB/OL]. http://en.wikipedia.org/wiki/Computer_hardware_and_software.

[55] Marshal Brain. How Microprocessors Work [EB/OL]. HowStuffWorks, Inc. 2008 [2009-12]. http://computer.howstuffworks.com/microprocessor.

[56] Wikipedia, the free encyclopedia. Computer network [EB/OL]. [2009-12]. http://en.wikipedia.org/wiki/Computer_network.

[57] Wikipedia, the free encyclopedia. Digital signal processing [EB/OL]. http://en.wikipedia.org/wiki/Digital_signal_processing.

[58] Omega Engineering. Data Acquisition [EB/OL]. http://www.omega.com/prodinfo/DataAcquisition.html.

[59] Kerry Lacanette. A Basic Introduction to Filters—Active, Passive, and Switched-Capacitor [EB/OL]. National Semiconductor Application Note 779, 1991. http://www.national.com/an/AN/AN-779.pdf.

[60] Courseware [EB/OL]. http://www.ider.herts.ac.uk/school/courseware/content.html.

图书在版编目(CIP)数据

测控专业英语/王丽君,梁福平主编. —武汉:华中科技大学出版社,2010.3
ISBN 978-7-5609-6045-6

Ⅰ.①测…　Ⅱ.①王…　②梁…　Ⅲ.①测量系统-控制系统-英语-高等学校-教材
Ⅳ.①H31

中国版本图书馆 CIP 数据核字(2010)第 030391 号

测控专业英语　　　　　　　　　　　　　　　　王丽君　梁福平　主编

策划编辑:万亚军
责任编辑:陈　峰　　　　　　　　　　　　　　　　封面设计:范翠璇
责任校对:张　琳　　　　　　　　　　　　　　　　责任监印:周治超

出版发行:华中科技大学出版社(中国·武汉)　　电话:(027)81321913
　　　　　武汉市东湖新技术开发区华工科技园　　邮编:430223

录　　排:华中科技大学惠友文印中心
印　　刷:武汉市籍缘印刷厂

开本:787 mm×1 092 mm　1/16　　　印张:17.5　　　字数:420 000
版次:2010 年 3 月第 1 版　　　　　印次:2018 年 7 月第 6 次印刷　　定价:38.00 元
ISBN 978-7-5609-6045-6/H·715

(本书若有印装质量问题,请向出版社发行部调换)